Research

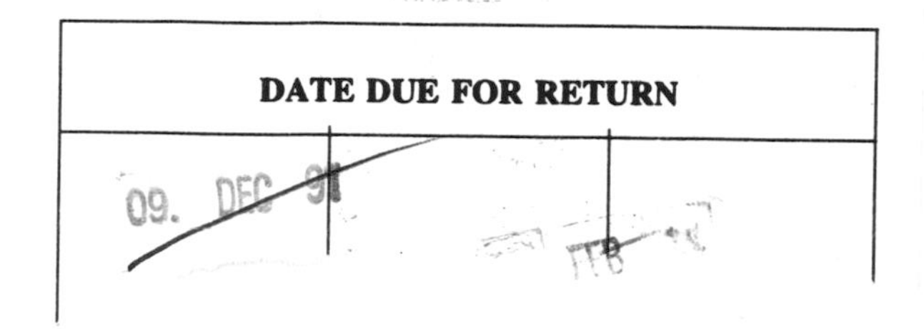

URBAN ECONOMICS

Edited by William H. Leahy, David L. McKee, and Robert D. Dean

URBAN ECONOMICS

Theory, Development and Planning

THE FREE PRESS, NEW YORK · Collier–Macmillan Limited, London

A DIVISION OF THE MACMILLAN COMPANY

Printed in the United States of America

The Free Press
A Division of the Macmillan Company
866 Third Avenue, New York, New York 10022

Collier Macmillan Canada Ltd., Toronto, Ontario
Library of Congress Catalog Card Number: 75-88859

printing number
2 3 4 5 6 7 8 9 10

Contents

Preface

The problem of the urban areas is currently the major domestic problem facing this country and an ever-growing problem in other countries, both developed and developing. Faced with a myriad of problems, from sociological ones to legalistic ones, the city functions as an economic entity in a spatial dimension as well as a historical dimension. The urban area is basically the wheel of economic activity. Without the city a developed economy could not properly function today.

This volume seeks to expose to those interested in the urban area a concise and analytical introduction to economic and spatial aspects of the city. In preparing this volume, we were not able to include all the articles that we would have liked because the size of the book would have been encyclopedic. Therefore, there are included only the most important articles. All of the articles except one have been published since 1958, reflecting the increasingly sophisticated attention given this area in recent years. Professor Edward L. Ullman's article in Part II, written in 1941, is the exception. It is included because it gives an excellent background of central place theory and centrality.

This volume complements our *Spatial Economic Theory*, which examines the effects of space on the location decisions of firms and industries. There we analyze the spatial dimensions of transportation and operating costs, interfirm competition, and the firm-residence interrelation. A third book, *Regional Economics: Theory and Practice*, deals with regional economy, of which the urban area is a part.

We have divided this book on urban areas into five parts. The Introduction consists of two articles by Professors Ullman and Lynch. These articles present an overview of the city's problems, including its changing structure, the urban dispersion of people and firms, and the resulting effects on employment. Possible solutions and objectives of urban planning and development are proposed.

The first part, Urban Location and Land Use Theory, presents a theoretical approach to the use of urban land for various activities. Alonso's article using bid rent curves develops an economic model of land use for a single-centered city in order to arrive at various prices, locations, and densities. Professor Moses examines the dispersion of manufacturing from the city's business center in terms of transportation costs. Muth's article analyzes changing land values in terms of a two-firm model.

Part II is concerned with Central Place Theory as an explanation of the size and composition of cities. In addition to showing the development and operation of Christaller's early central place theory, Ullman's article reveals its relevancy as a theory of location for non-agricultural cities. The article by Berry and Garrison adds to Christaller's theory by dropping the assumption of a uniform transportation plane. Professor Curry's article examines central place theory under the assumption of an imperfect market for both firm and consumer. Finally, the two articles by Professors Berry and Olson give a good background to central place theory and add important dimensions to an understanding of central place systems.

We move from theoretical models to a more pragmatic and empirical view of Urban Economic Development in the third part of this book. Professor Manners' article discusses the historical and present urbanizing process in the older and newer cities of the United States with an emphasis on the crucial role of transportation. The important interplay between the growth and structure of a city in terms of the city's development is stressed in Winsborough's article. The diverse factors accounting for the development of two cities is investigated by Professor Chinitz in his article.

The last part of this book is concerned with Urban Planning. The article by Perloff and Wingo analyzes three levels of urban development and their resulting implications for economic resources. Professor Harris' article discusses the often overlooked problems of design and sequential planning.

We wish to thank the authors and publishers for their permission to reprint the enclosed articles. Without their cooperation, this book would not have been possible. Finally, a special word of appreciation is due to Jerome W. Blood, Editor of the Free Press, for his encouragement and assistance.

W. L.
D. McK.
R. D.

URBAN ECONOMICS

INTRODUCTION

EDWARD L. ULLMAN

1

The Nature of Cities Reconsidered

Are cities really necessary? . . . or even farms, for that matter? Recent trends prompt one almost to raise this question or at the least to ask what kind. This does not necessarily mean that most people will live nowhere and do nothing (but it might help!). Cities have been growing in size, expanding even more in area, and declining in overall density. Analysis of these developments will bring up to date some of "The Nature of Cities" written in 1944,[1] which emphasized, among other facets, that "The support of a city depends on the services it performs not for itself but for a tributary area. Many activities merely serve the population of the city itself." In this presentation the degree to which a city actually is "supported" by performing services for itself will be measured and related to the size and growth of cities. The second and larger part of this study will analyze the expansion of urban areas and bring up to date the increasing importance of the "Multiple Nuclei" concept of urban structure first suggested in the earlier study.

THE GROWTH OF CITIES

Not only is rural and much small town population declining absolutely, but the very largest cities appear to be increasing more rapidly than any others. Actual figures for relative growth of metropolitan areas in the U.S. between 1950 and 1960, however, indicate that small and large have all grown about the same in terms of percentage increase. Rates are: over 3,000,000, 23 percent increase; 1,000,000 to 3,000,000, 25 percent; 500,000 to 1,000,000, 36 percent increase (the largest); 100,000 to 500,000, 26 percent. Still other groupings indicate about the same.

However, if the absolute amount of growth is allocated by groups still another interpretation can be made. For example, the five cities over 3,000,000 had an absolute increase of about 5,000,000. The second group also had an increase of about 5,000,000, but this was spread out over 16 cities. The next smaller groups had about 5,000,000 increase but the increase was distributed over still more cities. Thus

1. Chauncy D. Harris and Edward L. Ullman, "The Nature of Cities," *Annals of the American Academy of Political and Social Sciences* (Nov. 1945), pp. 7–17.

Reprinted from Papers and Proceedings of the Regional Science Association, *9 (1962), 7–23, by permission of the publishers and the author.*

an increasing quantity of U.S. population was concentrated on the average in each of the largest cities. This, then, is presumably the justification for emphasizing metropolitan growth.

If, in general, each of the largest cities on the average have been growing somewhat more, what is the explanation? No pat answer is possible but the following three factors may be involved: (1) Mere size attracts size—a mass, gravity effect; the larger the center the more innovators, the more persons who have relatives and friends who are attracted as in-migrants, etc. (2) The external economies of larger centers provide a greater range of interdependent specialities and facilities. (3) A relative improvement in internal, urban transit has occurred, primarily because of the short haul advantages of the auto and truck; this latter factor has been particularly significant in the expansion of urban area. Leon Moses suggests that the truck allows suburban factories to develop and thus enables the metropolitan area now to compete with outlying regions by providing not only relatively cheap land, but also urban nearness and access to the scale economies just noted.

All three of these forces presumably are given greater scope to influence growth because of the well known shift from primary, to secondary, and particularly to tertiary activities—toward more processing and consequent lesser orientation of production to resource locations.

SCALE ECONOMIES

What is the evidence for the scale economy factor, which has been mentioned so much recently by Vernon, Hoover, and others? In this connection some new findings will be advanced, indicating the degree to which a city is self-contained—takes in its own washing, if you please—which varies according to size and other particulars.

According to studies which Michael Dacey and I, and others, have made using what we call the "Minimum Requirements" method, there is, on the average, a definite relationship between size of a city and its degree of self-containment (Figure 1). [2] Thus, towns of 10,000 have about one-third of their employment serving internal needs and two-thirds external, for an Export-Internal or Basic-Service ratio of about 1:0.5; cities of 500,000 are about evenly divided, one-half internal, one-half external, etc.

This exponential relationship also fits approximately other logical

2. Edward L. Ullman and Michael F. Dacey, "The Minimum Requirements Approach to the Urban Economic Base," *Papers and Proceedings of the Regional Science Association*, 6 (1960), pp. 175–94.

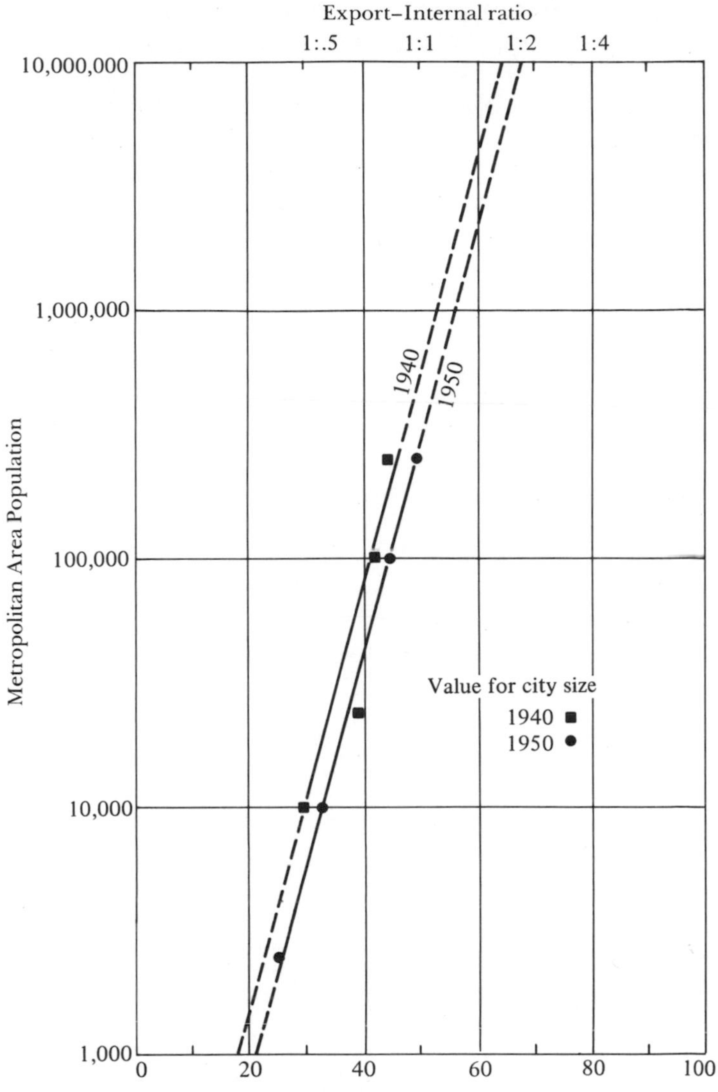

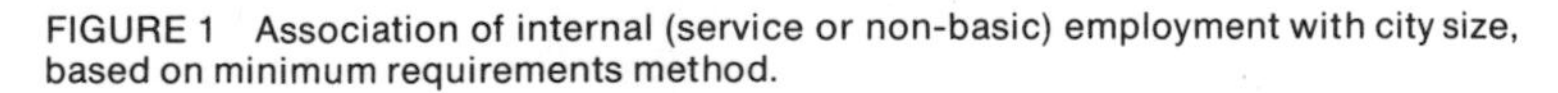

FIGURE 1 Association of internal (service or non-basic) employment with city size, based on minimum requirements method.

relationships. When extended downward it crosses 0 percent at about four persons, where it should according to logic, since a family unit can sell nothing to itself; when extrapolated upward, a more dubious procedure, it crosses within about 10 percent of the expected for the United States population, as a whole, if one assumes the United States to be about 90 percent self-contained.

If this relationship holds, then the only deduction one can make about the optimum size of cities is that the larger cities are, the more self-contained they are. By extension, on the basis of this measure *alone*, we tentatively conclude that the larger the city, the more efficient it is, since it can trade more with itself and save transport costs to and from other places. We cannot say there is an optimum size, other than that the larger the better, by this measure.

Table 1 indicates some other measures of the gain. Thus the amount of "external" employment "captured" increases, but is the increase really proportionate in effective terms to increase in size of city? For example, is there more "scale economy" gained in increasing from 10,000 to 100,000 than from 1,000,000 to 10,000,000? We do not know and will not know until we know a great deal more about the workings of urban economies.

TABLE 1

	APPROXIMATE % TOTAL EMPLOYMENT		APPROXIMATE % OF "REMAINING" EXTERNAL EMPLOYMENT "CAPTURED" BY INCREASING CITY SIZE TEN-FOLD
CITY SIZE	INTERNAL	EXTERNAL	
1,000	21	79	—
10,000	32	68	14
100,000	43	57	16
1,000,000	54	46	19
10,000,000	65	35	24

In any event it does not mean that many metropolises will become multi-million population centers in the next fifty years, first for the obvious reason that the total population of the U.S. will not be large enough to accommodate many, and secondly because many activities are top hierarchical, one-of-a-kind functions—national headquarters, United Nations, etc. They cannot pyramid in numerous cities. Does the latter consideration mean that one city, New York, (or two or three) will become the super giants, as Haig speculated some years ago?[3]

In considering this possibility we encounter other factors—persistence of some resource orientation, whether it be the old ones of minerals and agriculture or the newer role of resort climate, and possible *diseconomies* of scale, or simple lack of scale economies in a significant number of activities, as in government. Foremost among the diseconomies today *may* be environmental limitations—increasing cost of controlling air, and secondly water pollution from large

3. R. M. Haig, Toward an Understanding of the Metropolis: "Some Speculations Regarding the Economic Basis of Urban Concentration," *Quarterly Journal of Economics*, XL (1926), 179–208.

concentrations, although future technology may alter this in unknown ways.[4]

Still other forces are at work in individual cities, as the rapid growth of aviation and electronics centered in the attractive climate of Los Angeles which in turn grows as a second center of the U.S. in its own, somewhat protected, western territory. With the small number of giant cities over 5,000,000 (three in the U.S.) it is impossible to single out one common force more important than the individual influences at work on each of the cities. To a lesser degree this is true also of the nineteen cities from 1,000,000 to 5,000,000, which range from Dallas to Seattle to Philadelphia. The individual differences outweigh the similarities, but the scale economy factor would appear to be an underlying force of varying magnitude. Just how this operates and the magnitude of the effect of increasing size, now and in the future, is an explicit question needing further research.

THE INTERNAL EXPANSION OF URBAN AREAS

As our cities grow in size paradoxically their overall densities appear to decline. Suburbs and satellites boom, some fringe areas are by-passed, blight produces a gray area around most of the closer-in parts of central cities, and downtowns decline. This unsettles land values and existing tax bases and alarms powerful groups. The central cities are particularly hit because most of them are unable to expand their city limits. Some conclude that cities are therefore suffering from some unknown disease. There is, however, a logical explanation, already alluded to, related to improved circulation and communication, and particularly to the nature and widespread use of the automobile. Improvements in transportation and communication have benefited short hauls and especially self-loading and unloading commodities like passengers or telephone messages dialed by the individual. These are improvements at metropolitan scale distances.

Before analyzing the forces promoting change, let us attempt to establish what actually has been happening in our cities, a somewhat difficult task both for statistical reasons and because of the recency of the change.

For the country as a whole the census bureau indicates that

4. A highly urbanized region may also have scale economies. *Cf.* Chauncy D. Harris, "The Market as a Factor in the Localization of Industry in the U.S.," *Annals of the Association of American Geographers*, 44 (1954), pp. 315–48, and Edward L. Ullman, "Regional Development and the Geography of Concentration," *Papers and Proceedings of the Regional Science Association*, 4 (1958), pp. 179–98. See also references to Gottmann and others in note six.

SMSA's (all central cities and their counties over 50,000) have increased 26 percent in population, but the central cities alone, based on holding city limits constant to 1950, increased only 1.5 percent as compared to 62 percent in the remainder of the metropolitan areas. This is natural; as cities grow, they might be expected to expand in all directions. However, even within the 1950 city limits there is vacant land, especially on the edges, so that actually the innermost portions of cities have declined. In some areas increase in other activities has pushed out residences, but, as will be seen, on an overall basis, probably not even this has compensated for the loss. A net, although unevenly distributed, decline is evident.

For other measures beyond population, it is difficult to obtain data from the census, except for retail trade, and for the office function on a consistent basis it is impossible. To obtain as much consistency as possible a representative group of cities, of all size classes has been chosen and changes in the central city have been compared to the whole metropolitan area (Tables 2 and 3). The measures were limited to eighteen cities which from 1947 to 1958 had virtually no change in boundaries. Percentage calculations for the average of these cities are given in Table 2.

These eighteen metropolitan areas and their central cities grew slightly faster than all U.S. metropolitan areas, with the central cities showing a 6 percent increase compared to 1½ percent nationally. This probably means, therefore, that the other measures of decline of central city proportion of all metropolitan activity are slightly understated in Table 2. Also, as noted for population, the measures used probably actually understate the degree of inner decline since the city limits themselves are drawn fairly far out. Finally, the figures are for 1958; later data would show still more relative decline.

Even with these qualifications, relative decline of the central city is apparent. The decrease from 1948 to 1958 in the degree of central city concentration as a percentage of the metropolitan area is shown in the last four figures (28, 29, 30, 31) where Manufacturing in 1958 is 88 percent of 1947, Wholesale Trade 91 percent of 1948, Selected Services 93 percent, and Retail Trade 91 percent, as compared to 84 percent for Population.

The actual percents of population or employment in the central city in 1958 were as follows: Population about 54 percent, Manufacturing 60 percent, Wholesale Trade 82 percent, Selected Services 80 percent, Retail Trade 72 percent.

It is clear that population leads the way to the suburbs, but jobs are not far behind, especially in manufacturing. Factories appreciate the roominess of the suburb just as much as ranch houses. One-story structures with ample parking are the rule. Walk-up or elevator

TABLE 2 Changes in proportion of selected activities for eighteen U.S. central cities and metropolitan areas, various dates 1929–1960.[a]

NO.[b]		UNWEIGHTED MEAN PERCENT
1	*Population*: proportion of SMSA located in central city, 1948	64
2	1960	52
3	change in SMSA/Central City concentration, 1960/1948 (1948/1958:84)	81
4	change, SMSA 1960/1948	133
5	change, central city 1960/48	106
6	*Manufacturing*: production workers in central city, 1929	74
7	1939	71
8	1947	70
9	1954	64
10	1958	60
11	establishments in central city, 1947	75
12	1954	69
13	1958	67
14	*Wholesale trade*: paid employees in central city, 1948	89
15	1954	88
16	1958	82
17	establishments in central city, 1948	86
18	1954	83
19	1958	80
20	*Selected services*: paid employees in central city, 1948	86
21	1954	82
22	1958	80
23	establishments in central city, 1954	72
24	1958	69
25	*Retail trade*: paid employees in central city, 1948	79
26	1954	77
27	1958	72
28	*Manufacturing*: change in concentration of prod. workers, 1958/1947	88
29	*Wholesale Trade*: change in concentration of paid employees, 1958/1948	91
30	*Selected services*: change in concentration of paid employees, 1958/1948	93
31	*Retail trade*: change in concentration of paid employees, 1958/1948	91

[a]Central cities chosen were those with virtually no boundary change 1947–58: metropolitan area (SMSA) figures adjusted to 1958 area.

[b]Numbers refer to numbers of columns in following table for individual cities.

Sources: U.S. Census of Manufactures 1947, 1954, 1958; Census of Business 1948, 1954, 1958; Census of Population 1960.
D. J. Bogue, "A Technique for Making Extensive Population Estimates," *Journal of the American Statistical Association*, 45 (June, 1950), pp. 149–163.

factories in town are abandoned as soon as conditions permit by most industries, save some with high labor requirements and production processes not sensitive to poor layout or with light weight raw materials and end products. Wholesaling, especially warehousing, should increasingly join manufacturing in low density structures, although its traditional nature, and especially greater market within the city, in contrast to manufacturing, probably explains the greater urban concentration up to now.

The number of individual establishments in manufacturing are more concentrated in the city than is employment, indicating that the larger, more self-contained industries, requiring more space, have led the way to the suburbs. In wholesale trade the reverse appears,

Table 3 Ratios of activities of selected central cities to SMSA's.

	1[a]	2	3	4	5	6	7	8	9	10	11	12	13	14	15	16	17	18	19	20	21	22	23	24	25	26	27	28	29	30	31
Buffalo	56	41	73	124	93	60	50	48	43	42	69	62	61	87	85	80	84	80	75	81	72	70	60	55	70	65	59	88	92	86	84
Chicago	66	57	86	115	99	74	72	70	65	59	83	75	71	88	87	79	88	83	77	85	81	76	71	63	70	70	64	84	90	89	91
Cleveland	65	49	75	123	93	89	86	83	70	68	87	80	76	93	93	87	92	87	81	88	84	83	70	69	78	74	69	82	94	94	88
Detroit	61	44	72	129	94	75	58	60	53	49	69	56	52	86	77	74	87	77	73	86	78	75	66	59	71	65	56	82	86	87	79
Philadelphia	57	46	81	122	98	66	61	61	56	55	71	65	62	89	82	77	85	75	70	75	75	72	62	57	69	63	58	90	87	96	84
St,Louis	52	36	69	126	88	70	71	71	63	56	78	71	68	—	86	80	80	73	70	77	76	73	58	55	70	62	59	79	80	95	84
Akron	68	57	84	125	103	89	82	82	81	67	71	64	59	87	92	85	88	86	82	91	88	82	74	69	81	78	74	82	98	90	91
Miami	53	31	58	209	124	79	77	74	70	50	72	66	57	94	79	72	93	77	70	73	46	45	60	54	66	63	55	68	77	62	83
New Orleans	85	72	85	131	111	78	77	77	68	61	89	83	79	95	91	88	93	90	87	96	90	90	86	82	93	90	86	79	93	94	92
Portland	54	45	83	126	107	68	63	63	60	58	68	56	59	81	91	89	78	85	84	89	84	85	73	68	79	79	77	92	110	96	97
Rochester	69	54	78	123	97	92	94	95	94	92	90	87	84	95	95	92	93	92	91	97	93	87	88	84	85	90	82	97	97	90	96
Syracuse	64	51	80	131	105	76	71	47	43	40	55	49	49	84	79	71	76	74	71	82	78	69	54	51	67	65	60	85	85	84	90
Baton Rouge	79	66	84	145	121	18	17	28	23	37	57	77	83	87	94	92	88	95	93	89	98	95	97	89	91	96	94	132	106	107	103
Des Moines	79	78	99	122	121	91	95	86	77	69	93	84	85	—	96	94	91	93	92	98	96	95	92	90	92	95	92	80	94	97	100
Erie	62	55	89	121	107	67	69	54	56	57	70	67	64	90	90	87	83	82	79	89	85	83	72	67	82	81	77	106	97	93	94
Flint	62	53	85	147	125	96	99	98	80	68	62	56	65	—	89	54	82	83	79	89	90	89	69	71	85	83	79	69	54	100	93
Salt Lake City	67	49	73	150	111	70	61	70	71	72	84	80	77	92	95	93	91	90	90	89	90	91	78	81	85	87	85	103	101	102	100
South Bend	59	56	95	122	115	82	81	80	81	73	74	66	66	83	77	81	81	79	78	77	81	83	73	71	81	79	75	91	98	108	93
Average	64	52	81[b]	133	106	74	71	70	64	60	75	69	67	89	88	82	86	83	80	86	82	80	72	69	79	77	72	88	91	93	91

[a]Numbers at top of columns are identified on Table 2.
[b]Adjusted to 84 for 1958.

indicating probably relatively more warehouse, low labor activity in suburbs.

These general trends in themselves are not conclusive evidence of expansion and lower density, but several studies of individual cities, among them New York, Chicago, Boston[5] indicate the dispersal as well as the classic example of Los Angeles, a city which has grown up in the recent period.

REASONS FOR THE PRESENT AND FUTURE REARRANGEMENT OF CITIES

Before citing other evidence of the expansion and rearrangement of cities, let us examine the fundamental changes in background which have made this possible. As is well known, improvement in transportation and circulation has changed the nature of urban space, allowing greater distances to be covered[6] and particularly the development of *favored sites*—parts of the city more on the basis of their intrinsic natural and cultural characteristics, and less because of their location or situation. For example, before the automobile, some poor water recreation areas reached by streetcar or train on the edges of cities were very popular. Since the automobile has taken over, these nearby areas, if of poor quality, have declined drastically and visitors travel up to 100 or 200 miles to new impoundments or natural water bodies with better water and scenery, or build swimming pools. In this case, both the opportunity to travel and the ability to pay for something better in our increasingly affluent society have created a change.

5. Perhaps the most significant finding along these lines of the New York Regional Study is buried in a footnote added after the study was completed and using last minute, 1960 census returns: ". . . . the tendency to fill up the previously by-passed land of the inlying counties does not appear to be quite as strong as our projection assumes . . . . In general the dispersive population forces in the region seem even stronger than those built into our model." Raymond Vernon, *Metropolis 1985*, Harvard University Press, Cambridge, 1960, footnote, p. 222.

Examples of two earlier but recent quantitative studies proving the shift in urban structures are: John R. Hamburg and Robert Sharkey, "Chicago's Changing Land Use and Population Structures," *Journal American Institute of Planners*, XXVI (Nov. 1960), pp. 317–323, and *A Report on Downtown Boston*, Greater Boston Economic Study Committee, 1959.

6. *Cf.* the prophetic statement of H. G. Wells in "The Probable Diffusion of Great Cities" in *Anticipations* (London, 1901) where, in discussing urban growth promoted by improved methods of transport he says, "It is not too much to say that before [2000]—the vast stretch of country from Washington to Albany will be all of it available to the active citizen of New York and Philadelphia—This does not for the moment imply that cities of the density of our existing great cities will spread to these limits" (quoted by K. C. Edwards, "Trends in Urban Expansion," *Advancement of Science*, No. 62 [Sept. 1959], p. 60).

Jean Gottmann (*Megalopolis*, New York, Twentieth Century Fund, 1960) eloquently

Thus the stage is set for urban areas. First, as is well known, provision of streetcars and mass transit enabled cities to expand especially out along radial corridors; the volume required for this type of transport tended to focus on one large center—downtown. With the widespread use of the automobile, not dependent on large volume, the interstices could also be served which provided access to enormous additional amounts of land on the expanding circumference. The area of a circle increases by πr^2, which means, for example, that doubling the distance from the center increases the area four times.

Most of the inventions in communication also seem to favor a more open pattern. The telephone with its postage stamp rate over wide areas freed dependence on messengers, the movie made it possible to bring entertainment into the communities and neighborhoods from downtown, and the TV now brings it into the individual house and makes the home even more independent of other localities in the city.

What is happening in cities can be compared to what happened to world land use in the nineteenth and twentieth centuries when improved transport enabled distant fertile lands to produce for the world market and in the process compete with less fertile lands nearer the market. Thus, the steamship and railway brought agricultural products to Europe from fertile prairies in America, Argentina, or Australia and either forced abandonment or drastic alteration of agriculture in many less fertile lands in the European market. Thus the present subsidy to European agriculture might be compared to the subsidy to cities through redevelopment programs, although no value judgment is implied.

Cities might thus initially be compared to the Von Thünen model of land use around a city, with intensity generally decreasing as

describes the human geography of the whole area from Boston to Washington as one unit. Norton S. Ginsburg, "The Dispersed Metropolis: The Case of Okayama", *Toshi Mondai*, [Municipal Problems, in Japanese] (June 1961), pp. 67–76, equally eloquently proposes a new type of city based on several centers and improved transportation.

Some less careful enthusiasts have overplayed the urban explosion however, partly sparked by a change in definition of metropolitan areas in 1950 by the U.S. Bureau of the Census from a minor civil division basis to a county basis. When mapped it appeared as though urbanization had taken a gigantic leap into the countryside. Actually open country still surrounds all major metropolises even on the eastern seaboard of the U.S., even though the built-up area and ribbon development, much of it low density, has spread greatly. *Cf.* Lester E. Klimm, "The Empty Areas of the Northeastern U.S.", *Geographical Review*, XLIV (1954), pp. 25–45. What has happened is more to be measured by invisible indicators in the landscape: commuting, shopping and other trips, telephone calls, TV, etc., spreading out and beyond suburbia and exurbia. (For an example of quantitative indicators of this see: Edward L. Ullman, Ronald R. Boyce and Donald J. Volk, *The Meramec Basin*, Washington University Press, St. Louis, Mo., 1962, Chapter 1.

distance increased from the central market. Urban transportation, especially the automobile, removes much of the handicap of distance just as the steamship and railway did for the world's regions.[7]

One might thus paraphrase and add to some well known economic principles by coining a new law of *urban expansion* and *specialization* as follows: As urban transport improves cities not only can expand in area, but the range of location choice is widened; the more desirable sites within a city can be reached and developed according to their intrinsic advantages.

The second part of the generalization, relating to *site* qualities rather than *situation* qualities, as geographers would define them, is just as important as the first, or expansion part of the law. The monopoly quality of close-in urban locations is weakened.

Even in parts of Europe the same phenomenon is occurring as witness a statement in 1960 by Dr. Aage Aagesen of the Geography Department of the University of Copenhagen:

> The Intensive urbanization which has developed in proximity to the railway stations seems to have been transformed into a more general, less pronounced urbanization of more extensive areas; this is a natural result of the fact that the importance exercised by motor-cars and other motor-vehicles on the daily transport is constantly increasing. Another consequence is that there are almost no limits to the choice of residence; this allows preference to be given to *esthetic* considerations by choosing the site in coastal regions, in undulating land, at the edge of a wood or of a lake. A combination of these factors has caused the expansion of the Copenhagen district toward the north, in the sub-glacial stream-trenches of North Zealand filled with lakes and woods. To the west and to the southwest of Copenhagen, in a flat and fertile moraine-land, the relief of the landscape is far from being as attractive and, therefore, has not invited an expansion of the same dimensions.[8]

The same occurs in American cities where waterfront property, as on Lake Michigan in Chicago or Lake Washington in Seattle, is sought, or attractive wooded hill lands in part draw high class residence as in western St. Louis or north-western Washington, D.C. Likewise, close in hilly sites are by-passed by factories in favor of out-lying, level lands.

Thus specialization on the basis of natural site qualities occurs, whereas 100 years ago, before the streetcar or auto, close-in Back Bay in Boston was filled in for high class residential use, or centrally located Nob Hill in San Francisco was built up in mansions and

7. Homer Hoyt anticipates me somewhat in this interpretation (as he constantly does) in "Changing Patterns of Land Values," *Land Economics*, XXXVI (1960), p. 114.

8. Aage Aagesen, "The Copenhagen District and its Population," (paper presented to 1960 Symposium on Urban Geography, Lund, Sweden, August, 1960), published in *Geografisk Tidsskrift*, 59 (1960), pp. 204–13 (citation on p. 210).

Leland Stanford reportedly got cable car service, an invention of the time uniquely fitted to serve hills. Today many, if not most, of these residents have moved to more spacious sites in the suburbs. Thus different natural factors may apply to urban sites than to rural areas, such as scenically attractive land for high grade housing or level land for factories rather than fertile land for crops.

Urban sites, however, for various reasons, probably cannot be rated so much on their natural characteristics as rural lands, but rather more because of certain man-made or *cultural* attributes. The result is a *push-pull* relationship.

First, close-in locations generally are relatively unattractive because of smoke, noise, traffic, crime, and other well known attributes of crowding.

Secondly, closer in lands may be by-passed by new building for two principal reasons: (1) the generally smaller size of parcels close-in compared to large outlying tracts suitable for large subdivisions and the lower cost mass building techniques of today, and (2) the greater cost of acquiring old structures and paying high land prices near the center as opposed to using raw land farther out.

The cost of acquiring close-in sites may run from $100,000 to $200,000 and more per acre[9] as compared to $10,000 to $25,000 per acre for outlying land. As a result, few one story or even two story structures can afford costs of close-in sites, whether for house or factory; at the same time the demand for multi-story apartments or other intensive uses is simply not great enough to cover all the gray areas. As a further result the government must subsidize redevelopment, contributing two-thirds or more and the local government the remainder to get site costs down to competitive levels. Even so, the temptation is to build to high densities, which in the past has produced high rise, low income housing, in many cases of dubious attractiveness.

Furthermore, anywhere in the city it appears that low density—that is two story group houses—are the cheapest way to house people because of lower construction costs, lack of elevators, etc. Even in England this is claimed.[10] As Hans Blumenfeld notes the cheapest cost building in a country is apt to be the type which is built most.[11] The higher standard buildings may last somewhat longer, but even the average annual payments do not appear to be significantly less.

9. Raymond Vernon, "The Economics of the Large Metropolis," in "The Future Metropolis," *Daedalus, Proceedings of the American Academy of Arts and Sciences*, 90 (Winter 1961), p. 44.

10. *Cf.* "The two story house on new land is still the cheapest form of development in Britain," Myles Wright, "Further Progress" in *Land Use in an Urban Environment*, Liverpool, 1961, p. 251.

11. Hans Blumenfeld, *Urban Land*, 21, 7 (Aug. 1962).

It is argued that cost of utilities—sewers, water, electricity, is higher if dispersed building is allowed on the fringes. As Lovelace remarks, "The underground system of sewers and water mains is about all that is holding [the city] together.[12] Even this is questionable, as Lovelace also notes.

Cheaper methods of lagoon sewage treatment or small package plants have been developed for small subdivisions, septic tanks at low densities are suitable on many soils, and even farmhouses have electricity and telephone at not excessive rates. It is true that new schools and other community facilities may have to be built, but these may replace similar facilities close-in which have outlived their usefulness. One story schools, requiring more land, are preferred to the old urban two, or three story structures with inadequate playgrounds.

As a concrete example, Lovelace points out that much of southwestern Michigan outside the cities is developed for low density, nonfarm uses in an area of sandy soils with high water table so that sewers and water mains are not required.[13] This illustrates graphically natural site advantage which can now play a role with cheap transportation. Areas unsuitable for septic tanks can be skipped over.

Furthermore, low density, sprawl on the fringes of a city is not unattractive simply because it is low-density, but rather because of the way it is done with ribbon development, removal of trees, growth of junk yards and the like. It is not the low density itself that is to blame. Restraining cities to dense, contiguous settlement is not the only answer, nor even the best answer to unsightly sprawl. Sprawl does however produce some obvious inefficiencies.

THE CENTRAL BUSINESS DISTRICT

The core of the city is generally declining relatively and in many cases absolutely. The best data indicating these trends are for retail sales. The top part of Table 4 shows change in CBD sales and SMSA sales in terms of constant value dollars from 1948 to 1958. The decreases for CBD's range from 16 percent for cities over 1,000,000 down to about 10 percent for those from 100,000 to 250,000. At the same time the remainder of the SMSA's outside the CBD's were increasing from 33 to 64 percent. The lower portion of Table 4 shows what percentage CBD sales are of total SMSA's. Note the decline from 16 percent to 10 percent for those over 3,000,000, from 26 to

12. Eldridge Lovelace, "Urban Sprawl Need not be a Tragedy," *Landscape Architecture*, 51 (1961), pp. 230–1.

13. Lovelace, *op. cit.*

TABLE 4 Central business district sales data.

I. *Changes in retail sales CBD and metropolitan areas, 1948–58 adjusted to 1948 dollars and for 1960 SMSA's.*

SMSA POPULATION (1960)	*All Retail Sales*						*Women's Specialty Stores (Clothing)*					
	CHANGES IN CBD SALES			*CHANGES IN SMSA SALES (LESS CBD SALES)*			*CHANGES IN CBD SALES*			*CHANGES IN SMSA SALES (LESS CBD SALES)*		
	1948–54	1954–58	1948–58	1948–54	1954–58	1948–58	1948–54	1954–58	1948–58	1948–54	1954–58	1948–58
3,000,000 or more (5 cities)	−11.6%	−5%	−16%	+21%	+11%	+33%	−2.1%	+11.5%	+9.3%	+13%	+4%	+17%
1,000,000–3,000,000 (14 cities)	−7.8%	−7.8%	−16.3%	+31%	+17%	+50%	−16.8%	−5%	−21%	+12%	+32%	+48%
500,000–1,000,000 (25 cities)	−7%	−8%	−14.4%	+38%	+23%	+64%	−11.7%	−6.7%	−17.5%	+16%	+29%	+49%
250,000–500,000 (32 cities)	−4.3%	−6.7%	−10.6%	+35%	+18%	+55%	−10.3%	−13.7%	−23%	+60%	−3%	+55%
100,000–250,000 (14 cities)	−2.3%	−7.1%	−9.7%	+30%	+18%	+50%	−10%	−10%	−20%	+101%	+13%	+118%
U.S. Average	−6.6%	−7%	−13.4%	+30.4%	+16.8%	+51%	−10%	−4.8%	−14.4%	+40.2%	+15%	+57%

Source: Calculated from U.S. Census of Business, 1958, 1954, *Central Business District Statistics.*

II. *CBD retail sales as percentage of SMSA sales, 1948–58.*

SMSA POPULATION (1960)	*All Retail Sales*			*Women's Specialty Stores (Clothing)*		
	% OF SMSA SALES IN CBD			*% OF SMSA SALES IN CBD*		
	1948	1954	1958	1948	1954	1958
3,000,000 or more (5 cities)	15.6%	11.4%	9.6%	33.8%	27.4%	26.8%
1,000,000–3,000,000 (14 cities)	26%	18.8%	15.4%	58.8%	47.5%	41.1%
500,000–1,000,000 (25 cities)	34.3%	24.3%	19.7%	78.3%	65%	55.3%
250,000–500,000 (32 cities)	38.7%	28.5%	24.4%	84.8%	75.6%	70.8%
100,000–250,000 (14 cities)	44.5%	37.2%	32.1%	91.7%	81.8%	77.8%
U.S. Average	31.8%	24%	20%	69.5%	59.5%	54.4%

Source: Calculated from U.S. Census of Business, 1958, 1954, *Central Business District Statistics.*

15 percent for 1,000,000 to 3,000,000, etc. Note also the lower percentage of total SMSA sales in the CBD in the larger cities, as would be expected, ranging from 9.6 percent in the largest group to 32 percent in the smallest. Pre-war, the only firm figure we had, was the special census under Proudfoot for Philadelphia which reported 37.5 percent in 1937.

These figures show the effect of the construction of large branch department stores and shopping centers and the general movement of shopping to customers. If much of the retail trade leaves downtowns what will replace it?

Before attempting to answer this question, two fundamental points about downtowns should be noted:

1. Most large cities have developed on water and have grown more in one direction than another so that the central business district is not now centrally located in many cities. As a result it loses sales and economic activities as cities grow away from it.[14] Street grids and mass transport focussing on the CBD mitigated this handicap in the past and the construction of radial superhighways to downtown will probably help overcome it to some extent in the future, especially if the parking problem can be solved.

2. Even more serious than the off-center location, in many cases, is the surrounding of the CBD by the low income, blighted, "gray area" of cities. Redevelopment, therefore, in many cases is pushed in part as a means of providing customers. In addition, a market for high and medium income apartments can be developed around downtowns, especially as older people with grown children come onto the market, as well as a new wave of post-high school and young college graduates. This market in most cities, however, does not appear large enough to affect a significant change. Probably a larger natural apartment market for retired persons exists in suburbs and other centers.

The remaining large activity for CBD's is the office function. This is growing, and growing particularly in New York which has witnessed a boom in central office and other activities locating there for national control, in part made possible by the airplane. To a degree the same is happening in Washington. For most cities this does not appear so likely. Even Chicago's recent expansion and planned new construction will only result in the same per capita office space as in 1930, although it will help the Loop.[15] Most other cities are worse off.

14. *Cf.* Ronald R. Boyce's forthcoming study suggested this point of the relation of CBD retail sales to CBD centrality. Also note William Weismantel, "A Multicenter Transportation Plan," *Washington University Law Quarterly* (June, 1962), pp. 310–37, for an excellent discussion of St. Louis' growth patterns in relation to transportation.

15. *Urban Land*, April, 1961, p. 8.

The unknown question is how much is face-to-face contact—linkages of various kinds—necessary for various functions, especially outside New York City. Many activities apparently do not require it, particularly in insurance and in single-function office buildings.

In some cities, even beside Los Angeles, notably St. Louis, outlying office centers are now starting to develop. Clayton, seven miles west of the CBD and more centrally located in reference to the high income area, has many modern, city-wide or nation-wide office buildings, with rents as much as three times higher than downtown, but with land values only about 1/3; Clayton illustrates a location nearer the geographic center of a city as well as closer to executives' homes. Ancillary businesses and social services, including luncheon clubs, have sprung up, although the center is not as large as downtown St. Louis. Executives, however, can still go downtown for luncheon club conferences. They drive to their offices in Clayton, then drive downtown for lunch and return in the afternoon, avoiding all rush hour traffic.

Many activities are downtown just because they are there, or in response to linkages which disappeared years ago. Many could be served better elsewhere. In any case, the average downtown should be greatly improved in order to compete with the greater number of sites now accessible by modern transportation. This will be increasingly difficult in view of the outward movement of housing, retail trade, manufacturing, and other activities which now begin to reinforce each other elsewhere in the city.

It looks as though the CBD may become one of the many centers in a city, in many cases the most important, but a center of much less relative importance than in the past. A logical development would make it the shopping center for the large, low income area around it and an office center on a reduced scale for older activities or smaller concerns needing poor, vacant space or using large amounts of cheap labor. The high grade activities characteristic of the top hierarchical position of the CBD will abandon it for centers better located to serve the high income areas.[16]

Other centers elsewhere will develop on a regional or specialized basis, strengthening the multiple nuclei generalization suggested in the earlier "Nature of Cities." Conventions and out of town visitors will find it increasingly more convenient to locate near the airport which, because of its own space needs locates on the periphery; outlying shopping centers will handle retail trade; large factories and employment centers will be on the outskirts on large tracts of land;

16. This will eliminate some of the cross hauling now occurring as executives travel from the residential suburbs into the center and workers travel from the center outward to suburban industrial sites.

special entertainment, educational, cultural, and recreational centers will be scattered all over the city to serve the whole population.

Many have said that a city cannot exist without a heart, the CBD. The metropolis of today and increasingly in the future is not only one city, but a federation of general and special centers. As such it is likely to have several hearts better located than one, and basically will be better off because of reduction in travel time, congestion, and utilization of better sites.

CONCLUSION

The generalizations about urban growth and re-arrangement will vary with individual cities because individual natural environments, economic bases, and civic actions vary. Many of the location changes in cities hinge on small margins with inertia and tradition holding many activities in uneconomical, old areas. Identical offices and industries can thrive in CBD's, suburbs, and small towns. They adjust accordingly.

If we were to start over, however, we would not build our cities as they are today. If we were to apply private enterprise depreciation principles to the inner portions of cities we would write them off—just as machinery is scrapped, and throw them away, but where would we throw them?

As a citizen I recognize that the major problem of cities—slums and the gray area—cannot be tolerated. We may well have to eliminate them before we eliminate all the causes, including poverty, ignorance, and racial discrimination against the new arrivals, or the other manifold ills of our society both old and new.

Some might say that the new pattern of our cities is the result of a plot hatched by Detroit, the sub-dividers, and land speculators. Inflated land values are a part of the "pernicious" process of urban sprawl.[17] The auto does not pay its fair share for use of the city and hidden costs are passed on to the public in urban expansion. This may be true, but three points seem germane: (1) the magnitude of the underpayment is probably not enough to result in anything more than a slowing down in the process, even if corrected. (2) Countervailing forces are already deployed on the other side, sparked in part by the threatened decline in land values in the center. Urban redevelopment is subsidized, and priority is given a radial pattern for the interstate highway system focussing on downtown, reflecting old

17. *Cf.* the thoughtful article by Mason Gaffney "Urban Expansion—Will it even Stop?" *1958 Yearbook of Agriculture* (Washington, Govt. Printing Office, 1959), pp. 503–22.

flow patterns, with generally only one circumferential, when some inner or intermediate belts are also required. (3) Even if the whole process is a plot, it is our foreseeable institutional arrangement and as a geographer I see it producing the future expansion–specialization–federation patterns sketched above.

A key question then will be the interrelations between the centers and parts. How much will they benefit from being adjacent, or would separate cities of 100,000 to 500,000 be as good or better? The latter seems unlikely since there are still some specialized services, such as jet aircraft flights, that are better performed for millions than thousands. The problem remains to design cities to take advantage of scale economies and the other advantages of concentration, and at the same time to provide optimum livability.

2

KEVIN LYNCH

The Pattern of the Metropolis

The pattern of urban development critically affects a surprising number of problems, by reason of the spacing of buildings, the location of activities, the disposition of the lines of circulation. Some of these problems might be eliminated if only we would begin to coordinate metropolitan development so as to balance services and growth, prevent premature abandonment or inefficient use, and see that decisions do not negate one another. In such cases, the form of the urban area, whether concentrated or dispersed, becomes of relatively minor importance.

There are other problems, however, that are subtler and go deeper. Their degree of seriousness seems to be related to the particular pattern of development which has arisen. To cope with such difficulties, one must begin by evaluating the range of possible alternatives of form, on the arbitrary assumption that the metropolis can be molded as desired. For it is as necessary to learn what is desirable as to study what is possible; realistic action without purpose can be as useless as idealism without power. Even the range of what is possible may sometimes be extended by fresh knowledge of what is desirable.

Let us, therefore, consider the form of the metropolis as if it existed in a world free of pressures or special interests and on the assumption that massive forces can be harnessed for reshaping the metropolis for the common good—provided this good can be discovered. The question then is, how should such power be applied? We must begin by deciding which aspects of the metropolitan pattern are crucial. We can then review the commonly recognized alternative patterns, as well as the criteria that might persuade us to choose one over another. Finally, we may hope to see the question as a whole. Then we will be ready to suggest new alternatives and will have the means of choosing the best one for any particular purpose.

THE CRITICAL ASPECTS OF METROPOLITAN FORM

There are at least three vital factors in our judging the adequacy of the form of the metropolis, once its total size is known. The first of all is the magnitude and pattern of both the structural density (the

Reprinted by permission of Daedalus, *Journal of the American Academy of Arts and Sciences, Boston, Massachusetts, 90 (Winter, 1961), pp. 79–98.*

ratio of floor space in buildings to the area of the site) and the structural condition (the state of obsolescence or repair). These aspects can be illustrated on a map by plotting the locations of the various classes of density ranging from high concentration to wide dispersion, and the various classes of structural condition ranging from poor to excellent. Density and condition provide a fundamental index of the physical resources an urban region possesses.

A second factor is the capacity, type, and pattern of the facilities for the circulation of persons, roads, railways, airlines, transit systems, and pathways of all sorts. Circulation and intercommunication perhaps constitute the most essential function of a city, and the free movement of persons happens to be the most difficult kind of circulation to achieve, the service most susceptible to malfunction in large urban areas.

The third factor that makes up the spatial pattern of a city is the location of fixed activities that draw on or serve large portions of the population, such as large department stores, factories, office and government buildings, warehouses, colleges, hospitals, theatres, parks, and museums. The spatial pattern of a city is made up of the location of fixed activities as well as the patterns of circulation and physical structure. However, the distribution of locally based activities, such as residence, local shopping, neighborhood services, elementary and high schools, is for our purpose sufficiently indicated by mapping the density of people or of buildings. Hence, if we have already specified structural density and the circulation system, the remaining critical fact at the metropolitan scale is the location of the city-wide activities which interact with large portions of the whole.

When we come to analyze any one of these three elements of spatial pattern, we find that the most significant features of such patterns are the grain (the degree of intimacy with which the various elements such as stores and residences are related), the focal organization (the interrelation of the nodes of concentration and interchange as contrasted with the general background), and the accessibility (the general proximity in terms of time of all points in the region to a given kind of activity or facility). In this sense, one might judge that from every point the accessibility to drugstores was low, uneven, or uniformly high, or that it varied in some regular way, for example, high at the center and low at the periphery of the region. All three aspects of pattern (focal organization, grain, and accessibility) can be mapped (see Figures 1–3), and the latter two can be treated quantitatively if desired.

It is often said that the metropolis today is deficient as a living environment. It has suffered from uncontrolled development, from too rapid growth and change, from obsolescence and instability.

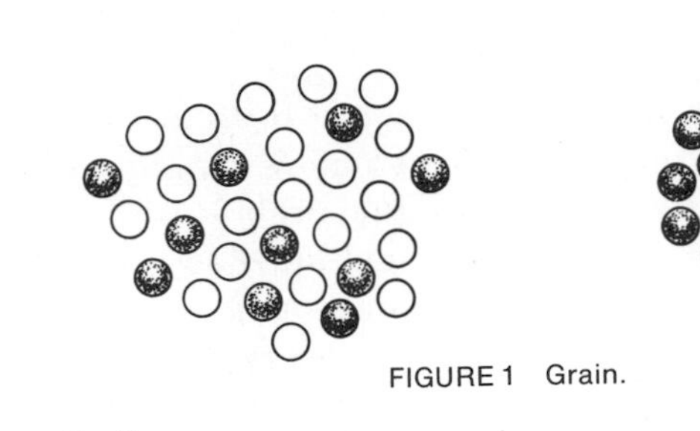

FIGURE 1 Grain.

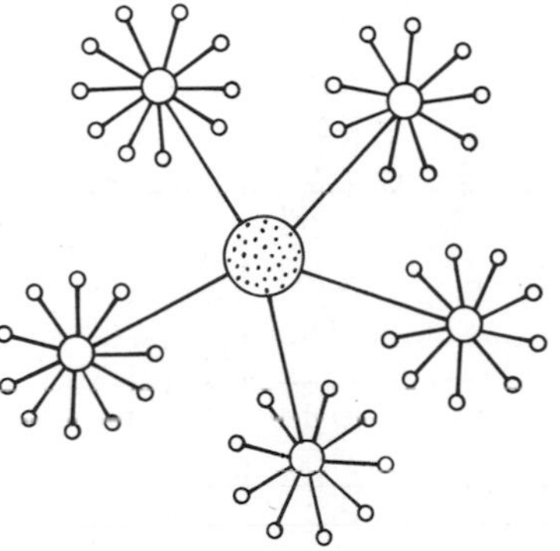

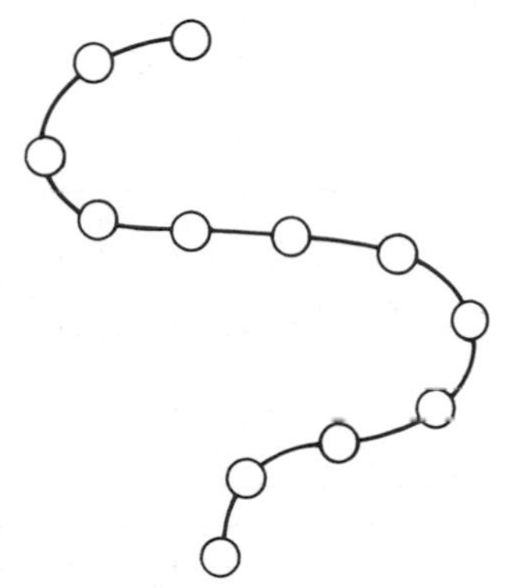

FIGURE 2 Focal organization.

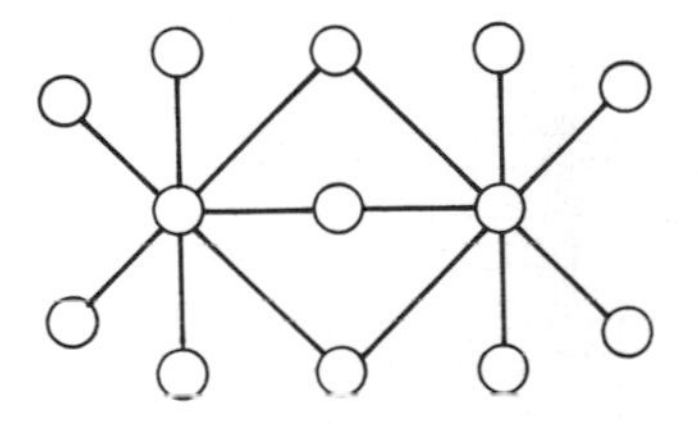

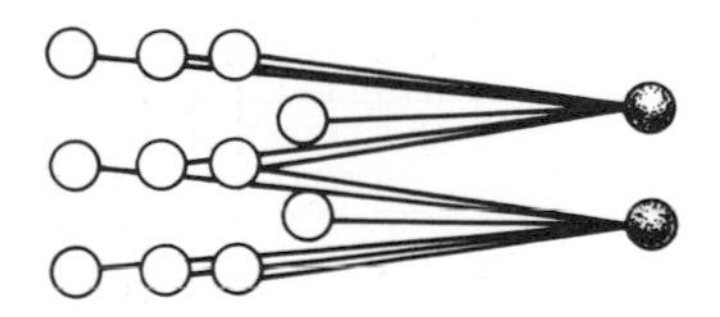

FIGURE 3 Accessibility.

Circulation is congested, requiring substantial time and a major effort. Accessibility is uneven, particularly to open rural land. The use of facilities is unbalanced, and they become increasingly obsolete. Residential segregation according to social groups seems to be growing, while the choice of residence for the individual remains restricted and unsatisfactory. The pattern of activities is unstable, and running costs are high. Visually, the city is characterless and confused, as well as noisy and uncomfortable.

Yet the metropolis has tremendous economic and social advantages that override its problems and induce millions to bear with the discomforts. Rather than dwindle or collapse, it is more likely to become the normal human habitat. If so, the question then is, what particular patterns can best realize the potential of metropolitan life?

THE DISPERSED SHEET

One alternative is to allow the present growth at the periphery to proceed to its logical conclusion but at a more rapid pace. Let new growth occur at the lowest densities practicable, with substantial interstices of open land kept in reserve. Let older sections be rebuilt at much lower densities, so that the metropolitan region would rapidly spread over a vast continuous tract, perhaps coextensive with adjacent metropolitan regions. At the low densities of the outer suburbs, a metropolis of twenty million might require a circle of land one hundred miles in diameter (Figure 4).

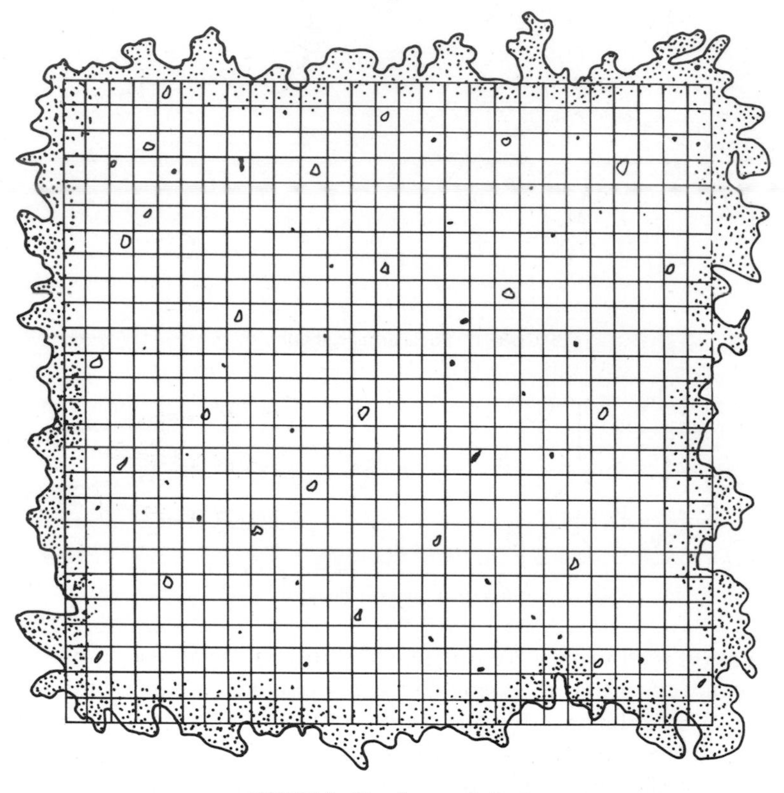

FIGURE 4 The dispersed sheet.

The old center and most subcenters could be dissolved, allowing city-wide activities to disperse throughout the region, with a fine grain. Factories, offices, museums, universities, hospitals would appear everywhere in the suburban landscape. The low density and the dispersion of activities would depend on and allow circulation in individual vehicles, as well as a substantial use of distant symbolic communication such as telephone, television, mail, coded messages.

Accessibility to rural land would become unnecessary, since outdoor recreational facilities would be plentiful and close at hand. The permanent low-density residence would displace the summer cottage.

The system of flow, concerned solely with individual land (and perhaps air) vehicles, should be highly dispersed in a continuous grid designed for an even movement in all directions. There would be no outstanding nodal points, no major terminals. Since different densities or activities would therefore be associated in a very fine grain, the physical pattern similarly might encourage a balanced cross-section of the population at any given point. Work place and residence might be adjacent or miles apart. Automatic factories and intensive food production might be dispersed throughout the region.

Frank Lloyd Wright dreamed of such a world in his Broadacre City.[1] It is this pattern toward which cities like Los Angeles appear to be moving, although they are hampered and corrupted by the vestiges of older city forms. Such a pattern might not only raise flexibility, local participation, personal comfort, and independence to a maximum, but also go far toward solving traffic congestion through the total dispersion and balancing of loads. Its cost would be high, however, and distances remain long. Accessibility would be good given high speeds of travel and low terminal times (convenient parking, rapid starting); at the very least it would be evenly distributed. Thus communication in the sense of purposeful trips ("I am going out to buy a fur coat") might not be hindered, but spontaneous or accidental communication ("Oh, look at that fur coat in the window!"), which is one of the advantages of present city life, might be impaired by the lack of concentration.

Although such a pattern would require massive movements of the population and the extensive abandonment of equipment at the beginning, in the end it might promote population stability and the conservation of resources, since all areas would be favored alike. It gives no promise, however, of heightening the sense of political identity in the metropolitan community nor of producing a visually vivid and well-knit image of environment. Moreover, the choice of the type of residence would be restricted, although the choice of facility to be patronized (churches, stores, etc.) might be sufficiently wide.

THE GALAXY OF SETTLEMENTS

We might follow a slightly different tack while at the same time encouraging dispersion. Instead of guiding growth into an even

1. Frank Lloyd Wright, "Broadacre City," in *Taliesin*, I, *1* (October 1940), 1.

distribution, let development be bunched into relatively small units, each with an internal peak of density and each separated from the next by a zone of low or zero structural density (Figure 5). Depending on the transport system, this separation might be as great as several miles. The ground occupied by the whole metropolis would increase proportionately; even if the interspaces were of minimum size, the linear dimensions of the metropolis would increase from thirty to fifty percent.

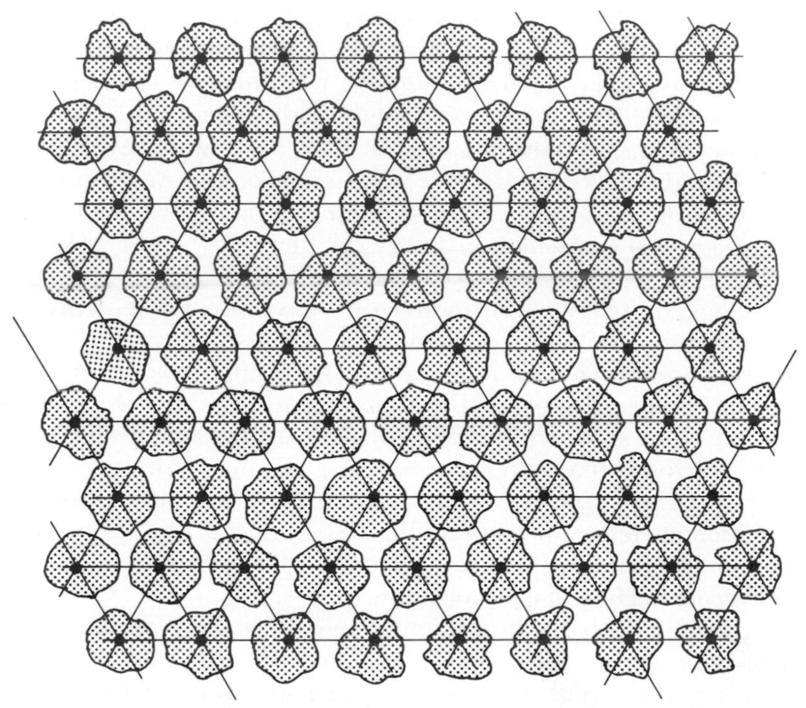

FIGURE 5 The Galaxy.

City-wide activities could also be concentrated at the density peak within each urban cluster, thus forming an over-all system of centers, each of which would be relatively equal in importance to any of the others. Such a metropolitan pattern may be called an "urban galaxy." The centers might be balanced in composition or they might vary by specializing in a type of activity, so that one might be a cultural center, another a financial center.

The system of flow would also be dispersed but would converge locally at the center of each cluster. It might be organized in a triangular grid, which provides such a series of foci while maintaining an easy flow in all directions over the total area. Since median densities remain low, while the centers of activity are divided into relatively small units, the individual vehicle must be the major mode of transportation, but some supplementary public transportation such as buses or aircraft running from center to center would now be feasible.

While it retains many of the advantages of the dispersed sheet, such as comfort, independence, and stability, this scheme probably enhances general communication, and certainly spontaneous communication, through creating centers of activity. It would presumably encourage participation in local affairs by favoring the organization of small communities, though this might equally work against participation and coordination on the metropolitan scale. In the same sense, the visual image at the local level would be sharpened, though the metropolitan image might be only slightly improved. Flexibility might be lost, since local clusters would of necessity have relatively fixed boundaries, if interstitial spaces were preserved, and the city-wide activities would be confined to one kind of location.

The factor of time-distance might remain rather high, unless people could be persuaded to work and shop within their own cluster, which would then become relatively independent with regard to commutation. Such independent communities, of course, would largely negate many metropolitan advantages: choice of work for the employee, choice of social contacts, of services, and so on. If the transportation system were very good, then "independence" would be difficult to enforce.

This pattern, however, can be considered without assuming such local independence. It is essentially the proposal advocated by the proponents of satellite towns, pushed to a more radical conclusion, as in Clarence Stein's diagram.[2] Some of its features would appear to have been incorporated into the contemporary development of Stockholm.

The pattern of an urban galaxy provides a wider range of choice than does pure dispersion, and a greater accessibility to open country, of the kind that can be maintained between clusters. This pattern has a somewhat parochial complexion and lacks the opportunities for intensive, spontaneous communication and for the very specialized activities that might exist in larger centers. Local centers, too, might develop a monotonous similarity, unless they were given some specific individuality. That might not be easy, however, since central activities tend to support and depend on one another (wholesaling and entertainment, government and business services, headquarters offices and shopping). A compromise would be the satellite proposal proper: a swarm of such unit clusters around an older metropolitan mass.

2. Clarence Stein, "City Patterns, Past and Future," *Pencil Points* (June 1942).

THE CORE CITY

There are those who, enamored with the advantages of concentration, favor a completely opposite policy that would set median structural densities fairly high, perhaps at 1.0 instead of 0.1; in other words, let there be as much interior floor space in buildings as there is total ground area in the city, instead of only one-tenth as much. If we consider the open land that must be set aside for streets, parks, and other such uses, this means in practice the construction of elevator apartments instead of one-family houses. The metropolis would then be packed into one continuous body, with a very intensive peak of density and activity at its center (Figure 6). A metropolis of twenty million could be put within a circle ten miles in radius, under the building practice normal today.

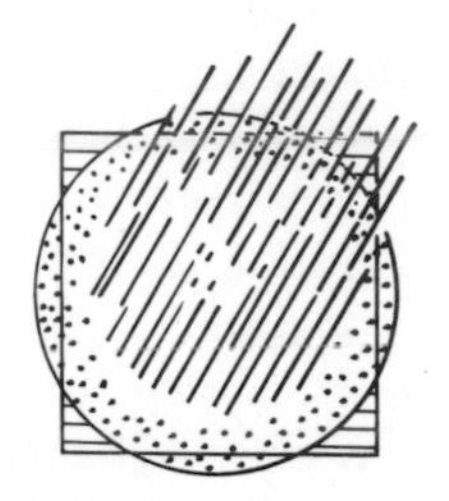

FIGURE 6 The core.

Parts of the city might even become "solid," with a continuous occupation of space in three dimensions and a cubical grid of transportation lines. (The full application of this plan could cram a metropolis within a surprisingly small compass: twenty million people, with generous spacing, could be accommodated within a cube less than three miles on a side.) Most probably there would be a fine grain of specialized activities, all at high intensity, so that apartments would occur over factories, or there might also be stores on upper levels. The system of flow would necessarily be highly specialized, sorting each kind of traffic into its own channel. Such a city would depend almost entirely on public transport, rather than individual vehicles, or on devices that facilitated pedestrian movement, such as moving sidewalks or flying belts. Accessibility would be very high, both to special activities and to the open country at the edges of the city. Each family might have a second house for weekends; these would be widely dispersed throughout the countryside and used regularly three or four days during the week, or even longer, by mothers and their young children. The city itself, then, would evolve into a place for periodic gathering. Some of the great European cities, such as Paris or Moscow, which are currently building large numbers of high-density housing as compact extensions to their peripheries, are approximating this pattern without its more radical features.

Such a pattern would have an effect on living quite different from that of the previous solutions. Spontaneous communication would be high, so high that it might become necessary to impede it so as to preserve privacy. Accessibility would be excellent and time-distance low, although the channels might be crowded. The high density might increase discomfort because of noise or poor climate, although these problems could perhaps be met by the invention of new technical devices. As with the previous patterns, the choice of habitat would be restricted to a single general type within the city proper, although the population could enjoy a strong contrast on weekends or holidays. The nearness of open country and the many kinds of special services should on the whole extend individual choice. Once established, the pattern should be stable, since each point would be a highly favored location. However, a very great dislocation of people and equipment, in this country, at least, would be required to achieve this pattern.

Such a metropolis would indeed produce a vivid image and would contribute to a strong sense of the community as a whole. Individual participation, on the other hand, might be very difficult. It is not clear how running costs would be affected; perhaps they would be lower because of the more efficient use of services and transportation, but initial costs would undoubtedly be very high. The segregation of social groups, as far as physical disposition can influence it, might be discouraged, although there is a level of density above which intercommunication among people begins to decline again. Certainly this solution is a highly rigid and unadaptable one in which change of function could be brought about only by a costly rearrangement.

THE URBAN STAR

A fourth proposal would retain the dominant core without so drastic a reversion to the compact city. Present densities would be kept, or perhaps revised upward a little, while low-density development at the outer fringe would no longer be allowed. Tongues of open land would be incorporated into the metropolitan area to produce a density pattern that is star-shaped in the central region and linear at the fringes. These lines of dense development along the radials might in time extend to other metropolitan centers, thus becoming linear cities between the main centers. The dominant core, however, would remain, surrounded by a series of secondary centers distributed along the main radials (see Figure 7). At moderate densities (less than the core pattern, and more than the sheet), the radial arms of a metropolis of comparable size might extend for fifty miles from its own center.

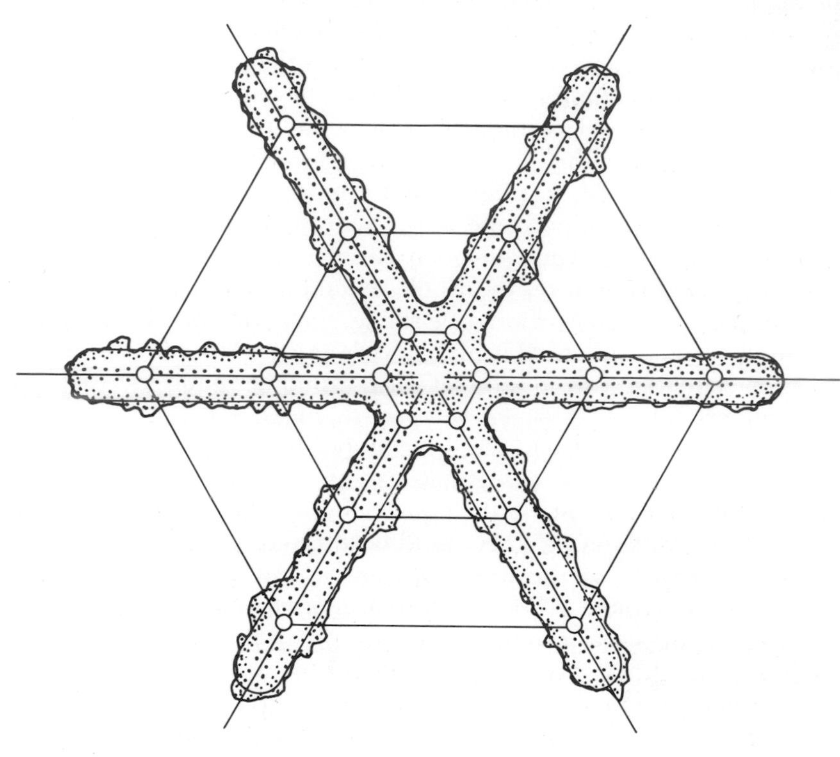

FIGURE 7 The star.

The metropolitan center of the star pattern would again contain the most intensive types of city-wide activity. Elsewhere, either in the subcenters or in linear formations along the main radials—whichever proved the more suitable—these activities would be carried on at a less intense level. The system of flow would logically be organized on the same radial pattern, with supplementary concentric rings. An efficient public transportation system of high capacity could operate along the main radials, whereas the ring roads could accommodate public transit of lower intensity. To some degree, travel by individual vehicles, although discouraged for centrally bound flows, would be practicable in other directions.

This pattern is a rationalization of the manner in which metropolitan areas were developing till the individual vehicle became the usual means of travel. It is the form the city of Copenhagen has adopted as its pattern for future growth;[3] Blumenfeld has discussed it at length.[4] This form retains the central core with its advantages of rapid communication and specialized services yet permits the location of other kinds of major activities. Lower residential densities are also possible. Individual choice should be fairly wide, both in regard to living habitat, access to services, and access to open land—this land lies directly behind each tongue of development, even at the core, and leads continuously outward to rural land.

Movement along a sector would be fairly fast and efficient, although terminals at the core might continue to be congested and, with continued growth, the main radials might become overloaded. Movement between sectors, however, would be less favored, especially in the outer regions; there distances are great, transit hard to maintain, and channels costly, since they would span long distances over land they do not directly serve. Accessibility to services would be unequal as between inner and outer locations.

The visual image is potentially a strong one and should be conducive to a sense of the metropolis as a whole, or at least to the sense of one unified sector leading up to a common center. Growth could occur radially outward, and future change could be accomplished with less difficulty than in the compact pattern, since densities would be lower and open land would back up each strip of development. The principal problems with this form are probably those of circumferential movement, of potential congestion at the core and along the main radials, and of the wide dispersion of the pattern as it recedes from the original center.

THE RING

In the foregoing, the most discussed alternatives for metropolitan growth have been given in a highly simplified form. Other possibilities certainly exist—e.g., the compact high-density core-pattern might be turned inside out, producing a doughnut-like form. In this case the center would be kept open, or at very low density, while high densities and special activities surround it, like the rim of a wheel. The principal channels of the flow system would then be a series of annular rings serving the high-intensity rim, supplemented by a set of feeder radials that would converge at the empty center. In fact,

3. *Skitseforslag til egnsplan for Storkobenhaven:* Copenhagen regional plan. Summary of the preliminary proposal, 1948–1949, with list of contents and notes explaining all illustrations of the preliminary proposal, translated into English.

4. Hans Blumenfeld, "A Theory of City Form," *Society of Architectural Historians Journal* (July 1949).

this is essentially a linear system, but one that circles back on itself and is bypassed by the "spokes" crossing the "hub." (See Figure 8.) This system is well-adapted to public transportation, both on the ring roads and the cross radials, while individual vehicles might be used for circulation outside the rim.

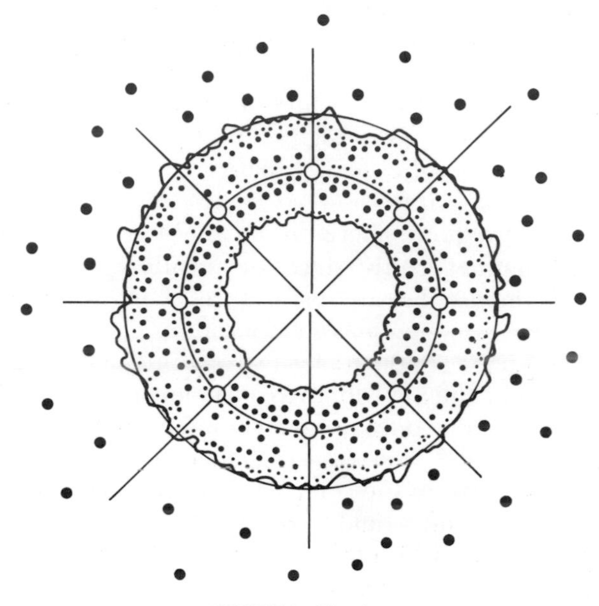

FIGURE 8 The ring.

Densities within the rim would have to be rather high, while those beyond the rim could be low. A system of weekend houses might also be effectively employed here. The central area could either be kept quite open or devoted to special uses at low densities. City-wide activities could be spotted round the rim in a series of intense centers, supplemented by linear patterns along the annular roadways. There would be no single dominant center but rather a limited number of strong centers (an aristocracy rather than a monarchy). These centers might also be specialized in regard to activity—finance, government, culture, etc.

This pseudo-linear form, like the radial tongues of the star plan, has the linear advantages: a high accessibility, both to services and to open land; a wide choice of habitat and location of activities; and a good foundation for efficient public transit. Congestion at any single center is avoided, yet there is a high concentration. In contrast to the galaxy or satellite form, the variety and strong character inherent in the specialized centers would have some hope of survival because of the relatively close proximity of these centers.

The visual image would be strong (though perhaps a little confusing because of its circularity), producing a particularly clear impression of the centers around the rim, in contrast to the central openness, and of their successive interconnections. The whole metropolis would seem more nearly like one community. One of the most difficult problems would be that of growth, since much development beyond the rim would soon blur the contour and require a new transportation system. A second concentric ring might be developed beyond the first, but it would negate some of the advantages of the first ring and would demand massive initiative by the central government to undertake its development. Another difficulty would be that of control. How can the belts of open land or the accessible center be kept free of building? Even if this problem were solved satisfactorily, a dilemma is also likely to arise in regard to the size of the ring: should it be small enough for the major centers to be in close proximity to one another or big enough to allow all the residences and other local activities to be related to it?

One classic example of this form exists, although on a very large scale—the ring of specialized Dutch cities that surround a central area of agricultural land, Haarlem, Amsterdam, Utrecht, Rotterdam, The Hague, and Leiden. This general pattern is now being rationalized and preserved as a matter of national policy in the Netherlands. In our own country, the San Francisco Bay region appears to be developing in this same direction.

The ring tends to be rather rigid and unadaptable as a form. It would require an extreme reshaping of the present metropolis, particularly with regard to transportation and the central business district; but it might dovetail with an observable trend toward emptying and abandoning the central areas. The plan could be modified by retaining a single major center, separated by a wide belt of open space from all other city-wide activities to be disposed along the rim. It may be noted that this use of open land in concentric belts ("green belts") is exactly opposite to its use as radial tongues in the star form.

THE OBJECTIVES OF METROPOLITAN ARRANGEMENT

Many other metropolitan forms are hypothetically possible, but the five patterns described (the sheet, the galaxy, the core, the star, and the ring) indicate the variation possible. One of the interesting results of the discussion is to see the appearance of a particular set of values as criteria for evaluating these forms. It begins to be clear that some human objectives are intimately connected with the physical pattern of a city, while others are very little affected by it. For example, there has been little discussion on the healthfulness of the environment or of its safety. Although these factors are influenced by the detailed design of the environment, such as the spacing of buildings or the provision for utilities, it is not obvious that the specific metropolitan pattern has any significant effect on them so long as we keep well ahead of the problems of pollution and supply. Psychological well-being, on the other hand, may be affected by the shape of the urban environment. But again, we are too ignorant of this aspect at present to discuss it further.

We have not referred to the efficiency of the environment in regard to production and distribution. This represents another basic criterion that probably is substantially affected by metropolitan pattern, but unfortunately no one seems to know what the effect is. "Pleasure" and "beauty" have not been mentioned, but these terms are nebulous and hard to apply accurately. A number of criteria have appeared, however, and it may well be worth while to summarize them. They might be considered the goals of metropolitan form, its fundamental objectives, either facilitated or frustrated in some significant way by the physical pattern of the metropolis.

The criterion of choice heads the list. As far as possible, the individual should have the greatest variety of goods, services, and facilities readily accessible to him. He should be able to choose the kind of habitat he prefers; he should be able to enter many kinds of environment at will, including the open country; he should have the maximum of personal control over his world. These advantages appear in an environment of great variety and of fine grain, one in which transportation and communication are as quick and effortless as possible. There may very likely be some eventual limit to the desirable increase of choice, since people can be overloaded by too many alternatives, but we do not as yet operate near that limit for most people. In practice, of course, to maximize one choice may entail minimizing another, and compromises will have to be made.

The ideal of personal interaction ranks as high as choice, although it is not quite so clear how the optimum should be defined. We often say that we want the greatest number of social contacts, so as to promote neighborliness and community organization, minimize segregation and social isolation, increase the velocity and decrease the effort of social exchange. And yet, while the evils of isolation are known, we are nevertheless beginning to see problems at the other end of the scale as well. Too much personal communication may cause breakdown, just as surely as too little. Even in moderate quantities, constant "neighborliness" can interfere with other valuable activities such as reflection, independent thought, or creative work. A high level of local community organization may mean civic indifference or intergovernmental rivalry when the large community is involved.

In this dilemma, a compromise could be found in saying that potential interaction between people should be as high as possible, as long as the individual can control it and shield himself whenever desired. His front door, figuratively speaking, should open on a bustling square, and his back door on a secluded park. Thus this ideal is seen as related to the ideal of choice.

Put differently, individuals require a rhythmical alternation of stimulus and rest—periods when personal interchange is high and to some degree is forced upon them, to be followed by other periods when stimulus is low and individually controlled. A potentially high level of interaction, individually controlled, is not the whole story; we also need some degree of spontaneous or unpremeditated exchange, of the kind that is so often useful in making new associations.

The goal of interaction, therefore, is forwarded by many of the same physical features as the goal of choice: variety, fine grain, efficient communication; but it puts special emphasis on the oscillation between stimulus and repose (centers of high activity versus quiet parks), and requires that communication be controllable. In addition, it calls for situations conducive to spontaneous exchange. Storehouses of communication, such as libraries or museums, should be highly accessible and inviting, their exterior forms clearly articulated and expressive of their function.

These two objectives of choice and interaction may be the most important goals of metropolitan form, but there are others of major importance, such as minimum first cost and minimum operating cost. These seem to depend particularly on continuous occupation along the major transportation channels, on a balanced use of the flow system, both in regard to time and direction of flow, a moderately high structural density, and a maximum reliance on collective transport.

Objectives of comfort, on the other hand, related principally to a good climate, the absence of distracting noise, and adequate indoor and outdoor space, may point either toward generally lower densities or toward expensive ameliorative works, such as sound barriers, air conditioning, and roof-top play areas. The important goal of individual participation may also indicate lower densities and an environment that promotes an active relation between an individual and his social and physical milieu, thus giving him a world that to some extent he can manage and modify by his own initiative.

We must also consider that the urban pattern will necessarily shift and expand, and therefore it is important to ask whether the adjustment to new functions will be relatively easy, and whether growth as well as the initial state, is achievable with a minimum of control and central initiative and intervention. Adaptability to change seems to be greater at lower densities, since scattered small structures are readily demolished or converted. Both an efficient transport system and some form of separation of one kind of activity from another are also conducive to flexibility. Discontinuous forms like the galaxy or the ring require special efforts to control growth, for these patterns raise problems such as the appearance of squatters and the preservation and use of intervening open land.

Stability is a somewhat contradictory goal; it takes into account the critical social and economic costs of obsolescence, movement of population, and change of function. It is very possible that stability in the modern world will be impossible to maintain, and it runs counter to many of the values cited above. Yet stability may be qualified in this light: if change is inevitable, then it should be moderated and controlled so as to prevent violent dislocations and preserve a maximum of continuity with the past. This criterion would have important implications as to how the metropolis should grow and change.

Finally, there are many esthetic goals the metropolis can satisfy. The most clear-cut is that the metropolis should be "imageable," that is, it should be visually vivid and well structured; its component parts should be easily recognized and easily interrelated. This objective would encourage the use of intensive centers, variety, sharp grain (clear outlines between parts), and a differentiated but well-patterned flow system.

THE RELATION OF FORMS TO GOALS

We have now treated a number of objectives that are crucial, that are on the whole rather generally accepted, and that seem to be significantly affected by the pattern of the metropolis: the goals of choice, interaction, cost, comfort, participation, growth and adaptability, continuity, and imageability. Other goals may develop as we increase our knowledge of city form. What even these few imply for city form is not yet obvious; moreover, they often conflict, as when interaction and cost appear to call for higher densities, while comfort, participation, and adaptability achieve optimal realization at lower levels. Nevertheless, we have immediate decisions to make regarding the growth of urban areas, and if we marshall our goals and our alternatives as best we can, we can the better make these decisions.

The clarifying of alternatives and objectives has an obvious value, for this will permit public debate and the speculative analysis of the probable results of policy as related to any given form. Yet this kind of approach will soon reach a limit of usefulness unless it is supported by experimental data. Such experimentation is peculiarly difficult in regard to so large and complex an organism as a metropolis. To some degree we can form judgments drawn from such different urban regions as Los Angeles, Stockholm, and Paris, but these judgments are necessarily distorted by various cultural and environmental disparities. Possibly we can study certain partial aspects of city form, such as the effects of varying density or the varying composition of centers, but the key questions pertain to the metropolitan pattern as an operating whole. Since we cannot build a metropolis purely for experimental purposes, we can only build and test models, with some simplified code to designate pattern. By simulating basic urban functions in these models, tests might be run for such criteria as cost, accessibility, imageability, or adaptability. Such tests will be hard to relate to the real situation, and it is difficult to see how certain objectives (such as interaction or participation) can be tested, yet this technique is our best current hope for experimental data on the implications of the total metropolitan pattern.

DYNAMIC AND COMPLEX FORMS

Until we have such experimental data, what can we conclude from our imaginary juxtaposition of metropolitan form and human goals? Each of the alternatives proposed has its drawbacks, its failures in meeting some basic objectives. A radical, consistent dispersion of the metropolis appears to restrict choice, impair spontaneous interaction, entail high cost, and inhibit a vivid metropolitan image. A galaxy of small communities promises better, but would still be substandard as regards choice, interaction, and cost, besides being harder to realize. A recentralization of the metropolis in an intensive core appears to entail almost fatal disadvantages in cost, comfort, individual participation, and adaptability. The rationalization of the old metropolis in a star would work better if central congestion could be avoided and free accessibility maintained, but this form is less and less usable as size increases. The ring has many special advantages but raises great difficulties in cost, adaptability, and continuity with present form.

Of course, these are all "pure" types that make no concessions to the complications of reality and they have been described as though they were states of perfection to be maintained forever. In actuality, a plan for a metropolis is more likely to be a complex and mixed one, to be realized as an episode in some continuous process, whose form involves rate and direction of change as well as a momentary pattern.

For example, let us consider, on the basis of the little we know, a form that might better satisfy our aspirations, if we accept the fact of metropolitan agglomeration: this form is in essence a variant of the dispersed urban sheet. Imagine a metropolis in which the flow system becomes more specialized and complex, assuming a triangular grid pattern that grows at the edges and becomes more specialized in the interior. Many types of flow would be provided for. Densities would have a wide range and a fine grain, with intensive peaks at junctions in the circulation system and with linear concentrations along major channels, but with extensive regions of low density inside the grid. Through the interstices of this network belts and tongues of open land would form another kind of grid. Thus the general pattern would resemble a fisherman's net, with a system of dispersed centers and intervening spaces. (See Figure 9.)

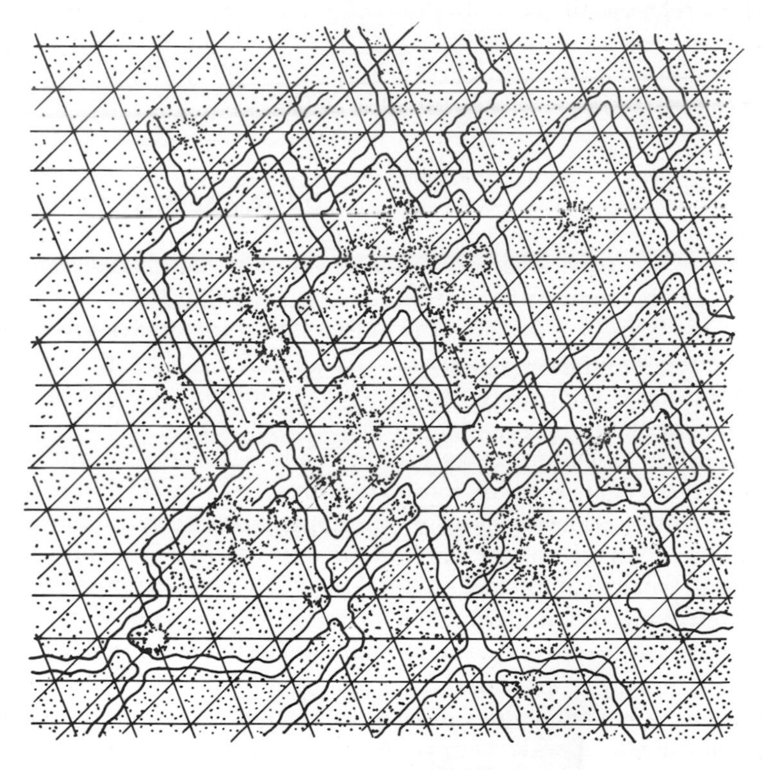

FIGURE 9 The polycentered net.

City-wide activities would concentrate in these knots of density, which would be graded in size. In the smaller centers the activities would not be specialized but the larger centers would be increasingly dominated by some special activity. Therefore the major centers would be highly specialized—although never completely "pure"—

and would be arranged in a loose central cluster, each highly accessible to another.

A metropolis of twenty million might have, not one such cluster, but two or three whose spheres of influence would overlap. These clusters might be so dense as to be served by transportation grids organized in three dimensions, like a skeletal framework in space. Elsewhere, the network would thin out and adapt itself to local configurations of topography. This general pattern would continue to specialize and to grow, perhaps in a rhythmically pulsating fashion. With growth and decay, parts of the whole would undergo periodic renewal. Such a form might satisfy many of the general criteria, but each particular metropolis is likely to encounter special problems. Even so, the description illustrates the complexity, the indeterminacy, and the dynamic nature of city form that are inherent in any such generalization.

Perhaps we can make such a proposal more concrete by stating it as a set of actions rather than as a static pattern. If this were the form desired, then the agencies of control would adopt certain definite policies. First, they would encourage continued metropolitan agglomeration. Second, they would begin to construct a generalized triangular grid of channels for transportation, adapting its interspacing and alignment to circumstances, but aiming at raising accessibility throughout the area as a whole. This grid would provide for many different kinds of flow and would have a hierarchy of its own—that is, the lines of circulation would be differentiated with respect to the intensity and speed of their traffic. Third, peaks of activity and density would be encouraged, but in sharply defined areas, not in rings whose density gradually declines from the center. The present metropolitan center would be encouraged to specialize and thus loosen into a cluster, while one or two major rival centers might develop elsewhere in the network, rather than allowing a general dispersal of city-wide activities. Such major specialized centers might be given even greater local intensity, with multi-level circulation, perhaps as a three-dimensional system of public rights-of-way.

Fourth, every effort would be made to retain, acquire, or clear a system of linked open spaces of generous size that pervaded the network. Fifth, a wide variety of activities, of accommodation and structural character, dispersed in a fine-grained pattern, would be encouraged. Once the concentration of special activities and the arrangement of higher densities in centers and along major channels has been provided for, then zoning and other controls would be employed only to maintain the minimum grain needed to preserve the character and efficiency of the various types of use and density, and large single-purpose areas would be avoided. Sixth, the form of centers, transportation channels, and major open spaces would be controlled so as to give as vivid a visual image as possible. Seventh, the agency would be committed to continuous rebuilding and reorganization of successive parts of the pattern.

Such a set of policies would mean a radical redirection of metropolitan growth. Whether this plan is feasible or worth the cost would require serious consideration. Even if this pattern were chosen, there would still be many crucial questions of relative emphasis and timing to be weighed. If life in the future metropolis is to be worthy of the massive effort necessary to build it, the physical pattern must satisfy human values. The coordination of metropolitan development, however obligatory, will not of itself ensure this happy result. Coordination must be directed toward some desired general pattern, and, to define this, we must clarify our alternatives and the goals they are meant to serve.

PART I URBAN LOCATION AND LAND USE THEORY

3

EDGAR M. HOOVER

The Evolving Form and Organization of the Metropolis: Principal Location Factors

It is a truism that socioeconomic organizations involve primarily mutual interrelations among decision units rather than the conveniently simple one-way impacts and sequential effects that we like to use whenever possible in building explanatory theories. And spatial organization in the urban setting presents this aspect of mutual interdependence of everything on everything to an expecially notable degree, precisely because the very raison d'être of a city is that it puts enormous numbers of diverse households, business firms, and other decision units cheek by jowl so that they may interact in fruitful and efficient ways.

So when we try to construct a conceptual model of how various residential and non-residential activities are spatially distributed in an urban area, we find a vast web of interdependence. Shopping centers locate primarily on the basis of access to consumers; people like to live close to their work, schools, shopping areas, and other types of facilities that they have occasion to use. Business firms of various types are attracted by access to labor supply, other related firms, or transportation facilities. In many kinds of urban activities, like seeks like. There are strong pressures for neighborhood homogeneity as such, as illustrated by the exclusive suburb, the garment district, and the automobile row. Every user of space has also to consider its price, and that will depend on how desirable the site is to other users.

Picturing all this even in greatly simplified terms as an equilibrium or dynamic system, the model builder or other theoretician trying to encompass the whole is likely to find himself hopelessly engulfed in myriad simultaneous equations in futile search of a useful solution or any solution. He has long since abandoned any attempt to elucidate by diagrams, since every important relationship seems to have many more than the graphically manageable two or three dimensions.

The situation is perhaps not quite as hopeless as this may imply.

Reprinted by permission of the publishers from H. Perloff and L. Wingo, Issues in Urban Economics *(Baltimore, Md.: Johns Hopkins Press, 1968), pp. 237–48. Only the first part of the article is reproduced.*

In tracing what determines what and how, there are a few welcome entries to and exits from the otherwise endless pretzel of causation. In the first place, some of the locations in an urban area can be regarded as determined exogenously and not just in response to the rest of the local pattern. Perhaps the most obvious example is a port and waterfront area, which is primarily determined by natural locational advantages. In the second place, it is clear that the actual spatial structure does not represent or even closely resemble a static equilibrium of the locating forces. Rather, it represents a snapshot of current states of mutual adjustment. Impacts of one change upon another, and spatial adjustments, take time, because long-lived physical facilities, habits, social and business ties, and political commitments are entailed. Consequently, at any given juncture a great many of the locations and locational shifts can pragmatically be viewed in terms of one-way, rather than reciprocal, impact. Actual decisions, even some planning decisions over substantial periods of time, can therefore take most of the current setting as given, and ignore a large part of the conceivable ultimate "feedback" effect.

It remains true that heroic and ingenious simplification of reality is necessary for any comprehensible image of the spatial structure. Throughout this paper, therefore, runs the question of how we can boil down facts and concepts and still have something nutritious left at the bottom of the kettle.

In this paper I shall try to describe the current state of understanding of economic forces affecting the spatial pattern of activities in urban areas. A vast amount of effort in recent years has been devoted to measuring those spatial distributions and their shifts, and constructing more sophisticated theories and quantitative models to interpret them. This effort, essential to any insight into coming problems and opportunities and to any co-ordinated planning and public policy, has been productive. We know a great deal more now about how the parts of urban areas fit together, about the processes of adjustment to changed conditions, and about the not-so-obvious effects of such specific major undertakings as freeway construction and urban renewal. Unfortunately, the problems also are growing and proliferating. It is not quite so clear that we have come much closer, in terms of knowing what should be done—to say nothing of actually doing it—toward real mastery of our urban destiny.

The first step in building a useful conceptual framework for understanding urban spatial patterns is to sort out the multifarious location factors that influence the preferences and placement of specific activities or types of decision units. What is suggested below is a logical way of reducing these factors to a manageably small number of groups.

"GIVEN" LOCATIONS

As already intimated, there are some kinds of locations within an urban area which are not determined primarily by where the other activities of the area are. Actually there are two distinct bases for exogenous determination of locations in an urban area.

For some kinds of activities, certain topographical or other natural site features are essential, which means that the lay of the land narrows down the choice to one or a very small number of locations. Ports for water traffic illustrate this, and there are some urban areas where the topography limits jet airport sites almost as drastically. In the past, defense considerations played a major part in locating the center of the city and the city itself. Localized recreational features such as beaches also illustrate this kind of factor, and in a few urban areas extractive industries (mainly mining) occur and are, of course, limited to certain special sites.

There is a further type of exogenously-determined location where the independent influence arises not from site features so much as from the fact that the activity in question is primarily concerned with contact with the outside world. Not just water ports but all kinds of terminal and interarea transport activities come under this head. Since there are great economies of scale in interregional transport and in terminal handling of goods, the urban area's gateways to and from the outside world constitute a set of focal points whose locations within the area help to determine—rather than just being determined by—the other activities of the area. This does not, of course, mean that such terminal locations (unless constrained by natural site features) are absolutely and permanently unresponsive to the changing pattern of other activities in the area served: such terminals are from time to time shifted to improve local accessibility or to make way for more insistent claimants for space. But the terminal locations do, in dynamic terms, play a primarily active role in shaping the pattern, and are to be viewed as part of the basic framework around which other activities are fitted.

Finally, in practice, we can generally take as given the focus of *maximum over-all accessibility* within the urban area. If we think of that as, for example, the place at which all the people of the area could assemble with the least total man-miles of travel, it is simply the median center of population, depending upon where all of the various types of residence are located. But travel is cheaper and faster along developed routes, and the cost and layout of these are affected by scale (traffic volume) and topography. So, evaluated in terms of travel cost and time, the focal maximum-access point can be regarded as a quite stable datum, even though the extent and importance of its access advantage over other points can change radically. We find in major American urban areas that, despite great over-all growth and far-reaching change and redistribution of activities, the focal point in this sense has usually shifted only a relatively short distance over periods measured in decades and generations, and that the earlier central foci are well within what we currently recognize as the central business district.

This concept of a single, most central focal point in an urban area is then significant and useful in developing simplified bases for understanding the over-all pattern. Obviously it has limitations. In the first place, there is in principle a variety of distinguishable central points of this sort, depending on what kinds of people or things we are imagining to be assembled with a minimum of total expense or effort. The employed workers of the area are not distributed in quite the same pattern as the total population, the shopping population, the school-attending population, the office workers, the industrial blue-collar workers, the theater-going or the library-using population; there might be a different optimum location from the standpoint of access for each of these types of people. Where goods rather than people are moving (as for example in the case of wholesale activity or production serving local needs such as daily newspapers or bread) the transport conditions are different and this may again mean a different optimum-access point. Finally, we have to recognize that, in varying degrees, the concept of one single point serving as the origin or destination for all flows of a specified type may be unrealistic and defensible only as a convenient fiction. Thus, if we identify some central point as having best access to the homes of the entire clerical office force of an urban area, this does not imply that all offices should logically be concentrated there. What it does imply is that, solely from the standpoint of commuting access for the clerical workers and ignoring claims of alternative space uses, it would make sense for the density of clerical employment to peak at that point. The significance of the focal point is determined, then, by the extent to which the activity involved is dependent upon (1) concentration in a single small district, and (2) access to the flow in question.

ACCESS LINKAGES

Since the function of an urban concentration is to facilitate contacts, the most important class of location factors shaping in the spatial pattern involves the advantage of physical proximity as measured by the money and/or time saved. This applies to cases in which such costs are substantially increased by added distance. Where they are not, they have nothing to do with urban concentration. For example, information in a widening sense (now including not only the printed word but sounds and computer signals and various types of pictures) can now be transmitted electronically over long distances just as quickly as over short distances, and sometimes just as cheaply to the user. This kind of contact, then, does not in itself depend upon, nor help to maintain or explain, intra-urban concentration.

Most relevant to the urban pattern are kinds of access for which costs are high and increase very rapidly with distance within the intra-urban range of distances (ranging from next door to a few dozen miles). Access involving human travel belongs par excellence to this category. Human beings require more elaborate and expensive vehicles (in dollars per ton of freight) than almost anything else. And, in particular, the time cost becomes generally even more important than the actual transport cost.

For people and things alike, the time cost to the passenger or the owner of the cargo is essentially an "opportunity cost," measured in terms of what useful services the person or thing being transported might otherwise be yielding. For commodities, we can measure this crudely in terms of interest on the investment represented by the value of the goods tied up in transit. For human beings, a commonly used yardstick is the rate of earnings while at work.[1] Thus, a man who earns $5.00 an hour would consider the time cost of a half-hour trip to be $2.50. This rate of time cost equals the accrual of interest (at 5 percent per annum) on an investment of about $880,000. So, calculated on that basis, human freight carries a time cost equivalent to that of a commodity worth at least $300 an ounce—perhaps not "more precious than rubies," but somewhere in the range between gold and diamonds.

The locational importance of an access linkage—i.e., the economic advantage of proximity—depends not only on how much the trip costs but also on how often the trip is made. Access to one's regular work place is likely to be a weighty consideration because it generally involves at least five round trips a week. It becomes somewhat less important if one shifts from a six day to a five day or shorter working week.

In the case of shopping trips, the costs of the trip should be related to the amount of the purchase in order to get a measure of the proximity advantage. Thus, if ten minutes' additional travel in each direction (twenty minutes round trip) is valued at, say, $1.50, it would be worthwhile making the extra travel in order to save $1.50. That is

1. This way of evaluating time cost is used for lack of anything better. We need more information on what value people of various sorts place upon time spent in transit under various circumstances.

15 percent on the purchase of $10 worth of groceries, but only 1½ percent on the purchase of a $100 television set. We could infer that it is logical to travel ten times as far to shop for television sets as to shop for groceries, if the amounts of purchases stated are representative and if the price differentials among shopping places are about the same for both types of goods. Here again, only time costs are considered; but this illustration illustrates the wide variations in the strength of the proximity incentive, even within the limits of one category of relationship, like retail trade.

The various kinds of access linkage that tie together the urban complex can be meaningfully classified in a good many ways: for example, by mode of transport of communication, or according to whether the incentive toward proximity is thought to influence predominantly the location of the sender or that of the receiver of whatever is being transported. Perhaps as useful a classification as any other can be based on the distinction between households and other decision units—i.e., between residential and non-residential activities.

Access among non-residential activities

This involves in part interindustry transactions such as those recorded in an input-output table. Business firms have an incentive to locate with good access to their local suppliers and their local business customers. To that extent, an interindustry transactions table gives us an idea of the relative volume and importance of the flows of goods and services between establishments[2] of the same and different industries, though this does not go very far toward measuring the relative strengths of locational attraction. Nor do these input-output figures take account of some strong business proximity ties that do not directly involve transactions at all. Thus, local branch offices or outlets of a firm are presumably located with an eye to maintaining good access to the main local office, while at the same time avoiding overlap of the sublocal territories served by the branches (for example, the individual supermarkets of a chain or branch offices of a bank). There are strong access ties between the central office of a corporation and its main research laboratory, involving the frequent going and coming of highly paid personnel, but no entries in the input-output tables.[3]

2. Although interindustry transaction (input-output) tables are organized in cross-tabulations of *industries*, the basic unit is the industrial plant or other *establishment*, and interestablishment transactions within the same industry are shown in the diagonal cells of the table.

3. It would be useful, I think, to try to construct tables showing the transport and communication charges incurred in the transaction flows between each pair of industries. This could lead to a still more useful cross-tabulation in which such charges were

Access among residential activities (interhousehold)

A significant proportion of journeys from homes are to the homes of others. Such trips are by nature almost exclusively social and thus involve people linked by family ties or closely similar tastes and interests. This suggests that the value of "interhousehold access" can also be expressed fairly accurately in terms of homogeneity preference—like seeks like. As we shall see later, however, the pressures toward neighborhood or "microspatial" homogeneity include a good many other factors in addition to simple access.

Access between residential and non-residential activities

This type of access is far and away the most conspicuous in the urban flow pattern. The entire labor force, with insignificant exceptions, is concerned with making the daily journey to work as quick and painless as possible. Such trips are much the largest single class of personal journeys within any urban area.[4] In addition, the distribution of goods and services at retail makes mutual proximity an advantage for both the distributors and the customers; some attention has already been paid here to the factors determining the relative strength of the attraction in the case of different types of goods and services. Trips to school, and for cultural and recreational purposes, make up most of the rest of the personal trip pattern. There is mutual advantage of proximity throughout: the non-residential activities dealing with households are most advantageously placed when they are close to concentrations of population, and at the same time residential sites are preferred (other things being equal) when they are in convenient access to jobs, shopping districts, schools, and other destinations.

The way in which these mutual attractions shape the locational pattern of activities within the urban area depends not so much on the strength of the attraction as on the degree to which the non-residential activity in question is concentrated at relatively few points (since

expressed as coefficients on a per-mile, per-unit-of-output basis. These coefficients would roughly measure the strength of spatial attraction between pairs of industries attributable to transport and communication costs. On this point, as on many others in the present paper, I am indebted to my colleague Professor David Houston for stimulating comments and discussion.

4. For relevant reference material, see J. R. Meyer, J. F. Kain, and M. Wohl, *The Urban Transportation Problem* (Harvard University Press, 1965), and Louis K. Loewenstein, *The Location of Residences and Work Places in Urban Areas* (The Scarecrow Press, Inc., 1965). Also, for a primarily bibliographical survey of the whole question of access, see Gunnar Olsson, *Distance and Human Interaction: A Review and Bibliography* (Bibliography Series, No. 2, Philadelphia: Regional Science Research Institute, 1965).

almost any such activity is much less evenly diffused over the area than residence is). At one extreme, there are non-residential activities that need access to a large fraction of the households of the urban area, but that are confined to one location, and perhaps one establishment or facility. Thus, a visit to a large department store or some kind of specialty shop, or to a main library, or to the opera, or to attend university classes may mean, in many urban areas, a visit to one specific location, without alternatives. All such trips within the area have a single common destination focus and the attraction, from the household side, is centripetal, or at least monocentric. From the standpoint of the non-residential activity in question, optimum access means the choice of a point of minimum total travel time for all of the interested households in the area.

At the opposite extreme are activities not subject to any compelling scale economies or other economics of concentration, which can therefore have a dispersed or many-centered pattern. Drugstores, barbershops, branch banking offices, and the like are basically neighborhood-serving rather than catering to a broad citywide clientele. A good location is simply one in which there is a sufficient amount of business within a short distance. And the attraction of such activities to the householder is within rather than between neighborhoods, being measured in blocks rather than in miles. The gradient of access advantage is a local one, replicated many times over in all parts of the area, rather than a single one peaking at some one point.

AGGLOMERATIVE FACTORS

Access considerations involve a mutual attraction between complementary parties: stores and customers, employees and firms, pupils and schools. But there are also economic incentives favoring the concentration and clustering of identical or similar units of activity. The simplest case of this is perhaps that of scale economies. A large electric power plant is more efficient than a smaller one. A large store can, in addition to possible cost savings, provide more variety and thus enhance its attractiveness to buyers. As already suggested, some kinds of activities (such as opera performances) are subject to scale economies to the extent that only in the largest cities can more than one establishment be supported. Business corporations as a rule find that they can best concentrate their research laboratories at one location, and the same applies somewhat more obviously to their central offices.

A different and more subtle case involves the basis for clustering of many similar business firms or institutions. The classic case is the mid-Manhattan garment center, but analogous complexes are found in every city, such as "automobile rows," the financial district, and various types of specialized whosesale districts.[5]

If we inquire more deeply into the reasons for these clusterings we find that the establishments in the cluster are sharing some common advantage that is generally a pool of especially suitable labor, a variety of specialized business services, or the congregation of customers seeking to compare a variety of offerings. Sometimes two or all three of these kinds of external economy are involved. If the individual small firms in the cluster have good enough access to these external advantages, they themselves can specialize narrowly in functions not requiring large-scale operation, while at the same time having passed on to them the economies of a large labor market, a large concentration of buyers, and specialized business services produced on an efficiently large scale.

It appears, then, that these external economies of certain clustered activities are really based on two factors previously discussed: access, and economies of scale. What is new is the extension of the concept of scale economies to labor markets and shopping comparison markets as operating mechanisms.

Finally, the clustering of like activities can reflect immediate environmental interdependence. A site has value according to its access but also according to its physical features and to the character of its immediate surroundings. Neighborhood character in terms of cleanliness, smells, noise, traffic congestion, public safety, variety interest, and general appearance is important in attracting some kinds of use and repelling others. Prestige types of residence or business are of course particularly sensitive to this kind of advantage, which often is more important than any access consideration as such. A high-income householder may be willing to lengthen his work journey greatly for the sake of agreeable surroundings.

As has been suggested earlier, the usual effect of this type of consideration is to make neighborhoods more homogeneous within themselves, and more unlike other neighborhoods—a tendency toward areal specialization by uses, or segregation in the broad sense. With few exceptions, a given type of activity finds advantage in being in a neighborhood devoted to reasonably similar kinds of uses, and disadvantage in being in violent contrast to the neighborhood pattern. Zoning controls and planned street layouts play a part in reinforcing this tendency.

5. Cf. Robert M. Lichtenberg, *One-Tenth of a Nation* (New York Metropolitan Regional Study, Harvard University Press, 1960) for a penetrating analysis of the "external-economy" industries in New York.

COMPETITION FOR SPACE: THE COST OF SITES

I have cataloged above the various kinds of locational pulls and pushes that affect activities in an urban area. Most of the relationships mentioned are pulls—they involve a mutual locational attraction among complementary or similar units of activity. This reflects the underlying rationale of a city as a device effecting close contact and interaction on a grand scale.

But every land use needs some space or elbow room on which to operate, and the sites with best access or environmental features command a high scarcity value. The market mechanism works (albeit imperfectly like most markets) to allocate locations to uses and users who can exploit them to best advantage as measured by what they are willing to bid for their use.

SIMPLIFICATION AND SYNTHESIS

The various determinants of location in an urban area have been discussed above. In a really complex analysis, each could be broken down much further. But we seek simplification. It appears that basically there are just three kinds of considerations that determine the relative desirability of locations for particular decision units such as households or business establishments. These are (1) access, (2) environmental characteristics, and (3) cost. They reflect the fact that the user of a site is really involved with it in three different ways. He occupies it, as resident or producer, and is thus concerned with its site and neighborhood, or immediate environmental qualities. He and other persons and goods and services move between this site and others; he is therefore concerned with its convenience of access to other places. Finally, he has to pay for its use and is therefore concerned with its cost.

Ruthless simplification along these lines makes possible the useful step of building a conceptual model of the spatial structure of an urban economy. For example, in such a model we can reduce the complex factor of access to the simple form of access to a single given focal point, as if all intra-urban journeys were to or from downtown and all shipments of goods also passed through downtown. We can in the interests of maximum simplicity even assume that the cost of transportation within the urban area is directly proportional to airline distance. Access is then measured simply in radial distance from the center.

We can assume away all differentiation of sites with respect to topography, amenity, and environmental advantage. These two simplifications also imply ignoring the manifold types of external-economy effects and environmental attractions and repulsions that have been discussed. In effect, we envisage each type of activity as *independently* attracted (by access considerations) toward the urban center; the only interdependence among the locations of the various activities arises, then, from the fact that they are bidding against one another for space.

It is also appropriate to develop a condensed classification of activities. No two households, factories, or other decision units are exactly alike in their location preferences, but they can be grouped into more or less homogeneous classes on the basis of similarity in access/space trade-off. Among households, for example, it appears from empirical studies that income level and family structure (presence or absence of young children) are the principal determinants of this trade-off.

With the above types of simplification as well as with others, it is possible to develop more or less systematic theories or frameworks of analysis for urban spatial patterns. Some of these patterns will be taken up here; Professor Harris' paper, elsewhere in this volume, is more specifically directed to this question. It is sufficient here to note that most such models are partial in the sense that they attempt to explain or predict the location of one type of activity in terms of its adjustment to given or assumed locations of the other activities, including transportation services. Thus, a retailing location model may analyze the way in which retail stores locate in response to the advantages of access to the homes of consumers, a residential location model may analyze the way in which residences locate in response to the desire to shorten the journey to work, and so on.

WILLIAM ALONSO

A Theory of the Urban Land Market

The early theory of rent and location concerned itself primarily with agricultural land. This was quite natural, for Ricardo and Malthus lived in an agricultural society. The foundations of the formal spatial analysis of agricultural rent and location are found in the work of J. von Thunen, who said, without going into detail, that the urban land market operated under the same principles.[1] As cities grew in importance, relatively little attention was paid to the theory of urban rents. Even the great Marshall provided interesting but only random insights, and no explicit theory of the urban land market and urban locations was developed.

Since the beginning of the twentieth century there has been considerable interest in the urban land market in America. R. M. Hurd[2] in 1903 and R. Haig[3] in the twenties tried to create a theory of urban land by following von Thunen. However, their approach copied the form rather than the logic of agricultural theory, and the resulting theory can be shown to be insufficient on its own premises. In particular, the theory failed to consider residences, which constitute the preponderant land use in urban areas.

Yet there are interesting problems that a theory of urban land must consider. There is, for instance, a paradox in American cities: the poor live near the center, on expensive land, and the rich on the periphery, on cheap land. On the logical side, there are also aspects of great interest, but which increase the difficulty of the analysis. When a purchaser acquires land, he acquires two goods (land and location) in only one transaction, and only one payment is made for the combination. He could buy the same quantity of land at another location, or he could buy more, or less land at the same location. In the analysis, one encounters, as well, a negative good (distance) with positive costs

1. Johan von Thunen, *Der Isolierte Staat in Beziehung auf Landwirtschaft und Nationalekonomie*, 1st. vol., 1826, 3d. vol. and new edition, 1863.

2. Richard M. Hurd, *Principles of City Land Values*, N.Y.: The Record and Guide, 1903.

3. Robert M. Haig, "Toward an Understanding of the Metropolis," *Quarterly Journal of Economics*, XL, 3 (May 1926); and *Regional Survey of New York and Its Environs* N.Y.: New York City Plan Commission, 1927.

Reprinted from Papers and Proceedings of the Regional Science Association, *6 (1960), 149–57, by permission of the publishers and the author.*

(commuting costs); or, conversely, a positive good (accessibility) with negative costs (savings in commuting). In comparison with agriculture, the urban case presents another difficulty. In agriculture, the location is extensive: many square miles may be devoted to one crop. In the urban case the site tends to be much smaller, and the location may be regarded as a dimensionless point rather than an area. Yet the thousands or millions of dimensionless points which constitute the city, when taken together, cover extensive areas. How can these dimensionless points be aggregated into two-dimensional space?

Here I will present a non-mathematical over-view, without trying to give it full precision, of the long and rather complex mathematical analysis which constitutes a formal theory of the urban land market.[4] It is a static model in which change is introduced by comparative statics. And it is an economic model: it speaks of economic men, and it goes without saying that real men and social groups have needs, emotions, and desires which are not considered here. This analysis uses concepts which fit with agricultural rent theory in such a way that urban and rural land uses may be considered at the same time, in terms of a single theory. Therefore, we must examine first a very simplified model of the agricultural land market.

AGRICULTURAL MODEL

In this model, the farmers are grouped around a single market, where they sell their products. If the product is wheat, and the produce of one acre of wheat sells for $100 at the market while the costs of production are $50 per acre, a farmer growing wheat at the market would make a profit of $50 per acre. But if he is producing at some distance—say, 5 miles—and it costs him $5 per mile to ship an acre's product, his transport costs will be $25 per acre. His profits will be equal to value minus production costs minus shipping charges: 100 − 50 − 25 = $25. This relation may be shown diagrammatically (Figure 1). At the market, the farmer's profits are $50, and 5 miles out, $25; at intermediate distance, he will receive intermediate profits. Finally, at a distance of 10 miles from the market, his production costs plus shipping charges will just equal the value of his produce at the market. At distances greater than 10 miles, the farmer would operate at a loss.

In this model, the profits derived by the farmers are tied directly to their location. If the functions of farmer and landowner are

4. A full development of the theory is presented in my doctoral dissertation. *A Model of the Urban Land Market: Locations and Densities of Dwellings and Businesses*, University of Pennsylvania, 1960.

viewed as separate, farmers will bid rents for land according to the profitability of the location. The profits of the farmer will therefore be shared with landowner through rent payments. As farmers bid against each other for the more profitable locations, until farmers' profits are everywhere the same ("normal" profits), what we have called profits becomes rent. Thus, the curve in Figure 1, which we derived as a farmers' profit curve, once we distinguish between the roles of the farmer and the landowner, becomes a bid rent function, representing the price or rent per acre that farmers will be willing to pay for land at the different locations.

We have shown that the slope of the rent curve will be fixed by the transport costs on the produce. The level of the curve will be set by the

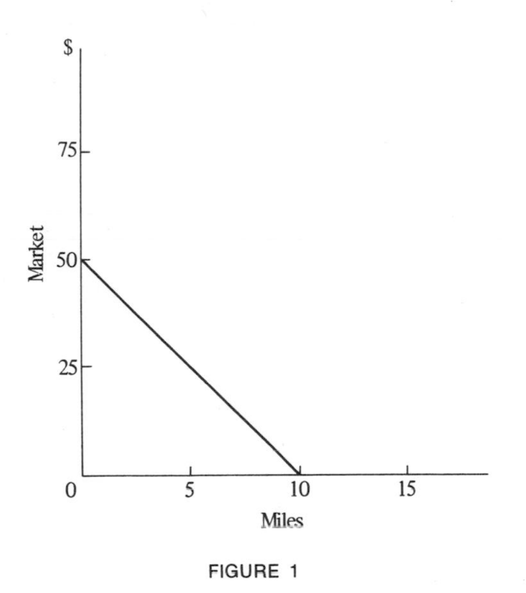

FIGURE 1

price of the produce at the market. Examine Figure 2. The lower curve is that of Figure 1, where the price of wheat is $100 at the market, and production costs are $50. If demand increases, and the price of wheat at the market rises to $125 (while production and transport costs remain constant), profits or bid rent at the market will be $75; at 5 miles, $50; $25 at 10 miles, and zero at 15 miles. Thus, each bid rent curve is a function of rent vs. distance, but there is a family of such curves, the level of any one determined by the price of the produce at the market, higher prices setting higher curves.

Consider now the production of peas. Assume that the price at the market of one acre's production of peas is $150, the costs of production are $75, and the transport costs per mile are $10. These

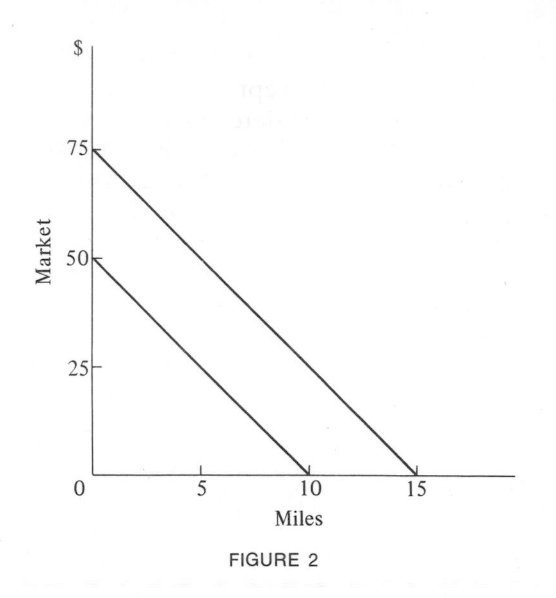

FIGURE 2

conditions will yield curve *MN* in Figure 3, where bid rent by pea farmers at the market is $75 per acre, 5 miles from the market $25, and zero at 7.5 miles. Curve *RS* represents bid rents by wheat farmers, at a price of $100 for wheat. It will be seen that pea farmers can bid higher rents in the range of 0 to 5 miles from the market; farther out, wheat farmers can bid higher rents. Therefore, pea farming will take place in the ring from 0 to 5 miles from the market, and wheat farming in the ring from 5 to 10 miles. Segments *MT* of the bid rent

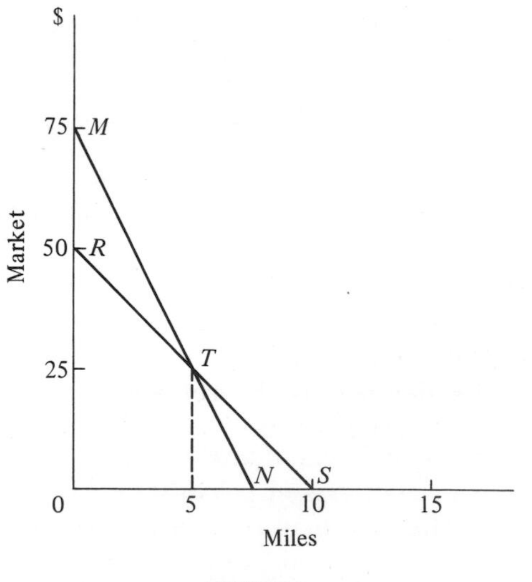

FIGURE 3

curve of pea farming and *TS* of wheat farming will be the effective rents, while segments *RT* and *TN* represent unsuccessful bids.

The price of the product is determined by the supply-demand relations at the market. If the region between zero and five miles produces too many peas, the price of the product will drop, and a lower bid rent curve for pea farming will come into effect, so that pea farming will be practiced to some distance less than five miles.

Abstracting this view of the agricultural land market, we have that:

1. Land uses determine land values, through competitive bidding among farmers;
2. Land values distribute land uses, according to their ability to pay;
3. The steeper curves capture the central locations. (This point is a simplified one for simple, well-behaved curves).

Abstracting the process now *from* agriculture, we have:

1. For each user of land (e.g., wheat farmer) a family of bid rent functions is derived, such that the user is indifferent as to his location along any *one* of these functions (because the farmer, who is the decision-maker in this case, finds that profits are everywhere the same, i.e., normal, as long as he remains on one curve);
2. The equilibrium rent at any location is found by comparing the bids of the various potential users and choosing the highest;
3. Equilibrium quantities of land are found by selecting the proper bid rent curve for each user (in the agricultural case, the curve which equates supply and demand for the produce).

BUSINESS

We shall now consider the urban businessman, who, we shall assume, makes his decisions so as to maximize profits. A bid rent curve for the businessman, then, will be one along which profits are everywhere the same: the decision-maker will be indifferent as to his location along such a curve.

Profit may be defined as the remainder from the volume of business after operating costs and land costs have been deducted. Since in most cases the volume of business of a firm as well as its operating costs will vary with its location, the rate of change of the bid rent curve will bear no simple relation to transport costs (as it did in agriculture). The rate of change of the total bid rent for a firm, where profits are constant by definition, will be equal to the rate of change in the volume of business minus the rate of change in operating costs. Therefore the slope of the bid rent curve, the values of which are in terms of dollars per unit of land, will be equal to the rate of change in the volume of business minus the rate of change in operating costs, divided by the area occupied by the establishment.

A different level of profits would yield a different bid rent curve. The higher the bid rent curve, the lower the profits, since land is more expensive. There will be a highest curve, where profits will be zero. At higher land rents the firm could only operate at a loss.

Thus we have, as in the case of the farmer, a family of bid rent curves, along the path of any one of which the decision-maker—in this case, the businessman—is indifferent. Whereas in the case of the farmer the level of the curve is determined by the price of the produce, while profits are in all cases "normal," i.e., the same, in the case of the urban firm, the level of the curve is determined by the level of the profits, and the price of its products may be regarded for our purposes as constant.

RESIDENTIAL

The household differs from the farmer and the urban firm in that satisfaction rather than profits is the relevant criterion of optional location. A consumer, given his income and his pattern of tastes, will seek to balance the costs and bother of commuting against the advantages of cheaper land with increasing distance from the center of the city and the satisfaction of more space for living. When the individual consumer faces a given pattern of land costs, his equilibrium location and the size of his site will be in terms of the marginal changes of these variables.

The bid rent curves of the individual will be such that, for any given curve, the individual will be equally satisfied at every location at the price set by the curve. Along any bid rent curve, the price the individual will bid for land will decrease with distance from the center at a rate just sufficient to produce an income effect which will balance to his satisfaction the increased costs of commuting and the bother of a long trip. This slope may be expressed quite precisely in mathematical terms, but it is a complex expression, the exact interpretation of which is beyond the scope of this paper.

Just as different prices of the produce set different levels for the bid rent curves of the farmer, and different levels of profit for the urban firm, different levels of satisfaction correspond to the various levels of the family of bid rent curves of the individual household. The higher curves obviously yield less satisfaction because a higher price is implied, so that, at any given location, the individual will be able to afford less land and other goods.

INDIVIDUAL EQUILIBRIUM

It is obvious that families of bid rent curves are in many respects similar to indifference curve mappings. However, they differ in some important ways. Indifference curves map a path of indifference (equal satisfaction) between combinations of quantities of two goods. Bid rent functions map an indifference path between the price of one good (land) and quantities of another and strange type of good, distance from the center of the city. Whereas indifference curves refer only to tastes and not to budget, in the case of households, bid rent functions are derived both from budget and taste considerations. In the case of the urban firm, they might be termed isoprofit curves. A more superficial difference is that, whereas the higher indifference curves are the preferred ones, it is the lower bid rent curves that yield greater profits or satisfaction. However, bid rent curves may be used in a manner analogous to that of indifference curves to find the equilibrium location and land price for the resident or the urban firm.

Assume you have been given a bid rent mapping of a land use, whether business or residential (curves $brc_{1,2,3}$, etc., in Figure 4).

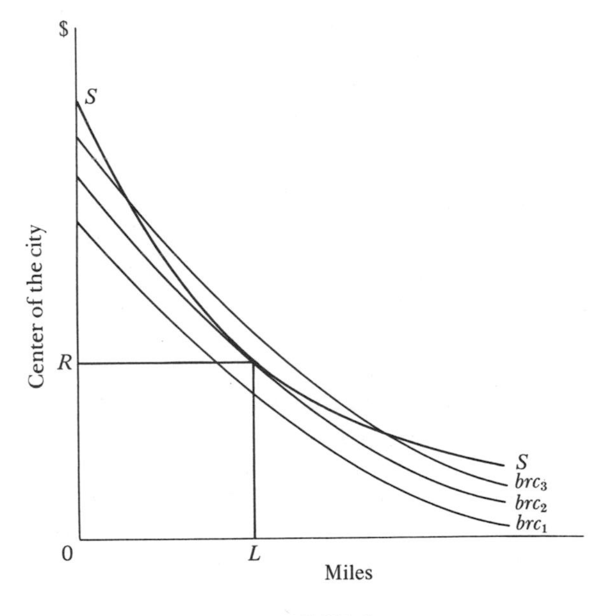

FIGURE 4

Superimpose on the same diagram the actual structure of land prices in the city (curve *SS*). The decision-maker will wish to reach the lowest possible bid rent curve. Therefore, he will choose that point at which the curve of actual prices (*SS*) will be tangent to the lowest of the bid rent curves with which it comes in contact(brc_2). At this point will be the equilibrium location (*L*) and the equilibrium land rent (*R*) for this user of land. If he is a businessman, he will have maximized profits; if he is a resident, he will have maximized satisfaction.

Note that to the left of this point of equilibrium (toward the center of the city) the curve of actual prices is steeper than the bid rent curve; to the right of this point (away from the center) it is less steep. This is another aspect of the rule we noted in the agricultural model: the land uses with steeper bid rent curves capture the central locations.

MARKET EQUILIBRIUM

We now have, conceptually, families of bid rent curves for all three types of land uses. We also know that the steeper curves will occupy the more central locations. Therefore, if the curves of the various users are ranked by steepness, they will also be ranked in terms of their accessibility from the center of the city in the final solution. Thus, if the curves of the business firm are steeper than those of residences, and the residential curves steeper than the agricultural, there will be business at the center of the city, surrounded by residences, and these will be surrounded by agriculture.

This reasoning applies as well within land use groupings. For instance, it can be shown that, given two individuals of similar tastes, both of whom prefer living at low densities, if their incomes differ, the bid rent curves of the wealthier will be flatter than those of the man of lower income. Therefore, the poor will tend to central locations on expensive land and the rich to cheaper land on the periphery. The reason for this is not that the poor have greater purchasing power, but rather that they have steeper bid rent curves. This stems from the fact that, at any given location, the poor can buy less land than the rich, and since only a small quantity of land is involved, changes in its price are not as important for the poor as the costs and inconvenience of commuting. The rich, on the other hand, buy greater quantities of land, and are consequently affected by changes in its price to a greater degree. In other words, because of variations in density among different levels of income, accessibility behaves as an inferior good.

Thus far, through ranking the bid rent curves by steepness, we have found the relative rankings of prices and locations, but not the actual prices, locations, or densities. It will be remembered that in the agricultural case equilibrium levels were brought about by changes in the price of the products, until the amount of land devoted to each crop was in agreement with the demand for that crop.

For urban land this process is more complex. The determination of densities (or their inverse, lot size) and locations must be found simultaneously with the resulting price structure. Very briefly, the method consists of assuming a price of land at the center of the city, and determining the prices at all other locations by the competitive bidding of the potential users of land in relation to this price. The highest bid captures each location, and each bid is related to a most preferred alternative through the use of bid rent curves. This most preferred alternative is the marginal combination of price and location for that particular land use. The quantities of land occupied by the land users are determined by these prices. The locations are determined by assigning to each successive user of land the location available nearest the center of the city after the assignment of land quantities to the higher and more central bidders.

Since initially the price at the center of the city was assumed, the resulting set of prices, locations, and densities may be in error. A series of iterations will yield the correct solution. In some cases, the solution may be found by a set of simultaneous equations rather than by the chain of steps which has just been outlined.

The model presented in this paper corresponds to the simplest case: a single-center city, on a featureless plain, with transportation in all directions. However, the reasoning can be extended to cities with several centers (shopping, office, manufacturing, etc.), with structured road patterns, and other realistic complications. The theory can also be made to shed light on the effects of economic development, changes in income structure, zoning regulations, taxation policies, and other. At this stage, the model is purely theoretical; however, it is hoped that it may provide a logical structure for econometric models which may be useful for prediction.

5

LEON MOSES and HAROLD F. WILLIAMSON, JR.

The Location of Economic Activity in Cities

The decentralization or suburbanization of economic activity in major metropolitan areas, particularly those which grew to immense size during the nineteenth century, is a familiar phenomenon. The problems, such as increasing central city budgetary difficulties, associated with this process are also familiar. In this paper the authors hope to provide additional insight into the development of such large, core-dominated cities and into the factors which have and are affecting the location of economic activity within them.

The paper begins with a summary of a theoretical analysis developed to examine the structure of factor prices and costs within a core-dominated city. This analysis does not directly incorporate the influence of agglomerative economies, though their importance is acknowledged. The model highlights the effects of certain technological lags and transport cost relationships that the authors feel have not been sufficiently well understood. The model, moreover, assigns to the automobile a more modest role in the suburbanization of metropolitan activity than is found in most studies.

The remainder of the paper presents the results of two empirical analyses of the manufacturing sector in a particular core-dominated city—Chicago. (The analysis of location is made for this sector since manufacturing is the largest employer in many of these metropolitan areas and has had the largest central city decline in employment.) The first analysis presents evidence on an early stage of decentralization, roughly 1900 to 1920. The second summarizes some preliminary conclusions on the location of economic activity in a more recent period.

THEORETICAL ANALYSIS OF THE CORE-DOMINATED CITY

The city is divided into two areas: the core where all economic activity initially takes place and the satellite or residential zone surrounding it where a known number of households are located.

Reprinted from American Economic Review *(May 1967), pp. 211–22, by permission of the American Economic Association and the authors.*

The satellite area is assumed to be a transport plane and all households are assumed to be identical in terms of tastes—they have identical utility functions—and income earned at the core.[1] An equilibrium distribution of households requires that each is maximizing utility subject to constraints on income and time, the entire satellite ring is settled, and no household can improve its level of satisfaction by changing location, meaning that all households are equally well-off.

It is the price of land which must vary so that these conditions are met since—as in the usual analysis of urban rent—incomes, transport costs, and the price of goods are fixed and known throughout the urban area. The result is a rent gradient—a function indicating the variation in the price of land as distance from the core varies. Since net income falls and the cost of goods rises as distance from the core increases, it can be shown that the rent gradient must decline with distance. Otherwise the equilibrium condition that utility is a locational constant would not be met.

Once the equilibrium distribution of households and the resulting rent gradient are established, a price gradient for labor—the wage rate gradient—can be determined. It measures the wage a firm has to pay at various locations in the satellite area to switch a given number of workers from core employment to employment at those sites, other things given, including the rent gradient.[2] The form of the wage rate gradient is not certain for all numbers of workers. It can, however, be shown to slope downward if a firm's employment were small relative to population in the vicinity of a potential site. The remaining factor price gradient, that for liquid capital, is invariant with respect to distance from the core. Capital is assumed to be perfectly mobile within an urban area so the interest rate is a locational constant.

The above analysis leads to the conclusion that factor costs tended to be lower in the satellite area. If this is the case, it is evident that other conditions must account for the growth of the core-dominated city. The agglomerative economies associated with proximity to competitive and complementary firms and to service industries are usually advanced to explain concentration of economic

1. The assumptions are similar to those used by other authors who have analyzed urban land rents. For example, see William Alonso's study [1] of land rent.

2. For a detailed development of the analysis concerning this gradient, see Leon N. Moses [11]. The assumption that the rent gradient is held constant means that the impact of the firm's relocation to an alternative site is not considered. This impact includes the changes in work trip lengths for the affected households and the development of a second rent gradient centered at the new employment site. This is not considered here since the analysis is sufficient without it to provide insights into the location of urban plants and the factors affecting their movement.

activity in the core. The authors acknowledge their importance but wish to focus attention on the structure of transport costs in the nineteenth century, and the influence this structure had on the form of large cities. It is a thesis of this paper that in the nineteenth century the cost of moving goods within cities was: (1) high relative to the cost of moving people within cities; and (2) high relative to the cost of moving goods between cities. Location in the satellite area involved moving away from the central goods handling facilities of the city. In general, the increased costs of transporting inputs from and outputs to the core (for shipment to other areas) outweighed the savings from the lower factor prices associated with location in the satellite area.[3]

This in fact tended to be the situation during the period when the core-dominated cities grew. Firms received from and shipped to other regions a significant proportion of their inputs and outputs. The economies of scale in rail transport—the main mode for interregional goods movement—were such that the receiving and sending of such shipments were concentrated at one or at most a few large, centrally located freight terminals. Within cities, the movement of people was relatively efficient, being carried out by modes which were closely related to the railroad: trolleys and street railways. Intracity movement of goods, however, took place by an inefficient mode, the horse and wagon. The cost of moving goods was, therefore, high relative to the cost of moving people. This relative cost relationship played a crucial role in the emergence of the core-dominated city. The lower transport costs associated with location in the core exceeded the reduction in cost possible from lower wages and rents at sites in the satellite area. A prerequisite for decentralization was the breaking of the transport tie to the core.

Only after technological changes occurred in transportation was the attraction of a non-core location strongly felt. The major change was the introduction of the truck which reduced the cost of moving goods within cities. Its effect on the spatial structure of cities can, roughly, be divided into two phases. During the first, the motor truck was introduced and became the dominant form of intra-urban carriage, but interurban carriage was still done by railroads. In this period—the first two decades of this century—firms could leave the core but were still tied to it for shipments to and from other regions. This tie was weakened during the second phase when improvements in the truck and in the interregional highway system meant this mode could be used for long-distance transport. The full impact of this change was probably not felt until the revival of a strong peacetime

3. For a study of freight costs and their impact upon the New York Metropolitan Region, see Benjamin Chinitz [6, Part II, particularly Chap. 6].

economy after World War II. The attractiveness of the satellite area in this period was increased by the automobile which allowed firms to draw labor from a broad area.[4]

In summary, the theoretical analysis emphasized the effect of changes in transportation cost structure. It implied that decentralization should have begun, roughly, during the first two decades of this century when the motor truck was first introduced, though this period is not usually thought to be one of suburbanization. The first part of the empirical analysis examines this period. The second part provides a more extensive examination of the spatial rearrangement of firms during the post-World War II period—the period during which the impact of interregional transportation was felt.

EMPIRICAL ANALYSIS: THE EARLY PERIOD

There is fragmentary evidence in support of the proposition that the introduction of the truck in the first two decades of the present century did reduce the cost of moving goods within cities relative to the cost of moving people. The cost of moving people—to judge from the fare—was fairly constant during this period. The passenger fare was almost universally five cents at the beginning of the century and remained in force until approximately World War I.[5] At the same time, motor carriage began to replace the horse and wagon in urban goods transport. Evidence of the relative efficiency of the two modes is seen in the rapid rise in truck registrations (800 in 1910 in Chicago to 23,000 in 1920) and decline in the number of horse-drawn vehicle registrations (58,000 to 31,000 during the same period).[6]

Reliable data on cost differences between motor truck and wagon are practically nonexistent for urban areas but Department of Agriculture surveys of farm use give some idea of relative costs. A survey in 1918 found that horse and wagon costs were $.33 per ton-mile. This was a bit higher than similar surveys had found it to be near the turn of the century. The ton-mile cost for truck was $.15. Another survey in 1920 found average hours per ton-mile were one-third to one-half as great for motor truck as for horse and wagon. The truck thus appears to have had a time as well as a direct money cost

4. The attractiveness of suburban locations was also enhanced by other technological changes during this period; for a discussion of such factors, see J. R. Meyer, J. Kain, and M. Wohl [10, pp. 10–18]. Improvements in data processing and communications, for example, meant that firms could remain "near" other firms though they had moved many miles away.

5. See American Transit Association [2, Chap. I].

6. Homer Hoyt [8, p. 485].

advantage.[7] These findings were, however, for hauls longer than those common in urban transportation during the period. They are, therefore, somewhat biased against the horse and wagon since its disadvantages increase as distance increases. Even with this qualification, the data do give rough evidence that the introduction of the motor truck reduced the cost of moving goods during a period when the cost of moving people was relatively constant.

Evidence of decentralization during this period of changing transportation costs is also limited. It is based on a survey made by the authors of 955 firms in four industry groups.[8] Information on location was obtained for 1908 and 1920.[9] There were 473 firms which could be identified at both dates. Two hundred eighty-five of these firms had shifted location during the period.

The behavior of these firms is in agreement with the conclusions reached in the theoretical analysis. While firms moved a short distance on average, the direction of movement was away from the core. The average distance from the core for firms which moved was 59 percent greater in 1920 than it had been in 1908, having increased from 0.92 miles to 1.46 miles. In addition, the average origin (1908) distance for firms which moved was less than the distance for nonmoving firms. This agrees with the implication that the introduction of the motor truck had a greater impact on core area firms than those already located somewhat outside the core.

EMPIRICAL ANALYSIS: THE RECENT PERIOD

For the years 1950 through mid-1964, it was possible to obtain rather detailed information for 2,000 firms in the Chicago area which had either relocated or expanded capacity at a site different from their existing one.[10] Information on the size, location, and

7. The money results from the 1918 survey are from George W. Grupp [7, pp. 38–39]; while the time results from the 1920 survey appear in H. R. Tolley and L. M. Church [12, p. 11].

8. The industry groups were printing and publishing, chemicals, nonelectrical machinery, and electrical machinery. They were chosen because of their importance to the city's economy and because firms in these industries could be most easily identified in the industrial directories used for gathering the sample.

9. Though it was hoped to cover the first two decades of this century, the study was begun in 1908 because this was the first for which a directory was available which provided an adequate industrial identification for the firms. The directories used were the *Membership Directory* (1908) and the *Blue Book of Chicago Commerce* (1920), both issued by the Chicago Association of Commerce.

10. The metropolitan area was defined to be the study area of the Chicago Area Transportation Study (CATS) and the geographic divisions used were those developed by CATS. For information on the geographic, land use and population characteristics of the study area, see CATS [3] [4] [5].

industry group of each firm was gathered from the files of the Chicago Association of Commerce and Industry and the Illinois State Employment Service. Destination for each movement was plotted by Chicago Area Transportation Study (CATS) zone and also by postal zone within Chicago and suburbs outside the city. Data on characteristics of the metropolitan area such as population and land use were obtained from CATS surveys and maps. With this information, it was possible to analyze the pattern of location and movement. This analysis is divided into three parts: the distribution of origins, the direction and distance of movement, and the pattern of destinations.

Distribution of Origins

Preliminary investigation revealed that the distribution of origins fell off sharply as distance from the core of the city increased. One interpretation of this result is that inner portions of the city have become undesirable as locations, so that firms located there have a higher propensity to move. This conclusion is somewhat misleading in that it ignores the fact that zones near the core also are likely to have larger numbers of firms in them. The critical issue, therefore, is not whether number of origins declines with distance but whether the percentage of origins behaves in this manner.

To see whether number of firms or distance was more highly correlated with number of origins, regressions were run with origins in each zone as the dependent variable and these two factors as the independent variables.[11] The geographic divisions used were postal zones within the city of Chicago and suburbs outside it. When number of origins was regressed on each variable alone, number of firms provided a much higher explanatory power (coefficient of determination between 0.51 and 0.90) than did distance (coefficient of determination between 0.19 and 0.43). When the regression was run for both independent variables, number of firms had the higher explanatory power. The additional explanation provided by the distance variable was not significant in over half the cases. Thus, number of origins is highly correlated with number of firms in a zone. The coefficient for number of firms was from ten to twenty times as large as its standard error; i.e., the t ratio was between ten and

11. Though the results were summarized without this distinction, there were actually four groups of firms examined. The division was by type of move—relocation or expansion at new—and by period—1950–59 and 1960–64. The latter division was made because the data for each period were gathered at different times by different groups though from the same sources. In general, the results are similar for all four groups.

twenty. Economic dispersal has not therefore occurred because firms that are closer to the core have a higher propensity to move. Instead, this propensity is fairly constant over the entire metropolitan area. Since this percentage of firms being "set loose" is relatively constant, the shifting pattern of industrial location must result from the spatial pattern of destinations—the percentage of firms which "set down" in each zone. Before turning to the analysis of this pattern of destinations, it is necessary to determine whether these firms are truly set loose from their origin site.

Distance of Movement

The preceding empirical work emphasized net change in distance from the core; i.e., distance from the core of a firm's destination minus its origin distance. Net change is a surrogate for the variation in land and labor costs and for the expense of maintaining linkages with the core which arose due to the move. A different measure of the connection between origin and destination is the distance actually moved by the firm. It reflects the costs associated with the linkage between these two sites. As distance moved increases, established ties with suppliers of raw materials and services, labor supply, and customers may be attenuated. Costs may then have to be incurred to establish new ties. If so, firms would not be set loose when they decided to move. Instead, there would be factors unrelated to the attributes of potential destination areas which influence whether location there is optimal. The distance which a potential destination is from the firm's origin appears to be a good proxy for these factors.

The distribution of firms falls off sharply when arranged by distance moved. The median distance moved for the four categories of firms described in note 11 ranged from four to six miles. The relationship resembled that of a gravity model in which the number of interconnections between zones diminishes as the distance between them increases. A regression fitted to the data for all firms in the sample yielded a significant negative relationship between number of firms and distance moved, particularly when the latter was expressed logarithmically. The coefficient of determination was at least 0.50 in all cases and between 0.81 and 0.95 for the logarithmic form. Further insight into distance moved was obtained by examining various characteristics of the firms.

Size of the firm influenced distance moved.[12] Smaller firms tended to move shorter distances than larger ones. This would seem to

12. Size was measured by the cost of land and construction associated with relocation or expansion at a new site.

support the conclusion that distance moved is generally short because it reflects the cost of moving. Larger firms can move longer distances, perhaps because they are more independent of suppliers or buyers at a particular location.[13] Size should therefore be taken into account when analyzing location patterns, since smaller firms may not be free to choose among all possible destination areas. Instead, they will be limited to those within a relatively short distance of their origin location.

Two conditions which did not seem to affect the pattern of distance moved were the origin distance of the firm and its industrial category. A regression with distance moved as a function of origin distance was run and the coefficient of determination was never as high as 6 percent. The search for an industry effect had to be conducted in terms of the two-digit Standard Industrial Classification in order to have enough observations. At this level of aggregation it was found that the distribution of firms by distance moved for each industry was never significantly different (at the 0.05 level) from the distribution of all firms.

The Analysis of Destinations

Decentralization is due largely to the pattern of destinations of firms that shift location.[14] The purposes of this section are to explain the method by which the authors are examining the pattern of destinations, to present some preliminary results, and to indicate the direction of additional empirical efforts.

The basic tool employed in the analysis of destinations was the following explanatory equation:

$$D = a + b_1L + b_2W + b_3T + b_4H + b_5V + b_6M + b_7C + u$$

where a is the constant term and u the error term. D, the dependent variable, is the density or number of destinations per unit area for the 582 CATS zones used as observations.

The independent variables are measures of the various factors which affect the location decision. The first two are proxies for the rent and wage gradients, since it is nearly impossible to measure

13. The regression of number of firms on distance moved provided a good fit for the small size categories but had a reduced and often insignificant coefficient of determination for large firms. In other words, the distribution of number of firms did not decrease sharply as distance moved increased for the latter group.

14. It also reflects locational patterns of firms that go out of business and of firms that are new to the area. Though a limited set of data is available for the latter group, it is not considered in this paper.

either of these.[15] In place of the rent gradient, the distance of the zone from the core, *L*, is used since this is inversely correlated with the rent gradient.[16] A surrogate for the wage gradient is the availability of labor for firms locating in a given zone. An initial measure of this is *W*, population density in the given zone.[17]

The percentage of land in a zone used for transportation other than highway, *T*, was used to measure access to such modes as rail and water. For highway service, the stress was upon availability of limited access freeways or tollways. Accessibility was measured by *H*, a dummy variable which was one if such a highway was in the given zone or one adjacent to it, and zero if this were not the case. The availability of land was measured by *V*, the percentage of vacant land zoned for manufacturing and commercial purposes, and *M*, the percentage of land in manufacturing use. The final variable, *C*, is a dummy variable which is zero if more than half the zone is within the city of Chicago and one if it is not. This is the major political division in the study area. It was introduced to catch the effects of such things as differences in zoning policy, property tax rates, etc., between the central city and the rest of the area.

This equation was run for the firms which moved during the years 1950–59 because data for the explanatory variables were collected during that period. The results are presented in Table 1. The first two rows indicate the values when the equation was run for expansions at new locations and relocations, respectively, for the entire area (582 zones). As indicated by the coefficient of determina-

15. Assessed valuations of land provide some information on the price of land but the problem of forming an index of price to account for variations in these prices and type of land seems insolvable. Wage rate figures, on the other hand, are rarely broken down for sufficiently small areas within the metropolitan area to be useful here, and the problem of forming an index if they were would be equally difficult.

16. A variant of distance from the core was used, for example, by John Kain [9] to approximate the relative price of residential space in an urban area. Distance from the core is actually a proxy for two, inversely correlated independent variables. The first is the rent gradient as theoretically derived from the household sector equilibrium. This gradient is negatively correlated with both distance and destinations. The second is the cost gradient reflecting the difficulty of contact with the core and the services offered there. This cost gradient is positively correlated with distance but negatively correlated with destinations. It is necessary to consider this dual interpretation of the distance variable when discussing the meaning of its coefficient.

17. It is intended to improve this variable by using, instead, an index of availability of labor to any zone *j*. This index will be the sum of the population in each zone *i* weighted by an inverse function of the distance or travel time of this population from zone *j*. Limited support for this proxy can be found in a Chicago labor market study being conducted by Professor Albert Rees at the University of Chicago. When distance to work was included as an explanatory variable for the wage rate, it was found to have a positive effect. The farther workers had to travel, the higher was their wage. Thus, a readily available labor force might indicate a lower wage rate. Even if wage rates are relatively constant in the urban area, availability may be an attracting factor since it can result in a reduction in the costs of finding and hiring new workers.

Table 1 Regression results for equation one.

	(1)	(2)	(3)	(4)	(5)	(6)	(7)	(8)	(9)
TYPE OF ANALYSIS		INTERCEPT	VALUES OF THE COEFFICIENTS FOR THE VARIABLES†						
	R^2	*a*	*L*	*W*	*T*	*H*	*V*	*M*	*C*
1. Expansion at new, total area	0.2471	1.778	−0.0956 (0.0174) **	0.0177 (0.0116)	0.7671 (0.9306)	0.2260 (0.1607)	−0.6144 (0.8615)	−6.8012 (1.2145) **	0.1490 (0.2458)
2. Relocation total area	0.2152	1.501	−0.0829 (0.0153) **	0.0148 (0.0102)	0.3412 (0.8187)	0.2610 (0.1413)	−0.4791 (0.7579)	4.5580 (1.0684) **	0.1097 (0.2612)
3. Expansion at new, north	0.6600	0.481	−0.0354 (0.0259)	0.0362 (0.0190)	−4.3679 (2.7080)	0.3317 (0.2662)	−4.6234 (4.3808)	42.9550 (3.5370) **	0.2442 (0.4112)
4. Expansion at new, west	0.4346	2.091	−0.0349 (0.0292)	−0.0066 (0.0241)	1.0869 (1.1848)	0.1451 (0.2581)	−0.4858 (2.2110)	12.1229 (2.3806) **	−1.4064 (0.5055) **
5. Expansion at new, south	0.2801	1.303	−0.0487 (0.0168) **	−0.0064 (0.0103)	3.1634 (0.8577) **	−0.5261 (0.1377) **	−0.0313 (0.5625)	1.3638 (0.8369)	−0.0789 (0.1994)
6. Relocation north	0.5536	0.121	−0.0162 (0.0220)	0.0434 (0.0161)	−1.7338 (2.2997)	0.1845 (0.2261)	2.4800 (3.7202)	24.9222 (3.0032) **	0.1639 (0.3492)
7. Relocation west	0.4662	1.482	−0.0292 (0.0220)	−0.0052 (0.0181)	0.8782 (0.8901)	0.1422 (0.1939)	−0.5638 (1.6613)	10.6777 (1.7885) **	−0.9129 (0.3797) **
8. Relocation south	0.2521	0.830	−0.0358 (0.0132) **	0.0028 (0.0081)	2.2491 (0.6727) **	−0.2696 (0.1080) *	0.0988 (0.4412)	0.9438 (0.6564)	−0.0596 (0.1564)

†Explanation of variables: *L*, distance in miles; *W*, population as thousands per square mile; *T*, percentage of land in transportation; *H*, dummy variable: one if highway, zero if not; *V*, percentage of vacant land; *M*, percentage of manufacturing land; *C*, dummy variable; zero if zone within city, one if not.

The number in parentheses below the value of the coefficient is the standard error. If the coefficient is significantly different from zero at the 0.05 level of significance, it is indicated by * while ** indicates a 0.01 level of significance.

tion (R^2), this equation accounted for between one-fifth (0.2152) and one-fourth (0.2471) of the variation in the dependent variable. The only significant variables were distance, *L*, and percentage of manufacturing land, *M*.[18] Before discussing them, it should be noted that all but one of the remaining coefficients have the expected sign. Other things equal, an increase in population or transportation land, the existence of a limited access highway near the zone or a change from the city to the suburbs will be associated with an increase in destinations. Only vacant land has an impact (negative) which is different from that expected. This may be because the inaccuracy of zoning definitions makes this variable a poor indicator of the availability of destination sites. The significant, positive coefficient for manufacturing land may indicate that this variable, instead, provides a measure of such availability. The significant, negative sign for the distance coefficient seems to indicate that it is a measure of the attraction of the core rather than a proxy for the rent gradient.

Though these explanations are logical, another more likely one for the signs of the latter two coefficients is suggested by the results of the distance moved analysis. Since most firms move short distances and most origins are near the core, distance and manufacturing land may merely be measuring the proximity of a zone to firms which are moving. Thus, increases in distance reduce the number of destinations since the zone is farther from firms which are moving. Similarly, as the percentage of manufacturing land rises, destinations rise, since more firms are located in that square. The ability of the equation to measure the influence of all the locational factors examined may be improved by introducing a variable for proximity. Two approaches suggest themselves. The first is to divide firms by size group and examine the equation for each separately. A second is to introduce a measure of proximity of each zone to firms. This measure could be similar to the one suggested above for availability of labor.

The importance of this and other improvements in the analysis can be seen from the results in the rest of Table 1. The equation was fitted to data for each of three sectors into which the city was divided.[19] This division was made because examination of the data indicated noticeable differences in these sectors, particularly with respect to

18. Significance is indicated by ** (0.01) or * (0.05). Although the necessary assumptions for such tests of significance may not be met, it is assumed that the ratio of the coefficient to its standard error (the standard error appears in parentheses below the value of the coefficient) – the *t* variable – provides a roughly accurate measure of the variable's significance.

19. The sectors were formed by dividing the metropolitan area outside the core (CATS ring-sectors 01 and 11) into the north sector (156 zones in CATS sectors 1 and 2); the west sector (136 zones in CATS sectors 3 and 4) and south sector (270 zones in CATS sectors 5, 6, and 7).

manufacturing land. Though this variable had a significantly positive coefficient in all but one of the regressions, the sector with the highest percentage of such land, the south, had the lowest density of destinations. The reverse was true for the north.[20] The result of the division into sectors is a noticeable improvement in the explanatory power of the regression, particularly for the north and west sectors.[21] This improvement in the statistical results is not conceptually significant in itself. It indicates that there are critical variables that have not been included. It is hoped that with their identification it will be possible to obtain results for the entire study area that are as good as those that have been obtained for the somewhat arbitrary geographic subdivisions of it. One of these variables is suggested by the results of the sector analysis. As has been noted, zones in the southern sectors tend to have a higher percentage of manufacturing land than zones in the remainder of the study area. Manufacturing land always has a significant, positive effect on destinations yet the southern sectors attract the fewest number of firms. The explanation may be that zones in these sectors also tend to have a higher proportion of nonwhite population. A variable that reflects population composition of zones will, therefore, be included in future empirical work.

REFERENCES

1. William Alonso, *Location and Land Use: Toward a General Theory of Land Rent* (Harvard Univ. Press, 1964).
2. American Transit Association, Committee on Fare Structures, *Fare Structures in the Transit Industry* (New York, 1933).
3. Chicago Area Transportation Study, *Geographic Reference System* (20,000) (Chicago, Aug., 1963).
4. ——, *Home Interview Population Manual* (31,210) (Chicago, June, 1959).
5. ——, *Land Use Survey Manual* (15, 210) (Chicago, 1956).
6. Benjamin Chinitz, *Freight and the Metropolis* (Harvard Univ. Press, 1960).
7. George W. Grupp, *Economics of Motor Transportation* (Appleton & Co., 1924).
8. Homer Hoyt, *One Hundred Years of Land Values in Chicago* (Univ. of Chicago Press, 1933).
9. J. F. Kain, *A Multiple Equation Model of Household Locational and Trip-making Behavior* (RAND Corp., Memorandum RM-3086-FF, Apr., 1962).

20. The number of destinations in both groups per square mile in the north, west and south sectors, respectively, was 1.21, 1.00, and 0.54, while the percentage of land in manufacturing was 1.9, 3.1, and 4.4.

21. When the regression is run for each of the seven CATS sectors, the explanatory power is further improved, especially in the southern sectors. Except for one case, the coefficient of determination is over 0.40 and ranges as high as 0.74.

10. J. R. Meyer, J. F. Kain, and M. Wohl, *The Urban Transportation Problem* (Harvard Univ. Press, 1965).
11. Leon N. Moses, "Toward a Theory of Intra-Urban Wage Differentials and Their Influence on Travel Patterns," *Papers of the Reg. Sci. Asso.*, 1962.
12. H. R. Tolley and L. M. Church, "Experience of Eastern Farmers with Motor Trucks," U.S. Dept. of Agric. *Bul. No. 910* (Washington, D.C., 1920).

6

RICHARD F. MUTH

Economic Change and Rural-Urban Land Conversions

I

With the rapid growth in urban populations that has taken place in recent years, the problem of the conversion of land from rural to urban uses has stimulated a great deal of interest among many persons. The extent of this conversion has received some empirical study; perhaps the best known is Donald J. Bogue's, which concluded that from 1929 to 1954 between 0.17 and 0.26 acres of rural land were converted to urban land for each additional member of the urban population.[1] To my knowledge, however, there has been no theoretical study of this problem and little consideration of the effects of forces other than population change on shifts in land uses near the boundaries of urban areas. In this paper I consider the problem of how land rents and uses are determined by a competitive market, giving particular attention to how the equilibrium uses and rents of land change with changing market conditions.

More specifically, this paper sets out a von Thünen-like model of land use determination which postulates a market for commodities at some fixed point in space, around which land of homogeneous physical characteristics extends to an infinite distance. Firms of two competitive industries locate on this land, and my problem is to determine the areas in which the firms of the two industries locate and how their areas of location change with changes in the underlying conditions of demand and supply for the two commodities. I discuss the application of the model to the problem of the conversion of land from rural to urban uses for the special case in which firms of one industry produce non-farm housing services and the other some agricultural commodity. Of course, urban land is used for many

1. *Metropolitan Growth and the Conversion of Land to Non-Agricultural Uses*, Studies in Population Distribution No. 11 (Oxford, Ohio: Scripps Foundation, 1956).

Much of the research summarized in this paper was undertaken while I was associated with Resources for the Future, Inc. I wish to thank my colleagues in this organization for their many helpful suggestions, especially Marion Clawson, Paul Cootner, John Krutilla, and Lowdon Wingo, Jr. Likewise, I wish to thank Lester Telser for several very useful comments. I, of course, accept full responsibility for any errors this paper might contain.

Reprinted from Econometrica *29 (January 1961), 1–23, by permission of the publishers and the author.*

purposes other than housing, but the latter is by far the most important; the other forms of urban land use have been neglected here for analytic simplicity.[2]

The model presented here is concerned only with long run equilibrium conditions and neglects many features of the real world which may be important in the short run. Perhaps the most important of these latter are rigidities due to fixed capital investment and land conversions in expectation of future urban growth. The analysis developed here involves consideration of four different kinds of equilibrium conditions. First, firm equilibrium requires that production be so organized as to maximize profits. Second, what I call locational equilibrium requires that the profits of identical firms be the same everywhere. Third, equilibrium in the market for land requires that land be allocated to that use that yields the highest rent. And, finally, for industry equilibrium it is necessary that the total quantity of a commodity supplied be equal to the quantity demanded at the price prevailing at the market.

While I discuss the problem in rather general terms in Section II, most of this paper is devoted to consideration of a model involving specific assumptions about the form of the functional relationships involved. These assumptions, it seems to me, are the simplest ones mathematically that embody the essential economics of the problem. These assumptions, first introduced in Section III, are:

1. Firms in a given industry have identical production functions which are logarithmically linear.

2. Price received at the point of production declines negative exponentially with distance from the market, hence at a decreasing rate with distance, because of transport costs.

3. The total land area available up to a distance k from the market is proportional to k^2.

4. The market demand functions are logarithmically linear.

With the aid of these assumptions one could, in principle, calculate precisely the changes in land use that result from changes in the given conditions of the problem. Whether or not these special assumptions I have made turn out to be useful, of course, depends upon the correspondence of the model's implications for rural-urban land conversions reached in Section IV with experience in the real world.

2. Harland Bartholomew, *Land Uses in American Cities* (Cambridge, Mass.: Harvard University Press, 1955) found that about three-fourths of privately developed land (including railroads) is devoted to residential use in the central and satellite cities he studied. See especially p. 121.

The principal implication of my analysis is that the price elasticity of demand for the agricultural commodity is of crucial importance in determining even the direction of change in rent and the areas in which firms of the two industries locate. To highlight this importance I have constructed two hypothetical limiting cases, which I discuss explicitly in Section IV. The first, which I call the "local food case," is that in which the farms in the area sell all of their output to consumers in the area and there is no other source of supply in this market. In the real world, such a situation might be approximated by farms producing dairy products or fresh produce for a large metropolitan market. In the local food case it is likely that the demand for farm products is inelastic, perhaps highly so. The other I call the "national food case," that in which the farms in question sell only a small portion of the total supply coming to some regional or national market. The latter condition may approximately characterize farms in, say, the corn and wheat belts. The demand elasticity for the products of local agriculture in this case tends to minus infinity. As will be indicated more fully in what follows, the changes in land use that take place with, say, a growth in the urban population in the two cases are considerably different.

While I make no attempt in this paper to test empirically the implications of my analysis, perhaps the best way to summarize them is to conceive of a regression analysis of changes in the land area used for urban purposes and to ask what the model would say about the form of the regression equation and its coefficients. The model implies that the regression equation would be approximately linear in the relative change in urban land area, the relative changes in demand for the products of the two industries, the relative change in non-land costs, the relative changes in the constant terms of the logarithmically linear production functions, which reflect changes in technology, and the relative changes in the two price gradients. The latter are parameters describing the rate at which price received at the point of production falls off with distance from the market; changes in them reflect changes in transport costs. The partial regression coefficients would depend upon the exponents of the production functions, the size of the city in terms of its area, the price gradients, and the elasticity of demand for the local agricultural commodity. With respect to the last of these, for example, if it is inelastic, a decrease in non-land cost or a neutral technological change in local agriculture would increase the land area used for urban purposes, and conversely if demand is elastic. Likewise, the more elastic the demand for the product of local agriculture the smaller is the growth in demand for housing relative to that for the agricultural commodity needed to increase the land area used for housing by any given amount.

II

Let us begin the analysis by considering a market for commodities at some fixed point in space, around which land of homogeneous physical characteristics extends to an infinite distance. Firms of two competitive industries locate on this land. The exact parts of this von Thünen plain inhabited by firms in a particular industry depend upon the rent they are willing to offer in relation to the rent that firms in the other industry would offer. Let there be for each industry a rent distance function which shows the rent firms in that industry would offer for land at any given distance k from the market. In what follows I shall show how this function is derived. Since equilibrium in the market for land requires that land be allocated to that use which yields the highest rent and only land yielding a nonnegative rent will be used at all, the regions in which firms of the two industries locate can be determined by comparing their rent-distance functions.

Figure 1 shows two possible rent-distance functions, one for each of the two industries, which show the rent, r, firms in the industry

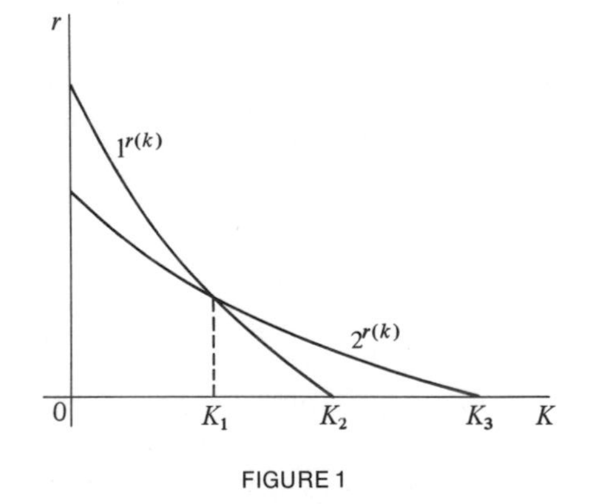

FIGURE 1

would offer for land at any distance, k, from the market. Since I implicitly assume that rent offered for land at any given distance is the same in all directions from the market, the rent-distance functions can be shown in two dimensions. The rent-distance function for the first industry, ${}_1r(k)$, as I have drawn it, shows that first industry firms would offer nonnegative rents for land up to a distance k_2 miles from the market, but they would be restricted in their location to land no more than k_1 miles from the market since second industry firms would offer a higher rent for land at any greater distance. The latter would locate on land from k_1 to k_3 miles from the market, since beyond k_3 land would yield a negative rent if used by them. Hence, under the conditions illustrated in Figure 1, a circular boundary would separate the areas of location of the two industries. I shall return to a more complete discussion of the conditions in which a circular boundary exists in Section III; first, let's consider two of the possible complications to the simple situation illustrated in Figure 1.

The first of these arises when the rent firms in a given industry offer for land depends upon direction as well as distance from the market. If such were the case my diagram would need to be three dimensional, with rent functions shown over a plane whose points are characterized either by north-south and east-west distance or by direction and distance from the market. In this case, the boundary between the areas of location of the two industries need not be circular, and might be quite irregular. A second complication is that the area in which firms of a given industry locate might not be contiguous. This possibility is illustrated in Figure 2; here the rent-distance function for the first industry dips below that for the second industry at k_1 and rises above it again at k_2 miles from the market. Hence, first industry firms would locate at distances up to k_1 miles and from k_2 to k_4 miles from the market. Certainly situations such as these

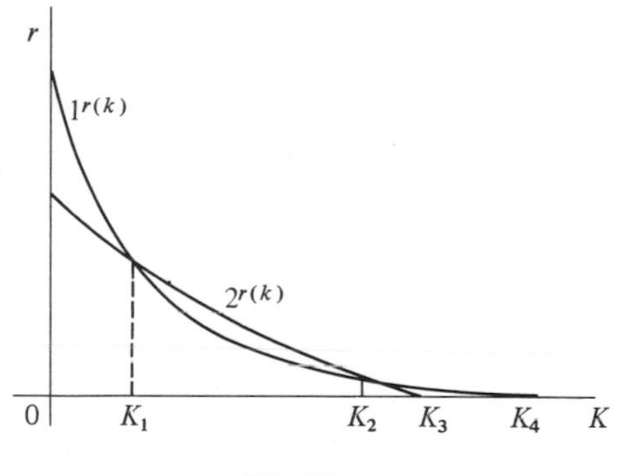

FIGURE 2

arise in the real world. They are ruled out, however, by the assumptions I make in Section III since I am not at all sure that taking explicit account of them would add materially to the conclusions reached about shifts in land from rural to urban uses which are reached later.

Let us consider now how the rent-distance functions for the two industries are derived. Firms locating on my von Thünen plain purchase land and labor inputs, R and L, respectively, at unit prices $_ir$ and w and sell their output, $_iq$, $i = 1,2$, at some price $_ip$ at the point of production. (The prescript i refers to (firms in) the ith industry throughout this paper.) I assume for simplicity that w is the same everywhere, although differences in w for the two industries could be easily handled. Now here, of course, labor stands for all inputs other than land; by assuming that the relative factor prices of all factors except land are fixed I may treat them as a single input. Hence, when I speak of the wage rate, w, I really mean the price per unit of the composite bundle of all factors other than land.

I shall further assume that all firms in the same industry have the same production function. Equilibrium of firms requires that, for given input and output prices, each firm adjust its purchases of land and labor so that profits, ${}_i\Pi$, are a maximum. Maximizing:

$${}_i\Pi = {}_ip_iq - wL - {}_irR,$$

subject to

$${}_iq = {}_iq(L, R),$$

yields the familiar necessary conditions for firm equilibrium:

$$w = {}_ip\frac{\partial_i q}{\partial L}, \qquad {}_ir = {}_ip\frac{\partial_i q}{\partial R}, \qquad {}_iq = {}_iq(L, R). \tag{1}$$

Of course, if firms of both industries use land of equal quality (a given distance from the market since we assume that the physical characteristics of land are the same everywhere), equilibrium in the market for land would require that they pay the same rent. Hence, the second of equations (1) may be interpreted as giving the maximum rent firms would be willing to offer given the price of their output and wages.

Secondly, locational equilibrium requires that the profits of firms in the same industry be the same everywhere and not vary with the distance from the market. From this condition and the conditions of firm equilibrium one can derive the proposition that the rent of land declines with distance from the market provided that price received net of transport costs declines with distance,[3] for the change in profits is given by:

$$d_i\Pi = ({}_iqd_ip - Rd_ir) + ({}_ipd_iq - wdL - {}_irdR).$$

The second parenthesis of the above is zero, as seen by substituting the conditions for firm equilibrium, (1). Hence,

$$d_i\Pi = 0 \qquad \text{implies that} \qquad d_ir = {}_i(q/R)d_ip. \tag{2}$$

3. In his study *The Location of Agricultural Production* (Gainesville: University of Florida Press, 1954), p. 27, Edgar S. Dunn, Jr., states that the price of land is not determined in a market external to the firm. Hence, he seeks to derive rent from the conditions of firm equilibrium alone. Actually, of course, land is bought and sold or rented in markets external to the individual firm just as any other non-human productive agent. As will be indicated below, it is transactions in land in external markets that determines the spatial pattern of land rents. But, while disagreeing with him on the point just noted, I am greatly indebted to Dunn for the analysis he developed.

I assume that price received at the point of production is a function of price at the market and distance from the market, ${}_ip = {}_ip({}_ip_0, k)$, and that price declines with distance from the market because of transport costs. Hence:

$$\frac{\partial_i r}{\partial k} = i(q/R)\frac{\partial_i p}{\partial k} < 0. \tag{3}$$

Further, from (3) I have:

$$\frac{\partial^2{}_i r}{\partial k^2} = i(q/R)\frac{\partial^2{}_i p}{\partial k^2} + \frac{\partial_i p}{\partial k}\frac{\partial}{\partial k}i(q/R).$$

If, as seems likely, price declines at a decreasing rate with distance, rent will decline at a decreasing rate if output per unit of land falls with distance. But, since wages are constant and rent declines with distance, land is increasingly substituted for labor with distance, and output per unit of land declines with distance.

The truth of the proposition that rent of land must decline with distance may also be seen as follows: suppose that price declines with distance from the market but that wages and rent are everywhere the same. Under these conditions the profits of firms would vary inversely with distance from the market. It would then be in the interest of those firms located, say, twenty-five miles from the market to offer a higher rent for land located, say, twenty miles. Hence, the rent of the more favorably situated land would rise and the profits of firms using this land would fall relative to those on the less favorably situated land. This process would continue so long as firms' profits tended to differ. Hence, locational equilibrium of firms—a situation in which no firm has an incentive to change its location—implies that rent must decline with distance provided that price does.

The conditions of firm and locational equilibrium discussed in the above paragraphs define for each industry a function ${}_ir(k) = {}_ir({}_ip_0, k)$, which shows the rent firms in the industry would offer for land at different distances from the market. The exact form of the function depends, of course, upon the production functions of firms in the industry and upon the price-distance function, which describes the variation of price received at the point of production with distance from the market. But in general the rent-distance function declines at a decreasing rate with distance if the price-distance function does. Likewise, the position of the rent-distance function depends upon the price received at the market. I remark in passing that the conditions discussed so far insure that land rents are maximized. Competition among firms in a given industry for land assures that in each given use the rent of a given plot of land could not be larger, for, if a plot of land were to receive a below average rent the firm using it would earn above average profits and other firms in the industry would bid up its rent. And, secondly, competition among industries assures that land is devoted to the use that yields the highest rent, as illustrated in Figures 1 and 2.

Once the areas ${}_iK$ in which firms of the two industries locate have been determined by comparing their rent-distance functions as discussed at the beginning of this section, their total outputs are obtained as follows. For the *i*th industry output per unit of land is:

$$ {}_i(q/R)(k) = {}_il({}_ip(k), w, {}_ir(k)) = {}_ig({}_ip_0, k), $$

in ${}_iK$ and zero elsewhere, so that total output is:

$$ {}_iQ = \int_{{}_iK} {}_ig({}_ip_0, k)\, R'(k)\, dk, $$

where $R'(k)$ is the marginal land supply function—the increase in total land area per unit increase in distance from the market. Hence, for any pair of prices at the market for the two commodities produced on my von Thünen plain, total output of both industries, their rent-distance functions and, hence, the rent of land everywhere and the areas in which firms of the two industries locate are determined. The condition of industry equilibrium, namely, that quantity supplied equal quantity demanded at the market, then determines the equilibrium prices of the two commodities as well as equilibrium land rent everywhere and the location of the two industries. Hence, it is seen that the problem of determining the equilibrium areas of location of firms is a part of the market process by which the prices of final products and productive factors—land being of special interest in this problem—are determined.

An even more interesting question is how changes in demand, non-land costs, technology and transport costs affect this equilibrium location. To tackle the latter question I prefer to limit consideration to a special case involving specific assumptions about the function relationships discussed above. These assumptions, it seems to me, are the simplest ones that embody the economically essential elements of the case. While somone possessing more mathematical cunning than I might proceed on a higher plane of generality, the special case discussed in the remainder of this paper does, I believe, yield several interesting conclusions about changes in land use. Whether or not the special model presented below turns out to be useful, of course, depends ultimately upon whether the predictions about land-use changes it yields accord with reality, a question I do not attempt to answer here.

III

In this section I consider the determination of market equilibrium and equilibrium land use for a special case of the analysis in the above section. This involves specific assumptions about the forms of production functions, price-distance functions, and market demand functions for each of the two industries and, though much less restrictive, the marginal land supply function. The questions of what changes in land use are brought about by changes in the underlying conditions of demand and supply are considered in Section IV.

Determination of equilibrium

First, I shall assume that the firms in a given industry have identical, logarithmically linear production functions; that is:

$$ {}_iq = {}_ia_0 L^{{}_ia_1} R^{{}_ia_2} \qquad (i = 1, 2) $$

This is perhaps the simplest production function which embodies the economically relevant condition of declining marginal physical productivity of each factor. It has been found to be a useful simplification for many empirical problems. Where ${}_ia_1 + {}_ia_2 < 1$, the second order conditions for maximization of profits by firms are satisfied. In this case entrepreneurial capacity is a limitational factor to the firm, profits per firm are greater than zero, and the size of the firm is determined by the first order conditions. In the limiting case where ${}_ia_1 + {}_ia_2 = 1$, entrepreneurial capacity places no limit on the size of the firms and profits are zero. While in this limiting case the size of the individual firm is indeterminate, the necessary or first order conditions for profit maximization describe the adjustment the firm must make for given prices and costs in order to produce. In what follows I shall assume that constant returns to scale characterizes the firms being considered, since it permits of some simplification, but assuming decreasing returns would make little difference in the conclusions.

Writing X^* for the natural logarithm of X, equations (1) are especially easy to handle; they become:

$$ {}_iq^* = {}_ia_0^* + {}_ia_1 L^* + {}_ia_2 R^*, \qquad (4) $$

$$ L^* = {}_ia_1^* - w^* + {}_ip^* + {}_iq^*, $$

$$ R^* = {}_ia_2^* - {}_ir^* + {}_ip^* + {}_iq^*. $$

Substituting the second and third of these into the first yields:

$$ {}_ir^* = \frac{1}{{}_ia_2}\,{}_ib_1^* - \frac{{}_ia_1}{{}_ia_2} w^* + \frac{1}{{}_ia_2}\,{}_ip^*, \qquad (5) $$

where

$$ {}_ib_1^* = {}_ia_0^* + {}_ia_1{}_ia_1^* + {}_ia_2{}_ia_2^*. $$

Equation (5) expresses the relation between rent per unit of land, price per unit of output, and the wage rate that must hold if firms are to earn zero profits. If, for given prices and wages, rent were greater than the amount shown by (5) profits would be negative and competition would force rents down; if rent were less, profits would be positive and rents would be bid up. Substituting (5) in the third of equations (4) we have:

$$ {}_i(q/R)^* = {}_ib_2^* - \frac{{}_ia_1}{{}_ia_2} w^* + \frac{{}_ia_1}{{}_ia_2} {}_ip^*, \tag{6} $$

where

$$ {}_ib_2^* = \frac{1}{{}_ia_2} {}_ia_0^* + \frac{{}_ia_1}{{}_ia_2} {}_ia_1^*. $$

This equation expresses the variation of output per unit of land with price and the wage rate on the assumption that rent varies with these two variables in the manner indicated by (5).

The second simplifying assumption made is that price as a function of distance from the market is given by:

$$ {}_ip = {}_ip_0 \exp. (-{}_ick). \tag{7} $$

This implies that price received at the point of production declines at a decreasing rate with distance from the market. If the firms in the ith industry produce some agricultural commodity, price received at the farm differs from price at the market because of costs of transporting the commodity to the market.[4] Since transport costs generally increase at a decreasing rate with distance, price received at the farm would decrease at a decreasing rate with distance. On the other hand, if the firms in the ith industry produce housing services, this assumption implies that the maximum price per unit of housing service people will pay declines at a decreasing rate from the center of the city. The explanation for the decline in the price of housing services with distance from the city center is to be found in the time and trouble of transport to this center or to other parts of the city. Since traffic generally moves more slowly the nearer one is to the center of the city, the time spent in travel would likely increase at a decreasing rate as distance from the center increases. The rate of fall of price with

4. Of course, the commodity might be shipped from the market to some other area, in which case further transport costs are incurred.

distance depends upon the parameter ${}_ic$, which I call the price gradient. Substituting (7) into (5) and (6):

$$ {}_ir^* = {}_ir_0^* - \frac{{}_ic}{{}_ia_2}k, \tag{8}$$

where

$$ {}_ir_0^* = \frac{1}{{}_ia_2}{}_ib_1^* - \frac{{}_ia_1}{{}_ia_2}w^* + \frac{1}{{}_ia_2}{}_ip_0^*;$$

$$ {}_i(q/R)^* = {}_i(q/R)_0^* - \frac{{}_ic_ia_1}{{}_ia_2}k, \tag{9}$$

where

$$ {}_i(q/R)_0^* = {}_ib_2^* - \frac{{}_ia_1}{{}_ia_2}w^* + \frac{{}_ia_1}{{}_ia_2}{}_ip_0^*.$$

Thus, like price, rent and output per unit of land decline at a decreasing rate with distance. The slopes of (8) and (9) depend upon the price gradient and upon the parameters of the production function.[5]

Given the rent functions for the two industries, equation (8), where will the firms of these two industries locate? The answer is suggested by Figure 3, on which the rent functions of the two industries are plotted. Suppose, first, that the maximum rent for land

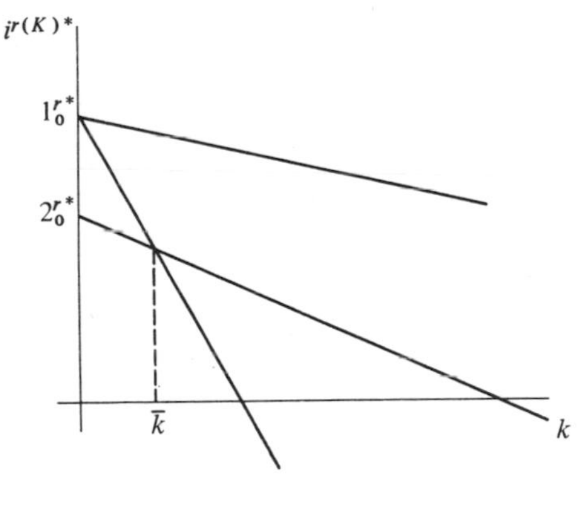

FIGURE 3

at the market that firms of one industry, call it the first, would offer exceeds that offered by the other firms. Then, for both commodities to be produced, the rent gradient for firms in the first industry must be steeper than that for firms in the second industry. If the maximum rent offered for land at the market were the same for

5. It is easy to verify that (8) satisfies equation (3) in the preceding section.

both industries, only one commodity would be produced if one of the gradients were steeper than the other; if the two gradients were the same, then both would be produced everywhere—or at least there would be no boundary separating the location areas of the two industries—and as far as this analysis is concerned the two industries produce essentially the same commodity. Hence, I will assume that ${}_1r_0^* > {}_2r_0^*$ and ${}_1c/{}_1a_2 > {}_2c/{}_2a_2$. Then $\bar{k}$, which is the boundary between the areas in which the firms of the two industries locate, is given by:

$${}_1r_0^* - \frac{{}_1c}{{}_1a_2}\bar{k} = {}_2r_0^* - \frac{{}_2c}{{}_2a_2}\bar{k}$$

or

$$\bar{k} = ({}_1r_0^* - {}_2r_0^*)/\left(\frac{{}_1c}{{}_1a_2} - \frac{{}_2c}{{}_2a_2}\right). \qquad (10)$$

In the case where firms in the first industry produce housing services and firms in the second produce agricultural commodities I shall refer to $\bar{k}$ as the "city limits."[6]

The third assumption I make relates to the supply function of land. As stated earlier I am assuming that all land surrounding the market is of the same quality. Furthermore, I assume that the total available land area up to a distance k from the market is proportional to k^2.[7] Therefore, the increment to the total supply of land per unit increase in distance, $R'(k)$, is given by:

$$R'(k) = \sigma k.$$

If land surrounded the market in all directions, σ would be equal to 2π; for a city like Chicago bounded on one side by a lake, σ would be closer to π. Actually, as will be shown below, so long as the price gradient is constant the conclusions of the model are independent of the specific form of the land supply function, so that this assumption is not very important.

Now the increment to total output per unit increase in distance from the market, ${}_iQ_k$, is simply output per unit of land multiplied by the increment to land area per unit increase in distance. Hence, for the first industry:

$${}_1Q_k = {}_1(q/R)R'(k) = \sigma_1(q/R)_0 k \exp.\left(-\frac{{}_1c_1a_1}{{}_1a_2}k\right)$$

6. In the economic sense, rather than in the sense of a political boundary.

7. In the special case of interest in this paper, the total land area devoted to urban uses is, thus, $\bar{K} = \frac{1}{2}\sigma h^2$, and so $d\bar{K}^* = 2d\bar{k}^*$. Hence, the relative change in the city limits uniquely determines that of urban land area, given the above assumption about the land supply function.

for $0 \leqslant k \leqslant \bar{k}$, and zero otherwise; so:

$$ {}_1Q = \int_0^{\bar{k}} {}_1Q_k dk = {}_1\lambda({}_1c, \bar{k})_1(q/R)_0, \tag{11} $$

where

$$ {}_1\lambda({}_1c, \bar{k}) = \left\{\sigma/\left(\frac{{}_1c_1a_1}{{}_1a_2}\right)^2\right\}\left\{1 - \left(\frac{{}_1c_1a_1}{{}_1a_2}\bar{k} + 1\right)\exp.\left(-\frac{{}_1c_1a_1}{{}_1a_2}\bar{k}\right)\right\}. $$

Aggregate output of the first commodity thus depends upon output per unit of land at zero distance, which is itself dependent upon the parameters of the production function for first industry firms, the wage rate, and the price of the first commodity at the market, and upon ${}_1\lambda$. The latter depends upon the price gradient for the first commodity and upon the boundary between the areas of location of the two kinds of firms, as well as upon the parameters of the production function. The location of the boundary, of course, depends upon the ratio of the rents the two kinds of firms would pay if located at the market and upon the difference between their rent gradients. It is through the boundary that the two industries are linked together on the supply side of the market. Similarly, for the second commodity:

$$ {}_2Q_k = {}_2(q/R)R'(k) = \sigma_2(q/R)_0 k \exp.\left(-\frac{{}_2c_2a_1}{{}_2a_2}k\right) $$

for $\bar{k} \leqslant k$, and zero otherwise; so:

$$ {}_2Q = \int_{\bar{k}}^{\infty} {}_2Q_k dk = {}_2\lambda({}_2c, \bar{k})_2(q/R)_0, \tag{12} $$

where

$$ {}_2\lambda({}_2c, \bar{k}) = \left\{\sigma/\left(\frac{{}_2c_2a_1}{{}_2a_2}\right)^2\right\}\left(\frac{{}_2c_2a_1}{{}_2a_2}\bar{k} + 1\right)\exp.\left(-\frac{{}_2c_2a_1}{{}_2a_2}\bar{k}\right). $$

Finally, I shall assume that the demand functions for the two commodities at the market are logarithmically linear:

$$ \begin{aligned} {}_1Q &= {}_1A_{01}p_0^{\,{}_1A_1} \\ {}_2Q &= {}_2A_{02}p_0^{\,{}_2A_2} \end{aligned} \tag{13} $$

Here ${}_1A_1$ is the elasticity of demand for the first commodity with respect to its own price, *etc.* For simplicity I am assuming that the cross elasticities of demand for the two commodities are zero. I do this because for the particular application I have in mind, I suspect this to be the case.[8] While nonzero cross elasticities of demand for the two commodities could easily be introduced into the analysis, the conclusions of the model would become much more complicated.

Displacement of equilibrium

Equations (8) through (13) define the joint equilibrium of the two industries. Their solution is illustrated diagrammatically in Figure 4.

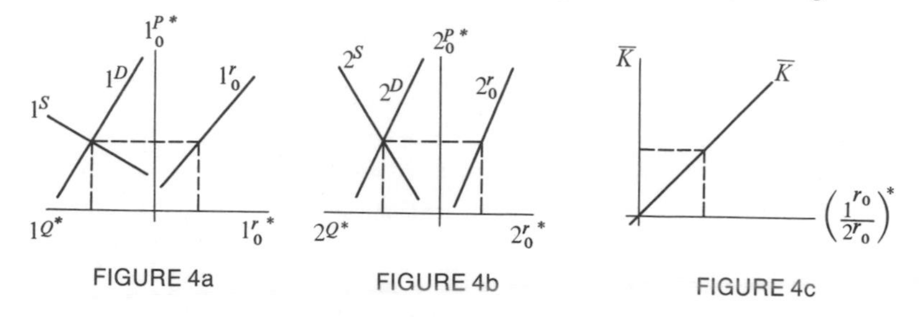

FIGURE 4a FIGURE 4b FIGURE 4c

The supply functions for the two commodities depend not only upon their prices and the wage rate, but also upon the boundary variable, $\bar{k}$. Hence, for a given wage rate, the positions of the supply schedules shown in Figures 4a and 4b hold only so long as the boundary is that value shown in Figure 4c. The boundary itself depends upon the ratio of the rents firms in the two industries would offer for land at the market. These rents in turn depend upon the prices of the two commodities and upon the wage rate.

The effects on the system of changing one or more of the exogeneous variables of the problem can be determined by differentiating equations (8) through (13). These may then be solved for the differential changes in the endogenous variables. Differentiating these equations we have (for ${}_ia_1$ and ${}_ia_2$ constant):

$$d_iQ = {}_i\lambda d_i(q/R)_0 + {}_i(q/R)_0\left[\frac{\partial_i\lambda}{\partial\bar{k}}d\bar{k} + \frac{\partial_i\lambda}{\partial_ic}d_ic\right],$$

$$d_i(q/R)_0 = \left[\frac{1}{{}_ia_2}d_ia_0^* - \frac{{}_ia_1}{{}_ia_2}dw^* + \frac{{}_ia_1}{{}_ia_2}d_ip_0^*\right]{}_i(q/R)_0,$$

$$\frac{\partial_1\lambda}{\partial\bar{k}} = {}_1Q_{\bar{k}}/{}_1(q/R)_0, \quad \frac{\partial_2\lambda}{\partial\bar{k}} = -{}_2Q_{\bar{k}}/{}_2(q/R)_0,$$

8. In a study of housing demand that I have made, I was unable to find any significant relationship between the demand for housing services and the price of food.

$$\frac{\partial_1 \lambda}{\partial_1 c} = -\frac{1}{{}_1c}\left[2_1\lambda - {}_1Q_{\bar{k}}\bar{k}/{}_1(q/R)_0\right],$$

$$\frac{\partial_2 \lambda}{\partial_2 c} = -\frac{1}{{}_2c}\left[2_2\lambda + {}_2Q_{\bar{k}}\bar{k}/{}_2(q/R)_0\right],$$

so that:[9]

$$d_1Q^* = \frac{1}{{}_1a_2} d_1 a_0^* - \frac{{}_1a_1}{{}_1a_2} dw^* + \frac{{}_1a_1}{{}_1a_2} d_1 p_0^* + \frac{{}_1Q_{\bar{k}}\bar{k}}{{}_1Q} d\bar{k}^* - \left(2 - \frac{{}_1Q_{\bar{k}}\bar{k}}{{}_1Q}\right) d_1c^*, \quad (14)$$

$$d_2Q^* = \frac{1}{{}_2a_2} d_2 a_0^* - \frac{{}_2a_1}{{}_2a_2} dw^* + \frac{{}_2a_1}{{}_2a_2} d_2 p_0^* - \frac{{}_2Q_{\bar{k}}\bar{k}}{{}_2Q} d\bar{k}^* - \left(2 + \frac{{}_2Q_{\bar{k}}\bar{k}}{{}_2Q}\right) d_2c^*,$$

$$d_iQ^* = d_iA_0^* + {}_iA_i d_i p_0^* \qquad (i = 1, 2),$$

$$d_i r_0^* = \frac{1}{{}_ia_2} d_i a_0^* - \frac{{}_ia_1}{{}_ia_2} dw^* + \frac{1}{{}_ia_2} d_i p_0^* \qquad (i = 1, 2),$$

$$d\bar{k}^* = \frac{1}{\left(\frac{{}_1c}{{}_1a_2} - \frac{{}_2c}{{}_2a_2}\right)^{\bar{k}}}\left\{(d_1 r_0^* - d_2 r_0^*) - \bar{k}\left(\frac{{}_1c}{{}_1a_2} d_1c^* - \frac{{}_2c}{{}_2a_2} d_2c^*\right)\right\}.$$

Equations (14) make it possible to trace the shifts of and movements along the functions exhibited in Figure 4 which result from a change in one of the exogeneous variables. They indicate, for example, that an increase in wages leads to rightward shifts in the supply functions of both commodities and leftward shifts in the rent functions. Obviously, an increase in the price gradient of the second commodity leads to a rightward shift in its supply schedule; it is less obvious but equally true that an increase in the price gradient of the

9. So long as the price gradients remain unchanged the output differentials do not depend upon the specific form of the land supply function. This is because, for the first industry:

$${}_1Q = {}_1(q/R)_0 \int_0^{\bar{k}} \exp.\left(-\frac{{}_1c_1a_1}{{}_1a_2}k\right) R'(k)\,dk$$

so that:

$$d_1Q = \left\{\int_0^{\bar{k}} \exp.\left(-\frac{{}_1c_1a_1}{{}_1a_2}k\right) R'(k)\,dk\right\} d_1(q/R)_0 + {}_1(q/R)_0 \exp.\left(-\frac{{}_1c_1a_1}{{}_1a_2}k\right) \times R'(k)\,dk$$

$$= \left\{({}_1(q/R)_0) \int_0^{\bar{k}} \exp.\left(-\frac{{}_1c_1a_1}{{}_1a_2}k\right) R'(k)\,dk\right\} d_1(q/R)_0^* + {}_1Q_{\bar{k}}\bar{k}d\bar{k}^*,$$

and similarly for the second commodity.

first commodity leads to a rightward shift in its supply schedule.[10] To determine the ultimate effect of changes in these exogeneous variables, of course, account must also be taken of the movements along these schedules and the further shifts in them. In the next section the effect of all these will be considered.

IV

In this section we shall be concerned with the ultimate effect on land use of changes in the underlying conditions of demand and supply for the two commodities. Since the primary concern of this paper is with the shifts of land from rural to urban uses, greatest attention will be concentrated upon changes in the boundary, $\bar{k}$, in the case where the first commodity being produced on the land around the market is (non-farm) housing. However, a similar analysis might equally well be made for the case where both industries produce agricultural commodities.

SHIFTS IN DEMAND

Suppose first that of the exogeneous variables, only the A_0's, the parameters determining the positions of the demand schedules, change. Looking at Figure 4, an increase in the demand for the first commodity leads initially to a bidding up of the market price of the first commodity and, consequently, to an increase in the rent which firms in the first industry would offer for land at zero distance from the market. But since the rent gradient for the first commodity is unchanged, firms in the first industry would offer a higher rent for land at all distances from the market. This leads to an increase in the land area used by firms in the first industry or an outward movement of the boundary, which in turn causes the supply of the second commodity to diminish and, hence, the price of the second commodity to rise at the market. The rent of land used in the production of the second commodity is thus bid up.

10. This follows from the observation that:

$$\frac{{}_1Q_{\bar{k}}\bar{k}}{{}_1Q} = \frac{\left(\frac{{}_1c_1a_1}{{}_1a_2}\bar{k}\right)^2}{\exp.\left(\frac{{}_1c_1a_1}{{}_1a_2}\bar{k}\right) - \left(1 + \frac{{}_1c_1a_1}{{}_1a_2}\bar{k}\right)} = \frac{2}{1 + \frac{1}{3}\left(\frac{{}_1c_1a_1}{{}_1a_2}\bar{k}\right)\exp.\xi} < 2, \text{ for } \bar{k} > 0,$$

where $0 < \xi < ({}_1c_1a_1/{}_1a_2)\bar{k}$ in the remainder term of the second order Maclaurin's series expansion of $\exp(({}_1c_1a_1/{}_1a_2)\bar{k})$.

This can be seen analytically as follows: substituting in equations (14) gives:

$$d_1 Q^* = \frac{{}_1a_1}{{}_1a_2} d_1 p_0^* + \frac{{}_1Q_{\bar{k}}\bar{k}}{{}_1Q} d\bar{k}^*, \qquad d_2 Q^* = \frac{{}_2a_1}{{}_2a_2} d_2 p_0^* - \frac{{}_2Q_{\bar{k}}\bar{k}}{{}_2Q} d\bar{k}^*, \quad (15)$$

$$d_i Q^* = d_i A_0^* + {}_iA_i d_i p_0^*, \qquad d_i r_0^* = \frac{1}{{}_ia_2} d_i p_0^*,$$

$$d\bar{k}^* = \frac{d_1 r_0^* - d_2 r_0^*}{\left(\frac{{}_1c}{{}_1a_2} - \frac{{}_2c}{{}_2a_2}\right)\bar{k}}.$$

Solving for the change in output supplied in terms of price changes gives:

$$d_1 Q^* = ({}_1m + {}_1a_1)\frac{d_1 p_0^*}{{}_1a_2} - {}_1m\frac{d_2 p_0^*}{{}_2a_2}, \qquad {}_1m = \frac{{}_1Q_{\bar{k}}/{}_1Q}{\frac{{}_1c}{{}_1a_2} - \frac{{}_2c}{{}_2a_2}} \gtrless 0,$$

$$d_2 Q^* = -{}_2m\frac{d_1 p_0^*}{{}_1a_2} + ({}_2m + {}_2a_1)\frac{d_2 p_0^*}{{}_2a_2}, \qquad {}_2m = \frac{{}_2Q_{\bar{k}}/{}_2Q}{\frac{{}_1c}{{}_1a_2} - \frac{{}_2c}{{}_2a_2}} \gtrless 0.$$

Equating the shifts on the demand and supply sides of the commodity markets yields the following two equations in the prices of the two commodities and in the shifts of the demand schedules:

$$({}_1m + {}_1a)\frac{d_1 p_0^*}{{}_1a_2} - {}_1m\frac{d_2 p_0^*}{{}_2a_2} = d_1 A_0^*, \qquad {}_1a = {}_1a_1 - {}_1a_2\,{}_1A_1 > 0,$$

$$-{}_2m\frac{d_1 p_0^*}{{}_1a_2} + ({}_2m + {}_2a)\frac{d_2 p_0^*}{{}_2a_2} = d_2 A_0^*, \qquad {}_2a = {}_2a_1 - {}_2a_2\,{}_2A_2 > 0. \quad (16)$$

The determinant of the coefficient matrix of the price changes is $D = {}_1m_2a + {}_2m_1a + {}_1a_2a > 0$, so a stable solution to (16) exists.

Now if only the demand for the first commodity increases we have:

$$d_1 r_0^* = \frac{d_1 p_0^*}{{}_1a_2} = \frac{({}_2m + {}_2a)}{D} d_1 A_0^* > 0, \quad (17)$$

$$d_2 r_0^* = \frac{d_2 p_0^*}{{}_2a_2} = \frac{{}_2m}{D} d_1 A_0^* \gtrless 0,$$

$$d\bar{k}^* = \frac{{}_2a}{\left(\frac{{}_1c}{{}_1a_2} - \frac{{}_2c}{{}_2a_2}\right)\bar{k}D} d_1 A_0^* > 0.$$

As the analysis above indicated, the market price and central rent of both commodities increase with an increase in the demand for the first, and the boundary moves away from the market. Given sufficient information about the given conditions of the problem the exact value of the partial derivative of the boundary with respect to the demand shift could be calculated. Its value depends upon the location of the boundary, the difference in the rent gradients, the elasticities of demand for the two commodities, the parameters of the production functions, and upon the m's. The m's themselves depend upon the value of $\bar{k}$. In particular, where the first commodity is housing, the change in the city limits and hence the rural-urban land shift depend upon the size of the city.

Likewise, if the demand for the second commodity increases while that of the first remains unchanged, the market price and central rent for both commodities tend to increase and the boundary tends to move toward the market:

$$d_1 r_0^* = \frac{d_1 p_0^*}{{}_1a_2} = \frac{{}_1m}{D}\, d_2 A_0^* \geqslant 0, \tag{18}$$

$$d_2 r_0^* = \frac{d_2 p_0^*}{{}_2a_2} = \frac{({}_1m + {}_1a)}{D}\, d_2 A_0^* > 0,$$

$$d\bar{k}^* = -\frac{{}_1a}{\left(\dfrac{{}_1c}{{}_1a_2} - \dfrac{{}_2c}{{}_2a_2}\right)\bar{k}D}\, d_2 A_0^* < 0.$$

The really interesting case is that in which the demand for both commodities increases. It is obvious from the above that the market price and central rent of both commodities rise, and the equations defining the extent of the increases can be found by adding the right members of the expressions in (17) and (18). The change in the boundary is not so simple, however. An increase in the demand for the first commodity tends to cause the boundary to move farther away from the market, the second causes it to move toward the market. The relative change in $\bar{k}$ is

$$d\bar{k}^* = \frac{({}_2a d_1 A_0^* - {}_1a d_2 A_0^*)}{\left(\dfrac{{}_1c}{{}_1a_2} - \dfrac{{}_2c}{{}_2a_2}\right)\bar{k}D} \gtreqless 0 \text{ as } d_1 A_0^* \gtreqless \frac{{}_1a}{{}_2a}\, d_2 A_0^*. \tag{19}$$

This means the more elastic the demand for the first and the more inelastic the demand for the second commodity, the larger must be the relative shift in the demand for the first commodity as compared with that of the second commodity for the boundary to increase. Hence, in the case where the first industry produces housing services and the second food used wholly in the city surrounding the market, it is not obvious that growth of the city in terms of population or income would result in an outward movement of the city limits.

Let's look at this case a little closer. To determine the direction of the shift in the city limits we need to know something about the parameters of the production function and the elasticities of demand for housing and food. With respect to the price elasticities I have concluded that for housing the value is about equal to -1,[11] while Rex F. Daly has estimated that the price elasticity of demand for food at the farm is about -0.1.[12] From a study of Iowa farms, Gerhard Tintner has estimated that the exponent of land in a logarithmically linear production function is about 0.3.[13] Taking these values as illustrative of the orders of magnitude involved, ${}_1a$ would be about 1, regardless of the value of ${}_1a_2$,[14] and ${}_2a$ about 0.7, or their ratio about 1.4. Hence, (19) implies the city limits would move out provided that the relative increase in demand for housing services was about one and two-fifths times as great as the relative increase in the demand for food.

The shifts in demand can be related to growth in per capita income, y, and population, P. I have estimated the income elasticity of demand for housing to be at least $+1$, it may be as much as $+2$, and Daly estimated the income elasticity of demand for food at the farm at about $+0.2$.[15] Then, where ${}_iA_y$ is the income elasticity of demand,

$$d_1A_0^* = {}_iA_y\, dy^* + dP^*,$$

and

$$d\bar{k}^* \gtreqless 0 \text{ as } ({}_2a_1A_y - {}_1a_2A_y)\, dy^* \gtreqless ({}_1a - {}_2a)^* dP^*.$$

11. See my "The Demand for Non-Farm Housing," (abstract) *Econometrica*, 25 (April 1957) pp. 365–66. This estimate refers strictly to structures alone, rather than structures plus land.

12. "Demand for Farm Products at Retail and the Farm Level: Some Empirical Measurements and Related Problems," *Journal of the American Statistical Association*, LIII (Sept. 1958), pp. 656–68.

13. See his *Econometrics* (New York: John Wiley & Sons, 1952), pp. 53–55. Of course, this value might be different for farms in other areas.

14. Actually, data gathered by the Housing and Home Finance Agency indicates that the site value of land was about 15 percent of the total value of FHA insured existing single family dwellings in 1956, *Tenth Annual Report* (Washington: U.S. Government Printing Office, 1957), Table III–46, p. 108. Since the cost of improvements may run as much as one to three times the raw land value, the latter would be 4 to 8 percent of total property value. Interest costs, in turn, are about one-half the cost of providing housing services, so that raw land costs probably are of the order of 5 percent of the cost of housing services.

15. See the references cited above.

Substituting the above values, so long as the growth in per capita income is at least three-fifths as large as the growth in population the city limits would tend to move out.

Contrast this case with what I call the national food case. Here the farms around the market account for a small part of the total supply on some national market. This means that the demand curve facing this group of farms is highly elastic and, hence, that even very small increases in demand for housing services would lead to an outward movement of the city limits. This contrast highlights the importance of the demand elasticities of the two commodities, particularly the agricultural commodity, in determining the changes in land use that result from shifts in demand for the products of the two industries.

Change in wages

As noted earlier, an increase in wages shifts both supply schedules in Figure 4 to the right and the market prices of both commodities tend to increase. The latter would tend to make rents at the market rise, but the rent functions in Figures 4a and 4b shift to the left. Hence, the changes in rent at the market and the boundary depend upon the extent to which the prices of the two commodities tend to increase with the initial shifts in supply.

Solving we find:

$$d_1r_0^* = -\frac{1}{{}_1a_2\,{}_2a_2D}\{{}_1a_1\,{}_2a_2({}_2m+{}_2a)({}_1a-1)+{}_1a_2\,{}_2a_1\,{}_1m({}_2a-1)\}dw^*, \qquad (20)$$

$$d_2r_0^* = -\frac{1}{{}_1a_2\,{}_2a_2D}\{{}_1a_2\,{}_2a_1({}_1m+{}_1a)({}_2a-1)+{}_1a_1\,{}_2a_2\,{}_2m({}_1a-1)\}dw^*,$$

$$d\bar{k}^* = -\frac{\{{}_1a_1\,{}_2a_2\,{}_2a({}_1a-1)-{}_1a_2\,{}_2a_1\,{}_1a({}_2a-1)\}}{{}_1a_2\,{}_2a_2D\left(\frac{{}_1c}{{}_1a_2}-\frac{{}_2c}{{}_2a_2}\right)\bar{k}}dw^*.$$

Since ${}_ia = {}_ia_1 - {}_ia_2\,{}_iA_i \gtreqless 1$ as ${}_iA_i \lesseqgtr -1$, the changes in rents and the boundary depend critically upon the elasticities of demand for the two commodities. Where the first commodity is housing, $({}_1a-1)$ is about zero, so the change hinge upon the elasticity of demand for the agricultural commodity. In the local food case ${}_2a$ is less than one, and with an increase in wages the rent of land devoted to the production of both commodities increases and the city limits move in toward the market. On the other hand, in the national food case the demand for the local agricultural product is highly elastic, and so

$({}_2a-1)$ is greater than zero. Here, the rent of land falls for both commodities and the boundary moves away from the market.

Neutral technological change

Suppose that a change in technology takes place in such a way that the relative marginal productivities of the two factors, labor and land, for any given input combination are unchanged. This leads, simply, to a renumbering of the isoquants of the production function or to a change in ${}_ia_0$. If ${}_1a_0$ only increases we have:

$$d_1r_0^* = \frac{({}_2m+{}_2a)({}_1a-1)}{{}_1a_2D}d_1a_0^* \tag{21}$$

$$d_2r_0^* = \frac{{}_2m({}_1a-1)}{{}_1a_2D}d_1a_0^*$$

$$d\bar{k}^* = \frac{{}_2a({}_1a-1)}{{}_1a_2D\left(\frac{{}_1c}{{}_1a_2}-\frac{{}_2c}{{}_2a_2}\right)\bar{k}}d_1a_0^*.$$

These can be interpreted in terms of Figure 4 as follows: an increase in ${}_1a_0$ causes the supply schedule in Figure 4a to shift to the left and the rent schedule to shift to the right. This leads to a fall in the price of the first commodity. If its demand is unit elastic, as where the first commodity is housing, the fall in price exactly balances the shift in the rent function so that rent offered by firms in the housing industry remains unchanged. Hence, there is no shift in the boundary and all conditions affecting firms in the second industry remain unchanged.

Now let ${}_2a_0$ only increase:

$$d_1r_0^* = \frac{{}_1m({}_2a-1)}{{}_2a_2D}d_2a_0^*, \tag{22}$$

$$d_2r_0^* = \frac{({}_1m+{}_1a)({}_2a-1)}{{}_2a_2D}d_2a_0^*,$$

$$d\bar{k}^* = -\frac{{}_1a({}_2a-1)}{{}_2a_2D\left(\frac{{}_1c}{{}_1a_2}-\frac{{}_2c}{{}_2a_2}\right)\bar{k}}d_2a_0^*.$$

Since the supply schedule in Figure 4b shifts to the left with the increase in ${}_2a_0$, the price of the second commodity tends to fall. But the rent function for the second commodity shifts to the right. If the demand for the industry's output is inelastic, the shift in the rent function less than counterbalances the fall in price and rent offered by firms in the second industry falls. The boundary then moves away from the market since, temporarily, rent offered by the first industry firms remains unchanged. The movement of the boundary leads to an increase in the supply of the first commodity, a fall in its price, and a decline in the rent offered by firms in the first industry. Hence, in the new equilibrium, the rent offered by both industries is lower than before and the boundary has moved out from the market. If, on the other hand, the demand for the output of the second industry is elastic, just the reverse holds.

Changes in the price gradient

Unlike the other cases examined so far, the effect of a change in the price gradient for either commodity depends upon the specific form of the land supply function. It is also somewhat more difficult to analyze than the other cases.

Suppose that only the price gradient for the first commodity increases. In terms of Figure 4, the supply function for the first commodity shifts to the right. This leads to a rise in price of the first commodity and in the rent that firms in the first industry would offer for land at the market. The rent gradient for the first industry increases, however, so that rent offered falls off more rapidly with distance. Analytically, we have:

$$d_1r_0^* = \frac{1}{{}_2a_2D}\left\{{}_2a_{22}m\left(2-\frac{{}_1Q_{\bar{k}}\bar{k}}{{}_1Q}\right)+(2{}_2a_2+{}_1m_2c\bar{k})_2a\right\}d_1c^*, \tag{23}$$

$$d_2r_0^* = \frac{{}_2m}{D}\left\{\left(2-\frac{{}_1Q_{\bar{k}}\bar{k}}{{}_1Q}\right)-\frac{{}_1c}{{}_1a_2}\bar{k}_1a\right\}d_1c^*,$$

$$d\bar{k}^* = \frac{{}_2a}{D\left(\frac{{}_1c}{{}_1a_2}-\frac{{}_2c}{{}_2a_2}\right)\bar{k}}\left\{\left(2-\frac{{}_1Q_{\bar{k}}\bar{k}}{{}_1Q}\right)-\frac{{}_1c}{{}_1a_2}\bar{k}_1a\right\}d_1c^*.$$

Recalling from the discussion of the displacement of equilibrium that the first term in the bracket of the first of equations (23) is positive, this equation indicates that rent at the market of the first commodity tends to increase. As the discussion above suggests, two factors affect the change in the boundary, the increase in ${}_1r_0$ and the increase in the rent gradient, and these work in opposite directions. Here it can be shown that the second tends to outweigh the first so that at the old boundary rent offered by firms in the second industry increases relative to rent offered by firms in the first. This leads to an increase in the supply of the second commodity, hence to a fall in its price and in the rent firms in the second industry pay.[16]

Next, consider the case where the price gradient of the second commodity increases while that of the first commodity remains fixed. Here:

$$d_1 r_0^* = \frac{{}_1m}{D}\left\{\left(2+\frac{{}_2Q_{\bar{k}}\bar{k}}{{}_2Q}\right)-\frac{{}_2c}{{}_2a_2}\bar{k}_2a\right\} d_2c^*, \tag{24}$$

$$d_2 r_0^* = \frac{1}{{}_1a_2 D}\left\{{}_1a_{21}m\left(2+\frac{{}_2Q_{\bar{k}}\bar{k}}{{}_2Q}\right)+(2_1a_2+{}_2m_1c\bar{k})_1a\right\} d_2c^*,$$

$$d\bar{k}^* = -\frac{{}_1a}{D\left(\frac{{}_1c}{{}_1a_2}-\frac{{}_2c}{{}_2a_2}\right)\bar{k}}\left\{\left(2+\frac{{}_2Q_{\bar{k}}\bar{k}}{{}_2Q}\right)-\frac{{}_2c}{{}_2a_2}\bar{k}_2a\right\} d_2c^*.$$

The increase in the price gradient of the second commodity leads to a rightward shift in the supply function in Figure 4b, which causes an increase in the market price of the second commodity and the rent offered by firms in the second industry for land at the market. Again there are two influences operating on the boundary. It can be shown that the rent offered by firms in the second industry for land at the market rises relative to that offered by first industry firms, and this in itself tends to make $\bar{k}$ decrease. However, the rent gradient of the second industry becomes steeper, and this tends to increase $\bar{k}$. The net effect of the two changes depends upon the location of the boundary and the elasticity of demand for the second commodity. For $\bar{k}$ small and a highly inelastic demand, the boundary moves to-

16. The proof is as follows: in (23), both of the two terms enclosed in braces in the second and third equations are positive. The first term is

$$\left(2-\frac{{}_1Q_{\bar{k}}\bar{k}}{{}_1Q}\right)=2\left[1-\frac{1}{1+\frac{1}{3}\left(\frac{{}_1c_1a_1}{{}_1a_2}\bar{k}\right) \quad \xi}\right]<2\left[1-\frac{1}{1+\frac{1}{3}\left(\frac{{}_1c_1a_1}{{}_1a_2}\bar{k}\right)\exp.\left(\frac{{}_1c_1a_1}{{}_1a_2}\bar{k}\right)}\right]$$

since $\xi < (({}_1c_1a_1/{}_1a_2)k)$ in the remainder term of the second order Maclaurin's series expansion of exp.$(({}_1c_1a_1/{}_1a_2)k)$. This upper bound of the first term can be written as

$$f(\bar{k})\,{}_1a_1\left(\frac{{}_1c}{{}_1a_2}\bar{k}\right), \text{ where } f(\bar{k})=\tfrac{2}{3}/\left\{\exp.\left(-\frac{{}_1c_1a_1}{{}_1a_2}\bar{k}\right)+\tfrac{1}{3}\left(\frac{{}_1c_1a_1}{{}_1a_2}\bar{k}\right)\right\}.$$

Examination of the first and second derivatives of $f(k)$ indicates that max $f(k) = 2/(1+\log_e 3) < 1$. But in the second term in the braces of the second and third terms of (23), ${}_1a \geqslant {}_1a_1$. Therefore, $f(k)_1a_1(({}_1c/{}_1a_2)k) < (({}_1c/{}_1a_2)k)_1a$ and the term in braces in these equations is negative.

ward the market, while for large $\bar{k}$ and a highly elastic demand, $\bar{k}$ tends to become larger.[17] Hence, in the national food case an increase in the price gradient of the agricultural commodity would lead to an outward movement of the boundary.

17. The reason for this is as follows: The first of the two terms in braces in the third of equations (24) can be written as:

$$g(\bar{k})_2a_1\left(\frac{_2c}{_2a_2}\bar{k}\right) \text{ since } \frac{_2Q_{\bar{k}}\bar{k}}{_2Q} = \left(\frac{_2c_2a_1}{_2a_2}k\right)^2 \Big/ \left(\frac{_2c_2a_1}{_2a_2}\bar{k}+1\right).$$

Now $g(\bar{k})$ increases without limit as $\bar{k}$ goes to zero and goes to one as $\bar{k}$ increases without limit. Also, $g(\bar{k})$ is a decreasing function everywhere. The second of the two terms in braces is $_2a_1$ for $_2A_2 = 0$, increases as $_2A_2$ decreases, and tends to infinity as $_2A_2$ tends to minus infinity.

PART II CENTRAL PLACE THEORY

7

EDWARD L. ULLMAN

A Theory of Location for Cities

I

Periodically in the past century the location and distribution of cities and settlements have been studied. Important contributions have been made by individuals in many disciplines. Partly because of the diversity and unco-ordinated nature of the attack and partly because of the complexities and variables involved, a systematic theory has been slow to evolve, in contrast to the advances in the field of industrial location.[1]

The first theoretical statement of modern importance was von Thünen's *Der isolierte Staat*, initially published in 1826, wherein he postulated an entirely uniform land surface and showed that under ideal conditions a city would develop in the centre of this land area and concentric rings of land use would develop around the central city. In 1841 Kohl investigated the relation between cities and the natural and cultural environment, paying particular attention to the effect of transport routes on the location of urban centers.[2] In 1894 Cooley admirably demonstrated the channelizing influence that transportation routes, particularly rail, would have on the location and development of trade centers.[3] He also called attention to break in transportation as a city-builder just as Ratzel had earlier. In 1927 Haig sought to determine why there was such a large concentration of population and manufacturing in the largest cities.[4] Since concentration occurs where assembly of material is cheapest, all business functions, except extraction and transportation, ideally should be located in cities where transportation is least costly. Exceptions are provided

1. Cf. Tord Palander, *Beiträge zur Standortsthcorie* (Uppsala, Sweden, 1935), or E. M. Hoover, Jr., *Location Theory and the Shoe and Leather Industries* (Cambridge, Mass., 1937).

2. J. G. Kohl, *Der Verkehr und die Ansiedlungen der Menschen in ihrer Abhängikeit von der Gestaltung der Erdoberfläche* (2d ed.; Leipzig, 1850).

3. C. H. Cooley, "The Theory of Transportation," *Publications of the American Economic Association*, IX (May 1894), 1–148.

4. R. M. Haig, "Toward an Understanding of the Metropolis: Some Speculations Regarding the Economic Basis of Urban Concentration," *Quarterly Journal of Economics*, XL (1926), 179–208.

Reprinted from The American Journal of Sociology *(May 1941), pp. 853–64, by permission of the publishers and the author.*

by the processing of perishable goods, as in sugar centrals, and of large weight-losing commodities, as in smelters. Haig's theoretical treatment is of a different type from those just cited but should be included as an excellent example of a "concentration" study.

In 1927 Bobeck[5] showed that German geographers since 1899, following Schluter and others, had concerned themselves largely with the internal geography of cities, with the pattern of land use and forms within the urban limits, in contrast to the problem of location and support of cities. Such preoccupation with internal urban structure has also characterized the recent work of geographers in America and other countries. Bobeck insisted with reason that such studies, valuable though they were, constituted only half the field of urban geography and that there remained unanswered the fundamental geographical question: "What are the causes for the existence, present size, and character of a city?" Since the publication of this article, a number of urban studies in Germany and some in other countries have dealt with such questions as the relations between city and country.[6]

II

A theoretical framework for study of the distribution of settlements is provided by the work of Walter Christaller.[7] The essence of the theory is that a certain amount of productive land supports an urban center. The center exists because essential services must be performed for the surrounding land. Thus the primary factor explaining Chicago is the productivity of the Middle West; location at the southern end of Lake Michigan is a secondary factor. If there were no Lake Michigan, the urban population of the Middle West would in all probability be just as large as it is now. Ideally, the city should be in the center of a productive area.[8] The similarity of this concept to von Thünen's original proposition is evident.

5. Hans Bobeck, "Grundfragen der Stadt Geographie," *Geographischer Anzeiger*, XXVIII (1927), 213–24.

6. A section of the International Geographical Congress at Amsterdam in 1938 dealt with "Functional Relations between City and Country." The papers are published in Vol. II of the *Comptes rendus* (Leiden: E. J. Brill, 1938). A recent American study is C. D. Harris, *Salt Lake City: A Regional Capital* (Ph.D. diss., University of Chicago, 1940). Pertinent also is R. E. Dickinson, "The Metropolitan Regions of the United States," *Geographical Review*, XXIV (1934), 278–91.

7. *Die zentralen Orte in Süddeutschland* (Jena, 1935); also a paper (no title) in *Comptes rendus du Congrès internationale de géographie Amsterdam* (1938), II, 123–37.

8. This does not deny the importance of "gateway" centers such as Omaha and Kansas City, cities located between contrasting areas in order to secure exchange benefits. The logical growth of cities at such locations does not destroy the theory to be presented (cf. R. D. McKenzie's excellent discussion in *The Metropolitan Community* [New York, 1933], pp. 4 ff.).

Apparently many scholars have approached the scheme in their thinking.[9] Bobeck claims he presented the rudiments of such an explanation in 1927. The work of a number of American rural sociologists shows appreciation for some of Christaller's preliminary assumptions, even though done before or without knowledge of Christaller's work and performed with a different end in view. Galpin's epochal study of trade areas in Walworth County, Wisconsin, published in 1915, was the first contribution. Since then important studies bearing on the problem have been made by others.[10] These studies are confined primarily to smaller trade centers but give a wealth of information on distribution of settlements which independently substantiates many of Christaller's basic premises.

As a working hypothesis one assumes that normally the larger the city, the larger its tributary area. Thus there should be cities of varying size ranging from a small hamlet performing a few simple functions, such as providing a limited shopping and market center for a small contiguous area, up to a large city with a large tributary area composed of the service areas of many smaller towns and providing more complex services, such as wholesaling, large-scale banking, specialized retailing, and the like. Services performed purely for a surrounding area are termed "central" functions by Christaller, and the settlements performing them "central" places. An industry using raw materials imported from outside the local region and shipping its products out of the local area would not constitute a central service.

9. Cf. Petrie's statement about ancient Egypt and Mesopotamia: "It has been noticed before how remarkably similar the distances are between the early nome capitals of the Delta (twenty-one miles on an average) and the early cities of Mesopotamia (averaging twenty miles apart). Some physical cause seems to limit the primitive rule in this way. Is it not the limit of central storage of grain, which is the essential form of early capital? Supplies could be centralised up to ten miles away; beyond that the cost of transport made it better worth while to have a nearer centre" (W. M. Flinders Petrie, *Social Life in Ancient Egypt* [London, 1923; reissued, 1932], pp. 3–4).

10. C. J. Galpin, *Social Anatomy of an Agricultural Community* (University of Wisconsin Agricultural Experiment Station Research Bull. 34 [1915]), and the restudy by J. H. Kolb and R. A. Polson, *Trends in Town-Country Relations* (University of Wisconsin Agricultural Experiment Station Research Bull. 117 [1933]); B. L. Melvin, *Village Service Agencies of New York State, 1925* (Cornell University Agricultural Experiment Station Bull. 493 [1929]), and *Rural Population of New York, 1855–1925* (Cornell University Agricultural Experiment Station Memoir 116 [1928]); Dwight Sanderson, *The Rural Community* (New York, 1932), esp. pp. 488–514, which contains references to many studies by Sanderson and his associates; Carle C. Zimmerman, *Farm Trade Centers in Minnesota, 1905–29* (University of Minnesota Agricultural Experiment Station Bull. 269 [1930]); T. Lynn Smith, *Farm Trade Centers in Louisiana, 1905 to 1931* (Louisiana State University Bull. 234 [1933]); Paul H. Landis, *South Dakota Town-Country Trade Relations, 1901–1931* (South Dakota Agricultural Experiment Station Bull. 274 [1932]), and *The Growth and Decline of South Dakota Trade Centers, 1901–1933* (Bull. 279 [1938]), and *Washington Farm Trade Centers, 1900–1935* (State College of Washington Agricultural Experiment Station Bull. 360 [1938]). Other studies are listed in subsequent footnotes.

Ideally, each central place would have a circular tributary area, as in von Thünen's proposition, and the city would be in the center. However, if three or more tangent circles are inscribed in an area, unserved spaces will exist; the best theoretical shapes are hexagons, the closest geometrical figures to circles which will completely fill an area (Figure 1).[11]

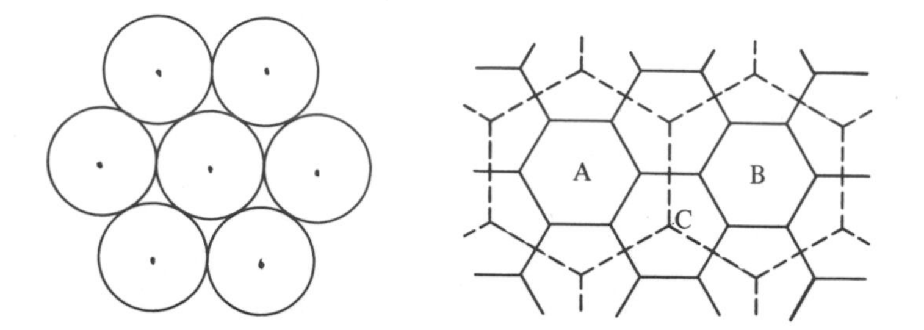

FIGURE 1 Theoretical shapes of tributary areas. Circles leave unserved spaces, hexagons do not. Small hexagons are service areas for smaller places, large hexagons (*dotted lines*) represent service areas for next higher-rank central places.

Christaller has recognized typical-size settlements, computed their average population, their distance apart, and the size and population of their tributary areas in accordance with his hexagonal theory as Table 1 shows. He also states that the number of central places follows a norm from largest to smallest in the following order: 1:2:6:18:54, etc.[12]

TABLE 1

CENTRAL PLACE	TOWNS		TRIBUTARY AREAS	
	DISTANCE APART (Km.)	POPULATION	SIZE (Sq. Km.)	POPULATION
Market hamlet (*Marktort*)	7	800	45	2,700
Township center (*Amtsort*)	12	1,500	135	8,100
County seat (*Kreisstadt*)	21	3,500	400	24,000
District city (*Bezirksstadt*)	36	9,000	1,200	75,000
Small state capital (*Gaustadt*)	62	27,000	3,600	225,000
Provincial head city (*Provinzhauptstadt*)	108	90,000	10,800	675,000
Regional capital city (*Landeshauptstadt*)	186	300,000	32,400	2,025,000

11. See August Lösch, "The Nature of the Economic Regions," *Southern Economic Journal*, V (1938), 73. Galpin (*op. cit.*) thought in terms of six tributary-area circles around each center. See also Kolb and Polson, *op. cit.*, pp. 30–41.

12. Barnes and Robinson present some interesting maps showing the average distance apart of farmhouses in the driftless area of the Middle West and in southern Ontario. Farmhouses might well be regarded as the smallest settlement units in a central-place scheme, although they might not be in the same numbered sequence (James A. Barnes and Arthur H. Robinson, "A New Method for the Representation of Dispersed Rural Population," *Geographical Review*, XXX [1940], 134–37).

All these figures are computed on the basis of South Germany, but Christaller claims them to be typical for most of Germany and western Europe. The settlements are classified on the basis of spacing each larger unit in a hexagon of next-order size, so that the distance between similar centers in the table above increases by the $\sqrt{3}$ over the preceding smaller category (in Figure 1, e.g., the distance from *A* to *B* is $\sqrt{3}$ times the distance from *A* to *C*). The initial distance figure of 7 km. between the smallest centers is chosen because 4–5 km., approximately the distance one can walk in one hour, appears to be a normal service-area limit for the smallest centers. Thus, in a hexagonal scheme, these centers are about 7 km. apart. Christaller's maps indicate that such centers are spaced close to this norm in South Germany. In the larger categories the norms for distance apart and size of centers appear to be true averages; but variations from the norm are the rule, although wide discrepancies are not common in the eastern portion of South Germany, which is less highly industrialized than the Rhine-Ruhr areas in the west. The number of central places of each rank varies rather widely from the normal order of expectancy.

The theoretical ideal appears to be most nearly approached in poor, thinly settled farm districts—areas which are most nearly self-contained. In some other sections of Germany industrial concentration seems to be a more important explanation, although elements of the central-place type of distribution are present. Christaller points out that Cologne is really the commercial center for the Ruhr industrial district even though it is outside the Ruhr area. Even in mountain areas centrality is a more important factor than topography in fixing the distribution of settlements. Christaller states that one cannot claim that a certain city is where it is because of a certain river—that would be tantamount to saying that if there were no rivers there would be no cities.

III

Population alone is not a true measure of the central importance of a city; a large mining, industrial, or other specialized-function town might have a small tributary area and exercise few central functions. In addition to population, therefore, Christaller uses an index based on number of telephones in proportion to the average number per thousand inhabitants in South Germany, weighted further by the telephone density of the local subregion. A rich area such as the Palatinate supports more telephones in proportion to population than a poor area in the Bavarian Alps; therefore, the same number of telephones in a Palatinate town would not give it the same central significance as in the Alps. He claims that telephones, since they are used for business, are a reliable index of centrality. Such a thesis would not be valid for most of the United States, where telephones are as common in homes as in commercial and professional quarters.

Some better measures of centrality could be devised, even if only the number of out-of-town telephone calls per town. Better still would be some measure of actual central services performed. It would be tedious and difficult to compute the amount, or percentage, of business in each town drawn from outside the city, but some short cuts might be devised. If one knew the average number of customers required to support certain specialized functions in various regions, then the excess of these functions over the normal required for the urban population would be an index of centrality.[13] In several states rural sociologists and others have computed the average number of certain functions for towns of a given size. With one or two exceptions only small towns have been analyzed. Retail trade has received most attention, but professional and other services have also been examined. These studies do not tell us actually what population supports each service, since the services are supported both by town and by surrounding rural population, but they do provide norms of function expectancy which would be just as useful.[14]

A suggestive indicator of centrality is provided by the maps which Dickinson has made for per capita wholesale sales of cities in the United States.[15] On this basis centers are distributed rather evenly in accordance with regional population density. Schlier has computed

13. In Iowa, e.g., almost all towns of more than 450 inhabitants have banks, half of the towns of 250–300, and 20 percent of the towns of 100–150 (according to calculations made by the author from population estimates in *Rand McNally's Commercial Atlas* for 1937).

14. See particularly the thorough study by B. L. Melvin, *Village Service Agencies, New York State 1925*; C. R. Hoffer, *A Study of Town-Country Relationships* (Michigan Agricultural Experiment Station Special Bull. 181 [1928]) (data on number of retail stores and professions per town); H. B. Price and C. R. Hoffer, *Services of Rural Trade Centers in Distribution of Farm Supplies* (Minnesota Agricultural Experiment Station Bull. 249 [1938]); William J. Reilly, *Methods for the Study of Retail Relationships* ("Bureau of Business Research Monographs," No. 4, University of Texas Bull. 2944 [1929]), p. 26; J. H. Kolb, *Service Institutions of Town and Country* (Wisconsin Agricultural Experiment Station Research Bull. 66 [1925]) (town size in relation to support of institutions); Smith, *op. cit.*, pp. 32–40; Paul H. Landis, *South Dakota Town-Country Trade Relations, 1901–1931*, p. 20 (population per business enterprise), and pp. 24–25 (functions per town size); Zimmerman, *op. cit.*, pp. 16 and 51 ff.

For a criticism of population estimates of unincorporated hamlets used in many of these studies see Glenn T. Trewartha, "The Unincorporated Hamlet: An Analysis of Data Sources," (paper presented December 28 at Baton Rouge meetings, Association of American Geographers; forthcoming, probably, in March number of *Rural Sociology*, Vol. VI [1941]).

15. *Op. cit.*, pp. 280–81.

the centrality of cities in Germany on the basis of census returns for "central" occupations.[16] Refinement of some of our census returns is desirable before this can be done entirely satisfactorily in the United States, but the method is probably the most promising in prospect.

Another measure of centrality would be the number of automobiles entering a town, making sure that suburban movements were not included. Figures could be secured if the state-wide highway planning surveys in forty-six states were extended to gather such statistics.

IV

The central-place scheme may be distorted by local factors, primarily industrial concentration or main transport routes. Christaller notes that transportation is not an areally operating principle, as the supplying of central goods implies, but is a linearly working factor. In many cases central places are strung at short intervals along an important transport route, and their tributary areas do not approximate the ideal circular or hexagonal shape but are elongated at right angles to the main transport line.[17] In some areas the reverse of this normal expectancy is true. In most of Illinois, maps depicting tributary areas show them to be elongated parallel to the main transport routes, not at right angles to them.[18] The combination of nearly uniform land and competitive railways peculiar to the state results in main railways running nearly parallel and close to one another between major centers.

In highly industrialized areas the central-place scheme is generally so distorted by industrial concentration in response to resources and transportation that it may be said to have little significance as an explanation for urban location and distribution, although some features of a central-place scheme may be present, as in the case of Cologne and the Ruhr already discussed.

In addition to distortion, the type of scheme prevailing in various

16. Otto Schlier, "Die zentralen Orte des Deutschen Reichs," *Zeitschrift der Gesellschaft für Erdkunde zu Berlin* (1937), pp. 161–70. See also map constructed from Schlier's figures in R. E. Dickinson's valuable article, "The Economic Regions of Germany," *Geographical Review*, XXVIII (1938), 619. For use of census figures in the United States see Harris, *op. cit.*, pp. 3–12.

17. For an illustration of this type of tributary area in the ridge and valley section of east Tennessee see H. V. Miller, "Effects of Reservoir Construction on Local Economic Units," *Economic Geography*, XV (1939), 242–49.

18. See, e.g., *Marketing Atlas of the United States* (New York: International Magazine Co., Inc.) or *A Study of Natural Areas of Trade in the United States* (Washington, D.C.: U.S. National Recovery Administration, 1935).

regions is susceptible to many influences. Productivity of the soil,[19] type of agriculture and intensity of cultivation, topography, governmental organization, are all obvious modifiers. In the United States, for example, what is the effect on distribution of settlements caused by the sectional layout of the land and the regular size of counties in many states? In parts of Latin America many centers are known as "Sunday towns"; their chief functions appear to be purely social, to act as religious and recreational centers for holidays—hence the name "Sunday town."[20] Here social rather than economic services are the primary support of towns, and we should accordingly expect a system of central places with fewer and smaller centers, because fewer functions are performed and people can travel farther more readily than commodities. These underlying differences do not destroy the value of the theory; rather they provide variations of interest to study for themselves and for purposes of comparison with other regions.

The system of central places is not static or fixed; rather it is subject to change and development with changing conditions.[21] Improvements in transportation have had noticeable effects. The provision of good automobile roads alters buying and marketing practices, appears to make the smallest centers smaller and the larger centers larger, and generally alters trade areas.[22] Since good

19. Cf. the emphasis of Sombart, Adam Smith, and other economists on the necessity of surplus produce of land in order to support cities. Fertile land ordinarily produces more surplus and consequently more urban population, although "the town .... may not always derive its whole subsistence from the country in its neighborhood ...." (Adam Smith, *The Wealth of Nations* [Modern Library edition; New York, 1937] p. 357; Werner Sombart, *Der moderne Kapitalismus* [zweite, neugearbeitete Auflage; Munich and Leipzig, 1916], I, 130–31).

20. For an account of such settlements in Brazil see Pierre Deffontaines, "Rapports fonctionnels entre les agglomérations urbaines et rurales: un example en pays de colonisation, le Brésil," *Comptes rendus de Congrès internationale de géographie Amsterdam* (1938), II, 139–44.

21. The effects of booms, droughts, and other factors on trade-center distribution by decades are brought out in Landis' studies of South Dakota and Washington. Zimmerman and Smith also show the changing character of trade-center distribution (see n. 10 of this paper for references). Melvin calls attention to a "village population shift lag"; in periods of depressed agriculture villages in New York declined in population approximately a decade after the surrounding rural population had decreased (B. L. Melvin, *Rural Population of New York, 1855–1925*, p. 120).

22. Most studies indicate that only the very smallest hamlets (under 250 population) and crossroads stores have declined in size or number. The larger small places have held their own (see Landis for Washington, *op. cit.*, p. 37, and his *South Dakota Town-Country Trade Relations, 1901–1931*, pp. 34–36). Zimmerman in 1930 (*op. cit.*, p. 41) notes that crossroads stores are disappearing and are being replaced by small villages. He states further: "It is evident that claims of substantial correlation between the appearance and growth of the larger trading center and the disappearance of the primary center are more or less unfounded. Although there are minor relationships, the main change has been a division of labor between the two types of centers rather than the complete obliteration of the smaller in favor of the larger" (p. 32).

roads are spread more uniformly over the land than railways, their provision seems to make the distribution of centers correspond more closely to the normal scheme.[23]

Christaller may be guilty of claiming too great an application of his scheme. His criteria for determining typical-size settlements and their normal number apparently do not fit actual frequency counts of settlements in many almost uniform regions as well as some less rigidly deductive norms.[24]

Bobeck in a later article claims that Christaller's proof is unsatisfactory.[25] He states that two-thirds of the population of Germany and England live in cities and that only one-third of these cities in Germany are real central places. The bulk are primarily industrial towns or villages inhabited solely by farmers. He also declares that exceptions in the rest of the world are common, such as the purely rural districts of the Tonkin Delta of Indo-China, cities based on energetic entrepreneurial activity, as some Italian cities, and world commercial ports such as London, Rotterdam, and Singapore. Many of these objections are valid; one wishes that Christaller had better quantitative data and were less vague in places. Bobeck admits, however, that the central-place theory has value and applies in some areas.

The central-place theory probably provides as valid an interpretation of settlement distribution over the land as the concentric-zone theory does for land use within cities. Neither theory is to be thought of as a rigid framework fitting all location facts at a given moment. Some, expecting too much, would jettison the concentric-zone theory; others, realizing that it is an investigative hypothesis of merit, regard it as a useful tool for comparative analysis.

For further evidence of effect of automobile on small centers see R. V. Mitchell, *Trends in Rural Retailing in Illinois, 1926–1938* (University of Illinois Bureau of Business Research Bull., Ser. 59 [1939]), pp. 31 ff., and Sanderson, *op. cit.*, p. 564, as well as other studies cited above.

23. Smith (*op. cit.*, p. 54) states: "There has been a tendency for centers of various sizes to distribute themselves more uniformly with regard to the area, population, and resources of the state. Or the changes seem to be in the direction of a more efficient pattern of rural organization. This redistribution of centers in conjunction with improved methods of communication and transportation has placed each family in frequent contact with several trade centers. . . . ."

In contrast, Melvin (*Rural Population of New York, 1855–1925*, p. 90), writing about New York state before the automobile had had much effect, states: "In 1870 the villages . . . . were rather evenly scattered over the entire state where they had been located earlier in response to particular local needs. By 1920, however, the villages had become distributed more along routes of travel and transportation and in the vicinity of cities."

24. This statement is made on the basis of frequency counts by the author for several midwestern states (cf. also Schlier, *op. cit.*, pp. 165–69, for Germany).

25. Hans Bobeck, "Über einige functionelle Stadttypen und ihre Beziehungen zum Lande," *Comptes rendus du Congrès internationale de géographie Amsterdam* (1938), II, 88.

V

Even in the closely articulated national economy of the United States there are strong forces at work to produce a central-place distribution of settlements. It is true that products under our national economy are characteristically shipped from producing areas through local shipping-points directly to consuming centers which are often remote. However, the distribution of goods or imports brought into an area is characteristically carried on through brokerage, wholesale and retail channels in central cities.[26] This graduated division of functions supports a central-place framework of settlements. Many nonindustrial regions of relatively uniform land surface have cities distributed so evenly over the land that some sort of central-place theory appears to be the prime explanation.[27] It should be worth while to study this distribution and compare it with other areas.[28] In New England, on the other hand, where cities are primarily industrial centers based on distant raw materials and extra-regional markets, instead of the land's supporting the city the reverse is more nearly true: the city supports the countryside by providing a market for farm products, and thus infertile rural areas are kept from being even more deserted than they are now.

The forces making for concentration at certain places and the inevitable rise of cities at these favored places have been emphasized by geographers and other scholars. The phenomenal growth of industry and world-trade in the last hundred years and the concomitant growth of cities justify this emphasis but have perhaps unintentionally caused the intimate connection between a city and its surrounding area partially to be overlooked. Explanation in terms of

26. Harris, *op. cit.*, p. 87.

27. For a confirmation of this see the column diagram on p. 73 of Lösch (*op. cit.*), which shows the minimum distances between towns in Iowa of three different size classes. The maps of trade-center distribution in the works of Zimmerman, Smith, and Landis (cited earlier) also show an even spacing of centers.

28. Table N = 1 gives the average community area for 140 villages in the United States in 1930. In the table notice throughout that (1) the larger the village, the larger its tributary area in each region and (2) the sparser the rural population density, the larger the village tributary area for each size class (contrast mid-Atlantic with Far West, etc.).

TABLE N = 1

REGION	COMMUNITY AREA IN SQUARE MILES		
	SMALL VILLAGES (250–1,000 POP.)	MEDIUM VILLAGES (1,000–1,750 POP.)	LARGE VILLAGES (1,750–2,500 POP.)
Mid-Atlantic	43	46	87
South	77	111	146
Middle West	81	113	148
Far West	–	365	223

concentration is most important for industrial districts but does not provide a complete areal theory for distribution of settlements. Furthermore, there is evidence that "of late .... the rapid growth of the larger cities has reflected their increasing importance as commercial and service centers rather than as industrial centers."[29] Some form of the central-place theory should provide the most realistic key to the distribution of settlements where there is no marked concentration—in agricultural areas where explanation has been most difficult in the past. For all areas the system may well furnish a theoretical norm from which deviations may be measured.[30] It might also be an aid in planning the development of new areas. If the theory is kept in mind by workers in academic and planning fields as more studies are made, its validity may be tested and its structure refined in accordance with regional differences.

Although 140 is only a sample of the number of villages in the country, the figures are significant because the service areas were carefully and uniformly delimited in the field for all villages (E. deS. Brunner and J. D. Kolb, *Rural Social Trends* [New York, 1933], p. 95; see also E. deS. Brunner, G. S. Hughes, and M. Patten, *American Agricultural Villages* [New York, 1927], chap. ii).

In New York 26 sq. mi. was found to be the average area per village in 1920. Village refers to any settlement under 2,500 population. Nearness to cities, type of agriculture, and routes of travel are cited as the three most important factors influencing density of villages. Since areas near cities are suburbanized in some cases, as around New York City, the village-density in these districts is correspondingly high. Some urban counties with smaller cities (Rochester, Syracuse, and Niagara Falls) have few suburbs, and consequently the villages are farther apart than in many agricultural counties (B. L. Melvin, *Rural Population of New York, 1955–1925*, pp. 88–89; table on p. 89 shows number of square miles per village in each New York county).

In sample areas of New York State the average distance from a village of 250 or under to another of the same size or larger is about 3 miles; for the 250–749 class it is 3–5 miles; for the 750–1,249 class, 5–7 miles (B. L. Melvin, *Village Service Agencies, New York, 1925*, p. 102; in the table on p. 103 the distance averages cited above are shown to be very near the modes).

Kolb makes some interesting suggestions as to the distances between centers. He shows that spacing is closer in central Wisconsin than in Kansas, which is more sparsely settled (J. H. Kolb, *Service Relations of Town and Country* [Wisconsin Agricultural Experimental Station Research Bull. 58 (1923)]; see pp. 7–8 for theoretical graphs).

In Iowa, "the dominant factor determining the *size* of convenience-goods areas is distance" (*Second State Iowa Planning Board Report* [Des Moines, April, 1935], p. 198). This report contains fertile suggestions on trade areas for Iowa towns. Valuable detailed reports on retail trade areas for some Iowa counties have also been made by the same agency.

29. U.S. National Resources Committee, *Our Cities—Their Role in the National Economy: Report of the Urbanism Committee* (Washington: Government Printing Office, 1937), p. 37.

30. Some form of the central-place concept might well be used to advantage in interpreting the distribution of outlying business districts in cities (cf. Malcolm J. Proudfoot, "The Selection of a Business Site," *Journal of Land and Public Utility Economics*, XIV [1938], esp. 373 ff.).

8

BRIAN J. L. BERRY and WILLIAM L. GARRISON

Recent Developments of Central Place Theory

In central place theory the term "central place" has meant "urban center." In the past the theory sought to account for these urban centers. It consisted of a series of assertions and definitions, logical consequences of which were a hierarchical ranking of urban centers according to functions (e.g., hamlets, villages, towns, and cities) and associated market areas and transportation networks.

Concern with the full array of urban centers and associated market areas and transportation routes remain basic to central place theory. Important recent work, however, has shown the usefulness of the theory in understanding the spatial structure of retail and service business (whether this business be located in alternate urban centers or in shopping districts within cities) and the content of the theory thereby has been increased. These changes have resulted in an increased generality of the application of the theory (*i.e.*, the theory may be more widely used; it serves as a theory of tertiary activity) and a more powerful theory (*i.e.*, its assertions are more plausible; its logical consequences are more explicit). Elaboration of these results is the purpose of the ensuing discussion.

Three topics are treated. First, the development of the theory is reviewed, especially in order to identify some important recent contributions. Second, some consequences of the theory are treated, especially in terms of results of recent empirical work and implications from this work for the reformulation of the theory. It is noted here how several concepts from economics serve to enrich work with central places. More important, it is noted that the theory may be formulated in terms of a simple concept of *threshold*. This frees the theory from complicating assumptions about the shape and homogeneous character of city trade areas. Finally, strategic research problems are identified from the standpoint of the present status of the theory and related theories.

NOTES ON THE FORMULATION OF CENTRAL PLACE THEORY

Schemes explaining urban growth and arrangement are many in number. Most of these likely stem from common origins. It seems

Reprinted from Papers and Proceedings of the Regional Science Association, *IV (1958), 107–20, by permission of the publishers and the author.*

likely, thus, that generic roots of central place theory extend in many directions and are joint with those of competing schemes. That these things may be true is taken for granted in the present discussion. The present discussion begins with the pragmatically taken position that central place theory began with Walter Christaller in 1933. To begin with Christaller and outline chief contributions of subsequent workers is a sufficient statement of the theory for present purposes. The complete statement of the growth of the theory awaits the never-to-be written definitive work on the development of ideas about urbanism.

Following the review of Christaller's work, contributions to the theory by August Lösch are reviewed. Following the discussion of Lösch's work the recent reformulation of central place theory is presented.

Initial Formulation of the Theory

Central place theory as formulated by Walter Christaller is his *Die zentralen Orte in Süddeutschland* [1] and presented elsewhere by Edward Ullman [2] is relatively well-known. The content of the theory may be stated in a summary way with an outline of its definitions, relationships, and consequences.

A. Terms defined included:
1. A central place.
2. A central good.
3. A complementary region.

B. Relationships specified included:
1. Variations in prices of central goods as distance from point of supply changes.
2. Explicit extremization behavior in the distribution and consumption of goods (*e.g.*, goods are purchased from the closest place).
3. Inner and outer limits for the range of distances over which central goods may be sold.
4. Relationships between the number of goods sold from a central place and the population of that place.

C. A statement which used the terms defined and relationships specified (within the simplifying assumption of homogeneous distribution of purchasing power in all areas) and described the

1. W. Christaller, *Die zentralen Orte in Süddeutschland* (Jena: Gustav Fischer, 1933).
2. E. L. Ullman, "A Theory of Location for Cities," *American Journal of Sociology*, 46 (1941), pp. 853–64.

arrangement of central places and complementary regions was made. Essential features of this statement were:

1. Hexagonal market areas for any set of central goods.
2. Overlapping sets of hexagons. The hexagons overlap in such a way that larger hexagonal market areas (resulting from a set of central goods) are divided into smaller hexagons when supplied by other central goods. The smaller hexagons nest into the larger according to a rule of threes (this is the K = 3 network described by Lösch).
3. Transportation routes serving the system of cities.

Generalization by August Lösch

A good portion of August Lösch's now classic *Die raumliche Ordnung der Wirtschaft*[3] was given to an evaluation and extension of notions of the arrangement of central places. Lösch's additions to the notions fall into three major divisions.

A. The explicit statement of two aspects of the system:

1. The derivation of demand cores over areas for goods.
2. Verification of the hexagonal-shaped complementary region as the "best" shape where purchasing power was uniformly distributed.

B. Clear linking of that arrangement of transportation routes among cities to central place notions.

C. The extension of the special case of a K = 3 network to a more general description of a system containing all possible relationships of evenly-spaced central places and nests of hexagonal shapes of complementary regions. In the system he develops he maintains: (1) that consumer movement must be minimized; (2) that no excess profits can be earned by any firm. Lösch further asserts, but does not demonstrate, that one outcome of his system is a hierarchical class-system of central places both as sources of central goods and as intersections upon the transport network.

Recent Developments

As developed, central place theory related only to alternate urban centers and the transport network linking urban centers. The

3. A. Lösch, *Die raumliche Ordnung der Wirtschaft*, translated by Woglom and Stolper as *The Economics of Location* (New Haven: Yale Univ. Press, 1954).

statement was in terms of homogeneously distributed purchasing power (hence, the hexagonal trade areas) and, thus, restricted in applicability in more realistic situations. Too, such assumptions as the absence of excess profits in the system were troublesome. Recent work tends to show, however:

A. That central place theory may be considered more readily, is more understandable, and definitely more viable, when reformulated in terms of a series of simple concepts.

B. That reformulation in terms of these concepts enables a hierarchical structure to be developed without the uniformity assumptions concerning purchasing power basic to the arrangement of hexagonal trade areas. One consequence of this is that the theory is applicable to areas within cities as well as areas without.

C. That the notion of no excess profits can be relaxed.

Empirical work associated with the developments listed above has shown how they simplify the problem of the empirical verification of the theory. The empirical work is also a good example of the value of such references in the refining of theory and better comprehension of the character of the hierarchical system of central place foci in the space-economy.[4]

The Concept of the Range of a Good A concept with an important role in present central place theory is that of the range of a central good. This range delineates the market area of a central place for the good. It has a lower limit which incorporated the *threshold* purchasing power for the supply of the good and an upper limit beyond which the central place is no longer able to sell the good. Each good will have different limits to its range because of competition between central places supplying the good (in the case of the upper limit) and differing internal economic characteristics of the supplying firms which determine threshold (in the case of the lower limit).

The Concept of Threshold Later in the present discussion it will be illustrated with a scale that there is some minimum size of market below which a place will be unable to supply a central good. On this scale this is the point where sales are large enough only for the firm to earn normal profits. This minimum scale, the lower limit of the range of a central place, is the minimum amount of purchasing

4. See Brian J. L. Berry and William L. Garrison, "The Functional Bases of the Central Place Hierarchy," forthcoming in *Economic Geography; idem*, "Central Place Theory and the Range of Good," forthcoming in *Economic Geography*; Brian J. L. Berry, *Geographic Aspects of the Size and Arrangement of Urban Centers*, unpublished M.A. thesis, University of Washington, 1956.

power necessary to support the supply of a central good from a central place, and is here termed the *threshold* sales level for the provision of that good from the center.

The Hierarchical Spatial Structure It can be argued that *whatever* the distribution of purchasing power (and whether in open countryside or within a large metropolis) a hierarchical spatial structure of central places supplying central goods will emerge. This argument requires only the concepts of range and threshold just given.

For the sake of exposition assume an area to be supplied with *n* types of central goods. Let these be ranked from 1 to *n* in ascending order of threshold sales requirements. The central place supplying good *n* will require the largest market area (in terms of amount of purchasing power) to support it. Let a central place supplying good *n* be called an *A* center.

As many *A* centers will exist in the area as there are threshold sales levels to support firms supplying good *n*. These firms compete spatially, hence are distributed so as to supply their own threshold most efficiently. If total sales levels are an exact multiple of thresholds for good *n*, market areas will be bounded by lower limits to the range of *A* centers. Firms will earn only normal profits, and these *only if* they minimize costs by: (a) locating to minimize distribution costs if the product is delivered, or (b) locating to minimize consumer movement if the consumer comes to purchase the products.

If sales in the whole area are slightly greater than an exact multiple of threshold, but not great enough to justify another *A* center, then excess profits may be earned. Ranges reach a more competitive upper limit.

The question arises as to how good $n-1$ will be provided. Presumably, it will be supplied from the *A* centers, which have sought out the most efficient points of supply. Too, there will be advantages from association with other establishments providing central goods. The threshold of good $n-1$ is less than that of good *n* and hence, spatial competition determines market areas (these are delimited by upper limit ranges)and excess profits may be earned. This argument will be the case for goods $n-2$ and down to good *1* as well.

But there may be one or more goods, say good $n-i$, in which case the interstitial purchasing power located between threshold market areas of *A* centers supplying good $n-i$ will themselves reach threshold size. In this case greater efficiency is reached if a second set of centers, which may be termed *B* centers, supply the good. These *B* centers again locate most efficiently relative to their threshold market area. If the market area is just at threshold only normal profits are earned by firms supplying good $n-i$. If part-multiples of threshold are present some excess profits are earned. Good $n-i$ may be termed a *hierarchical marginal good*. *B* centers will also provide lower threshold goods, $n-(i+1)$ through good 1.

Let us assume that good $n-j(j > i)$ is also a hierarchical marginal good, supporting a third set of central places designated as *C* places. These are a lower order of central places and provide only goods $n-j$ through good 1.

The pattern of provision of goods by centers in this hierarchical system may be displayed in an array (Table 1). The table displays how sets of goods build up hierarchies of types of central places. For example, the set of *C* places and places in the tributary areas of *C* places rely upon either *B* or *A* places for goods $n-i$ to $n-(j-1)$ and upon *A* places for goods n to $n-(i-1)$. *B* places rely upon *A* places for goods n to $n-(i-1)$. All places will be located at the point from which they most efficiently serve tributary areas with central goods.

TABLE 1 How n goods are supplied by M centers.

CENTERS	GOODS $n^a, n-1, \ldots$	$n-1^a, n-(i+1), \ldots$	$n-j^a, n-(j+1), \ldots$	$\ldots$	$k^a, (k-1), \ldots 1$
A	X	X	X	...	X
B		X	X	...	X
C			X	...	X
.				.	.
.				.	.
M					X

[a]Indicates hierarchical marginal good. X Indicates the set of goods supplied by the center.

Yet at the same time excess profits may be earned in the system. Where n goods are provided it is likely that the hierarchical marginal firm will tend to earn only normal profits. This is the firm which satisfies Lösch's condition that excess profits shall be at a minimum. However, all supramarginal firms in the hierarchy will have the opportunity to earn excess profits to the extent that they are able to compete spatially with other firms for the sub-threshold purchasing power which exists between threshold market areas in the spatial system.

The question may quite properly be raised, why argue a step hierarchy of functions and one with excess profits (profits over and above normal profits) when a system without excess profits can be argued (Lösch) using notions of nested hexagonal trade areas? The argument used was presented because recent empirical work indicates it is more like reality than the alternate argument. A discussion of this empirical work follows.

CONSEQUENCES OF RECENT EMPIRICAL WORK AND LINKS WITH OTHER THEORY

Formulation of central place theory using only simple concepts and readily comprehendable terms and with attention directed toward the arrangement in hierarchies of retail and service business rather than the hierarchical system of central places itself, was motivated by results of empirical work and has enabled empirical tests of theory to be formulated. Critical results from empirical work were the identification of hierarchies of central place functions and identification of threshold marginal goods.

Existence of a Hierarchy The existence of a hierarchical spatial structure has been asserted many times and many "tests" utilizing intuitive "indicators" of centrality, or assumed class-systems, have been utilized. [5] Given the notion of a basic hierarchical system of business, however, tests were designed to determine whether, indeed, a natural class system of types of business in alternate urban centers exists, and whether a hierarchy of urban centers was related to the classes of business. These tests have been reported elsewhere and will not be described here. [6] Suffice it to say that they were executed successfully and that a hierarchical system was proved to exist. The functional bases of the hierarchy and associated characteristics in the study area are discussed at length in the published reports of these empirical tests.

Excess Profits Likewise, the existence of a possibility to earn excess profits was demonstrated. Marginal hierarchical firms were identified with the nature and amounts of possible sub-threshold excess profits which could be earned by supramarginal firms in the hierarchy estimated. [7]

A Note on the Associated Transport Network The spatial pattern of central places and market areas is obviously indissolubly linked to a transport network. Problems of optimal design and utilization of such communication networks have been studied elsewhere. [8] What implications does central place theory provide for the understanding of such problems? Obviously, an hierarchical pattern of central places and an hierarchical pattern of business implies an

5. See the references in Berry and Garrison, "The Functional Bases," *op. cit.*, and the more complete bibliography in Berry, *op. cit.*

6. Berry and Garrison, *op. cit.*

7. Berry and Garrison, "Central Place Theory," *op. cit.*

8. One such study is R. E. Kalaba and M. L. Juncosa, "Optimal Design and Utilization of Communication Networks," *Management Science*, 3 (1956), pp. 33–44. This work contains further references. See also W. L. Garrison and Duane F. Marble, "The Analysis of Highway Networks: A Linear Programming Formulation," 38th Annual Meeting of the Highway Research Board, Washington, D.C., 1958.

hierarchical pattern of consumer movement. This in turn implies a like pattern for an optimal transport network to support such a system. Feeder roads to low order centers are supplemented by trunk lines between higher order centers. As many ranks of trunk lines occur as there are ranks of higher order centers. The higher the order of the center, the greater the convergence of routes. The denser the distribution of purchasing power, the denser the transport network.

Lösch maintained an associated characteristic would be an hierarchical pattern or route intersections. In his system of networks each metropolis would have twelve or more intersections and within its sphere of influence would be two centers with six intersections and three with four intersections.

This assertion was subjected to an empirical test by Wallace. [9] The 100 largest cities in the United States were taken and a count of all separate rail lines entering each of these cities within a radius of 25 miles made (Table 2). Some general validity for the Lösch assertion

TABLE 2 Railway intersections at the 100 largest cities in the U.S., 1955.

NUMBER OF RAYS AT THE INTERSECTION	NUMBER OF CITIES THAT HAD THE NUMBER OF RAYS
12 and more	10
11	2
10	6
9	3
8	2
7	10
6	22
5	19
4	19
3	6
2	0
1	1

is seen. Wallace reported that few intersection centers increased as more smaller centers were included in the sample. Hence an increase in sample size was thought to be needed to provide a better test of the theory. Nevertheless, it may be thought that if the concept of a hierarchical pattern of intersects has some merit, then too does the concept of an hierarchical transport network. Here is a subject for more empirical research.

Links With Other Theory

Empirical work tends to show that the formulation of central place theory free of the assumption of no excess profits and free of

9. W. C. Wallace, "A Note on Transportation Network Models," unpublished manuscript, 1957.

assumptions of the shape and character of trade areas is warranted. That is, the new formulation meets requirements of correspondence with reality. Another asset of the new formulation is its relation to alternate theories. Certain of these are explored below.

Theory of Retailing At first glance it appears that central place theory is compatible with the existing body of theory concerning the retail firm, as developed by such students as Aubert-Krier,[10] Smithies,[11] and Lewis,[12] since apparently central theory posits single types of business, or essentially single-product firms which reach a competitive state of spatial equilibrium.

The lack of sophistication of such a single-product approach has been pointed out by Holton.[13] He has argued that a far more realistic theory of retailing can be developed within the framework of a multi-product firm, and has developed a model for this case. His conclusion is that the long-run equilibrium pattern of the multi-product firm is one which requires that all products in which marginal revenue exceeds marginal cost be added to the product line and sales of each expanded to the point where marginal profits are all zero. Empirical tests in the case of supermarkets have verified the conclusions of his model and the further finding that profit maximization will result in price discrimination, since products will face demand functions of different elasticities.

Central place theory is compatible with this formulation of the equilibrium of the retail firm. Consider each rank of the hierarchy of central functions as a firm. Many products will be supplied by this rank (the number of stores supplying them will, of course, be substantially less). All products will be sold for which marginal revenue exceeds marginal cost, and marginal cost is defined upon the threshold sales volume of the hierarchical marginal product. Sales are expanded to the point where marginal profits are all zero as determined by the upper limits of the range of each product.

Generally, stores will be located in a manner which minimizes consumer movement and hence will maximize profits. But for all products other than those of the marginal hierarchical goods it is possible to earn excess profits. Central place theory posits that these are allocated by spatial competition. It is obvious that notions concerning this competition should be broadened to include competition through the practice of price discrimination according to the elasticity

10. J. Aubert-Krier, "Monopolistic and Imperfect Competition in Retail Trade," in E. H. Chamberlin, ed., *Monopoly and Competition and Their Regulation* (London: Hutchinson's University Library, 1949).

11. A. Smithies, "The Theory of Value Applied to Retail Selling," *Review of Economic Studies*, 6 (1939) 215–21.

12. W. A. Lewis, "Competition in Retail Trade," *Economics*, 12 (1945).

13. R. H. Holton, "Price Discrimination at Retail: The Supermarket Case," *Journal of Industrial Economics*, 6 (1957), 13–32.

of demand for different products. Ability to compete in these more general terms means that excess profits may be allocated in far from an equitable manner among existing firms.

Notions of Consumer Behavior It is interesting to consider correspondence between central place theory and recent work regarding shopping behavior by consumers. Baumol and Ide[14] have produced a simple model displaying the choice variables in the determination of a shopping center by the consumer. A customer will shop at a center when his demand function is such that

$$f(N, D) = wp(N) - v(C_d D + C_n \sqrt{N} + C_i)$$

is positive. $f(N, D)$ is a measure of the expected net benefit of the consumer from entering a store. It varies with D, his distance from the store, and N, the number of items offered for sale at the store. Assumed costs are C_d (a cost of transport assumed proportional to distance); $C_n \sqrt{N}$ is the assumed costs of actual shopping; and C_i represents the opportunity costs of other shopping opportunities foregone. $p(N)$ is the probabilistic satisfaction function. w and v are the subjective weights assigned by the consumer when he evaluates the size of each element in the equation.

The economic implications from this statement are many. For example, the minimum number of items necessary to induce a customer to shop at a given store will increase with D. Maximum shopping distance is given by the equation of the indifference curve which offers the consumer net zero benefit from shopping at a store and is obtained by setting $f(N, D) = 0$ and solving for D to yield:

$$D_n = \frac{w}{vC_d} p(N) - \frac{1}{C_d}(C_n \sqrt{N} + C_i)$$

Given the hierarchical spatial system of central place theory:

1. $p(N)$ will be a step-function related to levels of goods available at each rank of the hierarchy.
2. $C_n \sqrt{N}$ will be a like step-function.
3. C_i will be dependent upon the spatial distribution of an hierarchical system.

Hence any solution D_n will be a step-function related to levels of the hierarchy. The Baumol and Ide system is entirely compatible with

14. W. J. Baumol and E. A. Ide, "Variety in Retailing," *Management Science*, vol. 3, 1956, pp. 93–101.

central place theory. This statement is also true for their development of total retail sales, since they base this model upon the previous one of maximum consumer distance, and of their notions of maximization of profits, since these are based upon N. Not only do consumers discriminate among centers hierarchically and spatially, but retail varieties and sales levels and the extent of potential profits are likewise determined.

LOCATION OF STRATEGIC RESEARCH PROBLEMS

The preceding discussion has set forth in an expository manner several simple notions (especially, range of a good and threshold) and it has been argued that these notions satisfy the purposes of central place theory as well as do earlier formulations of the theory. One basis of argument was evidence from recent empirical research. Also, it was noted how notions of central place theory, when based on these simple notions, merge with other notions which bear on problems of retail business.

The discussion, thus, provides orientation and a useful way to end the discussion might be to elaborate needed research that may be identified at this time.

Nature of the Hierarchical System It has been argued that, whatever the areal circumstances, a hierarchical central place structure will exist. Put another way, it has been argued that a hierarchical structure will exist free of the assumptions of hexagonal tributary areas. Too, reference has been made to empirical studies which have tended to show the existence of hierarchies. These latter studies have been limited in scope and here is a place where much research is warranted. Namely, what is the nature of real world systems?

Several related problems are apparent. For example, city planners base actions on concepts of neighborhood and community shopping centers. How valid are these concepts on an empirical level? What is social gain and loss from planning other than "natural" locations? Another example question is, what relationship does a hierarchical structure bear to systems of urban rents? Here is yet another strategic and valid subject for both theoretical and empirical work. Indeed, both of these topics are the subject of studies at present being undertaken.[15]

Let us for the moment assume that there *is* an hierarchical structure of shopping centers. Other valid questions for research

15. Brian J. L. Berry, *The Spatial Structure of Intraurban Retail and Service Business*, in progress.

may be asked. One of these will now be explored at the theoretical level as an example. It relates to the relationships between the pre-equilibrium (*i.e.*, short-run) shopping habits of the consumer and the tendency for urban business to locate themselves in an hierarchical manner.

The Problem of the Pre-Equilibrium Spatial Connection Consider a hierarchical structure of urban shopping centers. This is a static pattern which masks a myriad of consumer movements to purchase goods and services. It is of such a nature that each individual movement is taken to be in equilibrium, with an optimal pattern of individual spatial connections existing. If a new consumer locates himself in the system the *ex post* view is taken that all his spatial connections must immediately be determinate.

But obviously this is not so. We know that a consumer newly locating himself in a city will tend to "shop around" and from personal experience will then develop his system of spatial connections. For goods which the consumer buys frequently the period of shopping around will be relatively short. A great number of contacts with stores will obviously lead to a rapid determination of some optimal shopping pattern. Accordingly we can think of stores which are visited quite frequently as being located within a framework of optimal spatial connections and therefore rationally within the hierarchical structure.

The same argument will apply to stores which are visited less frequently but which are few in number. They too will be positioned rationally within the hierarchical structure, for they will have relatively large proportions of their customers who have been in the city for long periods and hence stabilized their shopping habits.

However, there are certain types of business which are visited infrequently by the individual shopper and, because the purchase is large, visited by relatively few shoppers. For them the period of non-optimal spatial connection is long; indeed, the "shopping around" period may never cease. Many of the consumers will not have experienced sufficient shopping around to build up an optimal system of connections. For such types of business, advertising and product differentiation will be of particular significance. Since an optimal pattern of spatial connection is not present individual firms conceivably need not be located rationally relative to the hierarchical structure. Here is a force promoting the development of specialized shopping districts at one extreme, to facilitate the shopping around process, and apparently irrationally scattered business at the other, since no optimal patterns of spatial connections exist.

These ideas are extremely tentative, but they pose important problems for those concerned with spatial patterns of behavior.

9

LESLIE CURRY

Central Places in the Random Spatial Economy

> The problem (of atmospheric turbulence) is rather like that of finding some simple specification of the extent to which the population is divided between cities, towns, villages and isolated homes without making a map; for in the atmosphere a map of all eddies would be too bewilderingly complicated. (See Richardson [13].)

A central place is defined in terms of the "central" functions it performs for an area. These central functions have no procurement costs for raw materials and thus are oriented to the location of residences and concomitantly to the roads along which these people move. Writing theory about such places is predicated on the belief that centrality involves fairly general notions which, if valid, imply that the spatial distribution of the sizes and "mix" of activities of towns will show certain regularities in nature. In essence, then, central place theory attempts to state succinctly what is understood about those sectors of the array of settlement where centrality is important. Such work is facilitated by the fact that the operations of central activities are inherently simple to understand and that merely in living we obtain a wealth of experiential data about them.

ELEMENTS OF THE PROBLEM

Why Theory?

There appear to be two reasons why general theories are useful in understanding the real world. An ideal and still to be developed central place theory would, for instance, integrate the facts of location and operation of stores, of behavior of consumers, of flow of traffic, of the route network, of the flow of funds and all the myriad observations of the relevant parts of the urban economy. The greatest criticism by far of current theory is that it has apparently reached a dead end without achieving these objectives. First then, theory allows the integration at the conceptual level of events which do naively appear to be interrelated. Here the language of the theory is tailored to that of the events to be described.

Reprinted from the Journal of Regional Science, *7 (1967), 217–38, by permission of the publishers and the author.*

There is another pragmatic utility in general theory. Here, two or more sets of events not having any conceivable dependence can nevertheless be thought of as obeying the same "laws." As a simple example, all spatial interaction whether social, economic or physical must incur a frictional effect of distance. Much more complex processes may have analogues in different phenomenological fields with a common or similar mathematical formalizing. The possibility of the intellectual economy afforded by such theory is its justification. Clearly, at the formal level, it is advantageous to have the language divorced as far as possible from any phenomenological content. It is this type of theory which has fathered the "systems" approach where a "neutral" vocabulary is developed for discussing somewhat plausibly the pure symbolism of the mathematics. The possibility of having this type of theory available in geography is appealing, burdened as we are with such a wide range of phenomena.

The Central Place Quandary

Why do shopping centers exist? From a behaviorist viewpoint such a question hardly merits a reply. It seems that they have long existed to facilitate exchange on the one hand and to profit from the nodality of a site on the other. The whole structure of retailing has become institutionalized to the extent that the buying and inventory activities of both consumers and retailers have adapted to each other in a long and continuous learning process. Each of us knows that local hardware stores exist and approximately what might be bought there. The hardware store owner knows (in a statistical sense) the sort of inventory of goods that a householder is likely to keep, the sort of location that will support such a store and that consumers have accepted the idea of a store such as his. But to seek an explanation in terms of these institutionalized forms is missing the boat from an analytic viewpoint. An historical viewpoint would seem appropriate to explanation of institutions but this is not our aim. Rather we follow Koopmans [7] in looking for those indivisibilities or discontinuities in the human person, in residences, plants, equipment or in transportation from which our particular localization problem arises.

The major difficulty in writing central place theory is that the elements comprise a system without really independent variables so there are no fundamental determinants to use in understanding its logic. The locations of centers are suitable to a given road net while the roads can be understood relative to the places they connect. Centers are the focus of routes and crossroads suitable for the establishment of centers. Economic institutions must adapt themselves to social behavior but equally the latter has evolved within certain economic constraints. The stocks a consumer keeps at home and the standard of living which a shop-keeper expects to enjoy are more social than economic phenomena and will in large part determine the central place system, yet it is absurd to deny a reciprocal effect. Even the type of goods offered is sanctioned by the system as a whole: witness the reported decline of baked goods stores in New York as less frequent shopping trips induced by supermarket and refrigerator stimulate the sales of frozen baked products. The problem of writing theory in this context is one of obtaining postulates which do not contain the results in a direct manner so that insight is gained. Thus, for example, to postulate a certain pattern of social behavior and from this derive certain economic effect is not particularly enlightening. A term such as Christaller's "range of a good" [3] suffers from this conditionality of definition.

The fundamental hypothesis of any central place theory is that there are certain basic forces regulating the sizes, spacing and functions of such settlements. When one considers the large number of ways in which the retailer-consumer complex could achieve an equilibrium or balance between profitability and service in any particular case, the reasons why regularity should occur are not immediately apparent. Yet the quasi-universality of central place phenomena would seem to imply some simple allocation mechanism. Both Christaller [3] and Lösch [9] used a strong notion of economizing to describe spatial behavior with guidelines provided by prices. Their postulates must be capable of considerable relaxation. After all, it can be argued that pricing arrangements are but the posterior stamp of approval that society puts on a fairly efficient system. That similar spatial structures could develop in ancient Egypt, medieval Europe, and can recur in recent Iowa appears to attest fundamental "real" factors in operation rather than supporting the universality of current economic doctrine. Certainly within a city there is no systematic variation in price and no automatic economizing of shopping distance so that distinct market boundaries occur, and yet the same form of central place hierarchy develops here too.

This paper is largely a generalization of arguments used at the Lund Symposium (see Curry [4]) which will be briefly summarized. It was asserted then that the areal extent of the market for a good was dependent on the frequency with which it was demanded. The probability distribution of amounts demanded fixed the level of stocks required, with more frequently demanded goods allowing a lower level of inventory relative to sales. Profitability increased with size of area. An operating policy alternative to inventory management was delaying deliveries so that low stocks were possible. These arguments are retained in the present paper with some further generalization. However, the specifically spatial component of the approach, in which a finite area had centers for different orders of goods allocated by a subdivision of the market stemming from competition, lacked any generality. More important, the exact boundaries of the area had considerable effect in locating centers, a result which is not found in reality. Nevertheless, the basic approach of the current paper is similar to the first in that discrete hierarchical levels result from the boundedness of space. A much more general approach is now adopted however which allows a linkage with other aspects of the central place system. It is not perhaps sufficiently realized that to follow Garrison and Berry[6] in getting rid of Christaller's severe assumption of a uniform transportation plane also removes the explicit spatial dimensions of the analysis and renders it impotent for further geographical elaboration.

Behavior in Space

A theory of central places has to deal with four types of behavior: retailers' behavior over time and their locational policy in space plus consumers' behavior in time and in space. We assume a periodic and stationary time, i.e., no weekly or seasonal periodicity is apparent and no long term trend in sales or purchases occurs. The nature of the space will be discussed later but in general we regard it as homogeneous.

There are and there presumably always have been preferred spatial orientations in human traffic. Central places adapt to these preferences. A postulate on spatial behavior should not directly describe the behavior occurring within a central place system, since it is obvious that the system can then be directly derived without providing any insight. The behavior postulate must allow a central place system to be erected on it in a sufficiently indirect manner that a measure of initial surprise is occasioned by the results, and this postulate must still describe behavior after the system has been derived. If this last proviso is not met we are forced to describe a dynamic process—with the considerable chance of writing phony history. It is clear that the postulate must be extremely weak.

We do not need to describe individual behavior directly—only its spatial differentiation. Individual householders, having potential purchasing relations with a given point (or arbitrarily small area), will visit it with a certain frequency. As a measure of each individual's interaction with the point we shall use the number of his visits relative to his total travel pattern. We postulate that, while this ratio can be a random variable, an autocorrelation exists along a line away from the point in question. Thus, given a random variable $x(d)$ as a measure of an individual's relation to the point when he is situated at a distance d away, we assume that the expectation for interaction at a distance $d+\delta$, i.e., $x(d+\delta)$ will be smaller than $x(d)$. As δ is made larger, the autocorrelation will decline, and a point will be reached eventually at which $x(d+\delta)$ and $x(d)$ are uncorrelated so that they are independent random variables. A measure of the autocorrelation of a continuous sequence of values $x(d)$ of a random quantity x is

$$R_x(\delta) = \lim_{D\to\infty} \frac{1}{2D} \int_{-D}^{D} x(d+\delta)x(d)\,\Delta d$$

The product $x(d)x(d+\delta)$ is being averaged with respect to distance, and this mean will be a constant in homogeneous space. $R_x(\delta)$ depends on the spacing δ as well as on the random function $x(d)$. To be precise, $R_x(\delta)$ is best called the average lagged product, to use Tukey's term[1], and when an average of zero is used (so that only the effects of spatial variations occur, as is the case here) it should be called the autocovariance function. However, the conventional if imprecise term of autocorrelation function will be used although this is best reserved for $R_x(\delta)/Var[x(d)]$. We thus have a term to describe the spatial variation in the orientation of persons to a particular point in space. Note in particular that $x(d)$ is a random variable for the individual household and that the autocorrelation can only be defined and measured for groups of households. Such indeterminate behavior does justice to the difficulties facing a shopkeeper for whom uncertainty is a fact of life.

A retailer, in establishing himself in an area with so few constraints on location and not able to appreciate the nature of the behavior surface, will attempt to estimate his market. He cannot be certain that even the householder next door to his location will patronize his store; thus, individual demands can be seen to be random. However, he might assume that the nearer the household, the more likely that its shopping will be done at his store. Thus he weights customers inversely to their distance away from him; in statistical terminology this weighting is known as a lag window when weights start at unity and reach zero. The definitions of an autocorrelation function and of a lag window for uncorrelated variables are identical. Thus, whether we assume an unknown behavior surface and a retailer's estimate of his potential customers or whether we have a known surface we obtain the same results.

The Space

The assertion of homogeneity can only be accepted at certain scales of study. We propose to use Kolmogorov's notion of "local isotropy," as cited by Lumley and Panofsky [10]. For a representative distance l separating centers of a particular order, the region we consider shall be larger than l but of approximately the same order of magnitude. Small scale inhomogeneities of landscape and historic evolution will be relatively unimportant in affecting the spacing of the centers studied at this scale. Also, the major lineaments of countries or continents will be too large to affect the particular scale of analysis. At the scale chosen (and of course this scale will be different for different orders of center), the geography of service centers can be discussed *sui generis*. Strictly speaking, coastlines, political boundaries and similar conditions which can influence local isotropy should be avoided: in practice and in terms of central places these effects will be minor.

In the previous paper already referred to, it was argued that any theory concerned with settlement ordering must obtain closed space, either by postulate or by derivation. This question, although not of great import in observation, becomes so in explanation. For any aggregate of shops, it is not too extreme to assume an area to be served. No doubt a native of Detroit might some day buy an article in Birmingham, Alabama, or even in Hong Kong, but it is doubtful whether a retailer of interest to central place analysis takes this into consideration. It seems fair to assume that the territorial ambitions of the most aggressive of hucksters has a limit. To facilitate analysis, it will be assumed here that a local area ends abruptly at its edge and that beyond stretches the void. This is hardly realistic but then the real world is singularly mute in its suggestions of its logic.

Whereas at any one time the city can be regarded as having a limit, the exact boundaries have relatively little effect on the general distribution of its shopping centers. The spatial structure of such centers seems not to be a matter of dividing up and allocating the pie as was implied previously. This considerable independence of the bounds is due to the fact that cities develop through time and bounds change but centers maintain momentum.

The Time Equivalent of Locally Isotropic Space

For most of us, the future is a set of random variables and yet most of our actions are based on our forecasts of this future. Uncertainty or ignorance is a basic fact of life, and yet we must plan our activities in the face of this ignorance. Fortunately analysts share this ignorance—our ignorance is the same as those of whom we speak—so that we have a common bond in our calculus. Those phenomena of concern to geography are generally statistically motivated or controlled; they do not rely on a deterministic view of the future—an extreme gambling situation—but rather by basing themselves on the actions of collectives they achieve some degree of stability through time. But their viability is dependent on an ability to estimate the parameters of these random variables from which the future will come. The reatiler is entirely in this category, and the spatial structure of retail stores must manifest the manner in which the retail community achieves stability in the face of uncertainty.

The essential function of a spatial array of stores is to detect and transform the space and time dimensions of consumer demands. Any ordering of central places within a city, either perceived or imposed according to one's metaphysics, is to be found in the collective's response to an uncertain space-time environment. In this sense it should not formally be too different from other phenomena in such environments. In the face of an uncertain future, three adaptations appear possible: (1) some form of stock piles will even out fluctuations, (2) some form of delay mechanism will allow a conforming reaction, and (3) the maintenance of a variety of opportunity will allow a differential reaction to future conditions. This is essentially the same choice of variables to be found in a radio circuit: inductance, reactance and band width, or similarly in a biological species. These variables have, in our case, to be related to area or, more specifically, to the friction of distance, because the parameters of demand occurring at a place in the future will be affected by this factor, just as resistance occurs in an electrical network.

It is evident in the shopping problem that activities operating in the time domain such as inventory management must have spatial implications and cannot be divorced from a geographical analysis. The hindrance imposed by the postage stamp system of freight rate pricing to the development of Texas towns as distributing centers in the 1920's is an example of this interaction of space and time. The time equivalent of the space we have postulated requires: (1) boundedness, (2) homogeneity or stationarity for periods varying in size of the order of the representative intervals between purchases of the goods in question and (3) no periodicity. To assert closed horizons for time in the case of a retailer implies that he has a definite outer time limit in which he believes all goods will be sold. Since all purchases occur as "needed," there is clearly a limited horizon for consumers also. Periodicity, although important in the actual running of a store, can probably be ignored in our problem.

Assume that a shopkeeper keeps a running total of all sales and that he has a uniform interval between deliveries to stock which are then deducted from his tally. Amounts delivered are related to the size of his tally. It is this tally which we shall regard as indicating his stock position, the former being complementary to the latter, i.e., when the tally is large, stocks are low. Fluctuations, however, are the same.

With these equivalents defined, the location problem has its dual in the inventory problem. Solving one automatically solves the other; we may work with whatever problem seems convenient. The autocorrelation in spatial behavior implies an autocorrelation in temporal behavior. An areal grouping of households with a low probability of visiting a site will arrive there only rarely, whereas high probabilities mean frequent visits. Thus, whereas changes in the tally level are purely random (since probabilities for visiting a site are random), the autocorrelation constraint on behavior means that there is a similar correlation between tally levels. All this argument has been made to justify the total process as ergodic, a mathematical term meaning that sampling either through time at one point or at a number of places at an instant of time will give the same answer.

The Central Place System

Regard the householder as the generator of an *input* to the central place system. The central place system consists of a series of *filters*, at least two in number. The first, householders' stocks, is designed to filter out very high frequency components of demand. We cannot at present say much about this. Such stocks cut down on the number of shopping trips which would be necessary were every act of consumption followed by replenishment from outside. They are closely related to the existing market structure, including its spatial form and indeed can be regarded as the time transform of distance economies. It is only when demand for goods is translated into purchases at definite times and places that it can be defined operationally in a central place context. We shall thus exclude household stocks from consideration as an element of the central place system and look only at retailers, wholesalers etc. as the filtering agents.

Input to this system can be thought of as composed of two largely independent series of random variables: *signal* and *noise*. This idea can best be comprehended in a literally translated situation. A ship in harbor requiring water will hoist appropriate flags: the suppliers seeing such a signal will then send a water boat. Here there is signal and no noise. Suppose however that there are hundreds of ships asking not only for water but for many other commodities too and that there are a considerable number of competing companies each laying in supplies for the following month in anticipation of how many ships there will be and what their demands will be. It is evident that any one supplier will miss many of the hoisted signals, that he will often find demands have been met by another supplier by the time his boat gets near a ship, and that he has underestimated the number of ships found in the harbor in any day or week and overestimated the demand for butter or shirts. This uncertainty or ignorance will generate noise, that is, an input which masks the true signal. Noise and signal are likely to be independent because there is no reason why chance variation in the signals received by a supplier should affect or be affected by miscalculations on the part of the far-from-omniscient supplier.

Perhaps the introduction of a noise component should be justified further. In the literature relating probability theory to human affairs, there is sometimes a reluctance to regard probabilistic description of an activity as sufficiently describing the uncertainty attached to the series of events comprising such an activity. In decision theory, for example, the objection appears to be that conceptualization in probability terms oversimplifies the issue by allowing optimum solutions to be obtained. The assignment of measures to all alternatives is too close to a deterministic formulation. There is certainly some merit in this argument but no alternative method appears to have resulted. In the present model, the notion of a noise input to the system, uncorrelated to the probabilistic signal, is used as a means of increasing the uncertainty facing retailers. It is evident, for example, that the conditions affecting retailers' inventory and location policies within a metropolis must produce greater uncertainty than in a set of dispersed farms and villages. Yet a straightforward probabilistic description of demand does not appear to differentiate between these different circumstances: hence the introduction of the rather artificial notion of noise. It should be read as a measure of the difficulty in determining, even at the intuitive level, the probabilistic structure of the market. Alternatively or additionally it can be understood, as will be evident later, as the masking of consumer behavior, to which the retailer wishes to respond, by behavior to which he does not want to react.

Any filter which is operationally conceivable *distorts* the signal passing through it. There will be occasions when requests by the sailors for rental bicycles cannot be met by suppliers working under the prevailing pricing arrangements. There will be epidemics which flood the local hospitals or a few souls waiting to join bird watching expeditions who find they are never catered for. Distortion must occur spatially as well as temporally. This includes the sailor who would like to drink beer but cannot be bothered to make the trip ashore, or finds the ferry fare excessive from his position in the outer harbor, as well as the supplier who refuses to make a special trip to deliver a pack of chewing gum even were the price a hundred times what is usual. It may be seen that distortion will be difficult to define empirically especially in terms of our "real" variables which are usually vaguely formulated subjective appraisals of needs. In a sense all shopping or delivery journeys are distortions of a punctiform pattern of generated signals but it will be realized that such journeys are a concomitant of achieving a time collective for suppliers' inventories.

In order to treat signal, noise, and distortion, a further notion on the filter, the *bandwidth*, is introduced. We have intimated that a good is distinguished by the time intervals between successive purchases or the frequency of purchases per unit time. Frequently demanded goods have relatively low suppliers' inventory costs per item but this cost goes up as frequency goes down. Thus a supplier will find that for a given order of magnitude of potential customers, there will be certain frequently demanded goods which it is obviously worth his while to stock, others of infrequent demand which are clearly not worthwhile. Yet, in the intermediate frequencies there is a range of goods about which he must be uncertain, depending on price margins and holding costs per item. It is here that the disturbance of the signal by noise is particularly important.

To fix a definite but necessarily arbitrary upper limit to the goods stocked the term bandwidth is introduced, defined as the band of frequencies, i.e., the line, range or variety of goods, in which the ratio of mean output to mean input is not less than $1/\sqrt{2}$, i.e., .707. The assumption here is that the cost situation of the least frequently demanded item stocked is such that on the average the supplier will be out of stock three times in ten when the article is asked for. It may be noted that the bandwidth does not affect the management of stocks but is rather an adaptation to uncertainty about space and is thus at the heart of the central place problem.

MATHEMATICAL ARGUMENT

The Dimensions of Purchasing

We shall set down the dimensions of factors affecting the spatial structure of retail purchases. The only relevant dimensions appear to be length, time and dollars.

1. The propensity to purchase on a unit length trip within a unit time period will have dimensions $\$/LT$.

2. A certain rate of spending will occur in a unit area per unit period with dimensions $\$/L^2T$; the reciprocal will be the "space" required to provide unit value purchases.
3. Dividing (1) by (2), a measure of the movement necessary to generate a one dollar sale in a unit area is obtained with dimension L. Denote this by V. This quantity simply reflects density of population and income and common institutional factors such as technology, social mores and economic well-being.
4. The spatial relationships of a household with a point (interaction) can be expressed as a function of their relative position in Cartesian space and the frequency of visits to that point. In our two dimensional space, this vector has the dimensions L^2/T^2.
5. The gradient in interaction is obtained from (4) as dimensionally L^2/T^2L^2, i.e., T^{-2}.
6. Multiplying (3) by (5) a quantity of dimension L/T^2 is obtained. Movement to generate a one dollar sale times a gradient in interaction gives a measure of the average generation of sales per unit distance and period. Put another way, it represents the allocation of purchases at varying distances. Denote this by E.

Returning now to the autocorrelation in interaction at an arbitrary point,

$$R_x(\delta) = \overline{[i(d) - i(d+\delta)]^2}$$

i.e., the mean square of the differences between the interactions of two points with a datum point. The dimensions are clearly L^2/T^2.

Under the local isotropic central place mechanism, the autocorrelation in interaction depends only on the distance δ and the generation of sales effect E, i.e.,

$$R_x(\delta) \approx \delta, E.$$

These must be dimensionally equivalent

$$L^2T^{-2} \approx L, LT^{-2}.$$

No further calculation is needed to show that autocorrelation is a linear function of (1) the distance apart of the sampling points and (2) the sales generation effect; the former is the important finding, i.e.,

$$R_x(\delta) = K\delta E,$$

where K is constant.

If the space we are discussing is extremely large relative to purchasing behavior than we can make no more precise statement than this. If, however, the space is limited in extent as discussed earlier, the autocorrelation in interaction can be written

$$R_x(\delta) = \sigma^2 \left(1 - \frac{d}{D}\right), \quad d < D,$$

where D is the distance beyond which the autocorrelation declines to zero (or some arbitrary low limit) and d is the distance from the sampling point to the datum.

Spectrum of Purchasing: Infinite Space

It is well know that any time or spatial series can be broken down into a number of sine waves, i.e., the fundamental frequency and its harmonics. This can be done statistically so that the contribution of each harmonic to the total fluctuation of the series, i.e., to the variance, can be assessed. If we state that the frequency of the fundamental wave (w_1) is unity then that of any harmonic $w = nw_1$. Any sine wave can be considered as circular motion stretched out through time or space so that, for the fundamental frequency, the angular measure 2π, if divided by the distance occupied by a single wave, D, will give the value of the fundamental frequency, i.e., $w_1 = 2\pi/D = 1$. For the nth harmonic, $w_n = n2\pi/D$.

In the statistical fitting of these curves, an auto-regression analysis is used, i.e., the correlation between the value at distance d and distance $d+1, d+2, \ldots$, is calculated. Without going into this procedure (periodic regression or Fourier analysis), it is evident that there is a relationship between the autocorrelation displayed by the variable and the amplitude and phase of the harmonics. A generalized Fourier or spectral analysis carries this method a step further by no longer fitting the first few harmonics but instead using a whole spectrum of different frequencies. The contribution of smoothed bands of frequencies to total variance is considered without, however, paying attention to their phase. If $x(t)$ varies randomly in a stationary process, it may be shown that

$$x^2(t) = \int_0^\infty s(f)\,df,$$

when $s(f)$ is the spectral density of the function $x(t)$. The form of $s(f)$ shows the distribution of the harmonic content of the signal over the frequency range from zero to infinite frequency. Thus, a filter of bandwidth Δf will pass a mean square value of signal $x^2(t)$ equal to

$s(f)\Delta f$. If this is related to the whole harmonic content of the signal, we obtain the proportion of total variance contributed by Δf.

As might be expected, there is a direct relation between the spectrum of a random variable and its autocorrelation. The autocorrelation function is the inverse Fourier transform of the spectral density and vice versa. Thus, where we have the autocorrelation in interaction varying as the first power of distance, the spectrum will vary inversely as the square of the wavelength or directly as the square of frequency (Figure 1). We are simply saying that persons living close

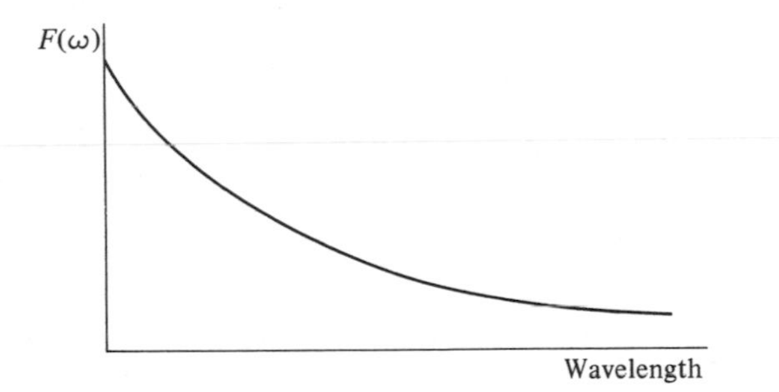

FIGURE 1 Form of spectral density of consumers' behavior in infinite space.

to the sample point will visit it more frequently (remember that we refer to groups and not individuals, whose behavior is random) and that frequency varies as the reciprocal of squared distance from the datum. This has clear affinities with empirical rules such as Reilly's "law" of retail gravitation but obviously is not identical with them since they are deterministic.

The personal orientation in space of an average person, (i.e., frequency of visit, which varies inversely as squared distance,) and the retailer's weighting function for potential customers, (i.e., inverse function of distance,) are compatible. The average person can be weighting his visits to all stores linearly with distance but since his range for movement in space for different distances increases linearly with the increase in distance (perimeter $= 2\pi r$), his likelihood of going to a particular spot d distance away will vary as d^{-2}. The retailer's lag window on the other hand represents an average likelihood for each perimeter of the concentric circles about his potential site and will thus increase linearly. It can be seen that they represent quite distinct notions.

If autocorrelation were zero, the spectrum would not vary with distance, i.e., it would be flat and be called "white noise." All wavelengths would be of equal importance so that there would be no reason for localization or store types to occur. As autocorrelation increases, the spectrum becomes a monotonically decreasing function of distance. All wavelengths are still present but the longer wavelengths are of less importance. Without further specification, all that we can say is that stores catering for infrequently demanded goods will be furthest apart and fewer in number; again, stores could carve out any wave band of goods to stock so that no "typing" of stores need exist. Central places need still not form. With an autocorrelation of unity, the signal is determinate, the spectrum is concentrated at a single wavelength, and we are in the world of Christaller.

If we assert a continuum of goods distinguished by the mean interval between purchases, then the frequency spectrum in the time domain should describe the contribution which each band of goods makes to sales variance. To try this out, assume that profitability per item purchased is unrelated to the characteristic interval between purchases of a good so that for bands of goods profitability will be greatest for those frequently demanded simply because more sales are made. Brown [2] has stated: "If you sell to the ultimate customer, you may find that only 50 percent of your income is derived from the topranking 20 percent of the items." Since the spectral density varies as the square of frequency, while it takes 100 percent of the items to provide 100 percent of the profits, 20 percent of the items will provide 45 percent of the profits or 25 percent of the items will provide 50 percent of the profits. This is a rough indication that the ergodicity assertion is not complete nonsense.

This spectrum is, or will be, regarded in several ways:

1. For a single good, this is the magnitude of the frequency of travel for it to a point as a function of distance.
2. For a single good, this is the magnitude of the frequency of purchases of it at a point as a function of time.
3. For the whole range of goods, defined in terms of the mean time interval between purchases, this is the number of purchases by a household, as a function of time.
4. For the whole range of goods ranked according to their mean time interval between purchases, this is the number of trips of various distances made by a household.

The Spectrum of Purchasing: Closed Space

The functions described depend on a very large size of area and number of customers. We have indicated that retailers operate in a closed space of relatively small size. This size of sample has a crucial effect on the spectrum and thus on location.

In taking the Fourier transform of our autocorrelation function in closed space, (see Lebedev [8]), the spectrum assumes the form

$$F(\omega) = \frac{2}{\pi}\sigma^2\left(\frac{1-\cos\omega d}{\omega^2 D}\right)$$

(see Figure 2). Mathematically, such behavior is simply a result of the postulates and does not require explanation but a plausible interpretation may be useful. This is easiest in the time domain because, whereas we can easily conceive of an observer recording repetitious behavior through time, the estimation of autocorrelation in spatial behavior from a single sample would be open to considerable error. One individual store or center could not obtain a stable estimate because it has only one random series of sample length T to examine (equivalent to D in the above equation).

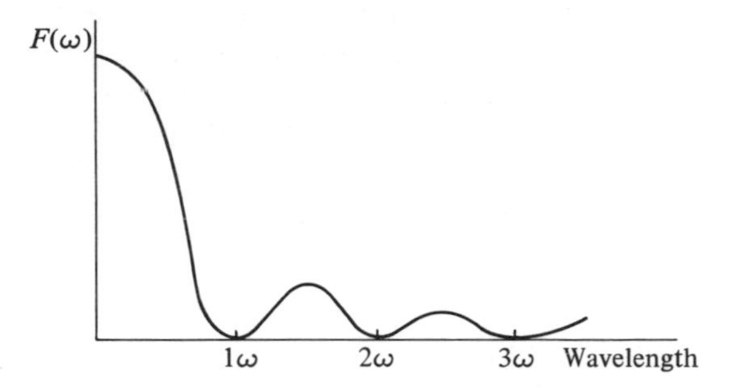

FIGURE 2 Spectral density of consumers' behavior in bounded space.

The period T is a result of the filter and not of the characteristics of the signal: periodicity is introduced into the output of the system with the period, T, of the fundamental frequency occurring between 0, and 2π so that $2\pi/T = 2\pi f = \omega_1$, the fundamental frequency. Harmonics are multiples of this frequency. Periodicity will not occur if the signal is of long duration so that sufficient averaging is done over all wavelengths – in areal terms, the sample space is large enough.

When a filter is being used to ascertain the characteristics of the signal it is necessary to choose a series long enough so that averaging over it will smooth out amplitude fluctuations created by the filter itself. Thus in the study of turbulence, for example, where the continuum is of concern, an effort is made to average out discontinuities in the spectrum. However in our problem, the discontinuities have a meaning evidencing the well-known dichotomy between the continuous function of the rank size rule and the step function of the central place hierarchy. If it were possible to have a filter responding to a single frequency only, i.e., a single-good store, then it would be possible to reproduce the signal exactly without distortion. For many goods, this corresponds to different single-good stores scattered over the landscape without localization. Increasing bandwidth increases distortion but allows a shopping list to be compiled, cutting down on shopping trips. This implies definite types of centers and characteristic distances between centers corresponding to the intervals between shopping lists. Harmonics of the fundamental frequency resulting from the boundedness of space-time correspond to higher order centers with their greater distance apart and larger market areas. We must invoke some notion of nodality to have higher order centers include lower order bandwidths.

Since discontinuities in the frequency envelope occur as the harmonics of the fundamental wavelength, opportunity is provided for centers to be equally spaced with second order centers being twice the distance apart of first centers, third order being thrice, and so on. However, this is inconsistent with any notion of a nested hierarchy: it is in fact analogous to Lösch's general case. We must introduce the further condition that *n*th order centers contain all lower order bandwidths; this suppresses some potential higher order centers. Just which multiplying function, Lösch's *K*, will be used seems to be a local idiosyncracy and hardly worth pursuing, at least in the present context.

Uncertainty: Noise and Error

We have introduced several notions informally—error, noise and bandwidth—which we shall now define rigorously following Lebedev [8]. It was pointed out that any filter will cause distortion of the signal so that error appears in the output, i.e.,

$$\epsilon(d) = u_{out}(d) - u_{in}(d),$$

which is, of course, a random function of distance. Allow σ_ϵ^2, i.e., the variance of the error, to be a measure of the error. It has been argued that it is the fluctuations or uncertainties in demand which are the important variables of the central place problem, so that mean values would be useless. Indeed our mathematics assume zero mean as the processes are stationary. Notice that the use of the variance is by no means a universal measure in filter design. It will only be valid when the importance of an error increases with its magnitude, in fact as the second power of its magnitude. In our problem the variance of the signal magnitude varies as d^{-2}. By using variance as a measure of distortion, we are measuring the extent to which far away customers are cut off by the filter. While, as has been said, error is a random function of distance for the individual purchaser, this is not so for groups. By the ergodic properties of the process, error variance also measures the extent to which infrequently demanded goods will be cut off by the filter.

Consider the process in the time domain. Call the time in which the inventory is reduced to ten percent of its initial value (assuming no deliveries) the inventory period, and denote it by α; i.e., the tally rises to ten times its initial value during the inventory period. It will be dependent on C, the size of the tally, and on the mean rate of purchases (and thus on store density). Denote by R the mean distance between stores. Thus $\alpha = 1/RC$. If a delay factor L were introduced, $\alpha = L/RC$, since clearly this will increase the inventory period. It is ignored, however, because it is unimportant. The mean square error of this filter can be shown to be

$$\sigma_\epsilon{}^2 = \frac{\sigma^2}{\alpha T}(1 - e^{-\alpha T}).$$

The relative root mean square error, i.e., the standard deviation of the error relative to that of the signal, is

$$\eta = \frac{\sigma_\epsilon}{\sigma} = \sqrt{\frac{1}{\alpha T}(1 - e^{-\alpha T})}.$$

The passband of the filter, denoted by P, has been defined as the range of goods in which mean output/mean input is not less than $1/\sqrt{2}$. The upper limit of this band corresponds to the wave length or wave number α, so that in terms of angular frequency

$$P = \alpha/2\pi.$$

Thus,

$$\eta = \left[\frac{1}{2\pi PT}(1 - e^{-2\pi PT})\right]^{1/2}.$$

It is clear that relative error increases as the passband of the filter PT is made smaller. However we have not considered noise, i.e., shopping which has an incoherent spatial behavior. Obviously a shopkeeper wants to make as many sales as possible and certainly does not care whether these be labelled signal or noise. However, noise should not affect his location and stock policy: it is the job of shopkeepers to arrange themselves so that only signal is responded to. This is an impossible task, but the "system" may go some way towards satisfying this condition.

Noise, by definition, is composed of uncorrelated random variables, i.e., there is no temporal or areal differentiation in shopping behavior in a statistical sense. Considering the temporal domain, it is clear that the inventory period will be very much longer than any correlation period for noise input, so that the exponential term categorizing the correlation of this input can be neglected.

It may be shown that the output from the filter as a result of noise is

$$\sigma_n{}^2 = \frac{\pi\alpha F_n}{2},$$

when F_n is the spectral density of the noise inputs. Total error in the output is

$$\sigma_{\epsilon n}^2 = \frac{\sigma^2}{\alpha T}(1 - e^{-\alpha T}) + \frac{\pi\alpha F_n}{\alpha}.$$

The relative root mean square error is

$$\eta_{\epsilon n} = \frac{\sigma_{\epsilon n}}{\sigma} = \sqrt{\frac{1}{\alpha T}(1 - e^{-\alpha T}) + \alpha TA},$$

where $A = \pi F_n/2\sigma^2 T$ is the relative noise input. Note that the relative error resulting from the filter is proportional to the reciprocal of the passband width αT, whereas the noise coming through the filter is directly proportional to the width. Thus a narrow bandwidth will have error resulting mainly from filter distortions with an unimportant noise component. If the passband is wide, error comes mainly from noise with negligible distortion. Recall what this means in our context. If the shopping centers offer a wide variety of goods, they will be more affected by incoherent (i.e., non-periodic) behavior and thus have a greater variance in inventory levels and location. When a small variety of goods is offered, they will be more regular in spatial pattern and inventory management but, of course, will not cater for large portions of shopping requirements.

IMPLICATIONS OF THE MODEL

Time-Space Coefficient and Rank Size Rule

Thus far it has been assumed that there is a direct and universal conversion between the time and space domains, between frequency and wavelength, between the inventory and location problems. However, it seems likely that such a time-space coefficient will vary by major regions according to the real factors expressed in the price structure. There should be some technological coefficient having an explicit or implicit price relative.

An analogy has already been drawn between the continuous

monotonic spectrum of purchasing behavior for large samples and the rank size rule for city size. Allow the latter ordering to describe central places for large samples; it has been pointed out that it conforms to the most probable distribution of a random arrangement of a given number of people in a given number of cities. (See Curry [5].) The degree of concentration of people in cities of various sizes will depend on the size of functional unit (i.e., requiring contiguity) which decides the minimum freedom of choice of location available to the population of the system. Thus the single parameter of the negative exponential series will determine the whole series. In deriving the most probable distribution, Lagrangian multipliers are used. It may be recalled that these are frequently interpreted in economic theory as price relatives.

Now recollect that the continuous spectrum above can be read as a set of bandwidth offerings at different points. Assuming that urban populations are proportional to bandwidths, the rank size rule can be related to the spectrum. More specifically, by fitting an exponential function to city sizes we obtain the parameter which is the multiplier used to give the maximum number of possible arrangements of locations and people. It may thus be regarded as a price relative minimizing the concentration of people in large cities, i.e., it ensures the maximum spread of people between cities. In this sense, it minimizes trips by maximizing bandwidth offerings.

Diffusion of Purchasing Power

In the remark quoted at the beginning of this paper Richardson drew an analogy between settlements of various sizes and turbulence. His main concern was with the diffusion of pollutants in the atmosphere and he pointed out that the process of separating two particles δ distance apart must be via eddies of a size similar to δ. The same process must go on in the central place system with regard to, say, purchasing power.

Consider two marked dollar bills spent by a householder at the local lowest order center as symptomatic of the diffusion of purchasing power and assume their track is due only to central place activities. Initially their distance apart is small, being affected only by circulation within the local "cell." However, there is a probability that one or both bills will be spent at higher order centers and again at still higher centers. This passage to higher order centers is the main diffusing medium, so that the hierarchical structure of central places will determine the extent of travel. Obviously the two bills could have been initially spent in Vancouver and New York but probabilities are small and the diffusion coefficient obtains its stability through the actions of the collective comprising all consumers in an area. Some properties of this diffusion process may be listed.

The diffusion coefficient cannot be time dependent since this implies, by taking several sources, that a particular area may be characterized by several different coefficients. The diffusion coefficient must be a property of the local space and cannot be defined by reference to points outside of that space. But local area has to be redefined to include an increased size at each step in the hierarchy. We may take as a measure of the appropriate local area, the distance apart of centers at various ranks in the hierarchy. Passage of the dollar bills through the hierarchy can best be measured relative to the distance separating the bills or, equivalently, the distance separating centers of various orders. To use Kolmogorov's phrasing, we refer diffusion to local isotropic conditions where local is continually redefined depending on the distance separating the diffusing particles. The principal diffusing agents separating two particles are "cells" of length comparable to the distance apart of the particles.

It is obvious that in an areally specialized economy most income in an area promptly leaves it again to pay for purchased goods. Some remains, however, and it may be postulated that for central place establishments this leakage will tend to be approximately constant, no matter what size of area is involved. Establishments with larger markets are much less certain in this respect; a steel mill will have huge flows directed towards iron ore, coal and heavy industrial areas, and even farms selling locally are often likely to have funds moving to absentee landlords. With central place establishments we are reasonably sure that householders' incomes will generate approximately similar demands for goods and services (i.e., be spent at establishments of similar areal extent when area is weighted for population). This feature could be important because it implies that, within this restricted range of establishments, it should be possible to obtain a lawful process of the diffusion of purchasing power. Obviously, we must leave out of account the larger scale currents of income provided by establishments having considerable orientation to non-local markets and sources.

Dimensions of Diffusion

Richardson proposed that the diffusion of a concentration of marked particles σ could be expressed by

$$\frac{\partial \sigma}{\partial t} = A \frac{\partial}{\partial l}\left(l^m \frac{\partial \sigma}{\partial l}\right).$$

Note here that A has the dimensions $t^{-1}l^{2-m}$.

In words, diffusion increases in efficiency in proportion to some power of the distance apart of the particles. Taylor [18] has shown how dimensional arguments can be used to evaluate m. Any universal rule regulating the allocation of incomes inside a central place system can only be dependent on the dissipation rate of one dollar, E, and the spatial agitation, V; their dimensions are $T^{-2}L$ and L respectively. V is the movement necessary to generate a one dollar sale in a unit area. It is determined by such locally variable phenomena as population densities, income levels, technological stage, social mores and economic well being. This "regional" effect could not be included in the definition of any "universal" diffusion coefficient. We need a formulation which considers only the proportionate allocation of income by a group of persons between different orders of center as expressed in generation of sales. Expressing A from Richardson's equation above in terms of E and V, its dimensions are $E^{1/2}V^{(3/2)-m}$. It is only when $m = 3/2$ that A does not depend on V.

We have pointed out that discontinuities in the spectrum leading to a stepped hierarchy only occur for restricted areas. As area is increased, the spectrum assumes a smooth downsloping form. Since the most useful diffusion coefficient is one for large areas and expressed as a continuous function of distance apart, we shall work at this general level.

This diffusion coefficient should be used only for fairly long tracks passing *upwards* through the *hierarchy*, i.e., it is not intended to apply to centers in the same step of the hierarchy or tracks bypassing the hierarchy. For objects diffusing downwards through the hierarchy, the diffusion coefficient would vary with the two-thirds power of distance apart (i.e., 1/1.5).

The derivation of a diffusion coefficient following a 1.5 power law is hard to justify or refute because of the lack of evidence. There is a clear need for some decisive experimentation here. That diffusive efficiency increases with distance (assuming that diffusion occurs via the hierarchy) appears entirely reasonable and corresponds with our notions of the city as the progenitor of change.

Economic Base

The economic base is a somewhat perverse notion probably because it is not usually discussed within a theoretical context. The trouble lies in the arbitrariness of the areal delimitation and industrial aggregation involved in measurement. It should, however, be pointed out that the ordering obtained by investigators such as Ullman and

Dacey[19] is apparently real and is not the result of sample size. The regularity found in the decrease in the economic base, stated as a percentage, with increase in size of city, is not accounted for by regarding size of city as size of sample drawn from the same population of trades. Thus for an economy composed of people engaged in N distinct trades, it can be shown that the expected size of sample required to obtain the fraction α of N is, for large N, approximately $N \log (1/(1-\alpha))$. (See Parzen[12].) The expected size of sample necessary to obtain all N elements is approximately $N \log N$. These results are at variance with Ullman and Dacey's regression equations of the form $\alpha/N = a + b \log$ (population), so that the regularities found in economic base percentages with city size do appear to mirror "real" forces.

The concept of the economic base or average multiplier is simply stated. Take a group of people living in a contiguous area and consider its trade relations both within and outside the "home" area. The value added by local employment (Y) will be equal to the amount it spends locally on consumption (C) and investment goods (I) plus the value of exports of consumption goods (E_c) and investment goods (E_i) less imports of consumption (M_c) and investment goods (M_i)

$$Y = C + I + E_c + E_i - M_c - M_i,$$

or

$$Y - (C - M_c) = I - M_i + E_c + E_i.$$

Write q for the proportion of local consumption expenditure absorbed by value additions made external to the region, M_c/C, and c for the proportion of income expended on consumption goods, C/Y. The proportion of income used to consume local products is $(C - M_c)/Y = c(1-q)$. The income earned locally and not expended on the product of local employment is $Y - (C - M_c)$, i.e., $Y[1 - c(1-q)]$. The above equation can be rewritten

$$Y = \frac{I - M_i + E_c + E_i}{1 - c(1-q)}.$$

Since the numerator represents expenditure offsetting the difference between income locally produced and income directly expended by local consumers on the products of local employment, the denominator is an average multiplier. It shows by how much total areal income is boosted above income derived from exports, taking the current rate of investment into account. To provide useful results it is clear that areas should not be defined to cut off residences from workplaces but otherwise they can be quite arbitrary: comparability is another matter.

If all producers provided only what they needed themselves, any groupings would be only social and there would be no inter- or intra-group trade. The economic base of all communities would be zero. Still let groupings be social but allow each producer to be so highly specialized that there is only one of a kind in the whole economy. Now the economic base of any community would depend only on the size of the latter, e.g., if the community totalled one third of the economy the economic base would be 0.66.

Considering only those activities of concern to central place theory we can be certain that such industries are local, provided that the area is suitably redefined in line with the previous arguments. Locational arrangement is not affected by factors external to the local areas of the operating units. It may be seen that economic base studies in such a context are the reverse face of diffusion of purchasing power studies. Area is being looked at relative to income flows rather than income flows in relation to area.

We have seen that the derived diffusion coefficient implies that n order centers are separated by a mean distance, $r_n = r_{n-1}^{1.5}$. Thus the sizes of areas served by centers of neighboring orders will be in the proportion r_{n-1}: $(r_{n-1}^{1.5})^2$ and the populations served will be in the same ratio. It is evident that the economic base (B) increases with increasing population (P) according to an exponential process, i.e.,

$$e^{B/2.25} = kP,$$

or

$$B = 2.25 \log_e (kP).$$

This expression is virtually identical with the average employment multiplier for retail trade found by Ullman and Dacey [19] in their minimum requirements approach to the urban economic base.

Spacing of Centers

Our postulates do not allow us to exploit the 1.5 power law for the spacing of centers in restricted areas as was done by Christaller and Lösch with their regular symmetric patterns. If this is done illegitimately, the hexagonal, $K = 3$ scheme does not fit whereas a $K = 7$ structure is in close accord. But other arrangements are also possible, and it is evident that a closer look at the dynamics of road nets is necessary before any advances can be made in this direction.

Only the statistical aspects of large areas can be considered, and we stay within a static framework. There are presumably an immense number of possible arrangements of people being served by the central place systems of different areas. Thus many probability series could be chosen to describe these arrangements. Assume that n-order centers (i.e., from a narrow band of the spectrum) are Poisson distributed so that the probability of a center being between x and dx yards away, given that the mean distance apart is $1/2\mu$ yards, is $2\mu e^{-2\mu x}dx$. (See Morse[11].) Let the $(n-1)$-order centers be arranged taking into account the existing distribution of n-order centers. These former centers are also assumed to be arranged in the same random fashion with the same mean so that if the n-order center is at x the $(n-1)$-order centers will be between $t-x$ and $t-x+dt$ with probability $2\mu e^{-2\mu(t-x)dt}$. Note, however, that the probability for the spacing of both orders of center is now no longer a negative exponential since some degree of statistical dependence has been introduced:

$$s(t)dt = (2\mu)^2 dt \int_0^t e^{-2\mu(t-x+x)}dx = 2\mu(2\mu t)e^{-2\mu t}dt.$$

The mean of this distribution is $1/\mu$ and the variance is $1/\mu\sqrt{2}$, i.e., the latter is less than the former whereas for n-order centers they are equal. Thus the lower order centers are more equally spaced than the higher orders. This argument can be continued for progressively lower order centers and the degree of regularity will be increased. Steinhaus[16] has presented some evidence that this occurs for cities in Poland and Rogers[15] for retail stores in Stockholm. Note that assertions are not being made about the priority of higher order centers or the universality of an initial Poisson distribution. One can begin with the regular distribution and, by introducing less dependent variables, approach the Poisson or even the clustered hyper-exponential distribution. This is what is implied in our previous argument where the noise level increased relative to the signal at longer wavelengths. In a locational context, uncertainty is greater and the white noise character of the locational guideposts becomes more and more important until it dominates at highest order centers.

Population Potential

Apparently the only method available for describing the orientation of an individual in space is that due to Stewart[17]. Using Warntz' notation[20], the total population potential at point i is

$$V_i = \int_0^\infty (D dA_j)/r_{ij},$$

where D is the density over the jth infinitesimal area dA_j and r_{ij} is the distance to point i. In practice the integration to infinity is replaced by a summation to large N. In terms of the contribution to potential at i, of an infinitesimal area with an assumed population of one, and assuming homogeneous space, we have $V_{ij}/V_i = 1 - (r_{ij}/r_{iN})$, which is analogous to our autocorrelation function. However, our term refers only to the area in which we assume local isotropy. While within any level of the hierarchy the population potential notion may be used as a deterministic equivalent of the lag window acting on the random behavior in space, it is not possible to apply it to all levels simultaneously.

This limitation follows from the rather peculiar character of the diffusion coefficient. We are saying that diffusion is equally efficient throughout each "cell" of the hierarchy to the outer limits of the cell. In terms of a distance measure, diffusion increases in efficiency at each level of the hierarchy. If we take the conventional notion that interaction is the reciprocal of friction, our formulation can lead to friction *decreasing* with distance. Assume that a metropolis has central place relations with all the settlements of an area. In the area in which it has first order relations diffusion is equal to, say, $d^{1.5}$. Second order relations for a larger area will occur with a coefficient of $(2d)^{1.5}$ and so on. When friction is defined as the reciprocal of diffusion, then it will actually decline for increments of distance. Riddell[14] has presented some evidence that this actually occurs for telephone traffic in Southern Ontario. Such traffic, while obviously not a diffusion process itself, can be interpreted as dependent on diffusion processes.

It should be recalled that we are concerned only with flows moving via the hierarchy of central places. We can say nothing of the many flows which do not use these routes, e.g., between centers of the same order and between centers of different orders where traffic is non-central.

CONCLUSIONS

The random spatial economy does encourage optimism about obtaining an overall coherence to the limited concepts describing its parts. A reconciliation has been obtained between the hierarchical continuum and the discreteness it exhibits for small samples. Inventories, consumer movements, the functions of centers, as well as their sizes and spacing, economic base and diffusion through interaction have been placed within a single scheme. It seems likely that a feature such as public transportation could also be handled as a problem of filters.

It is urged that the ergodic hypothesis be retained, even if it is found empirically incorrect, until an alternative translation between time and space has been found. In the social sciences, with their wealth of information and dearth of theory, the promise of a postulate for elaboration is at least as important as a fact. Consider, for example, the generalization that firms not selling directly to consumers are likely to have over 90 percent of their profits from 20 percent of their items. (See Brown [2].) Using our previous assumptions, the spectrum is steep and the autocorrelation fairly flat. In the space domain, deliveries would show only slight diminution with distance, implying competition over the whole area rather than in localized markets. The random spatial economy might thus be extended to include an important class of manufacturing and distributing activities.

While it is both justifiable and easy to call for a dynamic approach to location theory, it is extremely difficult to answer this challenge. Obviously, theory calls for some form of logical structure and although it is possible to conceive a synoptic logical structure for, say, a central place system, there is no reason to believe that this structure could have evolved by any conceivable process. And since today's date has no special relevance in an historical process, the synoptic pattern must be logical at all stages of its growth. History may never have had to solve such a problem but we must. Consider, for example, the evolution of the road system which must be the basis of any dynamic economic geography. A road net at any one time can only be understood in relation to a prior time, yet there is also an implication that roading decisions must take account of the future. Current optimizing decisions should allow similar decisions in the next stage ahead. Such a formulation is likely to be hopelessly unrealistic in the sense that its logic is not that of the individual decision maker and the evolution it produces is only partially associated with a particular history. Nevertheless, in spite of its unreality and its intractability, it seems to be what is required. That is as far as the theorist could go—the rest is for the historian.

REFERENCES

1. BLACKMAN, R. B. and J. W. TUKEY. *The Measurement of Power Spectra from the Point of View of Communication Engineering*. New York: Dover, 1959.
2. BROWN, R. G. *Statistical Forecasting for Inventory Control*. New York: McGraw-Hill, 1959.
3. CHRISTALLER, W. (C. W. BASKIN, trans.) *Central Places in Southern Germany*. Englewood Cliffs: Prentice-Hall, 1966.
4. CURRY, L. "The Geography of Service Centers within Towns: The

Elements of an Operational Approach," Proceedings of I.G.U. Symposium in Urban Geography, Lund, 1960, *Lund Studies in Geography*, B, 24 (1962), 31–53.
5. ——— "The Random Spatial Economy: An Exploration in Settlement Theory," *Annals of the Association of American Geographers*, 54 (1964), 138–146.
6. Garrison, W. L. and B. J. L. Berry. "Recent Developments of Central Place Theory," *Papers, Regional Science Association*, 4 (1958), 107–120 [Selection 8 of this volume].
7. Koopmans, T. C. *Three Essays on the State of Economic Science*. New York: McGraw-Hill, 1957.
8. Lebedev, V. L. *Random Processes in Electrical and Mechanical Systems*. Moscow: 1958. Translated and published by N.S.F. and N.A.S.A., Office of Technical Services, Washington, D.C.
9. Lösch, A. (W. H. Woglom and W. F. Stolper, trans.) *The Economics of Location*. New Haven: Yale University Press, 1954.
10. Lumley, J. L. and H. A. Panofsky. *The Structure of Atmospheric Turbulence*. New York: Interscience Publishers, 1964.
11. Morse, P. M. *Queues, Inventories and Maintenance*. New York: John Wiley and Sons, Inc., 1958.
12. Parzen, E. *Modern Probability Theory and Its Applications*. New York: John Wiley and Sons, Inc., 1960.
13. Richardson, L. F. "Atmospheric Diffusion on a Distance-Neighbor Graph," *Proceedings of the Royal Society of London*, A, 110 (1926), 709–737.
14. Riddell, J. B. *Toward an Understanding of the Friction of Distance: An Analysis of Long Distance Telephone Traffic in Southwestern Ontario*. Unpublished M. A. Thesis, University of Toronto, 1966.
15. Rogers, A. "A Stochastic Analysis of the Spatial Clustering of Retail Establishments," *Journal of the American Statistical Association*, 60 (1965), 1094–1103.
16. Steinhaus, H. *Mathematical Snapshots*. New York: Oxford University Press, 1960.
17. Stewart, J. Q. "Empirical Mathematical Rules Concerning the Distribution and Equilibrium of Population," *Geographical Review*, 37 (1947), 461–485.
18. Taylor, G. I. "The Present Position in the Theory of Turbulent Diffusion," in F. N. Frenkiel and P. A. Sheppard (eds.) *Advances in Geophysics*, Volume 6. New York: Academic Press, Inc., 1959.
19. Ullman, E. L. and M. F. Dacey. "The Minimum Requirements Approach to the Urban Economic Base," Proceedings of I.G.U. Symposium in Urban Geography, Lund, 1960, *Lund Studies in Geography*, B, 24 (1962), 121–144.
20. Warntz, W. "A New Map of the Surface of Population Potentials for the United States 1960," *Geographical Review*, 54 (1964), 170–184.

10

BRIAN J. L. BERRY

Cities as Systems Within Systems of Cities

This paper examines some of the ways by which understanding of cities and sets of cities has been advanced during the first decade of regional science. Originally, I was asked to prepare a paper which reviews the entire range of urban models but, for several reasons, decided to take a more limited view. The Social Science Research Council's Committee on Urbanization has recently completed a comprehensive review of urban studies, to be published shortly as *The Study of Urbanization*,[1] and to attempt to duplicate this work in a short paper would be as foolhardy as the result would be superficial. Other papers deal with certain kinds of urban models (for example, those related to metropolitan transportation studies, or those involving study of the urban economic base via input-output matrices) and I will not attempt to duplicate what they have to say.

What, then, is the scope of this paper? Three channels which lead towards development of sound urban models are explored and relevant implications drawn. By models, we mean *symbolic* models not those of the *iconic* or *analogue* kinds.[2] Further, the symbolic models of interest are those which provide idealized representations of properly formulated and verified scientific theories relating to cities and sets of cities perceived as spatial systems. Any scientific theory logically comprises two parts: (a) simple inductive generalizations drawn from observable facts about the world, and (b) abstract logical constructs. It is the coincidence of deductions drawn from the logical constructs and inductive generalizations drawn from fact that makes for a valid scientific theory. Ten years ago, urban studies were in an either/or situation—either inductive generalizations or logical constructs existed, the former as likely as not produced by urban geographers and the latter by urban economists. As the word "model" became fashionable, both called their products models, but neither had models of theories in the strict sense.

The importance of the last decade has been that the twain *have* met through the medium of regional science. Moreover, the meeting

1. This volume (33) includes review papers by historians, geographers, political scientists, sociologists, economists, and the like.

2. Ackoff[1] elaborates these terms.

Reprinted from Papers and Proceedings of the Regional Science Association, *13 (1964), 147–63, by permission of the publishers and the author.*

came just when quantitative methods of analysis, facilitated by rapid developments in computer technology, began a technological revolution which has wrought havoc throughout the sciences. What more shattering change could there be than one which facilitates the large-scale studies that lead to specification of strength of belief in inductive generalizations, allow objective testing of the degree of coincidence between inductive generalizations and deductions from logical constructs, and ease replication? The technological advance has meant more, however—virtual elimination of the once lengthy gap between problem formulation and evaluation of results, sharpening of the questions asked, initiation and completion of experiments of a size unthinkable under earlier technical conditions, and many more.

The meeting, then, was timely. Inductive generalizations could be eased toward theory, logical constructs could be faced with the ultimate test of reality, and new kinds of empiricism and experimentation could be developed. These are the three channels discussed in the following sections of the paper. Examples are presented in an expository rather than a rigorous manner, since each has been elaborated elsewhere. The conclusions of the paper are that urban models are the same kinds of models as appear in other kinds of systems inquiry. Urban theory therefore may be viewed as one aspect of general systems theory. Viable avenues for future urban research might therefore be identified by looking at those other aspects of general systems theory that are relatively well advanced to see how they reached this more developed position.

INDUCTIVE GENERALIZATIONS IN SEARCH OF A THEORY

Two of the better-known generalizations concerning cities are the rank-size relationship for sets of cities, and the inverse-distance relationship for population densities within cities. Both had been observed many times when they were formalized as empirical "rules" a decade or so ago, the former as the *rank-size rule* by G. K. Zipf and the latter as the *negative exponential density distance relationship* by Colin Clark. Yet as Isard noted in 1956, "How much validity and universality should be attributed to the rank-size rule is, at this stage, a matter of individual opinion and judgment."[3] Further, although Clark argued that the negative exponential "appears to be true for all times and places studied" he provided no theoretical rationale for his observations, only specified that they might have something to do with

3. Isard [34] in connection with a discussion of empirical regularities.

transport costs.[4] During the past decade, both inductive generalizations have been brought closer to the status of scientific models, with the range of their validity carefully specified.

Distribution of City Sizes

The rank size rule[5] says that for a group of cities, usually the cities exceeding some size in a particular country

$$p_r = p_1/r^2 \tag{1}$$

where p_1 is the population of the largest or first-ranking city, p_r is the population of the city of rank r, and q is a constant.[6] Whence it follows that

$$\log pr = \log p_1 - q \log r \tag{2}$$

so that a plot of rank against size on doubly logarithmic paper should give a straight line with a slope of $-q$.

Another way of expressing the foregoing is that the frequency distribution of cities by size seems to be highly skewed in the shape of a reversed-*J*. A whole series of probability distributions, among them the lognormal and the Yule, have a similar reversed-*J* shape, each bearing a general family resemblance through their skewness. Each is, in fact, the steady state distribution of a similar simple stochastic process. Could it be that rank-size regularities of city sizes also result from such a stochastic process? The tenor of arguments provided in the past decade is that stochastic processes do indeed provide such a framework, and both the Yule distribution and the lognormal have been proposed on the basis of rank-size regularities.[7] The two are, in fact, so similar that each could obtain when the cumulative distribution of cities, by size, plots as a straight line on lognormal probability paper. Whichever is applicable to the particular case depends upon whether a closed or an expanding system of cities is being considered.

Consider the transition matrix of a stochastic process in which the rows and columns are specified by city-size groups. If the probability density function of each size-class of cities is approximately the same,[8] then the steady-state of the stochastic process will be lognormal if the

4. See Berry [12] for review comments.

5. Berry [8] lists the relevant literature in some detail. Subsequent contributions include those of Bell [5], Friedmann [29], and Ward [51].

6. If the entire population were urban, then $p_t = p_1 \Sigma r^{-q}$. See Weiss [52].

7. Simon [48], Berry and Garrison [7], Thomas [49], Dacey [25], and Ward [51].

8. That is, so that the "law of proportionate effect" holds.

set of cities existing at the beginning of the process is the same as the set achieving the steady-state at the end. If, however, the smallest size class is augmented by new cities at a fairly steady rate throughout the process, the steady-state is that of the Yule distribution. If growth of cities within the set can be said to occur in small independent increments, with possibilities of growth the same for each size class (growth is the result of "many factors operating in many ways" and occurs such that if city sizes for time period *one* are plotted against sizes for time period n the resulting scatter of points is homoscedastic with a slope of $+1$), then the basic conditions of such a stochastic process can be said to have been met. One or another constraint leads to the lognormal or the Yule, in the former case a closed system of cities must exist, whereas in the latter the system must go on growing at a steady rate by addition of cities at the lowest level.

A recent study shows that the rank-size regularity applies throughout the world for countries which are highly developed with high degrees of urbanization, for large countries, and for countries such as India and China which, in addition to being large, also have long urban traditions. Conversely, "primate cities" or some stated degree of primacy obtains if a country is very small, or has a "dual economy."[9]

Moreover, additional studies have recently shown that many distributions with some degree of primacy take on more of a rank-size form as level of development and degree of urbanization increase.[10] By virtue of size and complexity, then, countries with rank-size distributions appear to satisfy the condition of "many factors operating in many ways," and increasing complexity of a space economy certainly brings the city size distribution closer to rank-size. A rank-size regularity is not found when few factors mold the urban system in a few simple ways: in small countries, where economies of scale accrue in a single "primate city"; or in "dual economies" where one or a few exogenous, colonial, cities of great size are superimposed upon an indigenous urban system of smaller places, etc. In such cases, growth patterns cannot be summarized in the form of a stochastic process of the simple kind outlined above.[11] For all large, complex systems of cities which exist in the world, however, aggregate growth patterns do conform to such a stochastic process, so that one macroscopic feature of these systems is a rank-size regularity of city sizes. The regularity may, in turn, be "explained"[12] by the stochastic process.

9. Berry [8].
10. Bell [5] and Friedmann [29].
11. Unless the process works, for example, to a random power of size, as with the log-lognormal, see Thomas [49].
12. Nagel [42] discuss the various modes of scientific explanation and the role of explanation in science.

Urban Population Densities[13]

No city has yet been studied for which a statistically significant fit of the expression

$$d_x = d_0 e^{-bx} \tag{3}$$

does not obtain. In this equation, which was derived empirically by Colin Clark, d_x is population density d at distance x from the city center; d_0 is central density, as extrapolated into the city's central business district; and b is the density gradient.

$$1\, nd_x = 1\, nd_0 - bx. \tag{4}$$

Alonso and Muth have provided a satisfactory "explanation"[14] of the observed regularity recently in terms of the rent-transport-cost-trade-off of individuals in different stages of the family cycle at different income levels and at different distances from the city center.[15] Thus, what Clark speculated might have something to do with transport costs, when he advanced the regularity a decade ago, in fact, does so. Apparently, the bid-rent function is steeper for the poorer of any pair of households with identical tastes in the American city, so the poor live toward the city center on expensive land consuming little of it and the rich on the periphery consuming much.[16] The negative exponential shape of the decline stems from the nature of the production function for housing and the shape of the price-distance function.[17] Expression (3) is thus an equation of some generality which can be derived as a logical implication of the theory of the urban land market.

This being so, a variety of conclusions may be drawn. For example, the population residing at distance m from the city center is

$$p_m = \int_0^m d_0 e^{-bx} (\pi 2x)\, dx \tag{5}$$

which becomes

$$p_m = 2 d_0 \pi b^{-2} [1 - e^{-bm}(1 + bm)]. \tag{6}$$

This implies that the population pattern of an urban area can be described by two parameters alone, b and d_0. Winsborough has called the former a measure of the *concentration* of the city's population and the latter an index of its *congestion*.[18]

13. Berry [12] lists the relevant literature. Also see Winsborough [54].
14. Alonso [2] and Muth [41]. Also see note 12.
15. *Ibid.*
16. Alonso, *op. cit.*
17. Muth, *op. cit.*
18. Winsborough [54].

Now for any set of cities and for any particular city through time, another empirical expression holds[19]

$$b = ap^{-c}. \tag{7}$$

Thus, b is in turn a function of city size. Central density, d_0, is on the other hand apparently a function of the form of the city as established at the particular stage at which it grew and is thus directly related to the city's age.[20] Knowing the population of a city and its age, it is possible to predict fairly closely the pattern of population densities within it.

In any system of cities for which the rank-size regularity obtains, the population p of a city of rank r, p_r, is a function of only p_1 and q, equation (1). Hence, b must likewise be a function of p_1 and q, equations (1) and (7). The distribution of population within cities is a function of the position of these cities within the entire system of cities and of age. If the larger system is Yule in form, age is simply the generation of the underlying stochastic process at which the city entered the system, so that congestion, d_0, as well as concentration, b, is given within the framework of the larger system. The preceding statement can thus be modified to read: the distribution of population within cities is a function of the position of these cities within the entire system of cities at some point in time, and the period of time for which they have been within the system.

LOGICAL CONSTRUCTS IN SEARCH OF A TEST

The preceding two models account for the size and the distributional characteristics of urban populations, but they say nothing of the locations of the cities concerned. Three sets of reasons for cities have been advanced, each with locational parameters more or less explicit: cities as strategic locations on transport routes; cities as the outcome of local concentrations of specialized economic activities; and cities as "central places" performing retail and service functions for surrounding areas. Only the latter is of interest here.

Central Place Theory

Central place theory[21] was formulated by Walter Christaller as a "general purely deductive theory" designed "to explain the size,

19. Berry [12], Weiss [52], and Newling [43].
20. Winsborough, *op. cit.*
21. Berry and Pred [9]. Later studies include [10], [11], [13], [22]. See also the parallel speculations of Rashevsky [46], [47].

number and distribution of towns" for reasons which also made it "the theory of urban trades and institutions."[22] A decade ago this theory was perhaps the only one concerning systems of cities that was at all well developed.[23] At that time, although many empirical studies of central places had been completed, the fact that no satisfactory test of the theory had been made largely reflects the fact that investigators looked for examples of theoretical implications drawn simply for exemplification by Christaller under the assumption of an isotropic plane. There also was a lively debate as to whether certain of the most fundamental theoretical implications, for example that of a hierarchy of central places, had any empirical validity. It has only been during the last decade that such questions have been settled. A thorough review of most aspects of the topic is to be found in *Central Place Studies. A Bibliography of Theory of Applications*, the first of the Regional Science Research Institute's Bibliography Series, and so will not be repeated here.[24] Subsequent to the *Bibliography*, the various postulates of the theory were drawn together in a model. Since the model appears to have some generality (implications drawn from the model have been verified independently, for example) it will be presented here.[25]

The model applies to systems of central places in which the elements are viewed aggregatively. A set of inequalities supplements the model, however, and these empirically derived expressions link aggregate patterns to local arrangements of central places under specified conditions of population density by specifying expectations as to the steps of the central place hierarchy. Random variations from ideal steplike patterns of central places in a series of local areas, combined with logical changes in location of the steps according to population density, interact to produce the regularities which may be observed in the aggregate. The definitions, equalities, structural equations, and implications of the model follow without lengthy comment.

Definitions:

p_t = the total population served by a central place;

p_c = population of the central place;

p_r = rural population and population of lower level centers served by the central place;

A = area of the trade area served;

Q_t = population density of the area served;

22. Christaller [21].
23. Berry and Pred *op. cit.*
24. *Ibid.*
25. See [10] and [14].

Q_r = population density of those parts of the area served lying outside the central place;
T = number of central functions performed by the center, and since central functions enter in a regular progression and can be ranked from 1 . . . T in decreasing order of ubiquity, also the highest level central function performed by the center;
E = number of establishments providing the T types of business;
D_m = maximum distance consumers will travel to a central place of size T, *or* the range of good T.

Equalities:

$$p_t = p_c + p_r \tag{E1}$$

$$p_t = AQ_t \tag{E2}$$

$$p_r = AQ_r \tag{E3}$$

$$A = kD_m{}^q \tag{E4}$$

Figure 1 shows, in five distinct study areas in the United States,[26] equality (E2). In each case, total population and total area served slope upwards to the right on doubly logarithmic paper with a slope of +1. Differences between study areas are simply a function of population densities.

Structural Equations:[27]

$$\log p_c = a_1 + b_1 T \tag{1}$$

$$\log D_m = a_2 + b_2 T \tag{2}$$

$$\log E = a_3 + b_3 \log p_t \tag{3}$$

These structural equations hold in any study area (i.e. at any level of density) and relate the population of a market center to the variety of central functions performed for surrounding areas, the drawing power of the center to its offerings, and the number of separate establishments performing the T functions (E exceeds T for all except the smallest villages and hamlets) to the total population served to account for nonbasic demands for goods and services from the population p_c as well as basic demands generated by the population of the area served, p_r.

Implications:

$$p_c = p_t{}^s w^{-s} Q_t{}^{-s} \tag{4}$$

where

$$w = k[\log^{-1}(qb_1^{-1}(a_2 - a_1 b_2))]$$

and

$$s = (b_1)/(qb_2)$$

26. See [10] or [11] for details.

27. Only a sample of the structural equations necessary to facilitate the present discussion is given here.

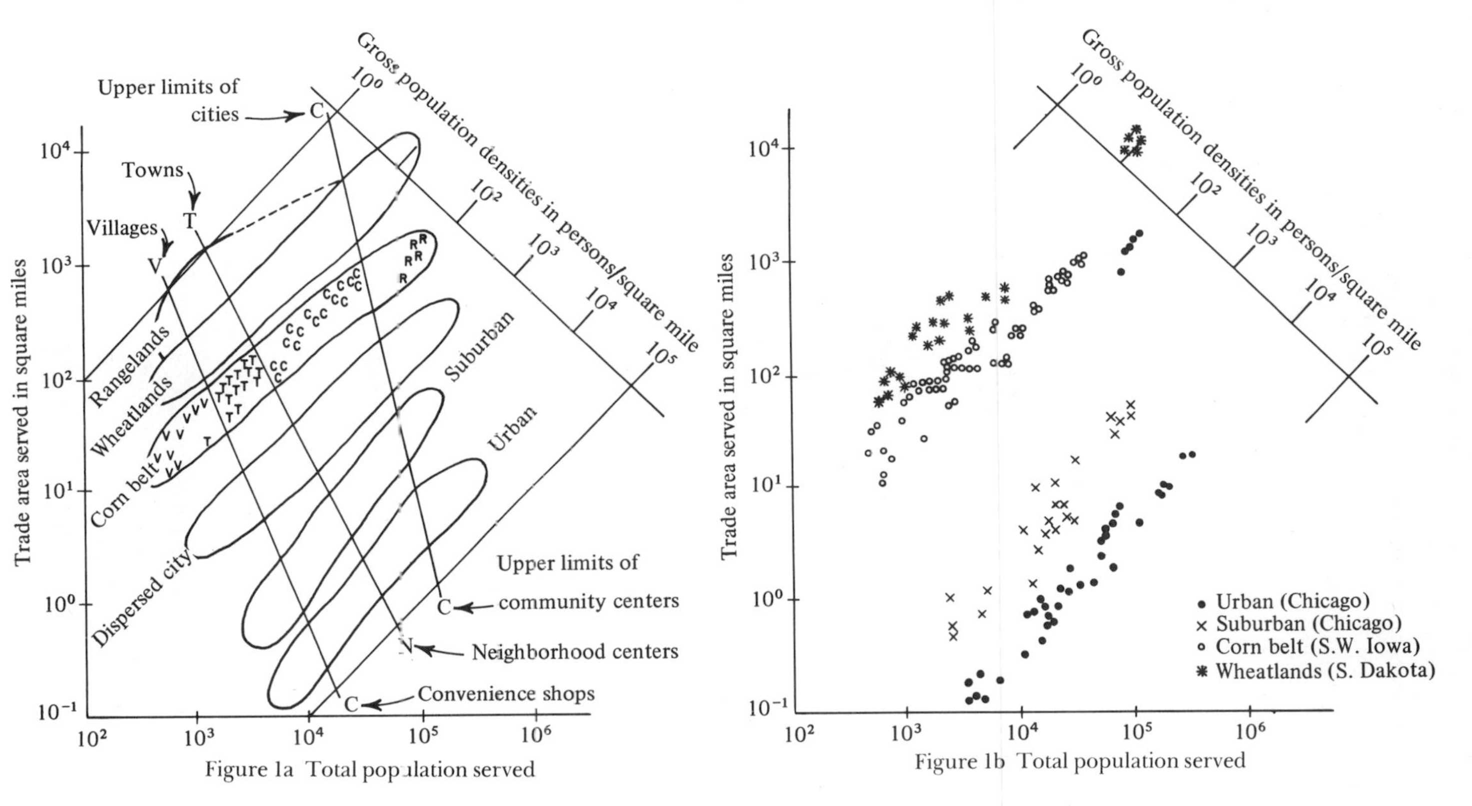

FIGURE 1 Gross trade area characteristics in the United States. Figure 1b shows sample data for central places in Chicago, Chicago's suburbs, the corn belt of southwestern Iowa, and the wheatlands of South Dakota. The "sausages," in Figure 1a encircle the scatters of points in each case, adding data for the "dispersed city" of southern Illinois, and the rangelands around the Black Hills of South Dakota. Note that, in the corn belt case, the factor analytic classification of the central places has been added, to illustrate how the inequalities representing the upper size limits of centers of each class under varying conditions of population density actually operate.

As total population served increases, the central population comes to assume an increasing proportion of the total, but this tendency varies inversely with population densities.

$$A = wp_c{}^x \tag{5}$$

where

$$x = s^{-1}$$

Area served increases exponentially with size of center.

$$E = mQ_t^{b_3}p_c^{b_3} \tag{6}$$

where

$$\log m = a_3 + b_3 \log w$$

Total number of establishments varies exponentially with both size of center and total population densities.

These and similar structural equations and implications have now been verified in several studies[28] and appear to be a reasonable summary of many of the aggregate features of central place systems. Each has particular implications within the framework of central place theory as well, particularly as it has been generalized. However, a set of inequalities is needed in combination with Figure 1 to lay out the steps of the central place hierarchy as it is found in local areas at different levels of density. These inequalities were established empirically by factor analyses of the functional structure of central places in each of several study areas, to determine the hierarchy individually within each of those areas, and then by discovering, unexpectedly, that limits to each of the levels varied consistently across the set of study areas as population density varied. With the second subscripts v referring to villages, t to towns and c to cities, these inequalities are:

$$\log A_{tv} \leqslant 10.4\text{–}2.67 \log p_t \tag{I1}$$

$$\log A_{tt} \leqslant 9.3\text{–}2.067 \log p_t \tag{I2}$$

$$\log A_{tc} \leqslant 22.25\text{–}4.75 \log p_t \tag{I3}$$

They are inserted into Figure 1, and, in the case of the corn belt study area, the individual observations are identified as they were classified in the factor analysis.[29]

28. See [10] and subsequent studies as yet unpublished by Karaska, Pitts, Murdie, and others.

29. The factor analytic results are presented in [14] and [10].

INNOVATION UNDER TECHNICAL IMPETUS

The decade has seen a variety of innovations, most facilitated by rapid developments in computer technology that made feasible kinds of research that could never have been contemplated prior to the developments. Beginnings are to be seen in the construction of urban simulators that will facilitate study of cities and sets of cities in laboratory-type experimental situations.[30] The most successful attempts so far have been those of Chapin in studies of land development[31] and Morrill in analyses of changing central place patterns,[32] although this statement is not intended to denigrate attempts along these lines in current urban transportation and economic studies. Out of these studies, particularly those undertaken in Chicago, Pittsburgh, and the Penn-Jersey region, and also those of the RAND Corporation and Resources for the Future, Inc. will surely emerge models of some predictive power and experimental capability. Another paper considers this topic however, recognizing what may be the most significant new dimension to urban research added during the past decade. We will concentrate here on another topic, the new empiricism of the decade, stimulated by advancing computer technology and consequent diffusion of multivariate analysis throughout the social sciences. We focus here on one form of multivariate analysis, *factor analysis*, and briefly review how, in the form of social area analysis, it has facilitated studies of the internal structure of cities.

Social Area Analysis

Social area analysis[33] is one approach to the classic problem of urban ecology, the succinct description of the location of residential areas by type within cities, in terms meaningful to persons interested in social differentiation and stratification. Over the years, several constructs have been developed in this context:[34] Hurd's concept of urban growth proceeding according to two patterns, central growth and axial growth; Burgess's concentric zone hypothesis of the location of residential areas by type, stemming from the nature of a growth process that proceeds outwards from the city center, accompanied by waves of residential invasion and succession; Hoyt's emphasis upon the axial growth of higher-income neighborhoods outwards from the

30. Garrison [30] has one of the first presentations.
31. See [20].
32. See [38] and [39].
33. Bell [6] has an excellent review.
34. See the review by Anderson [3].

city center along some sector; and Harris' and Ullman's notions of the multiple nucleation of the city. Both the social area analysts and their critics[35] have emphasized the difficulty of testing these hypotheses with the wide variety of socio-economic data available, for example, from censuses. Which variables should be used in the test? Will the story told by different but presumedly related variables be the same? What in fact are the stories told about the structure and differentiations of urban neighborhoods by the wide range of census data available?

Factor analysis can provide answers to questions of the latter kinds. Let us review the basic features of the method. Consider a data matrix ${}_nX_m$ is which are recorded the data for n observations (say, census tracts) over m variables. If the column vectors of X are normalized and standardized to yield ${}_nZ_m$ then $Z^TZ = {}_mR_m$ which is, of course, the correlation matrix of the m variables. Since the column vectors of X were standardized, R is the variance-covariance matrix of Z, and the trace of R, equaling m, is the total variance of the m variables.

Now assume that each of the m variables is regressed in turn upon the $m-1$ remaining. For each is then available a coefficient of determination expressing how much of its variance is held in common with the $m-1$ other variables; in factor analysis these coefficients of determination are called communalities, and denoted h^2. For each variable, then, in its standardized form $1.0-h^2=u^2$ is the proportion of variance unique to the variable. A diagonal matrix U^2 can thus be formed with individual u^2s along the diagonal. It follows that $[R-U^2]$ has communalities on its diagonal, and the trace of $[R-U^2]$ is the total common variance of the m variables. This total common variance plus the trace of U^2 equals m, the total variance.

Principal axes factor analysis provides a procedure whereby a matrix ${}_mA_r$ may be found such that

$$[R-U^2] = AA^T \qquad (1)$$

$$A^TA = \Lambda \qquad (2)$$

The dot product of each row vector of A yields one of the communalities, and the inner product of any pair of row vectors reproduces a correlation. Λ is a diagonal matrix, which implies that inner products of pairs of column vectors of A are zero. Such vectors are thus orthogonal (uncorrelated). The dot product of each column vector yields an eigenvalue λ. Since the sum of the eigenvalues must equal the sum of the communalities, these eigenvalues represent another

35. The Duncans write "students of urban structure have lived for some time with the uncomfortable realization that their theories, or rather their abstract, schematic descriptions, of urban growth and form are not very susceptible to empirical testing" [26].

way of parceling up the total common variance, the one (communalities) relating to the amount of the total common variance contributed by the association of any one variable with all other variables, the other (eigenvalues) to that part of the total attributable to one of the column vectors of A. These independent column vectors are the factors of factor analysis, the principal dimensions of variation underlying the original body of variables m.

Individual elements of A are factor loadings, the correlation coefficients between the original variables and each of the underlying common dimensions. The property of orthogonality of the dimensions is useful, because it means that each of the dimensions accounts for a different slice of the common variance, which slices are additive in any reconstruction of the whole; such additivity was not a property of the original intercorrelated m variables. Each dimension summarizes, then, one pattern of variation (one story told by) the original m variables. A further step which is useful is to form

$$ {}_nS_r = ZA\Lambda^{-1} \tag{3} $$

In S, the individual s_{ij} are factor scores of the original observations on each of the new dimensions formed by the analysis. S expresses all associations and common patterns found in X, but in a simpler form.

Factor analysis of census data for a whole series of United States cities by social area analysts has led to the conclusion that three dimensions are all that is required to summarize the stories told by the characteristics recorded for census tracts by the census. Study of the correlations between the original variables and the three dimensions has also revealed remarkably stable patterns from one city to another. One factor was consistently highly correlated with income, education, occupation, and wealth. A second was related to family structure, fertility, type of household, and position of women in the labor force. Finally, a third was associated with ethnic and racial structure of the population, age and sex composition, and measures of deterioration and blight. Speculation about the meaning of these regularities led social area analysts to identify the first as depicting variations in the *social rank* of individuals and families, the second as representing *urbanization* or *family status* of neighborhoods, and the third as resulting from *segregation*. The factor scores of tracts on these three dimensions could be used to characterize neighborhoods, since the three dimensions appear to be those responsible for the basic features of urban differentiation and stratification.

If the latter statement is true, then the three dimensions should enable research workers to test some of the classical constructs concerning such urban differentiation and stratification. A first study along these lines has revealed that factor scores of tracts with respect to social rank are differentiated in a sectoral fashion, as they should be if Hoyt's concepts apply, and that factor scores on urbanization and family status are differentiated in a concentric fashion, as they should be if Burgess's ideas are valid.[36] However, spatial variations in segregation show no regularity but are specific to each case. As Hurd had speculated much earlier, then, concentric and axial patterns are additive and independent sources of urban differentiation from city to city, with spatial variations specific to each city added by the third dimension of segregation.

It is clear that although social area analysts began simply in a "look-see" manner, with later work facilitated by advancing computer technology, their work has now laid the bases for a spatial model of the internal socio-economic pattern of cities in which the relevance and role of the traditional concepts are clear.[37]

A SYSTEMS FRAMEWORK

The previous findings point in one direction: that cities and sets of cities are *systems* susceptible of the same kinds of analysis as other systems and characterized by the same generalizations, constructs, and models. *General systems theory* provides a framework for such inquiry into the nature of systems; indeed Boulding calls it the "skeleton of science." Further, *information theory* has come to the fore as one of the foundations of general systems theory, contributing the two complementary ideas of *entropy* and *information* to the vocabulary of general systems research.[38] Entropy is achieved in the steady state of a stochastic process and is at its maximum if this process is unconstrained. Information is a measure of the order present if some systematic pressures for organization constrain the operation of the stochastic process.

Curry[39] has shown that given Z settlements, with Z_i having a population i, the numbers of ways people can be distributed among settlements is

$$p = Z! \Big/ \prod_{i=0}^{n} Z! \qquad (0 \leq i \leq n) \tag{1}$$

36. Anderson, *op. cit.*

37. This, in spite of criticism [26], has been the *accumulative* result. It is worthwhile to note some of the other contributions made possible by factor analysis: (a) more general urban typologies [40]; (b) clearcut evidence of the hierarchy of central places as an additive class system [10], [14]; (c) multivariate regionization [31]; and (d) metropolitan structure [32].

38. Bertalanffy [16], [17]; Boulding [19]; and Beer [4].

39. Curry [23]. Other cases he examines are the spacing of nearest neighbors, also see Dacey [24], the spacing of nearest neighbors of the same size, and the percent of manufacturing in an urban labor force.

and in a large system the entropy E is given by

$$E \underset{\text{def.}}{=} \log p = Z \log Z - \Sigma Z_i \log Z_i \tag{2}$$

E is maximized when

$$Z_i = (Z/N)\, e^{-(i/N)} \tag{3}$$

in which equation N is the mean population per settlement, or $N = n/Z$. Now if S is the size of the largest city,

$$Z_{i \leq S} = S\,(1 - e^{-(i/N)}) \tag{4}$$

in which case

$$E_{\text{max.}} = Z \log\,(eN) \tag{5}$$

and the most probable state of the system, giving maximum entropy, is one in which, given the size of the largest city, the probability of the $(q+1)$st city having a population which is a given ratio of the qth city is a constant. Under these conditions, the sum of the logarithms is a maximum, and of course it is the condition satisfied when the rank-size rule for cities obtains. If a system of cities assumes rank-size, then, entropy has been maximized and it has assumed its most probable steady-state.[40]

On the other hand, organization exists due to pressures for order in central place systems. If the per cent change in establishments in central places is constant with each addition of new business types, then[41]

$$dE/EdT = k. \tag{6}$$

Integrating yields

$$\log E = k_1 T + c_1. \tag{7}$$

If similar percentage ratios exist for the sizes of central places p_c then

$$\log p_c = k_2 T + c_2. \tag{8}$$

From the above

$$T = K_1 \log E - C_1. \tag{9}$$

$$T = K_2 \log P_c - C_2. \tag{10}$$

40. Curry points out that entropy in the same system constrained such that persons had to be allocated in threes, as families, would be $H' = Z \log\,(eN/3)$. Hence, a measure of order is $R = 1 - H'/E_{\text{max}}$.

41. Odum [44], Berry [11].

Now the equation

$$I = K \log (\text{number of states}) \tag{11}$$

has been identified as one measure of macroscopic negentropy, the inverse of entropy. It follows that the number of business types T is an index of the amount of information present in a set of establishments located in central places or of the population of those places. This is consistent with the use of types of functions to identify and classify the central place hierarchy. Many attempts have been made to assess the "centrality" of central places. It would seem that number of types of business, information content, provides such an index. In southwestern Iowa, very strong fits to (9) and (10) are found.

$$T = 55.56 \log E - 58 \quad (r^2 = 0.96). \tag{12}$$

$$T = 50.00 \log p_c - 105 \quad (r^2 = 0.91). \tag{13}$$

indicating that where urban centers are almost exclusively central places, necessary empirical bases for these arguments are to be found. It will be readily apparent that the above equations are compatible with those presented earlier for central place systems. Lösch and Christaller postulate such constant percentage relationships also with the addition of *levels* to the regular hierarchy ($k = 3$, $k = 4$, $k = 7$ networks and their implications); related measures of information should therefore exist for the order maintained by the step-like nature of the hierarchy.

It is not difficult to extend similar arguments to the situation within cities.[42] For example, urban population densities settle down to a most probable state in which densities are ranked with distance from the city center. Conversely, the model of central place systems also applies, indicating that certain aspects of urban life are constrained from reaching their most probable state.

Maruyama[43] has speculated about an apparent contradiction of the second law of thermodynamics in social phenomena, including those of cities. According to the second law, an isolated system will most probably trend to its most probable state, even if it begins in an inhomogeneous state. He points out that cybernetics, the study of equilibrating systems, considers many cases of self-regulation such that deviations are counteracted and the system is brought back

42. Meier [37].

43. See [35] for a review statement of Maruyama's ideas and other references of interest.

toward its equilibrium, usually a most probable state under constraint. But many instances can be cited in which feedback does *not* lead to self-correction towards some preset equilibrium (morphostasis). Rather, progressively greater contrasts appear, as between Myrdal's "rich lands and poor," or with progressively greater centralization of urban functions in fewer larger cities, or when the "growth of a city increases the internal structuredness of the city itself," in Maruyama's words. These are all examples of deviation *amplifying* processes (morphogenesis) which run counter to the second law.

Whether or not a system trends toward maximum entropy because processes working are deviation correcting, or toward maximum information because the processes are deviation, and therefore structure-amplifying, apparently depends upon the nature of the causal relationships at work and of their feedback characteristics. Maruyama concludes that any system, together with the subsystems into which it may be partitioned, contains many examples of both deviation-correcting and deviation-amplifying processes. One subsystem may be becoming more highly organized, another may be approximating its most probable state. To understand the system as a whole demands that each of the subsystems be understood, as well as the relationships between them.[44]

So be it in the urban field. It is clear that cities may be considered as systems—entities comprising interacting, interdependent parts. They may be studied at a variety of levels, structural, functional, and dynamic, and they may be partitioned into a variety of subsystems. The most immediate part of the environment of any city is other cities, and sets of cities also constitute systems to which all the preceding statements apply. For systems of cities, the most immediate environment is the socio-economy of which they are a part.

Whereas progress has been made in understanding various facets of these systems and subsystems, for other facets we stand much as we did a decade ago. In a systems framework, we should no longer worry about apparent contradictions between the kinds of conclusions reached for different subsystems, i.e. between the distribution of city sizes and the functional arrangement of market centers in a hierarchy, however, for the difference is understood to be one of the relative balance of entropy-approximating or order-generating processes in various parts of the system. In contradistinction, however, we have very little understanding of how to put these different patterns together in more general models that are broad in scope. Sound

44. Maruyama provides an example of the operation of deviation-amplifying mutual causal processes in a two-dimensional spatial distribution, and his discussion of systems, subsystems, and feedback is phrased in terms of cities.

models are providing the building blocks, but maximum progress during the next decade awaits the architectural systematizer.

BIBLIOGRAPHY

1. ACKOFF, R. L. *Scientific Method. Optimizing Applied Research Decisions*. New York: John Wiley & Sons, Inc., 1961.
2. ALONSO, W. "A Theory of the Urban Land Market," *Papers and Proceedings of the Regional Science Association*, 1960 [Selection 4 of this volume].
3. ANDERSON, T. R. and J. E. Egeland. "Spatial Aspects of Social Area Analysis," *American Sociological Review*, 1961.
4. BEER, S. "Below the Twilight Arch—A Mythology of Systems," in D. F. Eckman, ed., *Systems. Research and Design*. New York: John Wiley & Sons, Inc., 1961.
5. BELL, G. "Change in City Size Distribution in Israel," *Ekistics*, 1962.
6. BELL, W. "Social Areas: Typology of Urban Neighborhoods," in M. B. Sussman, ed., *Community Structure and Analysis*. New York: Thomas Y. Crowell Company, 1959.
7. BERRY, B. J. L. and W. L. Garrison. "Alternate Explanations of Urban Rank-Size Relationships" *Annals*, Association of American Geographers, 1958.
8. ———. "City Size Distributions and Economic Development," *Economic Development and Cultural Change*, 1961.
9. ——— and A. PRED. *Central Place Studies. A Bibliography of Theory and Applications*, Regional Science Research Institute, Philadelphia, 1961.
10. ———. "Comparative Studies of Central Place Systems," University of Chicago, processed, 1961.
11. ———, H. G. BARNUM and R. J. TENNANT. "Retail Location and Consumer Behavior," *Papers and Proceedings of the Regional Science Association*, 1962.
12. ———, J. W. SIMMONS and R. J. TENNANT. "Urban Population Densities, Structure and Change," *The Geographical Review*, 1963.
13. ———. *Commercial Structure and Commercial Blight*, Department of Geography Research Paper No. 85, University of Chicago, 1963.
14. ——— and H. G. BARNUM. "Aggregate Patterns and Elemental Component of Central Place Systems," *Journal of Regional Science*, 1963.
15. ———. "Research Frontiers in Urban Geography" in P. Hauser and L. Schnore, eds., *The Study of Urbanization*, Social Science Research Council, 1964.
16. BERTALANFFY, L. VON. "An Outline of a General System Theory," *British Journal of the Philosophy of Science*, 1950.
17. ———. "General System Theory," *General Systems*, 1956.
18. ———. "General System Theory: A Critical Review," *General Systems*, 1962.
19. BOULDING, K. "General Systems Theory—The Skeleton of Science," *Management Science*, 1956.
20. CHAPIN, F. S. and S. F. WEISS. *Factors Influencing Land Development*, Chapel Hill, 1962.
21. CHRISTALLER W. *Die zentralen Orte in Süddeutschland*, Jena: Gustav Fischer, 1933.

22. CLAVAL, P. *Géographie Générale des Marches*. Besançon, 1962.
23. CURRY L. "Explorations in Settlement Theory. The Random Spatial Economy. Part I." *Annals*, Association of American Geographers, 1963.
24. DACEY, M. F. and T. H. TUNG. "The Identification of Point Patterns, I," *Journal of Regional Science*, 1963.
25. ———. "Another Explanation for Rank-Size Regularity," Philadelphia, processed, 1962.
26. DUNCAN B. and O. D. DUNCAN. "The Measurement of Intra-city Locational and Residential Patterns," *Journal of Regional Science*, 1960.
27. ———. "Variables in Urban Morphology," in E. W. Burgess and D. J. Bogue, eds., *Research Contributions to Urban Sociology*, University of Chicago Press, 1963.
28. FRIEDMANN, J. R. P. *The Spatial Structure of Economic Development in the Tennessee Valley*, Department of Geography Research Paper No. 39, University of Chicago, 1955.
29. ———. "Economic Growth and Urban Structure in Venezuela," *Cuadernos de la Sociedad Venezolana de Planificacion*, 1963.
30. GARRISON, W. L. "Toward a Simulation Model of Urban Growth and Development," *Proceedings of the IGU Symposium in Urban Geography, Lund, 1960*. Lund: Gleerup, 1962.
31. GINSBURG, N. *An Atlas of Economic Development*, University of Chicago Press, 1961.
32. HATTORI, K., K. KAGAYA, and S. INANAGA. "The Regional Structure of Surrounding Areas of Tokyo," *Chirigaku Hyoron*, 1960.
33. HAUSER, P. and L. F. SCHNORE, eds., *The Study of Urbanization*, Social Science Research Council, New York, 1964.
34. ISARD, W. *Location and Space Economy*. New York: John Wiley & Sons, Inc., 1956.
35. MARUYAMA, M. "The Second Cybernetics. Deviation Amplying Mutual Causal Processes," *American Scientist*, 1963.
36. MCINTOSH, R. "Ecosystems, Evolution and Relational Patterns of Relational Patterns of Living Organisms," *American Scientist*, 1963.
37. MEIER, R. L. *A Communications Theory of Urban Growth*. Cambridge: Massachusetts Institute of Technology Press, 1962.
38. MORRILL, R. L. "Simulation of Central Place Patterns over Time," *Proceedings of the IGU Symposium in Urban Geography, Lund, 1960*. Lund: Gleerup, 1962.
39. ———. "The Development of Spatial Distributions of Towns in Sweden: An Historical-Predictive Approach," *Annals*, Association of American Geographers, 1963.
40. MOSER, C. A. and W. SCOTT. *British Towns. A Statistical Study of their Social and Economic Differences*. Edinburgh: Oliver and Boyd, 1961.
41. MUTH, R. F. "The Spatial Structure of the Housing Market," *Papers and Proceedings of the Regional Science Association*, 1961.
42. NAGEL, E. *The Structure of Science*. New York: Harcourt, Brace and World, 1961.
43. NEWLING, B. *The Growth and Spatial Structure of Kingston, Jamaica*, Ph.D. dissertation, Northwestern University, 1962.
44. ODUM, H. T., J. E. CANTLON, and L. S. Kornicker. "An Organizational Hierarchy Postulate for the Interpretation of Species—Individual Distributions, Species Entropy, Ecosystem Evolution, and the Meaning of a Species-Variety Index," *Ecology*, 1960.

45. PIERCE, J. R. *Symbols, Signals and Noise.* New York: Harper & Brothers, 1961.
46. RASHEVSKY, N. "Outline of a Mathematical Approach to History," *Bulletin of Mathematical Biophysics*, 1953.
47. ———. "Some Quantitative Aspects of History," *Bulletin of Mathematical Biophysics*, 1953.
48. SIMON, H. A. "On a Class of Skew Distribution Functions," *Biometrika*, 1955.
49. THOMAS, E. N. "Additional Comments on Population-Size Relationships for Sets of Cities," in W. L. Garrison, ed., *Quantitative Geography*. New York: Atherton Press, in press.
50. VAN ARSDOL, M. D., S. F. CAMILLERI, and C. F. SCHMID. "The Generality of Urban Social Area Indexes," *American Sociological Review*, 1958.
51. WARD, B. *Greek Regional Development*, Center for Economic Research, Athens, 1962.
52. WEISS, H. K. "The Distribution of Urban Population and an Application to a Servicing Problem," *Operations Research*, 1961.
53. WINGO, L. *Transportation and Urban Land*, Resources for the Future, Inc., 1961.
54. WINSBOROUGH, H. H. "City Growth and City Structure," *Journal of Regional Science*, 1963 [Section 13 of this volume].

11

GUNNAR OLSSON

Central Place Systems, Spatial Interaction, and Stochastic Processes

INTRODUCTION

"Systems analysis" and "general systems" have become *en vogue* with a school of spatial analysts, represented for instance by Chorley (1962, 1964), Ajo (1962), Ackermann (1963), and Curry (1964).[1] Very often, however, writers differ in their understanding of these notions, and, as a general background to the subsequent discussion, it might be illuminating to speculate about how these words came to enter our vocabulary. One source may be found in multivariate statistics, regional input-output analysis, regional linear programming, etc., i.e., with research techniques designed to further the understanding of functional interdependence amongst places or areas belonging to the same set or "system" of places and areas.

The idea of spatial systems may also be linked with general systems theory, as proposed for instance by von Bertalanffy (1951, 1962) and Boulding (1956b). These writers (as also the spatial analysts mentioned above) argued that the interdependence and functional relationships within a system (the problem of organization and interaction) should in particular be studied. But in the search for theory and adequate techniques, they also suggested that one looks to other and better developed disciplines. For example, von Bertalanffy used the physical concepts of open systems and steady states and applied them to biological problems. Ever since, general system theorists have followed the same challenging path, observing that similar mathematical formulations fairly frequently apply to quite different phenomena. For the regional scientist, the theories of economic equilibrium and social physics are familiar illustrations of the occasional fruitfulness of this approach. We need not emphasize,

1. In one way, this approach was officially sanctioned in the report by the *ad hoc Committee on Geography* (1965). However, this does not mean that all geographers necessarily approve of it and, in reviews of the report, both Thoman (1965) and James (1966) have been rather critical. (Numbers in parenthesis refer to References at the end of this paper.)

Reprinted from Papers and Proceedings of the Regional Science Association, *18 (1966), 13–45, by permission of the publishers and the author.*

however, the danger of too uncritical adoption of physical analogies to studies of social and human phenomena.

These introductory remarks have set the stage for the rest of this paper. Central place theory will be related to the more general theory of spatial human interaction. As in von Bertalanffy's studies, similarities in behavioristic underpinnings and mathematical formulations will be specifically stressed. This approach was chosen mainly because we surmise that knowledge accumulated in studies of general spatial interaction may also be of potential value in the quantitative estimation of central place parameters. Later, central place systems will be viewed as the outcome of various stochastic processes; observed deviations from "optimal" location patterns and their evolution over time will be emphasized.[2]

CENTRAL PLACE SYSTEMS AND GENERAL THEORIES OF INTERACTION

Simple Models of Spatial Interaction

Most discussions of central place theory begin with a detailed account of the classical model as formulated by Christaller (1933) and subsequently refined by Lösch (1954), and by Isard (1956). However, Berry and Pred (1961, supplemented 1965) have already reviewed this literature, while Olsson (1965 a) attempted to relate variants of the model to each other and to various location theories. This makes any introductory discussion of the Christaller-Lösch-Isard model superfluous. We can instead turn to the problem of whether the classical central place model can be fruitfully related to current theories of general spatial interaction.

In an important elaboration of central place studies, Berry and Garrison (1958 c) isolated "population thresholds" and the "range of a good" as the two basic concepts which determine the spatial organization of tertiary activities. The range of a good is said to delineate the market area of a central place for a specific good and so defined it can be interpreted as a distance measure determined as the maximum distance the average customer is willing to travel to procure a certain good. But the emergence of a central place system not only depends on decisions made by consumers but also on decisions of the entrepreneurs or suppliers. If it can be assumed that firms will go out of business when their market areas become too

2. Some inevitable overlap will be found with Berry (1964a). Also the present paper does not attempt to present empirical material—instead, citations to such studies will be made.

small to render a reasonable profit, there must also exist some minimum market size below which a place will no longer be able to supply a specific good. As Berry and Garrison (1958 c, p. 111) note, this minimum scale may be defined either as the lower limit of the range of a central place or, alternatively, as the minimum amount of purchasing power necessary to support the supply of a central good from a place. This minimum amount of purchasing power, simplified as the sales level at which firms either enter or go out of business, is generally termed the threshold sales level. Viewed in this way, the range of a good mainly influences the consumers' decision making, while the thresholds rather influence the decisions of the entrepreneurs.

In a very simplified manner, these notions can be depicted as in Figure 1, conceptually related to the demand cones of Lösch (1954,

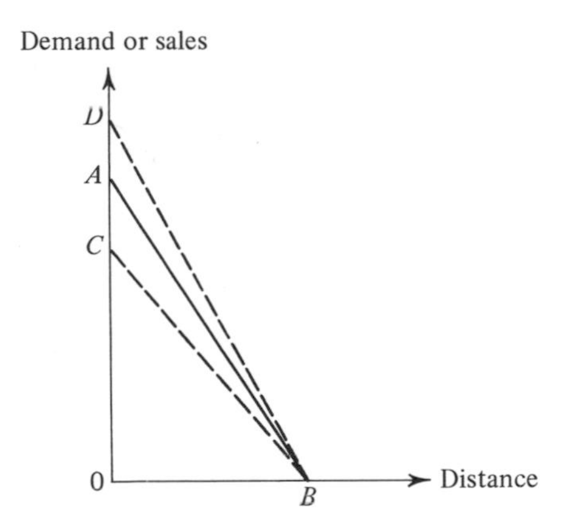

FIGURE 1 Variations in demand with variations in distance.

p. 105 ff.) and to the figures presented more recently by Smith (1966). It is seen from this sketch that sales from place O are assumed to diminish as one moves further and further out. In economic theory, this assumption is common and is based on the hypothesis that, as one moves away from the center, the delivered price increases because of transportation costs. Thus, less goods are bought. However, as pointed out by Curry (1962, p. 33), this is not usually the case for the type of goods normally understood as being the concern of central place theory. But it will be easier to follow the subsequent discussion if these objections are momentarily disregarded.

Under those circumstances, individuals living between O and B can be assumed to obtain the good in question at O, while persons living beyond B buy it elsewhere – probably at a place to the right of B in Figure 1. It follows that the distance OB may be interpreted as the range of the considered good, while the threshold is given as the area within the triangle *OAB*. Further, provided the satisfied demand in place *O* equals *A*, the system is in a state of equilibrium. In case demand (and sales) are less than *A*, for example *C*, the good will no longer be supplied by firms in *O*; if the satisfied demand is larger than *A*, for example *D*, it will be possible for firms in *O* to earn "excess profits". Since addition of new firms is a discrete process[3] while increases in demand are usually continuous, Berry and Garrison (1958 b) managed to demonstrate that excess profits tend to be greater in small than in large places.

This interpretation of Figure 1 directs our interest to the intercepts between the axes and the "demand or sales" line. Reformulated, this means that we will focus our attention on systematic variations in the value of the parameters in the (transformed) linear regression model, i.e.,

$$y = a + bd \tag{1}$$

where:

y = demand, arbitrarily set equal to sales; and
d = distance, measured either in physical or functional units.

But if it is reasonable to study the notions of thresholds and ranges via expressions of this type, it also seems reasonable to assume that people living between *O* and *B* satisfy their demand largely through shopping trips to *O*. Provided this is the case, equation (1) may, of course, be replaced by a gravity regression model, i.e.,

$$\log\left(\frac{I_{ij}}{P_i P_j}\right) = a - b \log D_{ij} \tag{2}$$

where:

I_{ij} = the level of interaction between place or area i and place or area j;
P_i = the number of inhabitants (purchasing power, etc.) in i;
P_j = the number of inhabitants (sales level, etc.) in j;
D_{ij} = the distance (physical or functional) between i and j;
a = an empirically derived constant denoting the intercept with the y-axis; and
b = an empirically derived exponent denoting the slope of the line.

By such a reformulation, the considerable knowledge gathered in gravity analyses becomes relevant for studies of spatial systems of

3. This is not entirely correct as new departments may be added to firms already in existence.

central places. It will be necessary, however, to comment on equation (2) and particularly on systematic variations in parameters *a* and *b*.[4]

An important finding in many gravity analyses has been that the exponent, or *b* in (2) tends to be a function of time. For instance, Hägerstrand (1957, p. 122) and Taaffe (1956, 1959, 1962) have demonstrated this and both suggest that there is a positive relationship between *b* and the technical, social and economic development in society. But *b* seems to vary systematically also in other ways. In a number of trip studies by Iklé (1954), Voorhees (1955), and Carroll and Bevis (1957) it was verified, for instance, that computed *b*-values vary with trip purpose. The latter investigated trip frequencies within urban regions; they demonstrated that the trip frequency gradient was steepest for trips to school, less steep for trips to shops and works, while trips for social recreation were least influenced by distance. Further, overwhelming evidence has been furnished by Claeson (1964), Olsson (1965 b), and Wärneryd (1965 a) that *b* is also a function of P_i and P_j, i.e., a function of the "masses" assigned to the interacting places. The smaller these masses, the larger the numerical value of *b* and the steeper the gradient of the interaction field. It is clear, however, that these variations may be a consequence of the fact that equation (2) only considers interactions between two places at a time, a problem to which we will return shortly. Claeson (1966) recently pointed out that the relationships between *b*-values and city size may to some extent also be due to mathematical characteristics of the model.

The variations in interaction gradients gain particular significance if (2) is treated as a simple regression model. This is so because observed differences in *b* can then be subjected to ordinary *t*-tests, as in the above mentioned studies by Olsson (1965 b, p. 25 ff.) and Wärneryd (1965 a). Unfortunately, similar tests of observed differences in *a*-values (the *y*-intercept) are not as easy to make, and in fact impossible if the regression lines are not parallel.[5] At the same time, the Pareto model (2) tends to exaggerate the intensity of close-in contacts, in other words is less reliable in areas close to the *y*-axis. As a consequence, (2) has often been replaced by non-linear functions, some of which were reviewed by Morrill (1963 a), Olsson (1965 c) and Malm, Olsson and Wärneryd (1966). The simplest of these functions is of course quadratic: employed for instance by Claeson (1964) and Helvig (1964, p. 6):

$$\log\left(\frac{I_{ij}}{P_iP_j}\right) = a - b_1 \log D_{ij} - b_2(\log D_{ij})^2 \quad (3)$$

4. The model is well-known and has already been fully treated by several writers including Carrothers (1956), Isard (1960, ch. 11) and Olsson (1965a).

5. For example, see: Hald (1952), p. 57 ff.); and Snedecor (1956, p. 398).

The high reliability of (3) as compared to (2) is due to a certain "plateau effect" close to the origin, where distance seems to have no effect on interaction intensity.[6] As an illustration of this effect, Garrison (1956) and Marble (1959), found that the correlation between shopping trip frequency and distance was almost negligible for short-distance trips. On the other hand, they also verified that purchases practically always were made in the closest town offering the demanded good.

While the lack of linearity in short-distance interaction data has led to the use of more complicated functions, the simpler linear model can still be employed in the modified form:

$$\log\left(\frac{I_{ij}}{P_i P_j}\right) = a' - b \log D_{ij} \tag{4}$$

where a' denotes that the initial value of the interaction field should not be defined as the intercept with the y-axis but rather as the intercept with another axis, parallel to the y-axis but at some distance from it. Instead of calibrating the field at a distance one unit away from the interacting place ($\log D_{ij} = 0$), this means that the calibration is performed at a distance of $1 + \Delta D_{ij}$ away. Nothing is explicitly said about the curve in the distance interval to ΔD_{ij}, but it is probably parallel to the x-axis. If this is so, interaction intensity within distance ΔD_{ij} is of course independent of distance. Claeson (1964, p. 73 ff.), who analyzed Swedish data on cinema visits, put ΔD_{ij} equal to 3.17 kilometers.

But, just as b in equations (2) and (4) is a function of P_i and P_j, Claeson (1964, p. 85 ff.) verified also that a' in (4) is a function of P_j, written as $(P_j)^\alpha$, where α in his case took on a value of approximately 0.3. He further concluded that this so-called mass exponent helps to characterize different regions and to measure to what degree an increase in population size of a place also is followed by an increase in its influence over the service area.

Does the gravity regression model have relevance for central place studies as well? Because of the characteristics of this model, we will have to make the simplifying assumption that the places under consideration are located along a line (e.g. a road or a river) and not over an area. If this holds, the discussion has made it clear that a modified version of equation (1) (referring to Figure 1 as well) may be used to determine theoretical values of thresholds and ranges. Most plausibly, this modified version of (1) should be written as:

$$y = (a')^\beta - (b)^\gamma d \tag{5}$$

where both β and γ vary with P_i, P_j, time, and type of good.

6. This relates to the assumption that sales from a place diminish as one moves away: i.e., the assumption previously questioned by Curry (1962).

But the derivation of (5) is, of course, based on too-restricted a set of assumptions. For instance, places are neither located one-dimensionally nor influenced only by one other place at a time, as hypothesized by the gravity regression model. Therefore, delimitations of nodal regions or service areas have not usually been based on expressions (1)–(5), but rather on some variant of the related model originally formulated by Reilly (1931). This model has later been modified,[7] and is generally written as:

$$I_{ij} = G \frac{\frac{P_j}{D_{ij}^b}}{\sum_{j=1}^{n} \frac{P_j}{D_{ij}^b}} \tag{6}$$

Available comments on (6) are mostly in line with those on the simple gravity regression model and need not be repeated. Unfortunately, however, (6) has not yet been as thoroughly studied as (2) and, although nothing clearly contradicts the supposition that b in (6) varies as b in (2), this has still to be proven. It should be recalled, though, that Huff (1963) employed (6) in predictions of demand in shopping trade areas verifying empirically that b varied for different types of good; for clothing shopping trips b was equal to 3.191 and for furniture shopping trips equal to 2.723 (p. 87). Since the type and number of functions in a central place is related to its population size, this also indicates that b in (6) is related to P_i and P_j much in the same manner as is b in (2).

Probability Models of Spatial Interaction

Gravity analysis, as has just been shown, may have value in the formulation of central place models. But it was also argued that these models are deterministic formulations based on very restrictive assumptions. Therefore, the possible value of interaction studies in location theory cannot be finally judged until these assumptions have been discussed in greater detail.

At the outset, let us agree that, although assumptions of rational behavior and perfect knowledge are helpful in the first stages of spatial theory building, these concepts are nevertheless utterly unrealistic. Since most theoretical derivations of normative and optimal location solutions have been based on these assumptions, it also follows that the feasibility of such deterministic derivations may be

7. For example by Converse (1949), Tuominen (1949), Godlund (1954), Ellwood (1954), Goosens (1963), Micklander (1964), Sweet (1964), Thompson (1966), and Smith (1966).

questioned.[8] Deterministic models resulting in normative and optimal solutions are not satisfactory. But such a conclusion should not lead to rejection of all concepts underlying current theories; it does suggest that future models must pay explicit consideration to the possibility of deviations from strict "optimality." This recognition caused Harris (1964) to reconsider the probability basis of the classical gravity model. We now turn to a discussion of this important point.

Harris based his derivation on an earlier paper by Schneider (1959), who suggested that, as one moves away from the origin of trips, the probability of trip termination is proportional both to the number of remaining or unsatisfied trip-makers and to the number of conceived opportunities. Formalized this may be expressed as;

$$P(I_{ij}) = Q_{j-i} - Q_j = e^{-LV_{j-1}} - e^{-LV_j} \qquad (V_0 = 0) \tag{7}$$

where:

$P(I_{ij})$ = the probability of interaction between an origin area, i, and a destination area, j, where the j's have been ranked according to access from i;

V = the cumulative number of opportunities already reached;

Q = the proportion of trip-makers continuing beyond opportunity V;

L = a fixed parameter specifying the rate of trip attenuation; and

e = the base of the natural logarithms.

In Harris' case, L was arbitrarily assumed to have a gamma distribution, i.e.:

$$f(L) = \frac{1}{\Gamma(a)b^a} \cdot (L-c)^{a-1} \cdot e^{-(L-c)/b} \qquad \begin{matrix} L \geqslant c \\ a > 0 \\ b > 0 \\ c \geqslant 0 \end{matrix} \tag{8}$$

with mean equal to $(ab+c)$ and variance equal to (ab^2+c). After manipulation of (7) and (8) the probability of a trip extending beyond V was derived as:

$$R = (1+bV)^{-a} e^{cV}. \tag{9}$$

8. This conclusion was already anticipated by Hotelling (1929), who clearly demonstrated that the optimal location of ice cream stands on a beach would not be the same for suppliers and customers. This was the more remarkable as all the actors had been blessed with rational behavior, perfect knowledge, and the other attributes of economic man. Social and individual optima may conflict; unstable solutions may well be generated.

From this it follows that the probability density function of trip termination is

$$\rho = -\frac{dR}{dV} = [ab/(1+bV)+c]R. \tag{10}$$

If c in these expressions approaches zero, (9) and (10) will become equivalent to a modified gravity model with a negative distance exponent greater than unity.

Later in his paper, Harris discussed the fact that the spatial distribution of opportunities is not a matter of indifference to the trip-maker.[9] More exactly, he assumed (p. 33) that L "is a behavioral parameter which not only depends on the trip-maker and his purposes, but is also proportional to the additional distance, D, he will at any point need to travel to the 'next' opportunity." This assumption is written:

$$L = M\frac{dD}{dV} \tag{11}$$

which subsequently leads to:

$$Q = e^{-MD} \tag{12}$$

Now, if also M has a gamma distribution, then:

$$R = (1+bD)^{-a}e^{cD} \tag{13}$$

which can immediately be compared with (9) and (10).

As demonstrated, Harris derived the gravity model entirely from probabilistic notions. This adds to the significance of the exposition in the previous section. Before the value of Harris' derivation can be fully appreciated, however, it will be necessary to reexamine his two basic assumptions. We will concentrate that reexamination first on his hypothesis that the rate of trip attenuation has a gamma distribution, and then on the behavioristic assumption of intervening opportunities made earlier by Schneider. Since few central place analyses have treated these problems, the discussion will draw mostly on a number of migration studies.

Järhult (1958 pp. 130 ff.) gave what may be the first description of observed variations in migration distances in terms of the gamma distribution (i.e., (8) above often called Pearson Type III).[10] The

9. This same idea earlier led us to favor the general gravity model (6) as compared to the gravity regression model (2), (3) and (4).

10. There is some doubt, though, whether his material, fitted to data from Olofström in southern Sweden, is representative of other areas: particularly as the exponent in the gravity regression model, (b in (2)) was found to equal 3.4. In other parts of the country, b has usually been smaller, indicating that Olofström's migration field is considerably steeper than normal.

gamma function was also successfully employed by Cavalli-Sforza (1962), while Dacey (1963) obtained a satisfactory fit when applying the incomplete or truncated gamma distribution to migration data from Asby, in Sweden.[11]

A slightly different approach to the use of gamma distributions in migration was recently attempted by Olsson (1965 b, p. 35 ff.), who first noted that central place theorists assume each good to be purchased in the nearest place which offers it and then drew attention to a study by Dacey (1964 b) showing that nearest neighbor distances within a set of places generally have the gamma distribution. With these observations as a background, Olsson then hypothesized that migrants tend to move to the nearest alternative destination. Provided the statistical distribution of migration distances could be shown to coincide with that of the nearest neighbor distances (i.e., with the gamma distribution) this hypothesis would of course be supported. Unfortunately, differences between observed and expected values became highly significant and the hypothesis had to be rejected, although a deterministic model based on identical behavioristic assumptions was later supported. In summary then, the validity of Harris' assumption, that the rate of trip attenuation follows a gamma distribution, has yet to be finally decided; meanwhile, empirical evidence suggests that this may well serve as a working hypothesis.

Schneider and Harris also based their models on the assumption that the concept of intervening opportunities influences the trip-maker's choice of destination. This assumption is of course simpler than the one involving the gamma distribution. It is also linked with earlier interaction models as those formulated by Stouffer (1940, 1960). In his earlier study, Stouffer only considered the concept of intervening opportunities, but in the latter he also introduced the concept of "competing migrants." Formalized, he stated that:

$$I_{ij} = K\frac{(P_iP_j)^{b_1}}{(O_{ij})^{b_2}(C_{ij})^{b_3}} \tag{14}$$

or:

$$\log I_{ij} = \log K + b_1 \log P_iP_j - b_2 \log O_{ij} - b_3 \log C_{ij} \tag{15}$$

with I_{ij}, P_i, and P_j defined as in (2) above, while

O_{ij} = the number of intervening opportunities, measured as the total number of out-migrants in the circle centered midway between i and j and passing through i and j;

11. The function was used in its truncated form because data on local or short-distance migration tend to be unreliable. Comparing Dacey's fits with those obtained by Järhult, it should be noted that the exponent in a Pareto curve for Asby was equal to 1.6, that is a "normal" value.

C_{ij} = the number of competing migrants, measured as the total number of in-migrants in the circle centered on j and passing through i; and K, b_1, b_2, and b_3 are parameters to be empirically estimated.

The Stouffer model (generally without the concept of competing migrants) has been repeatedly tested, though with varying degree of success.[12] The crucial point in Stouffer's model is of course the operational definition of O_{ij} and C_{ij}. This problem was discussed by among others, Anderson (1955) and Hägerstrand (1957) who both noted the danger of circularity in the above definition of O_{ij}. More recently, this problem was reconsidered by Porter (1964) who, by slight redefinitions of O_{ij} and C_{ij}, gained very good results. Satisfactory fits were also obtained by Ray (1965) in a study of U.S. investments in Canada.

The similarities between Harris' and Stouffer's formulations suggest that results gained with the intervening opportunity model may serve in part to verify the probability derivation of the gravity regression formula. Less directly, this holds also for the probabilistic migration model formulated by Porter (1956), who hypothesized that people migrate only in connection with changes in employment, while job vacancies are filled in a manner closely related to the suggestions by Stouffer, Schneider, and Harris. Porter further assumed that both job vacancies and job-seekers arise randomly over the area but in proportion to population. In periods with an excess of vacancies, the job-seeker was assumed to take the nearest position while in periods with an excess of applicants the applicant living closest to the working place is given the position. Thus, Porter suggested that if a vacancy occurs in an area centered at j when there exists a surplus of applicants, s, the applicant living closest to j migrates there. If P_{ji} denotes the probability that this applicant comes from the area centered at i, with population P_i and situated at distance D_{ji} from j, then:

$$p_{ji}(s) = s\frac{P_i}{T}(1-F_j)^{s-1} \tag{16}$$

where:

T = the region's total population; and
F_j = the fraction of the total population which resides within distance D_{ji}, i.e., the fraction of the total population living

12. Stouffer, as well as Bright and Thomas (1941), Isbell (1944), Folger (1953), Stewart (1960), and Galle and Taeuber (1966) all conclude that the intervening opportunity model is far more reliable than the simple gravity regression model. Strodtbeck (1949, 1950), Anderson (1955), and Hägerstrand (1957, p. 119 ff.) suggest that nothing essential is gained by replacing the simple distance model with the more cumbersome intervening opportunity model.

within a circle centered at j and passing through i. This circle is the same as that used earlier in estimation of C_{ij} in (14) and (15).

Equation (16) states that the probability of the applicant coming from i and going to j is equal to the probability that one of the job-seekers is living there, multiplied by the probability that each of the others is at a greater distance. Alternatively, if a time period with an excess of v vacancies is considered, i.e., a period when $v=-s$, an exactly analogous formula will hold. If the applicant lives at j, then the probability that he migrates to i equals

$$q_{ij}(v) = v\frac{P_i}{T}(1-F_j)^{v-1} \qquad (17)$$

Expressions (16) and (17) should be compared with expression (7) used by Harris (1964) but originally suggested by Schneider (1959).

Summing (16) and (17), the expected migration from i to j in a given period may be derived as:[13]

$$I_{ij} = kP_i \sum_{v=1}^{\infty} q_{ji}(v)\Pi(v) + kP_j \sum_{s=1}^{\infty} p_{ji}(s)\Pi(s) \qquad (18)$$

where

$\Pi(v)$ = the probability that there are exactly v vacancies;
$\Pi(s)$ = the probability that there are exactly s applicants; and
k = the average ratio of number of applicants (or vacancies) arising in the time period to the population of an area.

After specified assumptions about v and s, and after mathematical manipulations, Porter deduced the formula:

$$I_{ij} = K\frac{P_iP_j}{T}\left[\frac{1}{1-C(1-F_i)^2}+\frac{1}{1-C(1-F_j)^2}\right] \qquad (19)$$

where F_i is defined analogously to F_j given above. The parameters K and C can be estimated as:

$$\hat{K} = \frac{k(1-C^2)}{4} \text{ and } C = \frac{1-2c}{1+2c} \qquad (20)$$

where C is a restoring factor specifying how v and s vary over time.

The predictive power of (19) was tested on data from Sweden. The agreement between expected and observed numbers of migrants

13. It should be noted that the subscripts $q(v)$ in (18) have been reversed from the order in (17), indicating the probability that an applicant in area i, in periods with excess vacancies, will move to area j.

was found to be fairly satisfactory but, in his conclusions, Porter suggested that the model might be improved if it were disaggregated and each occupational group treated separately. He also warned that it would probably not be accurate for short distances, but this warning does not seem to have concerned him very much and he remarked that short-distance migration is a geometric rather than an economic problem.[14]

Finally, and to summarize this section, it follows from expressions (16)–(19) that Porter's tentative migration law can be related to Harris' probabilistic derivation of the gravity model, i.e., equations (7)–(13). It follows therefore that it can also be related to Stouffer's model of intervening opportunities and competing migrants, i.e., equations (14) and (15). More specifically, the three models all consider two sets of probabilities,[15] where the first probability specifies the number of opportunities already reached (e.g., settled migrants or satisfied trip makers), while the second probability specifies the proportion of unsatisfied migrants or trip makers who have to go beyond a certain point to reach an acceptable opportunity. In conclusion then, the deterministic gravity regression model has been shown to be closely related to a family of probability formulations—a fact which makes it far more attractive as a potential submodel in a more general stochastic central place theory.

Behavioristic Assumptions

It has been a great advantage that the models discussed thus far have been fully formalized. However, model building is always a matter of generalization or simplification and the mere fact that formalization has been successful does not immediately guarantee that a model also will give an accurate account of underlying human behavior. Bearing this in mind, the present section will scrutinize some of the behavioristic assumptions in current interaction and central place theory. First we refer to Wolpert (1965), who discussed the behavioral aspects of the decision to migrate. If it turns out that Wolpert's comments are reasonably applicable to central place problems as well, the suggested relationships between general interaction and central place systems will have been given further support.

Wolpert suggested three basic concepts of migration behavior: (1) the notion of place utility; (2) the field theory approach to search

14. The influence exerted on migration by the size and shape of areal units was only briefly discussed by Porter. For fuller and more elaborate treatments, see for instance: Bergsten (1951) and Kulldorf (1955).

15. This use of the word probability is not entirely correct, since Stouffer's model has no firm probabilistic basis.

behavior; and (3) the life cycle approach to threshold formation. These stem from organization theory. It becomes logical, therefore, to view migration as a process where the prospective migrant is evaluating the "utility" of various places, operationally defined as a measure of the individual's positive or negative satisfaction with respect to a particular place. Borrowing a concept from Simon (1963), one can assume that these evaluations have been based on intended rather than on objective rationality.

Although probabilistic interaction models can be said to implicitly consider this concept they largely focus on changes in interaction with changes in intervening distance. Similar distance functions were framed by Wolpert in the concept of "field theory approach to search behavior," a concept which becomes extremely important since the individual, in spite of his access in theory to a large number of alternative places, only manages to conceive of some rather limited portion of the environment. Most frequently, this so-called action space of the individual is limited to his immediate surroundings, but, as noted above, it varies both between different individuals and for different needs.

Wolpert's third concept, the "life cycle approach to threshold formation," holds that an individual's perception of his action space undergoes changes over time. Such changes are made probable partly because, as time goes by, the individual acquires more knowledge and experience, partly because he is influenced by his environment. The necessity of including such dynamic elements in spatial theory has already been stressed; it has been noted that observed variations in b, in the gravity model, suggest this may be operationally possible.

The wish to make central place theory more dynamic is not new. But little has yet been achieved and, even in very recent studies such as that by Hodge (1965) on the viability of trade centers in Saskatchewan or in the paper by Allpass et al. (1966), no formalization has been attempted. Notwithstanding, Allpass and his co-workers made the very strong point that central place theory should be abandoned because the model is based on outmoded assumptions of transportation technique and business structure. This is remarkable, since it appears most plausible that spatial distributions similar to those reported by both Hodge and Allpass can be generated simply by letting thresholds and ranges vary over time. In contradiction to Allpass' conclusion, this would rather lead us to accept than to reject the underlying theory.[16]

16. The possibility of such changes in parameters has long been recognized by Swedish planners, especially in their works on the new division of administrative areas. See, for instance: Statens Offentliga Utredningar (1961); and Jakobsson (1964).

As do most of the above studies, Wolpert's (1965) discussion of human behavior in spatial interaction centered on migration rather than on central place theory. Thus, the suggested relationships between general interaction and central place systems have been based largely on intuitive reasoning. It is of great interest, therefore, that Huff (1960, 1961) earlier arrived at similar conclusions to Wolpert, in spite of the fact that he chose his examples much closer to traditional central place topics.[17]

Summary

This section began with a review of basic central place concepts: population thresholds and the range of a good. Using a simplified sketch resembling Lösch's demand cone, it was then suggested that the study of general interaction models (the social gravity model, for example) may also be relevant for central place theorists. With this hypothesis we then turned to a brief discussion of systematic variations in parameter values of the gravity formulation.

It was soon recognized, however, that although this model is a good descriptive tool, it nevertheless fails in the explanation and prediction of spatial interaction patterns. Two reasons were given for this failure: first, the gravity regression model has no firm probabilistic basis, and second, it is not sufficiently anchored in the theory of human behavior and decision making. Because of this, probabilistic reformulations of the classical model were sought, and attention was drawn to Harris' (1964) derivation. The possible usefulness of this derivation caused us briefly to dwell on some of its underlying assumptions. Emphasis was given the hypothesis that the rate of trip attenuation has a gamma distribution and the supposition that a trip maker selects his destination partly with respect to the anticipated distance to the "next" opportunity. These behavioristic assumptions finally gave rise to selected comments on a family of related models.

The third section developed the theme that a scientific model can at best furnish only a simplified account of reality, since some relevant factors will have to be deleted in the process of formalizing a theory into an operational model. No simple or rigorous techniques exist for this critical stage. It was reassuring, therefore, that both the general interaction models and major portions of classical central place theory were consistent with the general behavioristic frameworks suggested by Huff (1960) and Wolpert (1965).

17. Based on earlier work of Isard (1956) and Marble (1959), Huff's model attempted to isolate the main factors affecting consumer space preferences, i.e., the behavioral aspects of consumer decisions. Other work in this direction can be found in: Murdie (1965); Malm *et al* (1966); and Rushton (1966); as well as Huff (1961).

It must be emphasized that the models discussed thus far have stressed the importance of spatial variables (e.g., distance) while other variables, probably more central to the actual decision-making process, have been largely neglected. Further, the distance analyses themselves have described existing empirical regularities rather than explained or predicted future patterns. But this is not to say that the many distance studies have been useless. Instead, they will probably prove extremely valuable in future formulation of submodels ultimately to be incorporated into more complex central place constructs. It may be that just these deterministic gravity regression models might facilitate the introduction of stochastic elements into classical central place theory.

CENTRAL PLACE SYSTEMS AND STOCHASTIC PROCESSES

Central Places as Points on a Hexagonal Lattice

We have noted relations between models of spatial interaction and central place theory and have focused on the behavior of consumers, specifically, on the range of a good. But classical central place theory is also based on the concept of population thresholds; one could well devote the rest of the discussion to such factors as influence decision making of entrepreneurs or suppliers. However, apart from the evident fact that parameters will take on other numerical values, nothing contradicts the assumption that the schemes suggested by Huff (1960) and Wolpert (1965) are relevant not only for consumers but also for entrepreneurs and producers. Therefore, we will not further discuss central place concepts per se, but rather turn to some technical comments on how the notion of nonoptimal locations can be operationally included in our models.

Both Christaller (1933) and Lösch (1954) maintained that, provided actions were taken upon a homogeneous plain and in a society with constant spatial behavior parameters, the economic game between consumers and suppliers would result in a state of equilibrium where all places were optimally distributed in a hexagonal network. Christaller (p. 63 ff.) arrived at this pattern inductively and without proof, while Lösch (p. 109 ff.) employed the concept of the demand cone to prove that central places were optimally distributed when located hexagonally.

Lösch's derivation has long been considered sufficient, but recently Dacey (1965 b, p. 112) commented that, although he finds Lösch's formulation suggestive, he can find "no precise statement of the locational conditions nor a subsequent demonstration that these conditions are satisfied by a hexagonal structure." Therefore, instead of determining the system of market areas in an areal and economic equilibrium system, he reformulated the geometry of central place systems into a purely mathematical problem, specified as the one of finding the tesselation of Dirichlet regions in which packing density is maximized.[18] Dacey also introduced the concept of Brillouin zones, extensively used in studies of physical waves and crystals to show that the hexagonal lattice in central place theory is a consequence of maximizing packing density.

It must be pointed out, though, that hexagonal place patterns are entirely theoretical solutions based on assumptions which are unrealistic both from the spatial and from the behavioristic point of view. Actually, the influence of institutional, personal, and environmental factors is so important that optimal spatial arrangements will rarely appear in reality. We will therefore turn to such non optimal spatial patterns, specifically focusing on the technique of cell counting.[19]

Deviations from the Hexagonal Network

Dacey (1964 c, 1964 d, 1965 a, 1966) has noted that nonoptimal, nonhexagonal place patterns may emerge even in areas which approach the homogeneous plain of theory. In the American Midwest, for instance, it is reasonable to hypothesize that the Land Survey Act not only influenced administrative areas and the partition of land between owners but also had a secondary effect on the location of service centers. It seems necessary to modify the structure of the underlying regular lattice. At the same time, it appears plausible that processes governing location of county seats are different from those which determine location of other places. This hypothesis led Dacey (1964 d) to derive a probability law for location of urban places in an inhomogeneous area as:

$$P(x) = \frac{(1-p)e^{-m}m^{x}}{x!} + \frac{pe^{-m}m^{(x-1)}}{(x-1)!} \qquad (x = 0, 1, \ldots) \qquad (21)$$

18. A primitive Dirichlet region is a mathematical concept defined as a polygon that contains a lattice point at its center and every point of the plane closer to that lattice point than to any other lattice point. Dirichlet regions become important for the spatial analyst mainly because they are identical with market areas in central place theory.

19. This has been treated by Olsson (1966). The traditional type of cell count analysis may be applied to such phenomena as can also be approximated as points on a map. Over that map, a grid of cells is placed and the number of points in each cell is observed. These observed frequencies are then compared with generated frequencies based on theoretical distribution functions, usually derived from the theory of generalized Poisson processes. The technique was originally developed by plant ecologists; it is usually necessary to supplement it with nearest neighbor and contiguity analyses.

where $P(x)$ stands for the probability that a county has x urban places, while p and m are parameters estimated as:

$$\hat{p} = \frac{z}{c} \quad \text{and} \quad \hat{m} = \frac{N-z}{c} \tag{22}$$

with:

z = the number of county seats in the sample (a place can be included in the sample only if it is classified as urban);
N = the total number of places in the sample; and
c = the number of counties in the sample. For (21) to hold, c must be large and all counties must be relatively homogeneous and of equal size.

Expression (21) is a double Poisson distribution; two random processes are assumed to be at work concomitantly. When added, these will give a more regular than random place pattern. The second term in (21) determines the distribution of county seats among counties by assuming that each county has an equal probability of receiving a county seat, but also that a county can never have more than one county seat. Formalized:

$$P(y=0) = 1 - z/c \tag{23a}$$

$$P(y=1) = z/c \tag{23b}$$

$$P(y \neq 0, 1) = 0 \tag{23c}$$

where $P(y)$ equals the probability that a county has y county seats.

Analogously, the first term in expression (21) determines the distribution of urban places other than county seats. As in the second term, it has been assumed that each county has an equal probability of receiving a place; only no limit is put to the number of noncounty seat places which can be assigned a county. It is immediately seen that the first term in (21) vanishes if $p = 1$, while the second term vanishes when $p = 0$. This makes it possible to interpret p as a measure towards evenness: if $p = 0$, the distribution is completely random, if $p = 1$ it is more regular than random (though even where p exactly equals 1 the distribution is not completely regular; though each county has been assigned a county seat, remaining places have still been distributed randomly).

Expression (21) demonstrates how the cell counting technique can be slightly reformulated and successfully applied to new problems. Its accuracy has been tested, and in Iowa—an area approaching homogeneity—the agreement between theoretical and observed distributions was almost perfect. This agreement is significant in that Lösch used Iowa as a type of laboratory for deriving and testing his model, and even more so inasmuch as Dacey's model is not primarily a central place model but rather a political model demonstrating how political factors may cause otherwise random place distributions to become more regular.

Dacey (1966) has suggested that expression (21), which only considers place distributions in homogeneous areas, can be shown to be a special case of another model, applicable also to inhomogeneous areas. It has long been known that a negative binomial distribution will be obtained for the universe, if that universe consists of several Poisson distributions with varying means.[20] More exactly, Greenwood and Yule (1920) demonstrated that the negative binomial:

$$P(x) = \binom{x+k-1}{k} p^k (1-p)^x \qquad (x = 0, 1, 2, \ldots) \tag{24}$$

arises if the Poisson parameter, i.e., m in (21) or, more generally, the mean or λ in the Poisson expression:

$$P(x) = \frac{e^{-\lambda}\lambda^x}{x!} \tag{25}$$

varies according to the gamma or Pearson Type III distribution, equation (8) above, with $2k$ degrees of freedom. As before, $P(x)$ in (24) and (25) may denote the probability of obtaining x places in a county.

Equation (24) contains two parameters, p and k.[21] If a somewhat unsatisfactory method of moments is used, then:

$$\hat{p} = \frac{\bar{x}}{S(x)} \tag{26a}$$

and:

$$\hat{k} = \frac{\bar{x}\hat{p}}{(1-\hat{p})} = \frac{(\bar{x}^2)}{S(x) - \bar{x}} \tag{26b}$$

where x stands for the mean of the observed distribution, and $S(x)$ represents the variance. It is clear, then, that a negative binomial distribution will be obtained for the whole area if the mean of a truly

20. See for instance: Feller (1943, and 1957, p. 263); and Bartlett (1960, p. 16, and 1962, p. 55).

21. Estimated in several ways discussed; see for example: Haldene (1941); Anscombe (1950); Evans (1953); Robinson (1954); Katti and Gurland (1962); and Williamson and Bretherton (1964).

random (Poisson) distribution varies according to Pearson Type III with $2k$ degrees of freedom. The equivalent of (21) for an inhomogeneous area could therefore be specified by Dacey (1966, p. 176) as:

$$P(x) = R\frac{(x+k-1)!}{x!(k-1)!}v^k(1-v)^x + S\frac{(x+k-2)!}{(x-1)!(k-1)!}v^k(1-v)^{(x-1)} \quad (27)$$

Apart from the assumption of homogeneity, all the above comments relative to expression (21) also apply to (27). Let us just note that the model was tested on a 10 percent sample of counties in the United States outside Standard Metropolitan Areas, and the agreement between observed and expected frequencies was satisfactory.

As noted equations (21) and (27) are important for the central place analyst mainly as a means of studying deviations from regular or hexagonal arrangements of places.[22] But these probability laws can only describe spatial patterns that are more regular than random, while the above discussion has made it clear that most phenomena are not really distributed in such a manner. Most patterns are in fact more clustered than random rather than being more regular than random. This requires mention of the most common of the clustered or contagious distribution functions.

One of the simplest of these distributions was originally derived by Thomas (1949) to describe the spatial distribution of a plant population in which the parent plants had been spread out randomly while offspring grew by root-development, a contagious process. Thomas showed that if the number of plants grows additively, the probability of obtaining x plants in a cell equals:

$$\left.\begin{aligned} P(x) &= e^{-m} && (x=0) \\ P(x) &= \sum_{r=1}^{x} \frac{m^r e^{-m}}{r!}\frac{(r\lambda)^{(x-r)}e^{-(r\lambda)}}{(x-r)!} && (x=1,2,\ldots,r,\ldots) \end{aligned}\right\} \quad (28)$$

The two parameters m and λ may be estimated in several ways.[23] These estimation techniques will not be discussed here, but it should

22. This is, of course, only one way in which such deviations may be analyzed; there exists a large body of literature on other techniques. Very relevant is the type of map transformations suggested by Tobler (1961, 1963), and used for instance by Getis (1963). The nearest neighbor technique seems promising (see: Dacey 1960 a, 1960 b, 1962, and Dacey and Tung, 1962), while the measure of shape, developed for instance by Bunge (1962, Ch. 3), Boyce and Clark (1964), and Hudson and Fowler (1966), should be applicable in analyses of market areas. Deviations from the hexagonal central place structure have, finally, concerned a number of writers interested in the "spacing" of central places. See, e.g.: King (1961 and 1962), Thomas (1962), and Olsson and Persson (1964).

23. See: Thomas (1949), Archibald (1950), Anscombe (1950), Thomson (1952), and Evans (1953).

be noted that Thomas gave the parameters a physical interpretation where:

m = the number of colonies or clusters per cell; and
λ = one less than the mean number of plants per colony or cluster.

A related distribution function, generally called the Polya-Aeppli distribution may be written:

$$\left.\begin{aligned} P(x) &= e^{-u} && (x=0) \\ P(x) &= e^{-u}p^{x}\sum_{r=1}^{x}\binom{x-1}{r-1}\frac{1}{r!}\left[\frac{u(1-p)}{p}\right]^{r} && (x=1,2,\ldots,r,\ldots) \end{aligned}\right\} \quad (29)$$

Methods for estimating the parameters u and p have been given, for instance, by Anscombe (1950) and Evans (1953). For our purposes, one need only note that the initial population of points (e.g., primary industries) are distributed randomly, while the number of contagious points (e.g., secondary industries) follows the geometric distribution. The parameters may be given a physical interpretation: thus u is the number of colonies or clusters per cell; and $(1-p)^{-1}$ is the mean number of individuals per colony or cluster.

If the total number of points grows in a multiplicative fashion, the Neyman Type A distribution will instead be applicable. This function was originally derived by Neyman (1939) and may be written in several alternative forms. One variation is:

$$\left.\begin{aligned} P(x) &= e^{-(m/a)(1-e^{-a})} && (x=0) \\ P(x) &= \frac{a^{x}}{x!}e^{-(m/a)}\sum_{r=0}^{\infty}\frac{r^{x}}{r!}\left[\frac{me^{-a}}{a}\right]^{r} && (x=1,2,\ldots,r,\ldots) \end{aligned}\right\} \quad (30)$$

Several ways have been developed to estimate parameters m and a.[24] Here it is sufficient to note the physical interpretation of these parameters: m/a is the number of colonies or clusters per cell; and a is the number of points per colony or cluster.

Compared with (28) and (29), (30) is probably the most useful; it has been applied in analyses of a number of phenomena; see the works of Neyman (1955), and Neyman and Scott (1957, 1959). But the negative binomial distribution, (24), has turned out to be even more valuable. It may seem puzzling that the negative binomial distribution is treated together with a family of contagious functions; as recalled, it was earlier used to describe a truly random distribution

24. See: Archibald (1948), Shenton (1949), Thomson (1952), Thompson (1954), Douglas (1955), and Katti and Gurland (1962).

where the mean of the different Poisson distributions varied in a specified way. It can be shown, however, that several other processes also may give rise to the negative binomial. For example, Bowen (1947), Quenouille (1949), Anscombe (1950), and Evans (1953), among others, have shown that it will arise if clusters are spread out randomly with the number of points per cluster following the logarithmic distribution. But this also demonstrates one of the main difficulties with cell count analysis; Feller (1943) and Anscombe (1950) have noted that it is sometimes impossible to tell which process gave rise to an observed distribution. It is necessary, therefore, to supplement cell counts with time studies in which the evolution of a pattern has been particularly considered.[25]

These difficulties were illustrated by Rogers (1964, 1965) who showed that the spatial distribution of shopping goods outlets in Stockholm could be fitted to the negative binomial. He suggested that two opposing processes may have been felt simultaneously; on the one hand he referred to the model of heterogeneous Poisson sampling, on the other hand to the model of randomly distributed colonies. The latter interpretation seems reasonable as retail firms may be hypothesized to gain from clustering with other firms selling the same products. The first interpretation is also plausible as retail outlets should be attracted to purchasing power and, if that is truly randomly distributed (but with varying means), the negative binomial would fit.

Rogers' studies also deserve attention in that he, following the plant ecologist Robinson (1954), noted that the exponent k in (24) can be interpreted as a measure of clustering: the variance of the negative binomial, $S(x)$, may be given as:

$$S(x) = \bar{x} + \frac{(\bar{x})^2}{k} \tag{31}$$

a rewriting of (26b). It must also be remembered that $\bar{x} = S(x)$ in the random or Poisson distribution, while distributions which are more regular than random have $\bar{x} > S(x)$, and those more clustered than random have $\bar{x} < S(x)$. It is immediately seen from (31) that as k approaches infinity, $S(x)$ tends to $\bar{x}$; it can be verified that the negative binomial in such cases converges to a Poisson distribution.[26] On the other hand, if k approaches zero from the positive side, the second

25. As noted by Archibald (1950), Curtis and McIntosh (1950), Skellam (1952), Evans (1952), Pielou (1957), Greig-Smith (1964, p. 83) and many others, the other main problem is that obtained fits are not independent of the size of the cells. This is not entirely disadvantageous, however, since it makes the technique particularly useful in analyses of spatial scale factors.

26. This was why (21) could be viewed as a special case of (27).

term in (31) approaches infinity and $S(x)$ gets larger and larger as compared to $\bar{x}$. This means of course that the smaller the k, the larger is the tendency for clustering. It agrees with our intuitive knowledge that Rogers (1965, p. 1100) computed $k = .1136$ for antique stores, $k = .4225$ for women's clothing stores, and $k = .4274$ for furniture stores.

Rogers also treated the distribution of convenience goods establishments, hypothesizing that these tend to repel each other and so will exhibit a spatial distribution which is more regular than random. However, convenience goods outlets (e.g., grocery stores and tobacconist shops) were also best fitted by a contagious distribution: more specifically by the Neyman Type *A*, (30) above. At a cursory examination, this could cause us to reject our hypothesis, but it must be realized that it was implicitly based on the assumption of a homogeneous plain and, if this assumption is violated, the regular pattern of places will of course be disturbed. Because of this, the conclusion that convenience goods outlets are clustered does not necessarily contradict the initial hypothesis. The opposite would instead be true if the underlying population distribution could also be approximated with the Neyman Type *A* or a related distribution function. It is of highest interest, therefore, that the spatial distribution of the Stockholm population could be satisfactorily fitted both to Neyman's Type *A* and to Thomas' double Poisson distributions.

Development of central place systems over time

As was shown above, cell count analysis can be useful as a means of detecting deviations from a theoretical location pattern. It was observed that different growth rates give rise to different distribution functions and, because of this, cell counts may also be used in studies of the evolution of spatial point patterns. Cell counts thus offer a method by which dynamic aspects may be introduced into central place models.

Most distribution functions can be related via physical urn models which specify how the number of points per cell is supposed to grow.[27] Knowledge of these growth rates was recently employed by Harvey (1965), who performed a cell count analysis of the maps of spatial innovations published by Hägerstrand (1953). Harvey tested several of these maps, finding that the negative binomial distribution persistently gave the best fit. He also noted that Thomas' double Poisson,

27. We noted in the previous paragraphs how the growth of a system is additive in Thomas' double Poisson, multiplicative in Neyman's Type *A*, geometric in Polya-Aeppli's, and logarithmic in the negative binomial distribution.

Polya-Aeppli, and the Neyman Type *A* functions all underestimated the frequencies in the tail of the distributions. This result is hardly surprising, since most innovations tend to grow in a logistic fashion; also logistic and logarithmic curves are closely parallel to the inflection point on the logistic. Provided there is no ceiling to the numbers accepting an innovation, the negative binomial should therefore be a good model. Under the restriction of a finite population, however, it can be ideal only up to the middle stages of the diffusion process.

But study of distribution functions is not the only way in which dynamic aspects may be introduced into central place models. Curry (1962) illustrates another approach: suggesting that the time factor in central place activities is the key to understanding of their geography. He claimed that the spatial pattern of service centers may be gainfully understood only through investigations of consumer behavior and its changes over time. Consistent with economic tradition, he assumed that consumers will make their purchases in the nearest center, but he added that the frequency of purchase for each good depends on the rate with which it is consumed and on the average level of stocks held at home. More specifically, he suggested that "the purchase of a good can be considered as an isolated event in a continuum of time so that, for a group of consumers, the number of the procurements of a good in unit time can be described by a Poisson distribution" (1962, p. 36). If this is so, the different curves could also represent different market areas; firms selling convenience goods having smaller market areas than firms selling goods normally bought once in a lifetime. This also makes it reasonable to suggest that each supplier must take cognizance of customer behavior and particularly of the number of goods normally bought each shopping trip. In essence, this brings down the supplier's problem to one of queuing and stocking policy. Instead of testing his ideas on empirical data, Curry employed a simulation approach by which it could be determined what repercussions his suggestions would have on the evolution of service centers and market area.

In summary then, Curry (1962) based his model of service centers on probability concepts derived from specific assumptions of human behavior. A related approach was used also in a more recent article (Curry, 1964). The spatial distribution of settlement, it was postulated, is governed by the law of randomness. In comparison with his first paper, it is interesting that he now (1964, p. 138) argued that such formulations are neutral as to rationality, since "every decision may be optimal from a particular point of view and the resulting actions as a whole may (yet) appear as random." Though Curry's paper raises many vital issues, our focus here will be on his attempt to relate the well-known rank-size or Zipf rule with the notion of entropy.[28]

The rank-size rule for a system of cities states:

$$P_1 = r(P_r)^q \tag{32}$$

or, in logarithmic form:

$$\log r = \log P_1 - q \log P_r \tag{33}$$

where

P_r = the population of the city of rank r;
P_1 = the population of the largest city, the city with rank 1; and
q = an empirically derived constant specifying the slope of the line in a double logarithmic diagram.[29]

As noted by Berry (1964 a, pp. 118–9), several distribution functions have been employed as approximations of this relationship, and, indirectly, these functions have also made it possible to arrive at conclusions about underlying processes. This is especially true about the Yule and lognormal distributions, which both can be shown to represent the steady state of the same stochastic process.[30] Other functions have also been tried as approximations of the rank-size relationship. Dacey (1964 a), for example, found the chi-square distribution gave a satisfactory fit.

In an earlier study, Berry (1961) investigated relationships between rank-size distributions and economic development for a number of countries; city-size distributions were found not to be related to economic development. Rosing (1966) came to a similar conclusion. Notwithstanding, there seems to be some doubt about this matter, and Berry (1964 a, p. 149), referring to Bell (1962) and Friedmann (1963), wrote that "additional studies have recently shown that many distributions with some degree of primacy take on more of a rank-size form as level of development and degree of urbanization increase." Boal and Johnson (1965) write in the same vein.

These comments suggest that a proper understanding of the rank-size rule might help to formulate a dynamic probability model

28. See also: Berry (1964 a, pp. 158 ff.). Meier (1962, ch. 8), on the other hand, discussed more generally how the notion of entropy together with other concepts from information theory may be used in studies of urban systems.

29. Olsson (1965 a, pp. 18–21) observed that the rank-size empirical regularity arises in many connections; income distributions, for example. Distribution of cities by population size has been analyzed, in addition to Zipf (1941, 1949), by Allen (1954), Stewart (1958), Moore (1959), Ward (1963), and others. Simon (1954) is a recent attempt to explain the rank-size regularity. For excellent overviews see: Berry and Garrison (1958 a) and Berry (1964 a).

30. The only difference is that the lognormal function assumes the growth to take place within a completely closed set of cities, while Yule's distribution arises if new towns are added at the lowest level.

of population settlement. This search for a better theory might be further aided by the concept of entropy; see Curry (1964).

Entropy is an outgrowth of the physical theory of thermodynamics. The first law of thermodynamics, the law of energy, states that all forms of energy are equivalent and interchangeable. The sum of total energy within a system is thus constant and unaffected by alterations in form. However, this law says nothing about the direction in which processes in nature are most likely to move, and it must therefore be supplemented by the second law, the law of entropy. This specifies the direction in which a closed system in disequilibrium will move in order to reach equilibrium: thus, energy moves from hotter to cooler bodies. This recognition enables us to define and compute physical entropy as:

$$S = c_v \log T + \frac{R}{m} \log v \qquad (34)$$

where:

S = the entropy;
v = the volume of a gas whose mass amounts to one unit;
c_v = the specific heat at constant volume;
T = the absolute temperature;
m = the molecular weight of the gas; and
R = the general gas constant.

It may be shown that if two systems with entropies S_1 and S_2 are brought together, the new entropy, S, becomes:

$$S = S_1 + S_2 \qquad (35)$$

The entropy of a closed physical system therefore tends to increase as long as the system has not yet reached equilibrium, and entropy may thus be taken as a measure of the degree of equalization reached within a system.[31] Since all processes are directed towards equalization, the entropy of a closed system can never decrease and the entropy of a system is maximized when the system is in equilibrium. It follows that, provided the second law of thermodynamics were a deterministic law, the concept of time could be defined and measured as the

31. To clarify: Reichenbach (1956, p. 53) asked his reader to consider "two equal quantities of the same gas which have different temperatures and are brought into thermal interaction by being put into adjacent containers. The heat flows through the walls from the gas of the higher temperature to that of lower temperature. According

increase. . . . . The temperature of both systems will finally assume a mean value; but the logarithm of the mean is larger than the mean of the logarithms, and the sum (35), taken after the temperature is compensated, is larger than the corresponding sum at the beginning."

direction towards higher entropy. However, in 1872, the Austrian physicist Ludwig Boltzmann found that the increase in entropy was not a deterministic but a statistical law. He argued that passage of heat from bodies with higher temperatures to bodies with lower temperatures should be understood as a statistical equalization of differences in molecular speed. This recognition enabled him to establish:

$$S = -k \sum_{i=1}^{n} p_i \log p_i \qquad \sum_{i=1}^{n} p_i = 1 \tag{36}$$

where:

p_i = the probability of finding an idealized physical system in the state i of n possible states; and
k = a constant (later named Boltzmann's constant).

By employing (36), the direction of physical processes may be interpreted as a statistical trend in which molecules are transformed from less probable to more probable states. It is self-evident that this interpretation leads to the conclusion that equilibrium is the most probable state.

But the law of entropy has concerned us here neither because of its physical merits nor because of its use in information theory.[32] Instead, it was presented because its socioeconomic analogue can further our understanding of the evolution of spatial patterns. Before this is demonstrated, it is only necessary to rewrite (36) as

$$S = k\left(p \log p - \sum_{i=1}^{n} p_i \log p_i\right) + \text{const.} \tag{37}$$

This reformulation of (36) is based on the probability law that the molecules in a container can be distributed among n possible states in P ways, such that:

$$P = \frac{p!}{p_1! \ldots . p_n!} \tag{38}$$

Using variants of (34) and (35), Curry (1964, pp. 144–5) noted that, given Z settlements, where Z_i has a population of i individuals, the number of ways in which N individuals can be distributed among settlements is determined by the same probability law as (38), i.e.:

$$P = \frac{Z!}{\prod_{i=0}^{N} Z!} \qquad (0 \leqq i \leqq N) \tag{39}$$

32. See, e.g., several articles in Dockx and Bernays (1965).

But it follows from (37) that a notion, conveniently termed entropy and denoted H, may be defined as:

$$H = \log P = Z \log Z - \Sigma Z_i \log Z_i \tag{40}$$

This expression is maximized when:

$$Z_i = (Z/N)e^{-(i/n)} \tag{41}$$

where:

$n = N/Z$, the mean population per settlement.

Since (41) is an exponential distribution, the same type of function as the rank-size rule (32), when (41) is rewritten as a cumulative function, it becomes

$$Z_{i \leq T} = T[1 - e^{-(i/n)}] \tag{42}$$

where:

T = the size of the largest city.

Under these circumstances, entropy is maximized when

$$H_{\max} = Z \log (\mathrm{eN}) \tag{43}$$

From the discussion above, it is evident that (43) represents the most probable or the equilibrium state of the system. But, according to Curry, it also corresponds to a situation in which, given the size of the largest city, the probability that the $(u+1)st$ city has a population $P_{(u+1)}$ is equal to q, where:

$$P = \frac{P_{(u+1)}}{P_{(u)}} \tag{44}$$

with:

$P_{(u)}$ = the population of the u largest city.

This ratio q is constant and does not vary with city rank.[33] Viewed in this way, (43) becomes equivalent to (32) or the rank-size rule. It also follows that a system of cities obeying the rank-size rule is in a state of equilibrium in which "entropy" has been maximized. It should be stressed, though, that this equilibrium is the result of a purely random process, and even if it is the most probable, it is in no way a determined state. It is for this reason that Berry and Garrison (1958 a, p. 90) and

33. Curry did not discuss this ratio, which may be compared to q in (32) and (33). It is noteworthy, therefore, that Calhoun (1957, p. 34) argued that optimal interaction within a system occurs when q equals -1.

Curry (1964, p. 145) argued that systems which deviate from the rank-size rule are worthy of more attention than are systems which follow.

If this is correct, it becomes very interesting to compare equilibrium solutions computed by the method of entropy with solutions computed otherwise. One way in which this might be done would be to apply a regular Markov chain analysis to city size distributions.[34] While the present writer knows of no study in which the rank-size rule for cities has been connected both with the law of entropy and with Markov chain analysis, the latter technique has been employed in several works related to central place theory.[35]

In summary then, we have demonstrated how the well-known rank-size distribution of cities may be entered as a useful submodel in a more general dynamic central place construct. Particular emphasis has been put on possible connections between the rank-size rule and steady state solutions derived through stochastic processes (those underlying the Yule and the lognormal frequency distributions) as well as via the concept of entropy and regular Markov chains.

But the rank size rule may be connected with still another dynamic concept. Beckmann (1958, pp. 246–8) proved its equivalence with the notion of allometric growth.[36] Such a model has been applied to geographic phenomena by Nordbeck (1965). The possibility of a similar relationship was also noted by Berry, Simmons, and Tennant (1963), Berry (1964 a), and Newling (1966), who further connected it with the hypothesis that intraurban population densities vary with distance from city center. This hypothesis, as originally expressed by Clark (1951), can be written:

$$D_x = D_0 e^{-bx} \tag{45}$$

or:

$$\log D_x = \log D_0 - bx \tag{46}$$

where:

D_x = the population density at distance x from city center;
D_0 = the extrapolated population density at city center; and
b = an empirically derived parameter, the "density gradient."

In several analyses, b has been shown to vary over time, much in the same manner as b in the gravity regression model, equation (2).

34. For general discussions of Markov chains, see, for example, Feller (1957), Kemeny and Snell (1959), Bharucha-Reid (1960), and Parzen (1962).

35. Brown (1963) analyzed diffusion of innovations, McGinnis and Pilger (1963) internal migration, Clark (1965) distribution of rental housing, and Fuguitt (1965) growth and decline of small towns.

36. The theory of allometric growth states that $y = ax^b$, where y stands for the relative growth of an organ and x stands for the growth of the entire body. In a general exposition, Boulding (1956 a) related allometric to other types of growth, concluding that the theories of growth, organization, and interaction are likely to constitute the main components of future general system theories.

Provided b in (45) and (46) is a negative exponential function of time, these variations can be expressed as follows—see Newling (1966, p. 214):

$$b_{t+n} = b_t e^{-c(t+n)} \tag{47}$$

where:

b_{t+n} = the density gradient at time $(t+n)$;
b_t = the density gradient at time t; and
c = a natural logarithm relating the change in the value of the density gradient to the passage of time.

From (45) and (47) it is now possible to deduce the rule of intraurban allometric growth as

$$(1+r_x) = (1+r_0)e^{gx} \tag{48}$$

where:

r_0 = the percentage rate of growth at city center;
r_x = the percentage rate of growth at distance x from city center; and
g = the "intraurban growth gradient," which measures the rate of change of the rate of growth with distance from city center.

Therefore Clark's formula (45) and the rank-size rule may be connected via the theory of allometric growth and thereby can become important tools in the formulation of a dynamic central place model. It should be noted, however, that no matter how appealing such a connection may seem, it brings into being a number of problems. This is so because (45) assumes population density to decrease symmetrically in all directions from the center: assuming a pattern of inner differentiation similar to the classic concentric zone theory. Since this theory is hardly realistic, it seems most plausible that equation (45) must be reformulated before it can be incorporated in an overall central place model. Recent work by Gurevich and Saushkin (1966) suggests directions for such a reformulation.

SUMMARY AND CONCLUSIONS

This paper first treated the classical central place model within a general theory of spatial interaction. At this point, it should only be reemphasized that today's spatial interaction models have focused mostly on the distance variable, biasing our knowledge somewhat. Future efforts should therefore be concentrated on the study of that type of behavior which gives rise to such distance variations.

Against this background, the paper next dwelt on the way intended rationality in human behavior could be operationally included in central place models. Attention was drawn to various derivations of the well-known hexagonal central place pattern, including its reformulation as a problem of maximizing packing density. It was then recognized how empirical place distributions tend to deviate from these theoretically optimal hexagonal networks; variants of the cell-counting technique were suggested as a means of introducing and analyzing such deviations.

The connections between cell counts and classical central place theory seem most evident in the case of the "more regular than random" distributions. However, most spatial distributions are, rather, "more clustered than random," and this recognition required a brief mention of a family of contagious distributions. In particular, it was noted that a number of distributions all may be satisfactorily fitted to the spatial distribution of central place functions. It was further pointed out that one of the main advantages of the cell counting technique is its firm anchoring in probability theory; this approach to location theory is preferable to one that is deterministic.

But the technique of cell counting may also prove helpful in the formulation of dynamic spatial models. This observation was followed in the last section by discussion of the way central place systems may be seen to develop over time. Specific attention was given to a number of probability models and to the problem of relating these models to each other: thus the rank-size or Pareto law can be treated as the steady state of a stochastic process. It was also shown how the concept of entropy and regular Markov chains may be used to compute statistical equilibrium solutions.

Finally, to draw some conclusions from the entire paper, it has persistently been argued that dynamic and probabilistic models should replace the classical central place theories. Such a reformulation has not yet been made. Meanwhile, however, the theorist has a host of valuable models at his disposal, and these may be entered as submodels into a more general simulation of urban systems. The utility of this approach was suggested by Garrison (1962), while Morrill (1962, 1963 b, 1965 a, and 1965 b) and others have demonstrated their use in practice. The characteristics of spatial simulations have recently been treated elsewhere.[37] Although it may seem strange to end one paper by referring to another, this appears to be the best solution at the present.

Simulation possesses at least four distinct features each of which satisfies certain needs of the central place theorist. First, the total

37. Malm, Olsson, and Wärneryd (1966). See, also, Wärneryd (1965 b, 1966).

simulation model is easily constructed as a set of submodels. Some of these submodels will almost certainly be variants of the formulations discussed in the main parts of the present paper. Second, simulations are, almost by definition, stochastic models in which an outcome depends on assigned probabilities and not on deterministic laws. This is important since the behavioristic assumptions underlying most deterministic models have been shown unrealistic. Third, simulation is an iterative procedure by which developments over time are readily analyzed. Again, such developments of model patterns may be governed by one or several of the mentioned submodels. Fourth and last, simulation is frequently used to study relationships too complex to be tied into exact mathematical expressions; if nothing else, the present paper has tried to make evident the complexity of central place relationships. As suggested in the introduction, only sophisticated systems analysis, of which simulation is a prominent tool, offers a feasible approach.

Although a general overview of the problem has been attempted, we must end with the same conclusion as Berry's (1964 a, p. 161): "we have very little understanding of how to put . . . different [submodels] together in more general models that are broad in scope. Sound models [as the ones mentioned above] are providing the building blocks, but maximum progress during the next decade awaits the architectural systemizer."

REFERENCES

ACKERMANN, EDWARD A. (1963): "Where is a Research Frontier?" *Annals of the Association of American Geographers*, vol. 53, pp. 429–440.

Ad hoc Committee on Geography (1965): "The Science of Geography." *National Research Council Publication*, no. 1277, Washington, D.C., National Academy of Sciences.

ADELMAN, IRMA G. (1958): "A Stochastic Analysis of the Size Distribution of Firms." *Journal of the American Statistical Association*, vol. 53, pp. 893–904.

AJO, REINO (1962): "An Approach to Demographical System Analysis." *Economic Geography*, vol. 38, pp. 359–371.

ALLEN, G. R. (1954): "The 'Courbe des Populations': A Further Analysis." *Bulletin of the Oxford University Institute of Statistics*, vol. 16, pp. 79–189.

ALLPASS, JOHN; ERIK AGERGÅRD; JESPER HARVEST; POUL ANKER OLSEN and SVEND SÖHOLT (1966): "Bycentre og aendringer i byfunktioners lokaliseringskrav." *Plan*, vol. 20, pp. 52–64.

ANDERSON, THEODORE R. (1955): "Intermetropolitan Migration: A Comparison of the Hypotheses of Zipf and Stouffer." *American Sociological Review*, vol. 20, pp. 287–291.

ANSCOMBE, F. J. (1948): "The Transformation of Poisson, Binomial, and Negative Binomial Data." *Biometrika*, vol. 35, pp. 246–254.

——— (1950): "Sampling Theory of the Negative Binomial and Logarithmic Series Distributions." *Biometrika*, vol. 37, pp. 358–382.

ARCHIBALD, E. E. A. (1948): "Plant Populations. I. A New Application of Neyman's Contagious Distribution." *Annals of Botany*, New Series, vol. 12, pp. 221–235.

——— (1950): "Plant Populations. II. The Estimation of the Number of Individuals per Unit Area of Species in Heterogeneous Plant Populations." *Annals of Botany*, New Series, vol. 14, pp. 7–21.

BARTLETT, M. S. (1960): *Stochastic Population Models*. Methuen, London.

——— (1962): *An Introduction to Stochastic Processes with Special Reference to Methods and Applications*. University Press, Cambridge.

BECKMANN, MARTIN J. (1958): "City Hierarchies and the Distribution of City Size." *Economic Development and Cultural Change*, vol. 6, pp. 243–248.

BELL, G. (1962): "Change in City Size Distribution in Israel." *Ekistics*, vol. 13, p. 98.

BERGSTEN, KARL-ERIK (1951): *Sydsvenska fodelseortsfält*. Gleerups Förlag, Lund.

BERRY, BRIAN J. L. (1961): "City Size Distributions and Economic Development." *Economic Development and Cultural Change*, vol. 9, pp. 573–587.

——— (1964 a): "Cities as Systems within Systems of Cities." *Papers and Proceedings of the Regional Science Association*, vol. 13, pp. 147–163 [Selection 10 of this volume].

——— (1964 b): "Research Frontiers in Urban Geography." In *The Study of Urbanization*, ed. by Philip M. Hauser & Leo F. Schnore, John Wiley, New York, pp. 403–430.

——— & WILLIAM L. GARRISON (1958 a): "Alternate Explanations of Urban Rank-Size Relationships." *Annals of the Association of American Geographers*, vol. 48, pp. 83–91.

——— (1958 b): "A Note on Central Place Theory and the Range of a Good." *Economic Geography*, vol. 34, pp. 304–311.

——— (1958 c): "Recent Developments of Central Place Theory." *Papers and Proceedings of the Regional Science Association*, vol. 4, pp. 107–120 [Selection 8 of this volume].

——— & ALLEN PRED (1961): *Central Place Studies: A Bibliography of Theory and Applications*. Supplemented 1965 by H. G. Barnum, R. Kasperson, & S. Kiuchi. Regional Science Research Institute, Philadelphia, Pa.

———, JAMES W. SIMMONS & ROBERT J. TENNANT (1963): "Urban Population Densities: Structure and Change." *Geographical Review*, vol. 53, pp. 389–405.

VON BERTALANFFY, LUDWIG (1951): "General System Theory: A New Approach to the Unity of Science." *Human Biology*, vol. 23, pp. 303–361.

——— (1962): "General System Theory: A Critical Review." *General Systems*, vol. 7, pp. 1–20.

BHARUCHA-REID, A. T. (1960): *Elements of the Theory of Markov Processes and Their Applications*. McGraw-Hill, New York.

BOAL, F. W. & D. B. JOHNSON (1965): "The Rank-Size Curve: A Diagnostic Tool?" *Professional Geographer*, vol. 17, pp. 21–23.

BOULDING, KENNETH E. (1956 a): "Toward a General Theory of Growth." *General Systems*, vol. 1, pp. 66–75.

——— (1956 b): "General Systems Theory: The Skeleton of Science." *Management Science*, vol. 2, pp. 197–208.

BOYCE, RONALD R. & WILLIAM A. V. CLARK (1964): "The Concept of Shape in Geography." *Geographical Review*, vol. 44, pp. 561–572.

BOWEN, M. G. (1947): "Population Distribution of the Beet Leafhopper in Relation to Experimental Field-Plot Layout." *Journal of Agricultural Research*, vol. 75, pp. 259–278.

BRIGHT, MARGARET L. & DOROTHY S. THOMAS (1941): "Interstate Migration and Intervening Opportunities." *American Sociological Review*, vol. 6, pp. 773–783.

BUNGE, WILLIAM (1962): *Theoretical Geography*. Gleerups Förlag, Lund.

CALHOUN, JOHN B. (1957): "Social Welfare as a Variable in Population Dynamics." *Cold Spring Harbor Symposia on Quantitative Biology*, vol. 22, pp. 339–356.

CARROLL, J. DOUGLAS & HOWARD W. BEVIS (1957): "Predicting Local Travel in Urban Regions." *Papers and Proceedings of the Regional Science Association*, vol. 3, pp. 183–197.

CARROTHERS, GERALD A. P. (1956): "An Historical Review of the Gravity and Potential Concepts of Human Interaction." *Journal of the American Institute of Planners*, vol. 22, pp. 94–102.

CAVALLI-SFORZA, L. (1962): "The Distribution of Migration Distances: Models and Applications to Genetics." In "Les déplacements humaines," ed. by Jean Sutter. *Entretiens de Monaco en Sciences Humaines*, Première session.

CHORLEY, RICHARD J. (1962): "Geomorphology and General Systems Theory." *Geological Survey Professional Paper*, No. 500-B.

——— (1964): "Geography and Analogue Theory." *Annals of the Association of American Geographers*, vol. 54, pp. 127–137.

CHRISTALLER, WALTER (1933): *Die zentralen Orte in Süddeutschland*. Gustav Fischer Verlag, Jena.

CLAESON, CLAES-FREDRIK (1964): "En korologisk publikanalys. Framställning av demografiska gravitationsmodeller med tillämpning vid omlandsbestämming på koordinatkarta." *Geografiska Annaler*, vol. 46, pp. 1–130.

——— (1966): "Gravitationsmodellen." In "Meddelande från ett simuleringssymposium." ed. by Gunnar Olsson. *Forskningsrapporter från Kulturgeografiska Institutionen*, Uppsala Universitet, No. 6, pp. 19–26.

CLARK, COLIN (1951): "Urban Population Densities." *Journal of the Royal Statistical Society*, Ser. A, vol. 114, pp. 490–496.

CLARK, WILLIAM A. V. (1965): "Markov Chain Analysis in Geography: An Application to the Movement of Retail Housing Areas." *Annals of the Association of American Geographers*, vol. 55, pp. 351–359.

CONVERSE, P. D. (1949): "New Laws of Retail Gravitation." *Journal of Marketing*, vol. 14, pp. 379–384.

CURRY, LESLIE (1962): "The Geography of Service Centres within Towns: The Elements of an Operational Approach." In *Proceedings of the IGU Symposium in Urban Geography, Lund 1960*, ed. by Knut Norborg. Gleerups Förlag, Lund, pp. 31–53.

——— (1964): "The Random Economy: An Exploration in Settlement Theory." *Annals of the Association of American Geographers*, vol. 54, pp. 138–146.

CURTIS, J. T. & R. P. MCINTOSH (1950): "The Interrelations of Certain Analytic and Synthetic Phytosociological Characters." *Ecology*, vol. 31, pp. 434–455.

DACEY, MICHAEL F. (1960 a): "The Spacing of River Towns." *Annals of the Association of American Geographers*, vol. 50, pp. 59–61.

——— (1960 b): "A Note on the Derivation of Nearest Neighbor Distances." *Journal of Regional Science*, vol. 2, pp. 81–87.

——— (1962): "Analysis of Central Place and Point Patterns by a Nearest Neighbor Method." In *Proceedings of the IGU Symposium in Urban Geography, Lund 1960* ed. by Knut Norborg. Gleerups Förlag, Lund, pp. 55–75.

——— (1963): "*An Observation in the Asby Area.*" Unpublished manuscript, Department of Regional Science, University of Pennsylvania.

——— (1964 a): "*Some Observations on Place Population.*" Mimeographed, Department of Regional Science, University of Pennsylvania.

——— (1964 b): "A Family of Density Functions of Lösch's Measurements on Town Distribution." *Professional Geographer*, vol. 16, pp. 5–7.

——— (1964 c): "Imperfections in the Uniform Plane." *Discussion Paper*, Michigan Inter-University Community of Mathematical Geographers, No. 4.

——— (1964 d): "Modified Probability Law for Point Pattern More Regular than Random." *Annals of the Association of American Geographers*, vol. 54, pp. 559–565.

——— (1965 a): "Order Distance in an Inhomogeneous Random Point Pattern." *Canadian Geographer*, vol. 9, pp. 144–153.

——— (1965 b): "The Geometry of Central Place Theory." *Geografiska Annaler*, vol. 47, Ser. B, pp. 111–124.

——— (1966): "A Compound Probability Law for a Pattern More Dispersed than Random and with Areal Inhomogeneity." *Economic Geography*, vol. 42, pp. 172–179.

——— & Tze Hsiung Tung (1962): "The Identification of Randomness in Point Patterns." *Journal of Regional Science*, vol. 4, pp. 83–96.

Dockx, S. & P. Bernays, ed. (1965): *Information and Prediction in Science.* Academic Press, New York.

Douglas, J. B. (1955): "Fitting the Neyman Type A (Two Parameter) Distribution." *Biometrics*, vol. 11, pp. 149–173.

Ellwood, Leon W. (1954): "Estimating Potential Volume of Proposed Shopping Centers." *The Appraisal Journal*, vol. 22, pp. 581–589.

Evans, P. A. (1953): "Experimental Evidence Concerning Contagious Distributions in Ecology." *Biometrika*, vol. 40, pp. 186–211.

Evans, Francis C. (1952): "The Influence of Size of Quadrat on the Distributional Patterns of Plant Populations." *Contributions from the Laboratory of Vertebrate Biology*, No. 54.

Feller, William (1943): "On a General Class of 'Contagious' Distributions." *Annals of Mathematical Statistics*, vol. 14, pp. 389–400.

——— (1957): *An Introduction to Probability Theory and Its Applications. Volume I.* John Wiley, New York.

Fisher, R. A. (1941): "The Negative Binomial Distribution." *Annals of Eugenics*, vol. 11, pp. 182–187.

Folger, John (1953): "Some Aspects of Migration in the Tennessee Valley." *American Sociological Review*, Vol. 18, pp. 253–260.

Friedmann, John (1963): "Economic Growth and Urban Structure in Venezuela." *Cuadernos de la Sociedad Venezolana de Planificacion*, Special Issue.

Fuguitt, Glenn W. (1965): "The Growth and Decline of Small Towns as a Probability Process." *American Sociological Review*, vol. 30, pp. 403–411.

Galle, Omer R. & Karl E. Taeuber (1966): "Metropolitan Migration and Intervening Opportunities." *American Sociological Review*, vol. 31, pp. 5–13.

Garrison, William L. (1956): "Estimates of the Parameters of Spatial Interaction." *Papers and Proceedings of the Regional Science Association*, vol. 2, pp. 280–288.

——— (1962): "Toward Simulation Models of Urban Growth and Development." In *Proceedings of the IGU Symposium in Urban Geography, Lund, 1960*, ed. by Knut Norborg. Gleerups Förlag, Lund, pp. 91–108.

GETIS, ARTHUR (1963): "The Determination of the Location of Retail Activities with the Use of a Map Transformation." *Economic Geography*, vol. 39, pp. 14–32.

GODLUND, SVEN (1954): *Busstrafikens framväxt och funktion i de urbana influensfälten*. Gleerups Förlag, Lund.

GOOSENS, M. (1963): "L'organisation du Nord-Est de la Belgique. Confrontation de quelques méthodes." *Bulletin de la Société d'Etudes Geographiques*, Tome 32, pp. 93–94.

GREENWOOD, M. & G. U. YULE (1920): "An Inquiry into the Nature of Frequency Distributions Representative of Multiple Happenings with Particular Reference to the Occurrence of Multiple Attacks of Disease or of Repeated Accidents." *Journal of the Royal Statistical Society*, vol. 83, pp. 255–279.

GREIG-SMITH, P. (1964): *Quantitative Plant Ecology*. Butterworths, London.

GUREVICH, B. L. & YU. G. SAUSHKIN (1966): "The Mathematical Method in Geography." *Soviet Geography*, vol. 7, No. 4, pp. 3–35.

HALD, ANDERS (1952): "*Statistical Theory with Engineering Applications*." John Wiley, New York.

HALDENE, J. D. S. (1941): "The Fitting of Binomial Distributions." *Annals of Eugenics*, vol. 11, pp. 179–181.

HARRIS, BRITTON (1964): "A Note on the Probability of Interaction at a Distance." *Journal of Regional Science*, vol. 5, pp. 31–35.

HART, P. E. & S. J. PRAIS (1956): "The Analysis of Business Concentration: A Statistical Approach." *Journal of the Royal Statistical Society*, Ser. A, vol. 119, pp. 150–181.

HARVEY, DAVID (1965): "Geographic Processes and the Analysis of Point Patterns: Testing Models of Diffusion by Quadrat Sampling." Mimeographed, Departments of Geography, University of Bristol and The Pennsylvania State University.

HELVIG, MAGNE (1964): *Chicago's External Truck Movements: Spatial Interaction Between the Chicago Area and Its Hinterland*. Department of Geography, University of Chicago, Chicago, Ill.

HODGE, GERALD (1965): "The Prediction of Trade Center Viability in the Great Plains." *Papers and Proceedings of the Regional Science Association*, vol. 15, pp. 87–115.

HOTELLING, HAROLD (1929): "Stability in Competition." *Economic Journal*, vol. 39, pp. 41–57.

HUDSON, JOHN C. & PHILLIP M. FOWLER (1966): "The Concept of Pattern in Geography." *Discussion Paper Series*, Department of Geography, University of Iowa, No. 1.

HUFF, DAVID L. (1960): "A Topographical Model of Consumer Space Preference." *Papers and Proceedings of the Regional Science Association*, vol. 6, pp. 159–173.

——— (1961): "Ecological Characteristics of Consumer Behavior." *Papers and Proceedings of the Regional Science Association*, vol. 7, pp. 19–28.

——— (1963): "A Probabilistic Analysis of Shopping Center Trade Areas." *Land Economics*, vol. 39, pp. 81–90.

HÄGERSTRAND, TORSTEN (1953): *Innovationsförloppet ur korologisk synpunkt*. Gleerups Förlag, Lund.

——— (1965 b): "The Negro Ghetto: Problems and Alternatives." *Geographical Review*, vol. 55.

MURDIE, ROBERT A. (1965): "Cultural Differences in Consumer Travel." *Economic Geography*, vol. 41.

NEWLING, BRUCE E. (1966): "Urban Growth and Spatial Structure: Mathematical Models and Empirical Evidence." *Geographical Review*, vol. 56, pp. 213–225.
NEYMAN, JERZY (1939): "On a New Class of 'Contagious' Distributions." *Annals of Mathematical Statistics*, vol. 10, pp. 35–57.
——— (1955): "Sur la théorie probabiliste des amas de galaxies et la Verification de l'expansion de l'universe." *Annales de l'Institut Henri Poincaré*, Tome 14, pp. 201–244.
——— & ELISABETH L. SCOTT (1957): "On a Mathematical Theory of Populations Conceived as Conglomerations of Clusters." *Cold Spring Harbor Symposia on Quantitative Biology*, vol. 22, pp. 109–120.
——— (1959): "Stochastic Models of Population Dynamics." *Science*, vol. 130, pp. 303–308.
NORDBECK, STIG (1965): "The Law of Allometric Growth." *Discussion Paper*, Michigan Inter-University Community of Mathematical Geographers, No. 7.
OLSSON, GUNNAR (1965 a): *Distance and Human Interaction: A Review and Bibliography*. Regional Science Research Institute, Philadelphia, Pa.
——— (1965 b): "Distance and Human Interaction: A Migration Study." *Geografiska Annaler*, vol. 47, Ser. B, pp. 3–43.
——— (1965 c): "Deterministiska och stokastiska interaktionsmodeller." In "Meddelande från ett symposium i teoretisk samhällsgeografi," ed. by Gunnar Olsson & Olof Wärneryd. *Forskningsrapporter från Kulturgeografiska Institutionen*, Uppsala Universitet, No. 1, pp. 6–14.
——— (1965 d): "Deductive and Inductive Approaches to Model Formulation." Paper presented at the First Scandinavian-Polish Regional Science Seminar, Szczecin.
——— (1966): "Beskrivning och testning av rumsliga simuleringsresultat." In "Meddelande från ett simuleringssymposium," ed. by Gunnar Olsson. *Forskningsrapporter fran Kulturgeografiska Institutionen*, Uppsala Universitet, No. 6, pp. 28–67.
——— & ÅKE PERSSON (1964): "The Spacing of Central Places in Sweden." *Papers and Proceedings of the Regional Science Association*, vol. 12, pp. 87–93.
PARZEN, EMANUEL (1962): *Stochastic Processes*. Holden-Day, San Francisco.
PIELOU, E. C. (1957): "The Effect of Quadrat Size on the Estimation of the Parameters of Neyman's and Thomas' Distributions." *Journal of Ecology*, vol. 45, pp. 31–47.
PORTER, HERMAN (1964): "Application of Intercity Intervening Opportunity Models to Telephone, Migration, and Highway Data." Unpublished PhD-dissertation, Department of Geography, Northwestern University.
PORTER, R. (1956): "Approach to Migration Through Its Mechanism." *Geografiska Annaler*, vol. 38, pp. 317–343.
QUENOUILLE, M. H. (1949): "A Relation Between the Logarithmic, Poisson, and Negative Binomial Series." *Biometrics*, vol. 5, pp. 162–164.
RAY, MICHAEL D. (1965): *Market Potential and Economic Shadow: A Quantitative Analysis of Industrial Location in Southern Ontario*. Department of Geography, University of Chicago, Chicago, Ill.
REICHENBACH, HANS (1956): *The Direction of Time*. University of California Press, Berkeley, Calif.
REILLY, WILLIAM J. (1931): *The Law of Retail Gravitation*. Knickerbrocker Press, New York.
ROBINSON, P. (1954): "The Distribution of Plant Populations." *Annals of Botany*, New Series, vol. 18, pp. 35–45:

Rogers, Andrei (1964): "A Stochastic Analysis of Intraurban Retail Spatial Structure." Unpublished PhD-dissertation, University of North Carolina.

——— (1965): "A Stochastic Analysis of the Spatial Clustering of Retail Establishments." *Journal of the American Statistical Association*, vol. 60, pp. 1094–1103.

Rosing, Kenneth E. (1966): "A Rejection of the Zipf Model (Rank-Size Rule) in Relation to City Size." *Professional Geographer*, vol. 18, pp. 75–82.

Rushton, Gerard (1966): *Spatial Pattern of Grocery Purchases by the Iowa Rural Population*. Bureau of Business and Economic Research, University of Iowa, Iowa City, Iowa.

Schneider, Morton (1959): "Gravity Models and Trip Distribution Theory." *Papers and Proceedings of the Regional Science Association*, vol. 5, pp. 51–56.

Shenton, L. R. (1949): "On the Efficiency of the Method of Moments and Neyman's Type A Distribution." *Biometrika*, vol. 36, pp. 450–454.

Simon, Herbert A. (1952): "A Behavioral Model of Rational Choice." *Quarterly Journal of Economics*, vol. 69, pp. 99–118.

——— (1955): "On a Class of Skew Distribution Functions." *Biometrika*, vol. 42, pp. 425–440.

——— (1957): *Models of Man*. John Wiley, New York.

——— (1963): "Economics and Psychology." In *Psychology: A Study of Science*, ed. by Sigmund Koch. McGraw-Hill, New York.

Skellam, J. G. (1953): "Studies in Statistical Ecology. I. Spatial Pattern." *Biometrika*, vol. 39, pp. 346–362.

Smith, D. M. (1966): "A Theoretical Framework for Geographical Studies of Industrial Location." *Economic Geography*, vol. 42, pp. 95–113.

Snedecor, George W. (1956): *Statistical Methods Applied to Experiments in Agriculture and Biology*. Iowa State University Press, Ames, Iowa.

Statens Offentliga Utredningar (1961): *Principer för en ny kommunindelning. Betänkande avgivet av indelningssakkunniga*. No. 9. Esselte, Stockholm.

Stewart, Charles T., Jr. (1958): "The Size and Spacing of Cities." *Geographical Review*, vol. 48, pp. 222–245.

——— (1960): "Migration as a Function of Population and Distance." *American Sociological Review*, vol. 25, pp. 347–356.

Stouffer, Samuel A. (1940): "Intervening Opportunities: A Theory Relating Mobility and Distance." *American Sociological Review*, vol. 5, pp. 845–867.

——— (1960): "Intervening Opportunities and Competing Migrants." *Journal of Regional Science*, vol. 2, pp. 1–26.

Strodtbeck, Fred L. (1949): "Equal Opportunity Intervals: A Contribution to the Method of Intervening Opportunity Analysis." *American Sociological Review*, vol. 14, pp. 490–497.

——— (1950): "Population, Distance, and Migration From Kentucky." *Sociometry*, vol. 13, pp. 123–130.

Sweet, Frank H. (1964): "An Error Parameter for the Reilly-Converse Law of Retail Gravitation." *Journal of Regional Science*, vol. 5, pp. 69–72.

Taaffe, Edward J. (1956): "Air Transportation and United States Urban Distribution." *Geographical Review*, vol. 46, pp. 219–238.

——— (1959): "Trends in Airline Passenger Traffic: A Geographic Case Study." *Annals of the Association of American Geographers*, vol. 49, pp. 393–408.

——— (1962): "The Urban Hierarchy: An Air Passenger Definition." *Economic Geography*, vol. 38, pp. 1–14.

Thomas, Edwin N. (1962): "The Stability of Distance-Population-Size Relationships for Iowa from 1900–1950." In *Proceedings of the IGU Symposium in Urban Geography, Lund 1960*, ed. by Knut Norborg. Gleerups Förlag, Lund, pp. 13–29.

THOMAS, MARJORIE (1949): "A Generalization of Poisson's Binomial Limit for Use in Ecology." *Biometrika*, vol. 36, pp. 18–25.

THOMAN, RICHARD S. (1965): "Some Comments on the Science of Geography." *Professional Geographer*, vol. 17, pp. 8–10.

THOMPSON, DONALD J. (1966): "Future Directions in Retail Area Research." *Economic Geography*, vol. 42, pp. 1–18.

THOMPSON, H. R. (1954): "A Note on Contagious Distributions." *Biometrika*, vol. 41, pp. 268–271.

THOMSON, GEORGE W. (1952): "Measures of Plant Aggregation Based on Contagious Distribution." *Contributions from the Laboratory of Vertebrate Biology*, No. 53.

TOBLER, WALDO R. (1961): "Map Transformations of Geographic Space." Unpublished PhD-dissertation, Department of Geography, University of Washington.

——— (1963): "Geographic Area and Map Projections." *Geographical Review*, vol. 53, pp. 59–78.

TOUMINEN, OIVA (1949): "Das Einflussgebiet der Stadt Turku im System der Einflussgebiete SW-Finnlands." *Fennia*, vol. 71, No. 5.

VOORHEES, ALAN M. (1955). "A General Theory of Traffic Movement." *Proceedings of the Institute of Traffic Engineers*, pp. 46–56.

WARD, BENJAMIN (1963): "City Structure and Interdependence." *Papers and Proceedings of the Regional Science Association*, vol. 10, pp. 207–221.

WILLIAMSON, ERIC and MICHAEL H. BRETHERTON (1964): *Tables of the Negative Binomial Distribution*. John Wiley, New York.

WOLPERT, JULIAN (1964): "The Decision Process in Spatial Context." *Annals of the Association of American Geographers*, vol. 54, pp. 537–558.

——— (1965): "Behavioral Aspects of the Decision to Migrate." *Papers and Proceedings of the Regional Science Association*, vol. 15, pp. 159–169.

WÄRNERYD, OLOF (1965 a): "Interaktion mellan urbaniserade regioner. Ett bidrag till diskussionen och användningen av gravitationsmodellen." Unpublished FL-thesis, Department of Geography, University of Gothenburg.

——— (1965 b): "Simuleringsteknik." In "Meddelande från ett symposium i teoretisk samhällsgeografi," ed. by Gunnar Olsson & Olof Wärneryd. *Forskningsrapporter från Kulturgeografiska Institutionen*, Uppsala Universitet, No. 1, pp. 38–43.

——— (1966): "Simulering inom geografin: En introduktion." In "Meddelande från ett simuleringssymposium," ed. by Gunnar Olsson. *Forskningsrapporter från Kulturgeografiska Institutionen*, Uppsala Universitet, No. 6, pp. 1–18.

Zipf, George K. (1941): *National Unity and Disunity*. Principia Press, Bloomington, Indiana.

——— (1949): *Human Behavior and the Principle of Least Effort*. Addison-Wesley, Cambridge, Mass.

PART III URBAN ECONOMIC DEVELOPMENT

12

G. MANNERS

Urban Expansion in the United States

During the decade 1950–60 the American population grew 18.5 percent. As a result of a high birth rate coupled with a steadily falling death rate this figure was considerably higher than it had been during the previous decades, although it still represented a slower rate of population increase than had persisted throughout the immigrant decades of the nineteenth century. The rural areas of America, however, in spite of their much higher birth rates than the country as a whole had a relatively stable population. This resulted from the persistent migration of people to the country's metropolitan areas, and the growing preference for living in cities and their suburbs. The magnetic effect of urban America lay mainly in its wide range of economic and social opportunities; however, the increasing social preference for an urban way of life, and the over-supply of labor in American agriculture were also influential. This increasing urbanisation of a rapidly expanding population, therefore, can be regarded as the first of three principal elements in the urban expansion of the United States. Projecting current trends forward, Pickard[1] has estimated that by the year 2000, the American population will be 320 million and that nearly two-thirds of these people will be located in three major zones of super-metropolitan growth, in the Northeast from the Atlantic to the Great Lakes, in California and in Florida. These three zones comprise a mere 17 percent of the country's land area.

A second aspect of urban expansion is the rather faster rate of urban growth in the 'newer' metropolitan areas of the West and South as compared with their 'older' counterparts in the East and North. Although the geographical distribution of the American population has remained remarkably stable since the turn of the century, changes have quickened since 1945. Between 1950 and 1960 the fastest rates of population increase in the United States were away from the 'traditional' centres of population in the manufacturing belt. New and reassessed resources, such as natural gas, metallic minerals and sunshine, have pulled people to the West and South, and as a consequence

1. J. P. Pickard, *Metropolitanization of the United States* (Washington, D.C. 1959), p. 30 *et seq.*

Reprinted from Urban Studies *2 (1965), 51–66, by permission of the publishers and the author.*

the economic colonialism of the Northeast is crumbling fast. Percentage rates of growth are deceptive, but it cannot be without significance that the twenty fastest-growing Standard Metropolitan Statistical Areas[2] between 1950 and 1960 were all in the West and South. Meanwhile the older industrial areas of New England, and the coal and steel communities of Pennsylvania and West Virginia, all lost people. Thus, whilst the population of California grew by 48 percent and that of Florida by 79 percent—both expansions were strongly influenced by large-scale migrations into these States—the number of people living in the manufacturing belt increased by only 20–25 percent. Projecting these trends of inter-regional population growth forward to the year 2000 (see Table 1), Pickard has estimated that Southern

TABLE 1 Distribution of U.S. population, by regions, 1910, 1956 and 2000 (mill.)

REGION	1910	1956	2000
Atlantic metropolitan	22.6	39.6	67.5
Great Lakes—Midwest metropolitan	24.0	43.9	84.0
Floridan metropolitan	0.8	3.8	14.5
Californian metropolitan	2.1	13.0	40.0
Metropolitan regions	49.5	100.3	206.0
North-east	0.7	0.7	0.8
South-east	18.1	27.5	42.0
Mid-South-west	7.5	13.6	24.5
Mid-West	11.0	13.3	18.2
West	4.4	9.5	20.5
South-west	0.6	2.3	8.0
Non-metropolitan regions	42.3	66.9	114.0
Total	91.8	167.2	320.0

Source: J. P. Pickard, *Metropolitanization of the United States*, Washington, D.C., 1959

California will have a population of 20 million and will begin to rival New York (23 million by that year); at the same time the urban areas of Florida will have a population of 11 million, a figure comparable with that of super-metropolitan Chicago at the end of the present century.[3]

The third aspect of urban expansion is the quickening rate of urban dispersion throughout America. This is partly the result of the growth of urban population which we have already noted, but it is in addition a response to powerful centrifugal forces within the urban economy. As metropolitan areas grow, so do their central areas decline in relative (and sometimes absolute) importance. Thus, between 1950

2. As defined by the U.S. Bureau of Census (see Figure 1).
3. Pickard, op. cit., p. 43.

and 1960 whilst the population living in the Standard Metropolitan Statistical Areas (see Figure 1) grew by 26 percent, that in the central cities within them increased by only 10 percent—and a quarter of those central cities actually lost population. The central city, therefore, is being rejected by an increasing number of Americans in favour of the space, the lower land values and the social norms of the suburbs, and a wide spectrum of economic activity is following them. The pace of dispersion is quickening. A modern house demands about twice the land used by a new house twenty-five years ago. Schools, shops, factories and the like are equally land-hungry. Every year well over a million acres of land is taken over for suburban developments, and it has been calculated that by the year 2000 urban land in the United States will occupy more than twice the space that it occupied in 1960.[4]

Each of these three aspects of urban expansion has created a series of major problems for the American people. The movement to the city has led to such social difficulties as overcrowding, the development of slums, and the emergence of large Negro and ethnic quarters in the central city. It has provided the setting for the West Side Stories and the Blackboard Jungles. The movement to the West and the South has raised crucial resource questions such as how to ensure the best allocation of scarce natural resources, and triggered off disagreements over river management and water allocation. Nevertheless, it is the regional dispersion of urban life which has led to the most formidable set of problems for urban America today, and it is the emergence of the dispersed city which is likely to raise some of the most challenging domestic issues in American politics in the next twenty-five years.

With the dispersion of urban life, resource problems are created not only by the rapid consumption of land but also by the high level of capital consumption which it involves. It has been estimated, for example, that each new home in suburbia demands between $2.5 thousand and $3.5 thousand of public investment in the form of roads, sewers, utilities and the like. Social problems stem readily from the emergence of 'two cities' within each metropolitan area. On the one hand there is suburbia with its white collar workers, its European stock, and its Parent-Teacher Associations; and on the other hand there is the central city with its working classes, its ethnic groups and segregated populations, and its zones of blight and decay. Political problems are also raised since the government of American metropolitan areas is balkanised and diffuse. Invariably there is a government for the central city itself, and then tens of small town local

4. H. H. Landsberg and others, *Resources in America's Future: Patterns of Requirements and Availabilities, 1960–2000* (Baltimore 1963), p. 371.

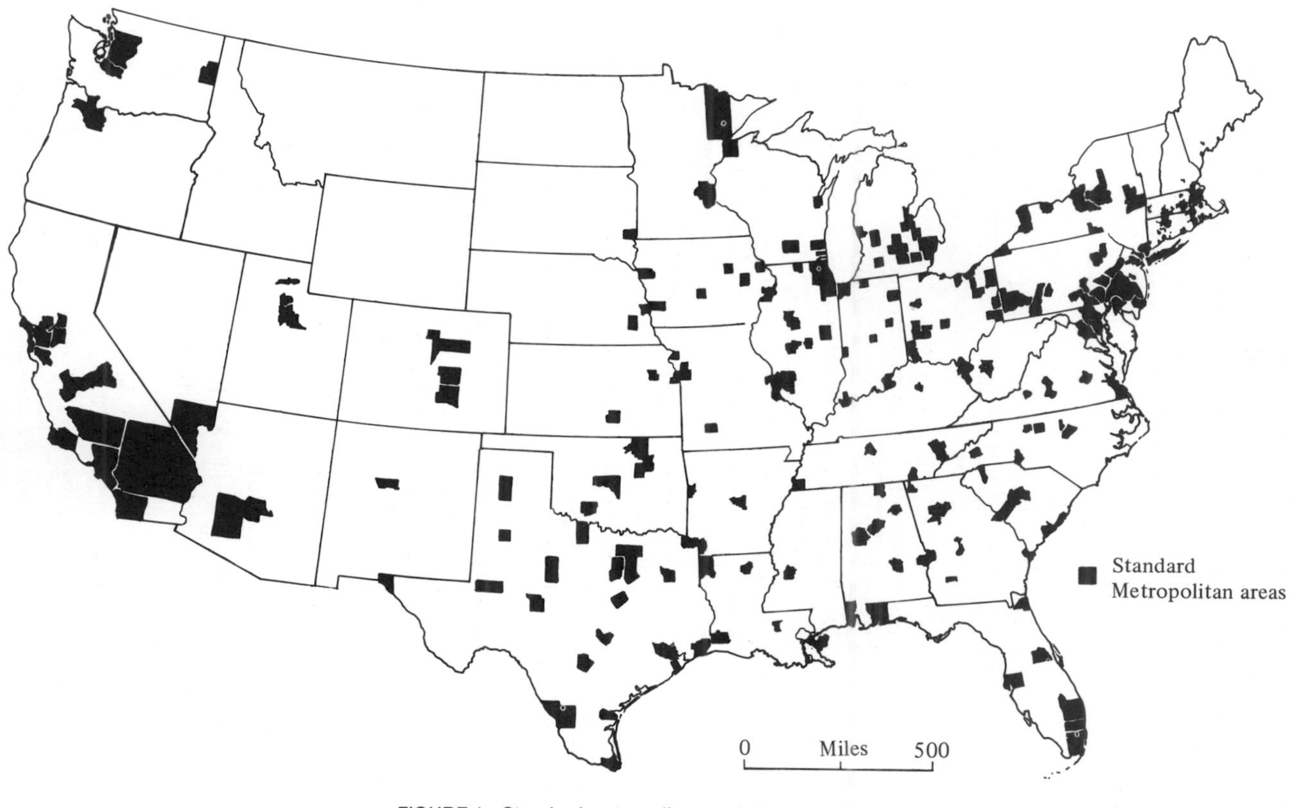

FIGURE 1 Standard metropolitan statistical areas, 1960.

authorities responsible for the surrounding suburbia. There are some 16,000 local jurisdictions in less than 200 urban areas in the United States. This in turn presents financial problems, since revenue is following people and economic life out into the suburbs and leaving the central cities relatively impoverished; and it also creates problems of planning and transport. Zoning regulations come within the province of the small local jurisdictions whose decisions tend to reflect the needs of the town rather than the wider metropolitan region of which they are a part, and the solution of traffic problems has also frequently been hindered by the limited vision of the same township authorities.

The complexity of the many problems related to all the three major aspects of urban expansion prevents their full consideration here. This essay therefore neglects those difficulties and issues associated with the drift to the city and the move to the sun, and concentrates upon the spread of metropolitan areas. It suggests the major forces which are molding the form of this urban growth, it emphasises the importance of public policy at both the metropolitan and federal levels in the present and future morphology of the American city, and it argues the possibility that there will be a growing geographical differential between the characteristics of the city in different parts of the country.

THE PROCESS OF URBAN DISPERSION

The story of the movement of people and economic life from the central city is well documented.[5] The vertical city of the nineteenth century, compact and intensive in its land-use, has been surrounded by a horizontal, land-devouring suburbia. As a consequence, the central city has lost something of its traditional role as the unifying factor in the region surrounding it. At the heart of the change lies a revolution in transport. Within any region, the economic structure, economic geography, pattern of land-use and methods of transport are intimately bound together by a set of forces acting and reacting upon each other. The full exploitation of the internal combustion engine, therefore, and the increasing control which man has come to have over distance with it, has meant that the whole meaning of space for human behaviour has radically changed. And suburbia has flourished. Of course, the motor car did not initiate the trends towards urban

5. See, for example, Editors of Fortune, *The Exploding Metropolis* (New York 1957); Amos H. Hawley, *The Changing Shape of Metropolitan America: Deconcentration Since 1920* (New York 1956); R. Vernon, *The Changing Economic Function of the Central City* (New York 1959).

dispersion. Earlier the commuter railway, the tramcar and the bus all had a comparable effect but it was on a very much smaller scale. They all meant that people were no longer required to live in close proximity of their work. As in Britain, however, the suburbs which they created were strung along major lines of communication, with housing located only a few minutes walk from the stations or termini. With the motor car, the super highway and the consequent decline in the use and the quality of public transport, however, the scale and the speed of change has been magnified dramatically. The result has been the creation of Mumford's 'formless urban exudation' in every section of the country.

First to move away from the compact nineteenth-century city in large numbers were the middle class—although they were soon to be followed by other sections of the community also. They were inspired by the simple need for living space following the steady growth of urban populations, and their migrations were facilitated by the new means of transport. Their exodus was reinforced, however, by social pressures and by a desire for better surroundings in which to bring up their children. This migration was not without its costs. But the growing wealth of America and the redistribution of incomes within the country, allowed an increasing number of people opportunity of suburban life; and large numbers accepted it. Thus the Man in the Grey Flannel Suit was born.

Retail trade soon followed people out into the suburbs. In the first instance it tended to move to the highways radiating out from the centre of the cities. More recently, however, its first preference has been for highly accessible sites adjacent to the intersections of radial and circumferential routes. Since the second world war the dispersion of retail trade has proceeded apace. Dessel has shown (see Table 2) how between 1948 and 1954 retail sales in forty-five of America's Standard Metropolitan Areas rose by 32 percent whilst the sales in

TABLE 2 Changes in retail sales in the United States, 1948–54.

CITY SIZE AT 1950 CENSUS	NO.	% CHANGE IN C.B.D. SALES 1948–54	% CHANGE IN S.M.A. SALES 1948–54	C.B.D. SALES AS % OF S.M.A. TOTAL 1948	C.B.D. SALES AS % OF S.M.A. TOTAL 1954
1,000,000+	5	− 1.5	31.9	15.5	11.6
500,000–999,999	13	0.9	29.3	22.7	17.8
250,000–499,999	15	3.3	28.4	12.0	9.7
100,000–249,999	15	11.4	43.0	35.3	27.5
Total	48	1.6	32.3	22.1	17.0

Source: M. D. Dessel, *Central Business Districts and their Metropolitan Areas: A Summary of Geographic Shifts in Retail Sales Growth, 1948–54*, Washington, D.C., 1957.

their Central Business Districts grew by less than 2 percent.[6] Today the suburban shopping centre is the characteristic source for most of the household goods of the American family. To the surrounding locality such centres are easily accessible; they provide ample car parking facilities; they best segregate pedestrians and traffic; and they have a range of shops from the small trader to the large departmental store. In other words, they offer a more convenient and pleasanter physical environment than most shopping districts at the heart of the city. Following this dispersion of retail trade, wholesaling was quick to follow. Now supplying shops located in both the suburbs and the central city, the wholesalers found their old sites both functionally cramped and geographically inconvenient. The multi-storey warehouse, for example, did not lend itself easily to mechanisation; the goods which they were handling were being moved increasingly by road rather than rail so operations were no longer tied to the rail termini; and the increasing traffic congestion downtown became a growing irritation. The suburbs on the other hand offered cheap land and ample space for both single-storey warehouses (with all their advantages for the mechanised handling of goods), ample room for car parking and, with the new metropolitan road networks, a good regional accessibility. The convenience and the economies to be derived from suburban location by many wholesale firms became increasingly apparent, and they began to move away from the central city.

Recent decades have also seen the release of manufacturing industry from the ties of the central city. Once again, the exploitation of road transport was especially important in this movement. It lessened, and in most cases obviated, the need for factories to be near rail or canal transport facilities. Further, the widening ownership of the motor car meant that labour was no longer dependent upon public transport to the same degree as before; and thus the need for a firm to locate near the centre of a metropolitan area in order that its workforce could take advantage of public transport—which invariably focuses there—no longer applied. As in the case of wholesale trade, the manufacturer saw in suburban sites positive attractions such as space for expansion, the possibility of replacing a multi-storey factory by a single-storey unit better adapted to assembly-line techniques, room for car parking, and (very often) lower taxes. Factors such as these caused many manufacturers from the inter-war years onwards to reassess their locational preferences within the metropolitan area. To many, the attractions of the suburbs were overwhelming.

6. M. D. Dessel, *Central Business Districts and their Metropolitan Areas: A Summary of Geographic Shifts in Retail Sales Growth, 1948–54* (Washington, D.C. 1957) see also Vernon, op. cit.

The most reluctant economic activities to move away from the central city were the white collar employments. Yet they too began reacting in the late nineteen-fifties to the same forces as did manufacturing industry two decades earlier. Research and development firms, serving industry in and drawing their workforce from the suburbs, began to find central city locations less attractive than they once were. Even some office employers, many of whose workers no longer used public transport, found that modern telephone and electronic communications could replace the need for a close physical juxtaposition to similar and related firms. They therefore began to show a keen interest in landscaped office parks, sited at highly accessible suburban locations, especially for their more routine operations. In sum, therefore, people, retail and wholesale trade, manufacturing, research and development firms and offices have all been, and are all being, attracted in differing degrees away from the centres of American metropolitan areas. Many factors have encouraged this trend, but above all others must be ranked the changing nature of transport facilities and preferences, both for moving goods and moving people.

This is not to argue that the central cities of contemporary America are *necessarily* doomed to relative or absolute stagnation or decay. Certain people still want to live there, and there are certain types of economic activity which continue to increase there. As far as people are concerned, a 'revolt against the suburbs' has for some time been evident. There are certain income and age groups, more especially the unmarried and the family whose children have grown up and left home, which have shown a distinct preference for a home at the heart of the metropolitan area with all the specialised amenities which it affords—the theatres, the specialised shops, the cinemas, the restaurants, the galleries, the clubs, the concerts and the like. Many of the cliff dwellers of New York like to be cliff dwellers! And there is no evidence that new luxury apartment housing in the heart of, say, Boston or Chicago has any difficulty in finding tenants.

The extent to which the central city retains a population clearly influences the degree to which it can retain its retail functions. In addition, however, it is noteworthy that certain types of retail trade continue to flourish in the central city irrespective of this. In particular, the speciality shops which serve the whole of a metropolitan area with such luxury goods as cameras, jewelry, foreign car imports and the like appear to retain a preference for a 'downtown' location. Fifth Avenue, in other words, is in no danger of losing its traditional role in New York City. Further, the success of suburban shopping centres has served in numerous instances to shock downtown retailing into the response of modernisation. Victor Gruen's work in Rochester, N.Y., for example, and his plans for Fort Worth, stand out in this regard. Extensive pedestrian shopping precincts, segregated from vehicle traffic, are the key to these schemes which have undoubtedly staged a revival of retail fortunes in those central cities where they have been put into effect. There are many other variables in this matter of the degree to which the central city can retain its retail trade. As a generalisation, it has been found that the success of the central city tends to fade as the size of the metropolitan area increases, as the use of private car transport grows and as the shortage of car parking space intensifies. On the other hand, it has been found that the retail activities of the central city are also in some measure a function of the size of the daytime working population. In nearly all of this, transport planning is clearly of crucial importance. And the degree to which retailing remains a central city activity influences the amount of wholesaling which tends to remain there also.

Just as there are certain types of retailing which remain attracted to the central city, so too are there some manufacturing enterprises which continue to prefer a central location. Particularly is this so in the case of those manufacturers of unstandardised products—goods such as ladies clothing, lithography, printing and publishing—where a day-to-day contact between buyers and sellers is essential to the successful functioning of the firm. Very often these firms have some difficulty in surviving in the central city and have to move away by default. They are invariably small, and occupy old quarters; yet with limited capital resources they cannot contemplate the redevelopment of their sites. They frequently find therefore that there is no alternative but to move away from the central city when they require new or enlarged premises. For this reason it has been suggested in the case of at least one American city that facilities should be provided in urban renewal schemes for such industries in order that they can be helped to retain a downtown location.[7]

Naturally office employments still tend to retain their preference for the central city, and the greater part of recent additions to American office floor space is to be found at the cores of metropolitan areas. Commercial firms, insurance companies, banks, finance houses, business services and government offices all continue to grow fast there. The advantages (both real and imagined) of such locations for office employers include the ease of obtaining female secretarial labor, geographical proximity of the similar and related activities, and the prestige offered by a central city site.

The continuing attraction of the central city for people and economic activity, therefore, is significantly biased towards the service

7. Great Boston Economic Survey Committee, *A Report on Downtown Boston* (Boston 1959).

sector of the economy.[8] It must be remembered, however, that it rests very heavily upon, first, transport facilities which are capable of drawing large numbers of people into the centre of the city each day, and, second, upon whether or not—and in which way—the older urban structures of the city are renewed. In both of these matters public policies are critically important. Over 50 percent of the land in a city lies in non-private hands. More important, it is local and central government bodies which lay the plans for, and provide much of the funds for, the building of roads. They also determine whether or not commuter railways are to be subsidised, and play a key role in the supervision (and subsidy) of urban renewal. In a very important sense, therefore, the economic and social geography of American metropolitan areas, and especially the fate of their central areas, lies in the hands of the politicians on the one hand, and the technocrats of traffic engineering, city planning and urban renewal on the other. The future shape of metropolitan America—in particular the degree to which the central city can retain its vitality and the focal role which it has traditionally played within the urban area—will depend to a very large extent upon their decisions.

THE CHALLENGE TO THE CENTRAL CITY

Until a few years ago, it was generally conceded that the task of the traffic engineers and city planners was to facilitate the flow of traffic within urban areas. In particular they were charged with solving the problems which were presented by the large and growing number of people commuting in and out of the central city each day. It was their task to try and discover means whereby new transport preferences, especially the swing to car transport, and new technological skills could be adapted in such a way as to retain older urban structures, in particular the role of the central city. This was received planning doctrine. Yet it turned out to be increasingly difficult. In response to public demand the car came to be treated as the chief concern of this type of planning; but after new roads had been constructed to satisfy their needs and alleviate congestion, it was found that the new highways generated even more traffic and so exacerbated the original problem. The planners if not the engineers came face to face with the nightmare realisation therefore that "Once wheeled traffic is treated as the chief concern of planning, there will never be enough space to keep it from becoming congested."[9] The multipli-

8. See G. Manners, "Decentralisation in Metropolitan Boston," *Geography*, 45 (1960) 276.

9. L. Mumford, *The City in History* (London 1961), p. 405.

cation of car ownership and use in metropolitan areas thus came to choke up whatever roads were provided and to demand more and more space for parking. In Los Angeles the multi-lane highways have laid waste almost the entire central business district to provide the most expensive system of roads and parking lots in the world—yet the peak hour transport problem there remains as frustrating as ever.

At the same time as more and more roads were built, an increasing proportion of commuter traffic was attracted away from public transport. Most individuals tend to measure the convenience and the marginal cost of car transport against the cost of commuter fares. The result is that where there is widespread car ownership and there are good roads, public transport can rarely compete in such distorted financial terms with the private car for commuting purposes. Throughout the United States, therefore, metropolitan railway and bus services with steadily falling traffic and with rapidly mounting losses began to decay both in terms of the quality of service which they could offer and the standard of capital equipment which they were able to afford. Mumford saw it this way,

> Municipal authorities, hypnotised by the popularity of the private car, feeling an obligation to help General Motors flourish even if general chaos results, have been in an open conspiracy to dismantle all the varied forms of transportation necessary to a good system; and [they] have reduced . . . facilities to the private car . . . and the airplane . . . . It is an absurdly impoverished technology that has only one answer to the problem of transportation.[10]

The problem was circular and self-perpetuating. It is all too familiar in Britain, also.

There have been three distinct responses to this problem of urban transport upon which the future morphology and functioning of the American metropolitan area hangs. The first response to the mounting transport crisis was the voting of subsidies for public transport in some urban areas, and even the installation of new—and potentially profitless—public transport facilities in others. Every year Chicago loses between $4 and $5 million on its public transit system, and Boston and New York lose even more—$20 and $100 million respectively.[11] In 1963 the Kennedy Administration proposed that the Federal Government should spend some $500 million to aid and renovate public transport in metropolitan areas, and the Boston and Maine Railroad, for example, accepted $2.2 million of this and Massachusetts funds to increase its services and reduce its fares by 30 percent. In the first year of the experiment the number of daily travellers on the railroad increased substantially—by as much as a third according to

10. Ibid., p. 509.
11. *The Economist* (9 March 1963), p. 890.

some reports, but the railway's deficit (in spite of the subsidy) remained at $3 million. Yet the alternatives would be even more expensive. The present expressways carry between 100,000 and 150,000 people in to the city of Boston each day (see Figure 2). To widen and supplement them to carry the entire daily commuting load of 500,000 would be highly expensive in itself. But to provide for the daily storage of

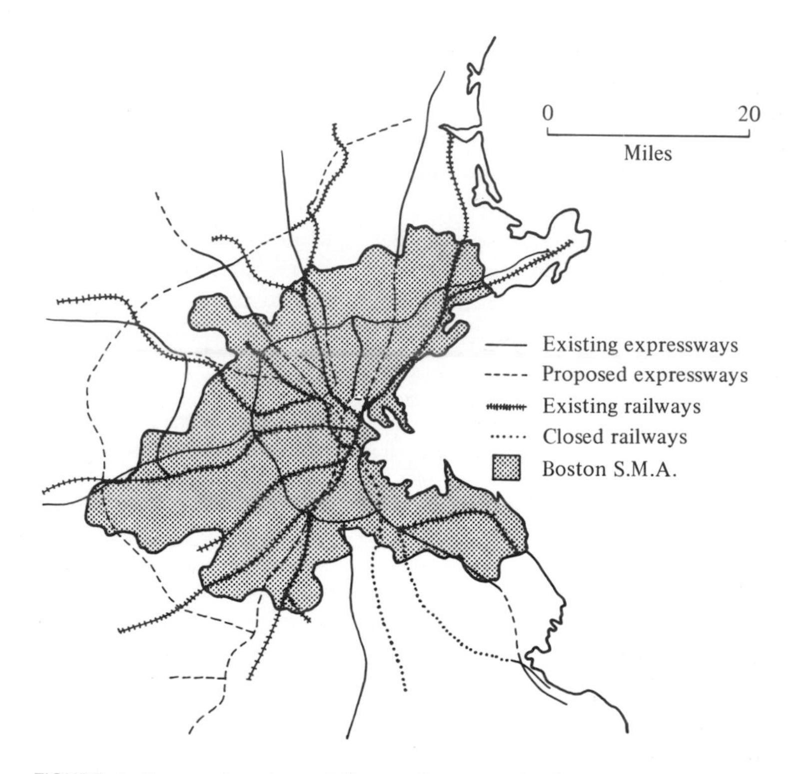

FIGURE 2 Transport system of Greater Boston, 1962. *Source*: Greater Boston Economic Study Committee, *Industrial Land Needs Through 1980*, Boston, 1962, p. 42.

their cars would be physically impossible without levelling much of the downtown area.[12] The same lesson has been learnt in San Francisco. When it was estimated that it would cost $5.5 billion to provide enough motorways to carry the ever-increasing traffic of the metropolitan area, the voters agreed to spend just over $.75 billion on a new rapid transit system for the Bay Area.[13] Even in this case, however, the original public transport plan for nine surrounding counties finally became one for three, partly for technical but also for political

12. *The Economist* (18 January 1964), p. 209.
13. *The Economist* (18 August 1962), p. 619, and (9 March 1963), p. 890.

reasons. The fashionable plea in some quarters today therefore is for—shades of Mumford—a better mix of public and private transport, to correct the imbalance created by the heavy emphasis upon the motor car in traffic planning over the past thirty years. In particular it is felt that rapid public transport facilities which can get commuters into the centre of cities faster than cars are an urgent necessity, and that some form of public subsidy is inevitable. This, then, is the first response to the mounting problem of urban transport.

The second response is closely related to the first. It follows from the appearance of a school of planning thought which rejects the present approach to urban transport in a vacuum. This school argues that regional land-use development plans should be considered at the same time as, and integrated with, the planning of new transport facilities. Self-evident though this need would seem, the proposition is little accepted in the country as a whole. The *Prospectus* of the Penn-Jersey Transportation Study[14] pointed out that "the recommended transport system should provide convenience and economy of travel, but also . . . (that) its influence on the development of the area should tend toward facilitating the desired pattern of regional development." In such an approach to urban transport, social as well as economic criteria can be evalued in the surveys prior to the formulation of a plan with the result that the urge for transport efficiency, which was tended to dominate planning objectives in the past, can be replaced by a search for what Perloff and Wingo of Resources for the Future have called "total socio-economic effectiveness." The phrase might be new, but the idea has distinguished precedents in the history of town planning. Another interesting example of work in this category is the study of Washington, D.C. projected to the year 2000.[15] Here is a metropolitan area which, it is anticipated, will grow from its present two million to a population of five million by the end of the century, and the study discusses the several possibilities which exist to handle this increase in geographical terms—the creation of new cities, the deliberate planning of urban sprawl, development of satellite new towns, the channeling of growth along radial corridors and the like.[16] The planning controls which exist to implement such plans as these, however, are either rudimentary or non-existent as yet, and the emotional resistance to them is strong. The public influence over the provision of new transport facilities on the other hand is a powerful weapon for influencing the pattern of land-use if it is exploited to the

14. Penn-Jersey Transportation Study, *Prospectus* (Philadelphia 1959), p. 2.

15. National Capital Planning Committee and the National Capital Regional Planning Council, *The Nation's Capital: A Plan for the Year 2000* (Washington, D.C. 1961).

16. The alternative urban forms are reproduced in *Traffic in Towns* (H.M.S.O. 1963), p. 187.

full. This, then, is the second response to the urban transport problem. It amounts to a plea for metropolitan regional planning.

There has been a third and even more revolutionary response to the problem as well. This is the first articulate challenge to the value of preserving the central city. It is now being argued that the highly centralised complex that is the central city no longer has a place in metropolitan geography, and that its artificial retention by transport policies should cease forthwith. The fundamental question which has been raised is whether the transport facilities—and more especially the primary roads—of a metropolitan area should necessarily lead to the central city and its central business district? In the past they have always tended to do so (see Figure 2). Yet, by molding the geographical pattern of communications upon what is basically a radial plan, one is inevitably directing people, traffic and economic activity into the central city even though they do not necessarily want to go there. Studies of radial plan Indianapolis, for example, have shown that some 70 percent of the traffic entering downtown is not in fact destined for that part of the city. In other words, the radial routes tend to channel unnecessary traffic and economic activity towards the centre of the city and hence to cause congestion there. Circumferentials, designed to avoid such congestion, merely make the radials more accessible to a larger suburban area and so intensify rather than ameliorate the problem. This traditional pattern of radials and circumferentials not only helps the central business district to become a focus of economic life in the metropolitan area, therefore, it also tends to make it a traffic switchyard and a vehicle store at the same time. Cleveland, for example, already has 25 percent of its downtown area devoted to parking facilities; and Los Angeles, it has been said, has given over 70 percent of its central business district to streets, freeways, car parks and garages. Unfortunately, with an extensive use of car transport there is rarely room for all these functions in anything above a relatively small urban community.

What, then, is the alternative? A new generation of traffic engineers and urban planners now argue that, largely as a result of the motor car and the personal mobility that it offers, modern urban life is an areal rather than a punctiform phenomenon. A transport and communications system for a city therefore should seek to serve all that area rather than a single point at its centre. Certainly there will always be high points of economic and social life within a metropolitan area, such as concentrations of banking and financial activites, of educational and recreational facilities, of manufacturing, retailing and research. But they need not all be in the same central locality. As a consequence, what is urgently required, the argument continues, is a new conception of urban form and its related pattern of transport facilities in which the radial and circumferential transport network is replaced by a road and possibly a rail pattern based upon a large-scale gridiron plan (see Figure 3). At some of the intersections of this transport net one would expect specialised concentrations of economic activities to develop, taking advantage of the regional accessibility which the grid would afford. H. T. Fisher has put it this way: "It may

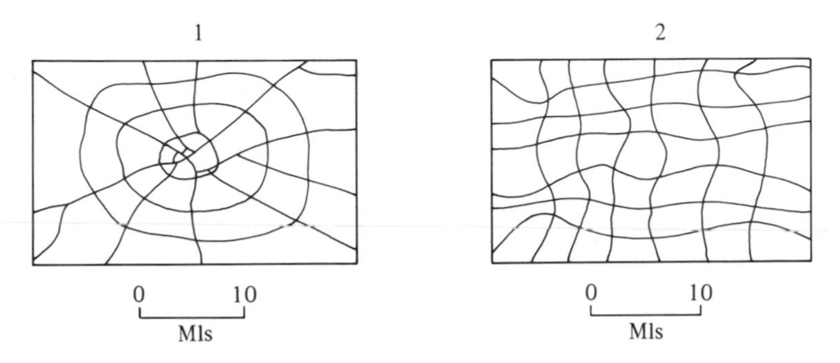

FIGURE 3 Major road plan of (1) traditional centralised city with radials and circumferentials, and (2) polynuclear metropolitan area with a gridiron coverage of transport facilities.

be said that in today's typical metropolitan complex there is no longer to be found, as in the past, one all-dominant mass destination–and, therefore, a specialised road system, designed primarily or largely to serve such a mass destination, is necessarily obsolete. In contrast, we increasingly have a plurality of destinations, and a road system designed more specifically to serve such a plurality is needed." He goes on, "Whether we like it or not, the land-use pattern for the accommodation of a large metropolitan population must be a *diffused* pattern. . . . The problem, therefore, is not whether it is best to have a diffused pattern, but rather how to achieve a diffused pattern that works well."[17]

Thus, for the first time since the coming of the motor car and the decline of public transport, the traditional form of the city is being challenged. Influential voices are now saying that the city (as it is conventionally understood) is no longer necessary or possible in twentieth-century America. In its place it is suggested that there must and will develop region-spanning metropolitan complexes in which what Scott Greer calls "urban villages"[18] will stand out as hills of economic and social intensity. In such a scheme the mountain of the central city has no place. The metropolitan area of tomorrow,

17. H. T. Fisher, "Radials and Circumferentials – An Outmoded Urban Concept?" in T. E. H. Williams, ed., *Urban Survival and Traffic* (London 1962), p. 58.

18. S. Greer, "Dispersion and the Culture of Urban Man," in Williams, ibid., p. 60; see also S. Greer, *The Emerging City: Myth and Reality* (New York 1962).

therefore, is envisaged as polynuclear and regional in contrast to the punctiform and local city of yesterday and today. Characterised by a low intensity of land-use, and held together by a transport system of super-highways arranged in a gridiron pattern, this diffuse city will take full advantage of modern means of communication such as the telephone, the F.M. radio and television, all of which will replace the more personal methods of communication of a former era. It is the logical extension of the Los Angeles phenomenon. Such an alternative to the conventional metropolis may seem unrealistic and unfamiliar. Yet an examination of the geography of economic life at the centre of traditional American or European cities reveals an interesting parallel. Within New York, or Boston, or London, there are clearly defined quarters of economic activity—manufacturing, banking, wholesaling, entertainment, commercial quarters—all distributed within the central city in accordance with an essentially pedestrian scale of life. Could not the polynuclear concept of future metropolitan geography simply reflect the shifting of this pattern of functional quarters onto an automobile scale?

THE FUTURE OF AMERICAN CITIES

The alternative aims which can be adopted by the traffic engineers and urban planners of American cities now range from the extremes of trying to preserve the highly centralised city, with its radial pattern of communications serving and supporting it, to deliberately fostering a polynuclear metropolitan area with a gridiron coverage of transport facilities. In the former, best represented today by, say, Boston or New York, public transport and careful land-use planning must inevitably play a large part in the functioning of the city and region. In the latter, best represented today by Los Angeles or Dallas, journeys become increasingly random (geographically) and it is difficult to see with any precision a distinctive role for public transport. Upon the decisions of the engineers and planners will depend the future shape and functioning of the American city. What is likely to be their choice? Obviously a variety of solutions will emerge throughout the country, and most of them will represent some form of compromise between the two extremes. The *Chicago Area Transportation Study* admits this. "A plan for the Chicago area would appear to be best constructed if it could have some blend of the attributes of the grid with those of the ring and radial system. To a large extent the region is heavily committed to the radial system. . . . On the other hand, the underlying arterial system is a strong influence for a gridded network of expressways. The need to meet distributed traffic demands without encouraging further concentrations of flow also argues for the grid-like design." [19] (See Figure 4.)

There are some indications, however, that the emphasis of transport planning will be towards the acceptance of the polynuclear type of urban form. This will not necessarily be the result of deliberate

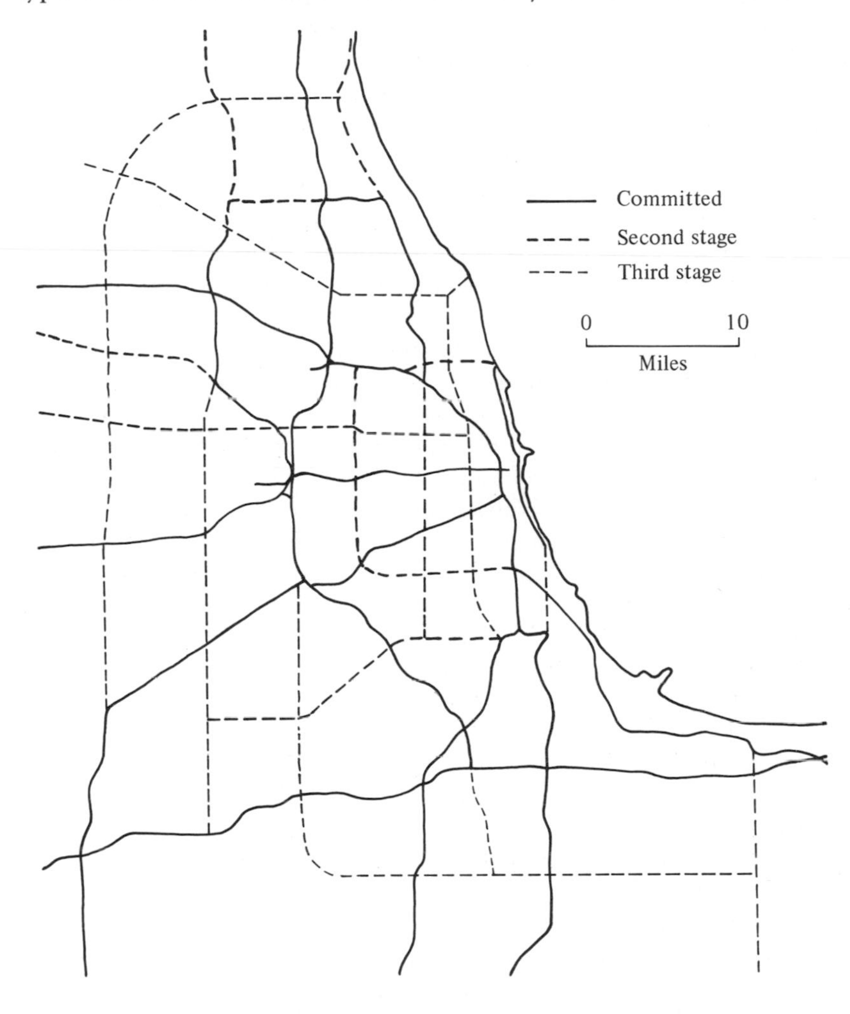

FIGURE 4 Recommended expressway plan for the Chicago Metropolitan Area. *Source: Chicago Area Transportation Study, Final Report, Volume III, Transportation Plan*, Chicago, 1962, p. 112.

choice on the part of the people and bodies concerned, but rather will follow from the absence of adequate physical planning machinery in

19. *Chicago Area Transportation Study, Final Report, Vol. III, Transportation Plan* (Chicago, 1962) p. 37.

metropolitan America. With the government of the Standard Metropolitan Statistical Areas so balkanised, and the organic growth (almost *laissez-faire*) attitude to the use of urban land ubiquitous, metropolitan planning is almost a dream. The result is that in many urban areas the provision of new transport facilities will continue to reflect public demand for bigger and better roads, and the relative—or even absolute—decline of public transport will continue apace. It is noteworthy than when the National Capital Transportation Agency of Washington, D.C., proposed in 1963 that before 1980 the percentage of rush hour trips into the centre of the city on public transport should be increased from forty-five to sixty, there was an immediate outcry from road haulage interests, bus companies, petrol station owners, motor car dealers, road-building firms and some local businessmen.[20] The interests vested in the motor car are extremely powerful.

Not only are regional and metropolitan attitudes likely to encourage the development of the diffuse polynuclear city. The priorities of the Federal Government are also liable to encourage the same end. Notwithstanding the progress made under the Kennedy and Johnson Administrations in the matter of urban transport, road building funds continue considerably to exceed those available for the subsidy of public transport and for urban renewal. Forty-one thousand miles of super (euphemistically called defence) highways are at present being built across the continent, and nine-tenths of the cost is being carried by the Federal Government. The present plans for helping metropolitan public transport are far less generous, and in urban renewal schemes only two-thirds of the cost can be billed to Washington. Whilst such a bias exists, once again the central city seems destined to decline.

Yet in addition it is possible to forecast a different emphasis in the solutions to the urban transport problem in the older cities of the East and the North as compared with those of the West and the South. As a generalisation, it seems highly likely that there will be a growing geographical differential between the form and the functioning of the cities of America based largely upon the age of metropolitan growth in different parts of the country. In the older type of American city, characteristically Boston, Philadelphia, San Francisco or New York, there are already heavy commitments to the urban structures of an older technology, especially in the central city. Public buildings, concert halls, offices, parks, libraries and the like all exist downtown and together they represent a considerable capital investment. There will be both a rational and an emotional desire to preserve

20. *The Economist* (6 July 1963), p. 38.

them. Through extensive urban redevelopment, and by attempting to solve their transport problems by the subsidy and renewal of public transport—and possibly with the help of regional planning—the social capital and the way of life of these cities is likely to be preserved at least to some extent. In the newer cities of the West and South, however, in cities such as Los Angeles, Dallas or Miami, there are fewer such structures and very much smaller amounts of social capital to preserve. And there is no such emotional attachment to the central city. It is highly likely therefore that the large-scale gridiron road plan will come to be more readily adopted, that an increasingly dispersed form of urban life will emerge, and that public transport will have little role to play. The central city, as a result, will tend to disappear in all except in name.

Now the interesting point is, and this brings us back to one of the first observations which was made about urban expansion at the beginning of this essay, that it is the cities of the West and the South which are growing the fastest. Consequently, it is highly probable that the diffused, polynuclear metropolitan area will come to dominate the American urban scene. The Bostons and the Philadelphias, in contrast, will be partially preserved as living memorials to an earlier phase of urban civilisation in America.

13

HAL H. WINSBOROUGH

City Growth and City Structure

In order to understand the growth of the city, it is necessary to understand its structural as well as its simple or populational growth. The distinction between these kinds of growth has been drawn by Boulding [2].

Boulding describes simple growth as the growth or decline of a variable by accretion or depletion. Populational growth occurs when it is not reasonable to regard the aggregate as homogeneous, but necessary to analyse it in terms of an age distribution. Structural growth, on the other hand, occurs when the aggregate consists of interrelated parts and the process of growth involves changes in the relations between the parts. Boulding describes structural growth as a complicated process but suggests several principles for its analysis. Two of these are important here. The first principle states: "At any moment the *form* of any object, organism, or organization is a result of its laws of growth up to that moment."[1] This principle also states: "Growth creates form, but form limits growth."[2] The second principle is called the principle of equal advantage and governs the distribution of "substance" among the parts of the structure.

Theories of the structural growth of the city seem to have relied on first one and then the other of these principles. Classical ecological theory stressed the importance of the interrelationship between growth and form. More modern theory seems to stress the principle of equal advantage.

THE RELATIONSHIP BETWEEN GROWTH AND FORM

The relationship between growth and form was brought out in the early studies of the city. Burgess seems to have been especially aware of the problems of this relationship. He stated that the structure of the city might be thought of as a series of concentric zones and that

1. Boulding [2; p. 120].
2. *Ibid.*

This is paper No. 17 in the series, "Comparative Urban Research," issuing from the Population Research and Training Center, University of Chicago, under a grant from the Ford Foundation. Some of the computations involved in this research were carried out in the Duke University Computing Laboratory which is supported in part by the National Science Foundation.

Reprinted from the Journal of Regional Science, 4 (1962), 35–49, by permission of the publishers and the author.

the structure grows by the expansion of zones and the invasion of one zone by another. Insofar as the Burgess schema accounts for the genesis of the zonal structure, it does so in terms of Boulding's first principle. Zones seem to be a product of the very growth of the city. Further, the invasion of one zone by another was not regarded as simply the forcing out of the old land use by the new, but rather was regarded in the light of the concept of succession. According to this concept, the occupancy of the land by one use tends to make in unsuitable for further occupancy by that use.

Disagreements with the foregoing style of analysis concentrated on its assumptions about the facts of city structure at a given time. It had early been noted that transportation routes radiate from the center of the city and that population tends to follow these routes.[3] It was also observed that business districts tended to follow transportation lines, with residential use occurring in the interstices.[4] Thus, it was argued, a segmented pattern of land use seemed more appropriate than a pattern of concentric zonation.

Both the patterns of zonation and segmentation assume that the city is mono-centered. In fact, however, there is usually one central business district, but also a number of sub-centers, providing for the retail needs of smaller sections of the city.[5] Perhaps residential units grade off from these smaller sub-centers. Thus a third type of pattern, that of multiple nucleation, is added to zonation and segmentation as possible kinds of city structure.

Keeping more within the Burgess line of thought, other students have suggested that zonation is only a crude representation of what should, in fact, be represented as a gradient. Clark [4] and [5], and Stewart and Warntz [17] have investigated the distribution of population density with distance from the center of the city. Both have fitted a negative exponential curve to this distribution and hold the fit to be satisfactory.[6] We shall discuss this finding presently.

THE PRINCIPLE OF EQUAL ADVANTAGE

Concomitant with, and growing out of, disagreements over the "facts" of the internal structure of the city, has been an increasing tendency to offer a synchronic explanation of why a given structure should exist. These explanations are frequently based on the principle

3. Hurd [13; pp. 56–74].
4. Federal Housing Administration [11].
5. McKenzie [14].
6. Other functions have been fitted to this distribution. Cf. Reinhardt [16]. In this work a function of the form:

$$d_r = k(1+r)e^{-r/b},$$

of equal advantage. The advantage to be equalized is the advantage—expressed through housing costs and transportation costs—in locating at any distance from the city center.

The various rationales for the differing descriptions of internal structure have been synthesized by Hawley [12; pp. 264–278]. He discusses the various descriptions of land use patterns in terms of competition for accessible land. In almost all cities, transportation facilities terminate in or near the center of the city. Thus, the center is the most accessible part of the city for trips originating both internally and externally. Owing to its accessibility, land in the center of the city is highly valued. Offices and specialized retail stores seek central location in order to minimize distance from employees and customers. Consumers want to locate near the center to minimize the cost of transportation to work and shopping. Producers want to locate near the terminals of transport routes from other cities. Competition for this accessible land increases its value. Hence, users who stand to gain the most economic benefit from accessibility will be most likely to acquire use of the land. It is also likely that the use of the land will be intensive. Hence, if residential use locates on highly accessible land, it is likely to be in the form of structures with many dwelling units. Manufacturing activities which require a good deal of space in proportion to value added will be less likely to locate on highly accessible land than will manufacturing requiring only a small amount of space in proportion to value added.

What has been said for location in the center of the city applies to all accessible sites, according to their accessibility. Thus locations on a major transportation route or at the intersection of transportation routes also tend to become valuable.

Data comparing the location of units which use land with varying degrees of intensity provide some empirical support for Hawley's formulation.[7] These data show the more intensive uses locating in the more accessible places nearer the center of the city.

Considering only competition between residential units, Muth [15] has formalized elements similar to Hawley's line of reasoning and produced a model which predicts an exponential form for the inverse relationship between population density and distance from the center of the city.[8] Thus, there is reason to suspect the

where d_r is the density at r distance from the center of the city and b and k are parameters estimated from the data, is fitted to the distribution of density with distance from the center of the city.

7. Duncan, Beverly [7], and Duncan, Otis Dudley [9].

8. Muth [15]. Muth's model is based on the following assumptions:

1. "Firm" Equilibrium. It is assumed that "firms" choose output and factor inputs so as to maximize profits.

Clark-Stewart finding mentioned earlier can also be interpreted in terms of a synchronic explanation of the internal structure of the city.

In order to offer empirical justification for his derivation of the exponential decline in density with distance from the center, Muth computed parameters of the decline for thirty-six cities in 1950, and investigated the relationship between one of these parameters and various indicators of availability of transportation. In computing the parameters, Muth transformed the equation for the exponential decline in density with distance, which can be given as:

$$d(r) = d(O)e^{-r/g}, \tag{1}$$

to the form:

$$\ln d(r) = \ln d(O) - r/g. \tag{2}$$

In these equations, $d(r)$ represents the density at r distance from the center, $d(O)$ the central density or the density extrapolated to the center, and g is the gradient of density. Elsewhere the parameter g has been described as a measure of concentration while $d(O)$ is called congestion.[9] To estimate the parameters g and $d(O)$, for each of the thirty-six cities Muth drew a random sample of twenty-five central city census tracts and estimated the parameters from a linear regression to fit equation (2). To investigate the relationship between the density pattern and the availability of transportation, Muth correlated the estimates of g with variables associated with characteristics of the local transportation system and the availability of automobiles in each city. The relationship between g and some of these variables remains even when many additional variables are held constant by partial correlation. Thus, Muth has fairly well demonstrated a considerable synchronic relationship between the degree of concentration of the city and the availability of transportation.

But what happens when transportation patterns change; when new modes of transit come into use during the course of a city's growth? Before a change in mode of transit, an elaborate structure appropriate to the old transportation pattern will have developed.

2. A Price-Distance Function. It is assumed that the price received for housing declines at a decreasing rate with distance from the city center.

3. Marginal Land Supply. It is assumed that the land area used for housing per unit increase in distance from the city center is proportional to distance.

4. Demand and Market Equilibrium. It is assumed that the demand function for housing is linear in the logarithm of price at the center and population.

In this model the "firm" is the unit to be housed, the household. Assumption (1) includes as assumption of the substitution of non-land inputs for land inputs.

9. Winsborough [20].

Buildings will have been built at a particular density in various parts of the city. These structures contain a given number of dwelling units. They occupy plots of land whose size had been determined when the area was plotted. They are located on streets of a size and spacing to accommodate the old transportation pattern. The advent of a new transportation technology probably renders many of these aspects of the physical structure of the city less appropriate than previously.

The first of our principles of structural change suggests that the growth of the city following a shift in transportation technology will be limited and its implications limited by the previously developed structure. Thus, one might suspect that a city undergoing the same stages of growth under the new transportation technology would develop differently.

The foregoing suggests that, out of the complicated welter of processes in the growth of the city, we ought to be able to find some kind of relationship between the timing of growth and characteristics of population distribution.

Muth's investigation offers some evidence to support this line of argument. He finds a significant zero-order correlation between the proportion of the standard metropolitan area population growth in the period 1920–1950 and the estimated value of g. He also finds a significant partial correlation between the decline in density and the proportion of central city dwellings classified as substandard. This latter correlation appears significant in partial correlation. Thus, some evidence suggests a relationship between the density pattern and variables likely to be associated with the timing of growth in the city.

In another investigation conducted from a rather different point of view, O. D. Duncan [9, p. 364] has investigated the relationship between the total density of cities and their population size for cities of differing ages. In order to permit age to be independent of size, he measured the age of a city in terms of the date at which it had achieved half of its 1950 population. Duncan summarizes his findings thus, "Older cities have somewhat higher average densities, and their densities respond more to increase in size than is the case for cities a major portion of whose growth has taken place since the inception of the automobile age."[10] Certainly this finding seems to support the argument that the growth pattern of a city influences its population distribution. The relationship between this finding and Muth's model of urban structure, however, can perhaps be clarified if that model is somewhat elaborated.

Elsewhere we have shown, and presented some empirical evidence to support the fact that in a model, circular, urbanized area in which

10. Duncan, O. D. [9; p. 364].

equation (1) holds, the population of the urbanized area is a function of the parameters g and $d(O)$ only.[11] We have reason to believe, therefore, that an increase in population size must be accommodated by an increase in congestion or a decrease in concentration, or some compensatory change in both. The total population density of a model urbanized area, however, can be shown to be a function of only the parameter $d(O)$, congestion.

This assertion can be justified as follows. As has been shown elsewhere,[12] the population of a model, circular, urbanized area out to the limits of the area at distance a, where density falls to some assigned value L, is given by:

$$P(a) = 2\pi g^2 d(O)\left\{1 - \frac{\ln [d(O)/L] + 1}{d(O)/L}\right\}. \tag{3}$$

In such a city, the area A, within distance a from the center is given by:

$$A = \pi a^2 \tag{4}$$

If a is substituted for r in equation (1), we have:

$$L = d(O) e^{-a/g} \tag{5}$$

and hence,

$$a = g \ln \left[\frac{d(O)}{L}\right]. \tag{6}$$

Therefore, substituting (6) in (4), we have:

$$A = \pi g^2 \ln^2 \left[\frac{d(O)}{L}\right] \tag{7}$$

The total population density of the area, therefore, is given by:

$$\frac{P}{A} = \frac{2d(O)}{\ln^2 [d(O)/L]}\left\{1 - \frac{\ln [d(O)/L] + 1}{d(O)/L}\right\}. \tag{8}$$

In a model, circular, urbanized area where equation (1) holds, then, total population density is a function of congestion. The parameter g does not enter into this equation at all.

Keeping in mind the fact that population increase in the model case must be accommodated by an adjustment in the degree of congestion and the degree of concentration, the foregoing clarifies Duncan's finding. It suggests that older cities adapt to population increase by increasing congestion Thus it would seem that in older cities the predilection for relatively higher central densities persists under the newer transportation regime.

11. Winsborough [19].
12. *Ibid.*

A certain amount of information about how population redistribution proceeds during the course of growth is presented by Beverly Duncan, et al.[8]. Drawing an analogy to cohort analysis of fertility, they divide Los Angeles census tracts into cohorts according to year built up. A tract was regarded as built up during the time period in which it achieved a density level of two dwellings per acre. The findings are summarized thus.

> The cohort built up before 1920 gained population in each period prior to the end of World War II and lost population in each postwar period. The 1920's cohort also grew during the prewar decade and lost population in the immediate postwar period, but a population increase was again recorded in the mid-1950's. The cohorts built up in the 1930's or more recently gained population throughout the observation period.[13]

Although no data on the distance of these cohorts from the city center are presented, inspection of the location of tracts by cohorts suggests considerable relationship between date built up and distance from the center of Los Angeles. The picture presented, then, suggests an increasing congestion up to the end of the war and a rather rapid deconcentration following the war. Some indication of a slowing of the rate of decongestion may be found in the lessened rate of decline in density from 1953 to 1956 in the cohort built up before 1920 and the increase in density during the same period in the cohort built up in the 1920's.

In investigating the mechanisms through which population growth is translated into redistribution, Duncan et al. focus on new construction and the vacancy rate as intervening variables. They find that during the Second World War, when population growth was high in Los Angeles but when new construction was low, the increase was housed in the existing inventory and, hence, the vacancy rate decreased markedly. The great surge of population deconcentration following the war, then, is attributed to pent-up demand developed during the war. In general, the authors hold: "Over the long run or under 'normal' circumstances, new construction will keep pace with population increase; the rapidity of population redistribution from mature to building-up areas then varies directly with the city-wide rate of population increase."[14]

To investigate the hypothesis that redistribution is a result of population increase, Duncan et al. recompute Bogue's[1; p. 75] correlation between population growth and change in percent of the SMA population in the suburban ring, adjusting city boundaries for changes in areal size. This adjustment markedly increases the correlation.

13. Duncan, Beverly et al.[8; p. 424].
14. *Ibid.*, p. 427.

Since change in the percent of the population in the suburban ring seems at least intuitively related to deconcentration, we may, perhaps, take this finding as suggesting that almost all cities are now adapting to population growth by the process of deconcentration. Duncan et al. extend the investigation by adding the population density of the central city and the population size of the SMA at the initial period to the growth rate in a multiple correlation to predict suburbanization. Each of these variables is found to have an independent relationship with suburbanization. The relationship of both growth and density is positive, while the relationship with population size is negative. Duncan et al. summarize their findings as follows: "... growth tends to take the form of outward expansion until the spread of the city begins to present a barrier to internal transportation and communication, at which juncture growth takes the form of upward expansion near the metropolitan core."[15] This latter interpretation finds additional justification in Muth's finding of a positive synchronic relationship between concentration and population size. Thus, larger cities are already more deconcentrated. Hence, they may be closer to the point at which existing transportation technology loses its effective ability to permit travel to the city center from greater distances in a reasonable length of time.

This series of findings by O. D. Duncan, Muth, and Beverly Duncan, then, leads us to the impression that population growth in cities can be accommodated by an increase in congestion or by a decrease in concentration or some combination of both. Beverly Duncan's findings suggest that deconcentration is currently a much-used adaptation. Muth's findings suggest that large cities have already used this technique and now have large average distances from the center of the city. Beverly Duncan's findings further suggest that large cities have just about reached the limits of deconcentration and are now showing signs of depending on increases in congestion to accommodate further growth. Dudley Duncan's findings suggest, however, that the extent to which cities have depended on deconcentration may be a function of their pattern of growth through time.

These results, then, lead us to an investigation of the mechanism through which the growth pattern affects the pattern of population density in the city.

Certainly Beverly Duncan's observation that new construction is an intervening variable in the relationship between growth and redistribution should provide some help. But previous construction to meet transportation and growth problems then current can have taken several forms. Construction can have been the building of

15. *Ibid.*, p. 428.

single family units or it can have been the building of multiple unit structures. Construction also entails a decision as to the amount of land allocated to each structure.

These observations can be formalized by noting that the population density of a given part of the city is the product of population per unit, units per structure, and structures per acre. Perhaps some insight into the relationship between timing of growth and population distribution can be gained by investigating the relationship of these components of density with both distance from the city center and some measure of the age of parts of the city. Since the logarithm of density is linearly related to distance from the city center, it seems reasonable to convert the components to logarithms. The sum of the logarithms, then, is equal to the logarithm of density.

For the City of Chicago in 1940 it is possible to find data necessary to investigate the relationship between these components, distance and age for the seventy-five community areas.[16] (See Table 1.) As a

TABLE 1 Components of the correlation between distance from city center and total population density, Chicago, 1940.
(Units of enumeration are Community Areas)

COMPONENT	CORRELATION WITH DISTANCE (1)	STANDARD DEVIATION OF COMPONENT AS RATIO OF STANDARD DEVIATION OF TOTAL DENSITY (2)	CONTRIBUTION OF COMPONENT TO CORRELATION OF TOTAL DENSITY AND DISTANCE (3)	PROPORTIONATE CONTRIBUTION OF COMPONENT TO CORRELATION (4)
$\text{Log}\,\frac{\text{Population}}{\text{Dwelling Units}}$	0.296	0.132	0.039	−0.059
$\text{Log}\,\frac{\text{Dwelling Units}}{\text{Structures}}$	−0.594	0.468	−0.278	0.419
$\text{Log}\,\frac{\text{Structures}}{\text{Area}}$	−0.517	0.821	−0.424	0.640
Total:				
$\text{Log}\,\frac{\text{Population}}{\text{Area}}$	−0.663	1.000	−0.663	1.000

measure of age, the percentage of dwelling units built before 1920 was used. Column (1) presents the correlations with distance from the city center of the logarithm of density and the logarithms of the components of density. Investigating the relationship between components of density and distance, we find that both structures per area and units per structure are negatively related to distance with the latter correlation being somewhat stronger. Population per unit,

16. Wirth and Bernert [21] and Chicago Plan Commission [3].

however, shows a significant positive relationship with distance. The relationsip between these correlations and the correlation of distance with total density, which is of higher absolute value than any of its components, can be explicated as follows:

For some variable z let:

$$z = x_1 + x_2 + x_3.$$

Then for some other variable y,

$$C_{yz} = \Sigma zy - \frac{\Sigma z \Sigma y}{N} = \Sigma(x_1 + x_2 + x_3)y - \frac{\Sigma(x_1 + x_2 + x_3)\Sigma y}{N}$$

Thus,

$$C_{yz} = C_{yx_1} + C_{yx_2} + C_{yx_3}. \tag{9}$$

Since the correlation between y and z is given by:

$$r_{zy} = \frac{C_{zy}}{(C_{yy})^{1/2}(C_{zz})^{1/2}} = \frac{C_{yx_1} + C_{yx_2} + C_{yz_3}}{(C_{yy})^{1/2}(C_{zz})^{1/2}}$$

where,

$$C_{yy} = \Sigma y^2 - \frac{(\Sigma y)^2}{N},$$

and

$$C_{zz} = \Sigma z^2 - \frac{(\Sigma z)^2}{N}$$

the correlation between y and z is given by:

$$r_{zy} = r_{x_1y}\frac{S_{x_1}}{S_z} + r_{x_2y}\frac{S_{x_2}}{S_z} + r_{x_8y}\frac{S_{x_8}}{S_z}, \tag{10}$$

where S is the standard deviation of the appropriate variable. Therefore, the correlation between distance and total density is given by the weighted sum of the correlations of distance with the components. The weights are the proportion that the standard deviation of the component is of the standard deviation of the total. Since the variance of total density is equal to the sum of the variances of the components plus twice the sum of the convariances, the sum of weights in the above equation does not necessarily add to one.

The relationships between distance and each component of density and between distance and total density are summarized in Table 1. Column (1) of that table presents the zero order correlations. Column (2) presents the ratio of the standard deviation of each component to the standard deviation of the total. Column (3) presents the contribution of the correlation of the component to the total correlation. Column (4) presents the proportionate contribution. In spite of the fact that the correlation of distance with population per unit is positive and significant, this relationship detracts very little from the total negative correlation with distance, because the standard deviation of this component is such a small proportion of the standard deviation of the total. We may also note that although the dwellings per structure component is more highly correlated with distance than is structures per unit of land, it makes a smaller contribution to the total correlation, because its standard deviation is a smaller proportion of the standard deviation of the total. It is somewhat surprising that within the city limits of Chicago, the standard deviation of structures per unit of land is about 82 percent of the standard deviation of total density.

Table 2 presents the correlations of each component with age and the correlation of total density with age. Here again, we find that dwellings per structure has the largest correlation and also is the largest contributor to the total correlation.

TABLE 2 Components of the correlation between percent of dwelling units built before 1920 and total population density, Chicago, 1940. (*Units of enumeration are Community Areas*)

COMPONENT	CORRELATION WITH AGE	STANDARD DEVIATION OF COMPONENT AS RATIO OF STANDARD DEVIATION OF TOTAL DENSITY	CONTRIBUTION OF COMPONENT TO CORRELATION OF TOTAL DENSITY AND AGE	PROPORTIONATE CONTRIBUTION OF COMPONENT TO CORRELATION
	(1)	(2)	(3)	(4)
$\text{Log}\,\frac{\text{Population}}{\text{Dwelling Units}}$	−0.099	0.132	−0.013	−0.033
$\text{Log}\,\frac{\text{Dwelling Units}}{\text{Structures}}$	0.466	0.468	0.218	0.559
$\text{Log}\,\frac{\text{Structures}}{\text{Area}}$	0.226	0.820	0.185	0.474
Total:				
$\text{Log}\,\frac{\text{Population}}{\text{Area}}$	0.390	1.000	0.390	1.000

This finding leads us to the suggestion that the effect of age on density may operate primarily through the component dwellings per structure. In Chicago we may investigate this suggestion further by looking at the partial correlations of density with distance holding age constant. Here again we find the partial correlation for total density to be larger than the partial for any of the components. By a logic similar to that presented above, it is possible to demonstrate that the partial correlation for total density is the weighted sum of the partial correlations of the components. In this case, however, the weights are the proportion that the residual standard deviation of the component is of the residual standard deviation of the total. Table 3 presents the details of this relationship. Column (1) presents the partial correlation, column (2) the ratios of standard deviations, column (3) the contribution of each component to the total correlation, and column (4) the proportionate contribution.

TABLE 3 Components of the partial correlation of density on distance holding age constant, Chicago, 1940.

COMPONENT	PARTIAL CORRELATION WITH DISTANCE	RATIO OF RESIDUAL STANDARD DEVIATIONS	CONTRIBUTION OF COMPONENT TO TOTAL PARTIAL	PROPORTIONATE CONTRIBUTION
	(1)	(2)	(3)	(4)
$\text{Log} \frac{\text{Population}}{\text{Dwelling Units}}$	0.270	0.143	0.039	−0.07
$\text{Log} \frac{\text{Dwelling Units}}{\text{Structures}}$	−0.473	0.435	−0.206	0.35
$\text{Log} \frac{\text{Structures}}{\text{Area}}$	−0.483	0.869	−0.420	0.72
Total:				
$\text{Log} \frac{\text{Population}}{\text{Area}}$	−0.584	1.000	−0.584	1.000

A comparison of the contribution of each component between Table 1 and Table 3 offers some additional evidence that the effect of age on density operates through the component dwellings per structure. This component contributes −0.278 to the zero-order correlation. It contributes less, −0.206, to the partial correlation. On the other hand, the contribution of population per dwelling to the two correlations is identical, 0.039, while the contribution of structures per area is very nearly identical; −0.424 for the zero-order versus −0.420 for the partial. Thus, almost all of the difference between the zero-order and the partial correlation of density and distance is due to the component dwellings per structure.

This finding leads us to the conclusion that, within the central city of Chicago, the influence of age on density operates primarily through the mechanism of the number of dwellings per structure. It suggests that the type of structure composition of many parts of the city was established under previously existing transportation conditions and then, despite new transportation conditions, remained relatively unflexible.

These results are based on the central city of only one large city. How might our findings be generalized? From O. D. Duncan we know that older cities have depended more on congestion to house their population than younger cities of the same size. Our finding suggests that the relationship between total density and the distribution of city growth in time, holding constant population size, should be explained by the type of structure composition of the city. A reasonable measure of the growth pattern of the city through time might be given by the age of dwellings composition of the city. Our investigation might be further refined if we took into account the fact that all our reasoning has been based on residential use of the land. Hence, it might be well to also hold constant the percentage of the labor force in manufacturing.

METHOD, DESIGN AND DATA

We are now presented with a rather interesting design problem. We are concerned with the influence of a variable (age of dwelling) represented by a percentage distribution, on another variable which is a single measure for our units of observation (population density). Further, we have reason to think that another variable also represented by a percentage distribution (type of structure), should be included in the analysis in order to hold constant its effect on the first compositional variable and to judge its influence on the relationship. We would also like to regard two other single measure variables (population size and percentage of the labor force in manufacturing) as independent variables and hold them constant in the relationship between density and age of dwellings. Our hypothesis, which states that the influence of timing of growth has its effect on density through the nature of dwellings built in another technological era but remaining to the present, suggests that holding constant the type of structure distribution should do away with the relationship between age of dwellings distribution and density.

The general problem of how to deal with compositional variables is a complex one. If one is interested in the relationship between two variables which are compositions, techniques of standardization seem appropriate. If one is interested in the relationship between a compositional variable and a variable which is a single measure, some quite clumsy techniques can be worked out.[17] When it is assumed that the compositional variable represents partitions of some sort of continuous variable and one assumes some regular, smooth, relationship between the scale and the single measure variable, then some single positional measure may be used. This was the approach taken in the analysis of the relationship between density and age within the city of

17. Duncan, O. D. et al. [10; pp. 46–81].

Chicago. There we used as a single, positional measure of age the proportion of dwellings built before 1920. This would also be a possible approach to the type of structure composition. We might, for instance, use as a summary measure, dwellings per structure. However, there may be some time-specific effect of growth on density. Also there may be no very orderly relationship between building in one decade and the type of structure composition it predicts.

The solution to this design problem will be to consider the percentage of dwellings in each age category as a separate variable and the percentage of dwellings in each type-of-structure category as a separate variable. We may then use multiple correlation and regression as our primary statistical tools. In order to use compositional variables in this fashion, it is necessary to drop one of the age-of-dwelling categories and one of the type-of-structure categories in order that these variables do not separately add to unity for each observation. By including all other categories in the compositions, however, we may presume all of its predictive power has been exhausted and that its influence on other variables has been held constant. Using the compositional variables in this way, we may compute:

$$R_{y(i,j,1,2)} \tag{11}$$

where y is a single measure, i the first compositional variable, j the second compositional variable, and two additional independent variables which are single measures.

Within this framework, our hypothesis can be tested by the use of the multiple-partial correlation developed by Cowden[6]. In this instance, the square of that statistic is given by:

$$R^2_{(y\cdot j,1,2)(i\cdot j,1,2)} = 1 - \frac{1-R^2_{y(i,j,1,2)}}{1-R^2_{y(j,1,2)}}. \tag{12}$$

In the present problem this statistic may be interpreted as the correlation between density and age of dwellings, holding constant type of structure, the logarithm of population and percentage of the labor force in manufacturing.

Data on the type of structure distribution for urbanized areas are taken from the 1950 Census of Housing, as are data for the age-of-dwelling composition. These latter data, however, include as one category dwellings built before 1920. In order to estimate data for earlier time periods, the percentage of dwellings built in 1919 or before was distributed into age categories as were the dwellings in 1940 for metropolitan districts.[18]

18. U.S. Bureau of the Census [18].

FINDINGS AND INTERPRETATIONS

Table 4 presents multiple correlations of the independent variables with population density. In this table, each row presents the multiple correlations of the dependent variable on the row variable and all preceding variables. Thus, 0.47 is the multiple correlation of density on all of the age-of-dwelling categories. We may note that the

TABLE 4 Multiple correlation coefficients for population density for 119 urbanized areas over 100,000 population, United States, 1950.

INDEPENDENT VARIABLES	DENSITY AS DEPENDENT	
	CORRELATION ON ROW AND ALL ABOVE	CORRELATION ON ROW AND ALL ABOVE
Percentage of dwelling units built:		
1940–44	0.044	
1930–39	0.268	
1920–29	0.272	
1910–19	0.352	
1900–09	0.380	
1880–99	0.436	
1879 or before	0.470	
Logarithm of population	0.600	
Percentage of dwelling units in structures with:		
1 dwelling unit attached	0.624	0.316
1 and 2 dwelling units semi-attached	0.628	0.332
2 dwelling units, other	0.651	0.433
3–4 dwelling units	0.651	0.433
5–9 dwelling units	0.651	0.449
10–19 dwelling units	0.657	0.497
20 or more dwelling units	0.657	0.576
Logarithm of population	—	0.625
Percentage in manufacturing	0.667	0.637

addition of population size to the age variable markedly increases the correlation. It explains an additional 14 percent of the variance of density. Addition of the type of structure variables to age and population raises the multiple correlation to 0.66. Thus they add an additional 7 percent to the explained variance. Addition of percentage in manufacturing to the battery of variables, completing the list, produces a correlation of 0.67. Thus, the whole battery of independent variables explains about 45 percent of the variance in density. Table 5 presents the multiple-partial correlations. For the relationship between density and age, we may note that holding population constant reduces the magnitude of the correlation somewhat. Addition of type of structure to the variables held constant reduces the magnitude of the correlation considerably. Thus, much of the effect of age on density is through type of structure, as we expected. The correlation remains significant, however, suggesting that age also operates through other mechanisms.

TABLE 5 Partial and multiple-partial correlation coefficients for population density, 119 urbanized areas over 100,000 population, United States, 1950.

VARIABLES	COEFFICIENT
Density and Age, Holding Constant:	
Nothing	0.47
Population	0.40
Population and Type of Structure	0.26
Population, Type of Structure, and Percentage Manufacturing	0.25
Density and Type of Structure, Holding Constant:	
Nothing	0.58
Population	0.30
Population and Age	0.34

Adding percentage in manufacturing does not diminish the correlation appreciably. It still remains significant. Thus, there is some evidence that the relationship between age and density is not dependent on the differential allocation of land to manufacturing by age of city.

The discovery that these variables do not explain all of the influence of age on density suggests that age of dwellings may be an index of influences of timing of growth external to the type of structure in which the dwellings exist. For instance, it may be that growth during a particular period determines, in part, the size of residential lots, the amount of land used for transportation, the amount of land allocated for business, education, or recreational use.

All in all, what have we accomplished by this somewhat lengthy and tortuous analysis? We have argued that the growth of the city is a complex process influenced heavily by more or less synchronic considerations of the relative cost of transportation and housing at various distances from the city center but also considerably influenced by the previous growth pattern of the city. We have shown further that the mechanisms through which previous form influences growth are not simple. We have investigated the hypothesis of a single mechanism for this relationship and been forced to reject that mechanism as the sole, but not as an important, way in which previous form influences contemporary structure. We submit the further elaboration of these mechanisms as an area of research in which both the nature of the data and the elaboration of theory make possible an interesting and sophisticated investigation of social change.

REFERENCES

1. Bogue, D. J. and D. L. Harris. *Comparative Population and Urban Research via Multiple Regression and Covariance Analysis*. Oxford, Ohio: Scripps Foundation, Miami University, 1954.

2. Boulding, K. E. "Toward a General Theory of Growth," in J. J. Spengler and O. D. Duncan (eds.), *Population Theory and Policy*. New York: The Free Press, 1956, pp. 109–124.
3. Chicago Plan Commission. *Residential Chicago*. Vol. 1 of the Report of the Chicago Land Use Survey directed by the Chicago Plan Commission and conducted by the Works Project Administration. Chicago: City of Chicago, 1942.
4. Clark, C. "Urban Population Densities," *Journal of the Royal Statistical Society*, Series A, 114 (1951), 490–496.
5. Clark, C. "Urban Population Densities," *Bulletin of the International Statistical Institute*, 36 (1957), 60–90.
6. Cowden, D. J. "The Multiple-Partial Correlation Coefficient," *Journal of the American Statistical Association*, 47 (1952), 442–456.
7. Duncan, B. "Intra-Urban Population Movement," in P. K. Hatt and A. J. Reiss, Jr, (eds.), *Cities and Society*. New York: The Free Press, 1957.
8. Duncan, B., G. Sabagh, and M. D. Von Arsdol, Jr. "Patterns of City Growth," *American Journal of Sociology*, 67 (1962), 418–429.
9. Duncan, O. D. "Population Distribution and Community Structure," Cold Spring Harbor *Symposia on Quantitative Biology*, 22 (1959).
10. Duncan, O. D., *et al. Metropolis and Region*. Baltimore: The Johns-Hopkins Press, 1960.
11. Federal Housing Administration. *The Structure and Growth of Residential Neighborhoods in American Cities*. Washington D.C.: U.S. Government Office, 1939.
12. Hawley, A. H. *Human Ecology*. New York: The Ronald Press Company, 1950.
13. Hurd, R. M. *Principles of City Land Values*. New York: The Record and Guide, 1911.
14. McKenzie, R. D. *The Metropolitan Community*. New York: McGraw-Hill, 1933.
15. Muth, R. "The Spatial Structure of the Housing Market," *Papers and Proceedings of the Regional Science Association*, 7 (1961).
16. Reinhardt, F. R. "A Test of Hypotheses Specifically Related to the Cross-sectional Distribution of Population Densities of Cities." Unpublished Master's Dissertation, Department of Sociology, University of Minnesota, 1950.
17. Stewart, J. Q. and W. Warntz. "Physics of Population Distribution," *Journal of Regional Science*, 1 (1958), 99–123.
18. U.S. Bureau of the Census. *Sixteenth Census of the United States*: *1940, Housing*, vol. II, "General Characteristics," parts 2–5. Washington, D.C.: U.S. Government Printing Office, 1943.
19. Winsborough, H. H. "A Comparative Study of Urban Population Density." Unpublished Ph.D. Dissertation, Department of Sociology, The University of Chicago, 1961.
20. Winsborough, H. H. "An Ecological Approach to the Theory of suburbanization," *The American Journal of Sociology*, 68 (1963), 565–570.
21. Wirth, L. and E. H. Bernert. *Local Community Fact Book of Chicago*. Chicago: The University of Chicago Press, 1949.

14

BENJAMIN CHINITZ

Contrasts in Agglomeration: New York and Pittsburgh

The natural inclination of a scientist when confronted with a new problem is to try to solve it with old tools. When he is finally convinced that the old tools will not do the job, he retreats to his shop to fashion some new tools. The burden of my argument in this paper is that we have reached the stage in regional economics when we must begin to fashion some new analytical tools.

When I say regional economics I have in mind specifically the analysis of the growth and structure of the economy of geographic subdivisions within a national economy. This type of analysis is now being carried on in at least a dozen metropolitan areas throughout the country and in numerous other types of subdivisions, large and small. I have been associated with two such studies: the New York Metropolitan Region Study, which just recently published its final report, and the Pittsburgh Economic Study, which is at its halfway mark, having been initiated in June, 1959, and being scheduled for completion in June, 1962. My observations, as the title of my paper suggests, are drawn from these two immersions in regional economics.

The basic-nonbasic approach to the analysis of a region has been under severe attack from many quarters in recent years. But I think it is fair to say that alternative approaches have differed in degree of refinement more than in kind. Fundamentally, we still go about our business in the same way. We try to identify the autonomous influences operating on the region and chart a network of interdependence between sectors within the region. I have no quarrel with this approach. I find it difficult to frame the problem otherwise. My quarrel is with the limitations of the maps of interdependence which are typically drawn.

I will surely be doing some of my colleagues an injustice with the following generalization but, begging their pardon, I state it anyway: our efforts so far have been almost exclusively devoted to the demand dimension of interdependence. The supply side has been virtually ignored. Let me elaborate.

The basic-nonbasic model is a way of coming to grips with the demand side of interdependence in one fell swoop. The links in the

Reprinted from American Economic Review *(May 1961), pp. 279–89, by permission of the Publishers and the author.*

output-income-consumption chain, the links in the output-capital-formation chain, the links in the output-tax revenues-government spending chain, and the links in the output-materials purchased-output (i.e., input-output) chain, are all subsumed under one grand link between the exogenous and the endogenous elements of the system. Sometimes we can get away with this leap over a lot of treacherous ground just as in football a seventy-yard pass from the thirty-yard line occasionally results in a touchdown. To maintain the metaphor, most of us prefer to gain more yardage on the ground before passing into the end zone.

So we move in small steps. We try to chart the flows between our sectors in greater detail. A dollar of output of industry A, we observe, generates a demand for the output of industry C which is not equal to the demand generated for the output of industry C by a dollar of output of industry B. We observe, further, that a dollar of output of industry A generates more or less personal income than a dollar of output of industry B. If we are really keen observers, we might even discover that a dollar paid out to workers in industry A generates demands for consumer goods, housing construction, and government services which are different from the demands generated by a dollar paid out to workers in industry B.

My point is that in the main we improve upon the crude basic-nonbasic approach by a process of flow disaggregation—a process which hopefully will reduce our margin of error. I characterize this activity as the application of old tools to new problems for the obvious reason that input-output relationships, consumption functions, investment functions, and the like are old tools which were fashioned to solve the problems of a national economy. Furthermore, all those tools are used to come to grips with the demand side of the interdependence between sectors in a regional economy.

When I say that the supply has been ignored, I mean simply that we have not come to grips with the following question: How does the level of activity in industry A in a given region influence the factor supply curves confronting industry B in the same region? Let me hasten to exclude one kind of effort from my indictment. We certainly have tried to incorporate the influence on industry B of the availability of the output of industry A as an input to industry B. Probably the best example of this kind of work is the Isard-Kuenne study of the impact of the Fairless Works. But this is only one of a number of supply relationships which need to be explored and, as far as I can tell, they have not received adequate attention from regional economists.

My former colleagues on the New York Metropolitan Region Study staff could certainly register a strong objection at this point.

After all, another term for supply interdependence is external economies and diseconomies, and there is certainly a lot of discussion about them in a number of volumes of the New York study.

But this discussion is limited to two problems: one has to do with intraindustry external economies and diseconomies the other has to do with the influence of the aggregate size of the region on the costs of individual firms. The first problem is too narrowly defined and the second too broadly defined from my point of view.

Nevertheless, I believe, regional economics owes a great debt to the New York Metropolitan Region Study for highlighting these external relationships. It was only after we were confronted with the problem of understanding certain features of the Pittsburgh economy that we at the Pittsburgh Study felt compelled to probe more deeply into the nature of these interindustry effects.

Pittsburgh, as a metropolitan economy, stands in sharp contrast to New York with respect to these three summary variables: size, industrial structure, and rate of growth in recent decades. New York is between six and seven times the size of Pittsburgh. New York has a much more diversified industrial structure. And, while New York has grown at just a bit less than the national rate for the last thirty years, Pittsburgh has grown at less than half the national rate in the same period.

Superficially, all these contrasts fit a familiar pattern. Large areas are more diversified than small areas. Diversified areas exhibit more stability in their growth because their fortunes are not tied to the fortunes of a few industries. In these terms, Pittsburgh's story seems easy to tell.

Unfortunately the matter cannot rest there. Pittsburgh is much more specialized than any large SMA with the exception of Detroit, including many which are no larger than Pittsburgh and many which are considerably smaller. The question, why is it not diversified, therefore, remains largely unanswered. Of course, if we could accept the lack of diversification as inevitable, we might not have to try to understand it. For it is difficult to quarrel with the proposition that the future of such an area can be safely projected once we project the future for its one or two dominant industries. But here we may be caught on the horns of a dilemma. Suppose we project a sharp decline in the dominant industries along with a modest decline in the region's minor industries. True, the dominant industries will retard the growth of the region but in the process they will also decline in relative importance. The region will then become more diversified in its old age, so to speak. What then? Do we correct for the increased diversification? Does it open up new opportunities to the region?

The need to understand the whys and wherefores of diversification should therefore be quite apparent. This has led us to consider the question which I posed earlier: How does the growth of one industry in an area affect the area's suitability as a location for other industries?

But we are not yet ready to assert that the latter question has to be answered. We might avoid it if we could show that different degrees of diversification in areas of comparable size are due simply to the fact that some areas have a variety of locational advantages which makes them attractive to a variety of industries while other areas offer advantages only to a small number of industries. Observe for example the figures in Table 1 for Cleveland and Pittsburgh.

TABLE 1 Employment in selected manufacturing industries, 1957.

	CLEVELAND	PITTSBURGH
Food	14,532	20,459
Textiles and apparel	14,130	3,550
Printing and publishing	14,618	10,042
Chemicals and products	17,959	6,823
Stone, clay and glass	3,260	21,372
Primary metals	46,894	154,215
Fabricated metals	38,378	31,298
Machinery, nonelectrical	52,552	23,534
Electrical machinery	20,746	27,652
Transportation equipment	55,570	11,047
Total	311,471	358,239

Source: Bureau of the Census, *Annual Survey of Manufactures, 1957.*

Pittsburgh is way ahead in glass and primary metals and leads also in food and electrical machinery. Cleveland, on the other hand, is ahead in textiles, printing, chemicals, fabricated metals, nonelectrical machinery, and transportation equipment. On the whole, Cleveland is a much more diversified manufacturing center. But maybe this is just the outcome of the process by which individual industries gravitate to those areas which are best for them. If Cleveland had attracted the 154,215 employees in primary metals, it might still look more like itself than like Pittsburgh in the rest of its manufacturing profile.

I cannot assert positively that this is an unsatisfactory way of approaching the matter, but I can suggest a number of reasons why I find it necessary to go beyond it. For one thing, this approach implies that location of industry is heavily determined by transportation factors or, as we say in our jargon, transport oriented. By this we mean that the location of markets and materials and the transport network determine the geographic distribution of industries. If a lot of industries end up in one place, presto, you have a diversified regional economy.

Nobody believes that the logic of location runs in these terms for the majority of manufacturing industries. My former colleague, Robert Lichtenberg, of the New York Study, after a painstaking review of factors influencing industrial location classified 50 percent of American manufacturing as nontransport oriented. P. Sargent Florence has repeatedly emphasized in his writings that transport orientation is a minor influence in location. There is also a fairly general consensus that the proportion of industry which is transport oriented is diminishing as time goes on.

Once we recognize that variations in production costs are important determinants of location, we cannot avoid the consideration of interindustry factor cost relationships. Production costs are not given by nature, except that nature may influence the cost of energy and the cost of plant. These are trivial determinants alongside the influence exerted by the way in which a region's natural advantages are exploited. If we ask why are wage rates higher in one area than another, it is only in rare cases that nature will provide the answer. In most cases the explanation will run in historical terms; that is, in terms of the heritage of each region as it bears on labor supply.

For many purposes it is sufficient to recognize the difference in wage rates, and there is no compulsion to explain why it exists. A firm which is seeking a maximum profit location for a new plant might very well take the wage-rate differential as given—a type of behavior which fits so well the textbook model of a competitive firm. Even so, a conscientious consultant might very well post a warning signal. After all, a plant represents a twenty-year commitment. What is the wage differential likely to be twenty years hence? Be that as it may, it is certainly inappropriate to take wage-rate differentials as given in a twenty-year projection for a region. A static atomistic approach will not do for a problem in aggregate dynamics.

I also find the multiple-locational-advantages theory of diversification unsatisfactory for another reason. It permits us to assess an area's potential for growth only with reference to industries with known locational requirements. But in a projection, it is difficult enough to anticipate the bill of goods, let alone to project the locational needs of the industries which will be producing them. This may suggest that we ought to give up the ghost. Those who have this alternative are blessed. The rest of us have to seek ways to mitigate the curse. One is to develop the concept of a region's capacity for attracting new industries with considerable freedom of location from a transport point of view. If we are to develop such a concept, we need to probe into the region itself more deeply than we do when we locate industries one by one.

I have said enough—perhaps too much—about my reasons for raising these questions. I will now proceed to the main business of this paper, which is to offer some hypotheses about interindustry influences on factor costs. To begin with, I think that the net has to be spread a lot wider than most people assume. I propose to consider all the traditional categories: entrepreneurship, capital, labor, and land, in that order.

Entrepreneurship

This is a production factor which, to my knowledge, no one has tried to price out at different locations. The implicit assumption, I suppose, is that the supply schedule of entrepreneurship is identical at all locations. Our colleagues studying international differences in growth reject this assumption explicitly. I am convinced that we need to reconsider its validity in regional economics.

When you tell a location analyst that a firm is where it is because its founders prefer to live there, he throws up his hands. Such cases, he claims, are outside his domain. Our own experience suggests that for many industries cost is almost invariant with location—or at least there is no "min min" location. Yet we are reluctant to treat such cases as random phenomena because we feel there are significant variations in the cost of entrepreneurship. Moreover, these differences may be large enough to offset other cost differences.

I came to this notion by reflecting on the differences between New York and Pittsburgh, but I hasten to say that area size is only one variable. For a given size of area, the entrepreneurial supply curve is also a function of certain traditions and elements of the social structure which are heavily influenced by the character of the area's historic specializations.

The proposition I offer is this: An industry which is competitively organized—in the neoclassical sense of the term "competition"—has more entrepreneurs per dollar of output than an industry which is organized along oligopolistic lines. The average establishment in the apparel industry, for example, has one-sixth as many employees as the average establishment in primary metals. Furthermore, multi-unit firms account for 82 percent of the employment in primary metals, while they account for only 28 percent of employment in apparel. Now you may have as much management per dollar of output in primary metals as you have in apparel, but you certainly do not have as many managers who are also risk-takers and this is my definition of an entrepreneur.

What is the consequence of this? My feeling is that you do not breed as many entrepreneurs per capita in families allied with steel as you do in families allied with apparel, using these two industries for illustrative purposes only. The son of a salaried executive is less likely to be sensitive to opportunities wholly unrelated to his father's field than the son of an independent entrepreneur. True, the entrepreneur's son is more likely to think of taking over his father's business. My guess is however, that the tradition of risk-bearing is, on the whole, a more potent influence in broadening one's perspective.

I think I have formulated a proposition which can at least theoretically be tested, although I confess that I have not tested it yet. For all I know, this may already be a well-established proposition in entrepreneurial history.

But if an oligopolistic environment has a lower entrepreneurial birth rate, there remains the question of how receptive it is to the in-migration of entrepreneurs. Here, too, I would argue that the competitively organized area has an edge. Receptivity as measured by factor costs we shall discuss under separate headings later on. What I have in mind now is receptivity as it relates to the entrepreneur's "utility function." There is an aura of second-class citizenship attached to the small businessman in an environment dominated by big business. It manifests itself in many small ways, such as the kinds of social clubs he can belong to, the residential areas he will comfortably fit into, the business organizations he can join, and so forth. The ease of entry, to borrow a concept from industrial organization, is considerably greater in an environment dominated—not dominated, to be more exact—by small firm industries. I am not sure that we can satisfactorily test this notion, but I am hopeful.

Capital

Many of the same observations are relevant to regional differences in the availability of capital. Here, too, we are dealing with a factor whose cost is typically assumed to be invariant with respect to location. This is surely not so. It is true that capital is almost perfectly mobile, provided the probability distribution of returns is approximately known. G.M. and U.S. Steel can raise capital almost anywhere with equal ease. But a small firm embarking on a new enterprise will find a much more receptive ear over the home counter than it will over-the-counter in "foreign" places. The cost of transferring confidence may be high enough to give us a capital-supply function which has distance as an important independent variable.

Once we admit of such immobility, it becomes relevant to inquire into differences in local capital supply among areas. Again the industrial organization of the dominant industries strikes me as an important variable. A major source of capital to new firms in general is the undistributed profit and unexpended depreciation allowance of old firms. Now, the surplus capital which accumulates inside large multiplant companies, I would argue, is more mobile interregionally within the company than intraregionally outside the company. A large corporation is more likely to respond to investment opportunities in its traditional activity at other locations than to investment opportunities at home in unrelated industries. The small firm, by contrast, is more likely to make its surplus capital available to other local enterprise in another industry than to a distant enterprise in the same industry. (Actually, I have overstated the case to avoid a complex formulation. All I need to argue is that the marginal rate of substitution between local and foreign outlets is greater [smaller] for the large multiplant firm [small firm]. Given an equivalent array of investment opportunities at home, the surplus capital of the multiplant industry is more likely to "leak" out to other areas.)

The commercial banks, of course, also play a vital role in the initial financing of new business. Are banks in one area more receptive than banks in another area to the demands of new business and, if so, are these differences in attitude shaped by the industrial traditions of the area? I say yes, on both counts. My conviction on this point is based less on deductive than on inductive reasoning. I have been told that this is the case. Having been told, I can think of some fairly good reasons why this might be the case. When banks cater to a competitively organized industry, they are more likely to accept the insurance principle of making money, not on each customer, but on the average customer. If you have U.S. Steel and Westinghouse on your rolls, you do not have to learn to make money on the insurance principle.

In the present state of my knowledge, I am not too optimistic about being able to test these hypotheses empirically. However, I am not prepared to pronounce them as untestable. This is an altogether too easy way out. I believe if we think hard enough, we can spell out some corollaries which, if we dig hard enough, we can subject to empirical test.

Labor

Now we come to what most will assume and I am prepared to concede is the cost factor, which is most sensitive to interindustry influence. Yet, even here, I suspect I will be spreading my net farther than most people would.

First, the wage level. My colleague on the Pittsburgh Study, Mel Bers, is exploring this question in great detail. The presumption that the wage level in the dominant industry influences the wage level in other industries is one which no one can seriously question. I am confident that Ber's research will throw more light on the network of interdependence than anything that has been done so far. Bers is also immersed in the study of the influence of labor organization in the dominant industry on the structure of wages in the region. These two issues are inseparable in this framework.

But there are other influences relating to labor cost and supply which are not generally recognized. Bers found, for example, that the rate of participation of married women in the labor force in the Pittsburgh region is far below the average for metropolitan areas. When standardized for industry mix, however, it turns out that the rate is as high as you would expect it to be. The question arises, therefore, do these women represent a potential supply or not? Why are not female-labor-using industries attracted by the surplus? Wages aside, there are at least two other factors relating to the character of the dominant industries which influence the outcome.

The first is the dispersion within the region of the plants of our dominant industries. The ratio of central city employment to SMA employment in manufacturing is much lower in Pittsburgh than in any of the large SMA's. Outside the Central City, the gradient in Pittsburgh is also flatter. The reasons are obvious. Our industries could not be piled up one on top of another as in the garment district even if our land were flat. The topography encourages still greater dispersion. But the importance of this for our purposes is that the early dispersion of manufacturing (plus the dispersion of mining) led to a dispersal of population which is also unmatched among our large SMA's. To the extent that pools of female labor are relevant to industrial location, Pittsburgh is at a disadvantage because a greater radius is required to form a pool of a given size. One must bear in mind that the areas in which the plants of the dominant industries operate are not exactly the most desirable as sites for other kinds of industry. (We shall return to this point later on.)

The second point has to do with the work schedule of the man in the family. Steel is a three-shift industry. The typical worker is not assigned to a particular shift for an indefinite period. Instead he works from 8:00 to 4:00 for some time, then 4:00 to 12:00 for some time, then 12:00 to 8:00 for some time. He also has to put in his share of weekends. It is reasonable to suppose that under these conditions the housewife is somewhat less willing to work than under ordinary conditions. Taken together, these factors tend to dissipate some of the labor force advantages we normally attribute to SMA's. And they are consequences of characteristics of the dominant industries.

Land

We normally assume than an SMA is large enough in area to nullify any considerations of site availability as a location factor except for industries with very special requirements like steel and chemicals. In general, I think this is a sensible approach. Nevertheless, I feel compelled to attach some importance to the impact of an industry's operations on the quality of the air and water in the surrounding area. Pittsburgh, as you all know, was notorious until recent years for its smoke and dust. There were three causes for this condition. The principal one was the use of soft coal as fuel in households and industry. A second was the steel industry. And a third was the railroads with their steam engines. All this has changed now and I do not mind using this forum as an opportunity to plug the radical improvement in the quality of Pittsburgh's air. A white shirt will now stay white in Pittsburgh for as long as it will in any city in the country. But it will take some time to work off our reputation. And furthermore, at a time when the reputation was founded in fact, it was bound to exercise a restraining influence on the growth of subsidiary industries in the region.

Intermediate Goods and Services

So much for the primary factors of production. I said earlier that location analysts have paid attention to a dominant industry's impact on the location of other industries which are oriented to the supply of the product of the dominant industry. But agglomeration is nourished more by the availability of a wide range of goods and services created in the first instance by the growth of the dominant industries. Transportation is the classic illustration of this phenomena. One industry attracts the service, and a second industry coming in finds that the service is available at costs which are lower than they would be in virgin territory. The second industry also finds already in existence a whole community of suppliers of business services such as legal, accounting, duplicating, etc.

The question I raise is whether the emergence of these services and their availability to other industries depends on the character of these industries which trigger development in the first instance. I think much depends on the internal organization of these industries. Large firms incorporate many of these services within their own operations because they can achieve scale economies within the firm. They are much more fully integrated and therefore depend less on outside suppliers. On the one hand, this means that, dollar for dollar, their business is less of a stimulus to the creation of a community of independent suppliers. On the other hand, the new entrant is not likely to find that the company is anxious to spread its fixed costs by making its services available to outsiders.

Again, consider the classic example of external economies: transport services. A firm which operates its own truck fleet on an exempt basis is specifically forbidden by the ICC to transport freight as a common carrier. Imagine then that you have two communities of equal size. In one of these, all the firms rely on common carriage. Hence service to and from a wide variety of places is available to all comers. In the other community, every firm has its private truck fleet. True, the roads are built and this helps a lot. But there is no service available to the new firm coming in unless it starts big.

We do know that Pittsburgh is not up to par in employment in ancillary services. This is indicated by the calculation of location quotients based on the 1950 Census of Population. The Duncans in their recent book, *Metropolis and Region,* also found that Pittsburgh had less than the national average per capita employment in service industries broadly defined. Only Detroit among the SMA's of 1,000,000 population or more shared this characteristic with Pittsburgh. It goes without saying, that much of my reasoning is applicable to Detroit as well.

Summary and Conclusions

It should be apparent by now that what I am reaching for is the specification of a function which relates external economies and diseconomies to industry structure, size being held constant. My feeling is that we have been too prone to associate external economies and diseconomies with size. We have been disturbed at not being able to derive a satisfactory correlation between the two. What I have tried to do is explore some of the residual variation around the size function. I recognize the difficulties of adequately formulating and testing these notions. But I do not think we can afford to ignore them because they are difficult if, as I maintain, they are relevant to an understanding of the dynamics of area development.

To come back to my first point: I think we are not using the optimal combination of tools in regional analysis. We know we can do a lot more to refine the methods we use to trap what I have called the demand side of interdependence. We need bigger and better regional input-output tables, regional capital coefficients, regional consumption functions. But we are not equating marginal returns in all directions if we do not, at the same time, push vigorously on the supply side of the problem.

I said we need new tools in regional analysis. I am prepared to modify that statement in favor of this one. We need to make better use of some old tools which we have not yet applied very extensively to regional analysis. We need to work out the regional implications of market organization.

PART IV URBAN PLANNING

15

HARVEY S. PERLOFF AND LOWDON WINGO, JR.

Planning and Development in Metropolitan Affairs

City planning in the United States has exhibited an historical responsiveness to emerging interests and social needs which has earned it a central position in urban policy-making and accounted for much of its continuing growth. It has more than once found itself happily identified with powerful social currents which have carried it to successively greater heights of influence in the complex web of urban affairs. In its infancy it was the appointed instrument for the creation of the City Beautiful. On this base, hand in glove with the architects, urban designers, and other practitioners of the fine arts, it has brought urban aesthetic into the stream of policy consciousness and has helped to firm up the notion of a satisfying physical environment as a prime community objective. Later it conspired with the angels of Reform to erect the City Virtuous, and the New Renaissance of Philadelphia is a late victory for this intrigue. The City Efficient is a more recent infatuation which it has contracted from the engineer and for which it has marched forth to do battle with the disorderly forces of scatteration. In each of these currents city planners have sensed powerful city-shaping forces which have now ripened and become part of the environment of urban decision-making.

Actually, it is absurdly easy for an "open-ended" activity like city planning to play the dilettante through superficial contact with activities which matter greatly to people, or the mandarin through an exorbitant preoccupation with matters, which, however precious to the professional, elicit at best a tepid ardor from people as a whole. In spite of the rapid growth and intellectual advances of the field, these are lively perils for city planning today; its contacts with economic development, with transportation, with social welfare and human development, and with other important fields tend to be desultory and ineffectual in many communities, while elsewhere "planning administration" and project design details frequently distract city planning from a truly vital role in the actual development of the metropolitan region.

If city planning is to avoid these pitfalls and play a significant role

Reprinted by permission of the Journal of the American Institute of Planners, *28 (May 1962), 67–90.*

in the urban life of the future, it must look to its relations with the socially important activities and movements which are now emerging to shape the future course of metropolitan development. As the past has shown, meaningful relations with these evolving areas of social concern will involve new functions and require more versatile planning concepts and tools than we now have available.

The Things that Matter to People: The Major Social Movements

Some conception of these new issues with which city planning must come to grips can be gained from a review of some of the social movements with large implications for city planning that have been gathering momentum in recent years. These movements have evolved largely outside of the traditional concerns of city planning—indeed, they are not essentially urban. However, each carries with it some challenge to the future of city planning simply because each is an expression of essential wants and aspirations of an evolving society in an urban age.

Among the movements which deserve special attention in this context we would find (1) area development, (2) community development, (3) recreation and open space, (4) mental health, (5) housing, and (6) transportation improvement. "City planning" itself also belongs in the list of modern social movements, and those who have been close to it during the last two generations have experienced the forceful dynamic aspects that such a movement can manifest. Being themselves the professional instruments of a popular movement, city planners should be particularly sensitive to the role of such movements in our democratic society.

Common to all such movements is a vagueness in definition, which—important as it may be in generating broad enthusiasms—makes the establishment of meaningful relations difficult at times. The "area development" movement, while always concerned with the central issues of jobs and business expansion, embraces almost everything from narrow inducements to attract manufacturing plants to a locality all the way to broad notions about strengthening every aspect of an area's economy. The endlessly flexible term *development* in the language of this movement can become "area *re*development" which describes efforts to help economically distressed regions cope with their basic problems (with recent federal legislation, under the guidance of the Area Redevelopment Administration). The semantic circle is closed by the need of these communities to rebuild their public and private plants, which locks into the city planner's "redevelopment." Confusing? Certainly, but suggestive of potentially strong common bonds which invite exploitation.

The "community development" movement has its own special focus in spite of its broad title. Its concern is with self-help and decentralized decision-making. This movement, with its origins in the efforts of rural communities for self-improvement, was based on the rural sociologists' "community" and has gradually become transplanted to the urban scene. Here it has lost the geographic simplicity of the rural environment, and here "bootstrap" types of operation have different content and meaning. It has ripened on the redevelopment of obsolescent and deteriorating neighborhoods, which, with the involvement of neighborhood groups, makes it a matter of considerable importance to city planning. Although the city planning and community development movements have generated at least as much tension and conflict as mutual support in the past (particularly highlighted in the Jane Jacobs formulation), each will depend on effective connections with the other to achieve its ends in any decisive way. A formula for a meaningful relationship should be high on the urban agenda.

The recreation movement is particularly diffuse; it has become involved with diverse social efforts of very different characteristics: urban parks and playgrounds, the development of landscape resources, urban open spaces, wild life conservation, leisure activities for almost every group in the community, and recreation aspects of multiple purpose river valley development. Up until now the main connection between city planning and recreation has been in building up the intrametropolitan stock of "recreation facilities." But the important dimensions of the picture are changing rapidly, as the growth of personal incomes, family leisure, and mobility build up extraordinary demands for a broad array of recreation services and opportunities extending geographically over a vast area. These trends will require revolutionary innovations in planning and policy-making to respond to the changing needs and wants of urban populations.

The mental health movement is one of the most difficult to describe in a few words, for it ranges all the way from the psychiatric social services to the therapeutic aspects of the leisure-time activities of all sorts of people. The mental health movement has an important, if largely unconsummated, tie to city planning in its concern for the mental and emotional responses of people to various urban environments. Because this mutual concern has never ripened into a viable relationship, city planning has been deprived of an understanding in depth of the psychodynamics of urban people, and the mental health movement has been excluded from any effective role to alter the physical environment within which people live and work. This is a critically important link to be forged, for if city planning yields up its concern for the emotional welfare of the urbanite, it may find itself reduced to the service of a few dusty canons of urban design.

The relationship of the housing movement to city planning in this country has a fascinating history. In its youth the housing movement crusaded militantly for housing for the poor ("public housing") and for reform of the capital markets to permit the vast expansions of home ownership and protection of the home buyer. It was only a step to the setting of construction standards on the one hand, and into the improvement of the older housing stock through urban redevelopment and rehabilitation on the other. It is an intriguing fact that the first cabinet level department of urban affairs will probably be built around the current housing activities of the federal government.

The movement for transportation improvement in this country is rooted deeply in American history—in the powerful drive of a growing nation to subdue the vast spaces which separated people, resources, and the productive plant of the nation. Today's urban transportation movement is of similar nature; the reduction of the costs of separating urban households from centers of employment and production is absorbing a major portion of the nation's transportation activities. This has led to contact with area development as well as with urban redevelopment. There are powerful emotional aspects to this movement. First and foremost is of course the American's love affair with his car. There are the strong feelings that emerge from traffic congestion—the number one irritant of modern urbanism. And more recently a strong drive for mass transit and the control of the car ("keep the downtown for pedestrians") has been gathering momentum.

In recent years all of these movements have converged on the urban sector of American society, if for no other reason than its increasing domination of the direction and tempo of national growth and development. We would, accordingly, expect that where urbanization exerts its most intensive consequences, there also we would find the most dramatic confluence of these movements. And, indeed, the major metropolitan regions of the nation without exception find these movements representing their most pressing problems and dramatizing the policy issues of most sensitive concern to the urban citizen. These movements and the issues they pose require of the city planner a new set of involvements. If he fails, his role and function will not disappear, but they will change as he is gradually dealt out of significant decisions in favor of other institutions with more persuasive visions of metropolitan development, with a keener sense of relevance, with a command of the rhetoric of urban public policy.

City planning has not been unconscious of the need to come to terms with these movements. It has in many cases sought to understand and assist the processes of economic development of the metropolitan region, as will be testified not only by the lengthy shelves of "economic base studies," but also by the participation of planning agencies in local industrial development programs and in the establishment of controlled industrial districts. It has joined forces with the housing movement in pressing for housing codes and in developing urban renewal programs. It has disputed with the transportation engineer the need to integrate urban transportation policies with land use plans and regulations. It has sought to aid and abet neighborhood and community efforts to pull themselves up by their own bootstraps. It has concurred with social psychiatry on the need for a more orderly, more "human-scaled" urban environment to maximize the opportunities for more rewarding human adjustments to metropolitan life. Most of these contacts, nevertheless, have been sporadic, unresolved, and vaguely unsatisfying; they have neither allowed the exploitation of the very special intellectual assets of city planning in the service of these movements, nor fostered for the city planner a broad-scaled developmental perspective which is indispensable for it to play a central role in the meaningful issues of metropolitan affairs.

In this article we try to make the point that the future effectiveness of city planning is directly bound up with its ability to establish meaningful relations with the broad movements rooted in the problems of intimate concern to the metropolitan citizen. To this end it must distinguish the essential elements in metropolitan development and treat them within a framework that can highlight the crucial ties among them as well as suggest strategies for the high priority items. It is only too easy to be "all over the map"—to mistake endless coördinating committees and advisory councils for really meaningful and relevant working relationships. The difference can be grasped by comparing the effective working contacts of city planning with the housing movement as compared to the present quite superficial ties to the other movements. This situation is not going to be resolved simply.

Given the magnitude of the problem involved in dealing with a truly vast spectrum of activities, policies, and values, the working out of a conceptual framework that can point the way to effective relationships becomes a top-priority need. In the remainder of this paper, we suggest, in outline and preliminary form, such a planning-development framework (or "model," to use the currently popular term), the product of a long-time search to arrive at some sense of coherence in the seemingly disparate elements that loom large on the metropolitan scene.

A Planning-Development Framework: The Metropolitan Assets

What are the essential elements in metropolitan development? Clearly they are *the attributes of a metropolitan region which determine the rate and direction of its development.* Human and natural resources can exert powerful, if varied, effects by setting significant constraints upon development or by endowing a region with a special competitive advantage among the great cities. The stock of capital which has accumulated from the historical flow of investment funds into and within the region determines in large degree the efficiency of the region as a setting for production. The manner in which it is organized—and its capacity for reorganization—will determine the degree to which it can control its development in favor of specific objectives. Resources, capital, organization—these seem to be the really powerful determinants of metropolitan growth and change. Hereafter we will refer to them collectively as *the metropolitan assets*.

It is well to note at once that basically these same elements are the crucial ones in development everywhere and under all conditions. We are now beginning to see, for example, that what happens to these elements will determine the rate of development of an underdeveloped country; and, quite belatedly, our Point Four aid is demonstrating appreciation of the role of human resources and political-administrative organization as well as of the better understood capital elements.

The truly fundamental importance of these factors suggests that they deserve the key place in a metropolitan construct as much as other developmental situations in a sense; we can say that these are the elements that "power" and give form to development.

The key assets need to be distinguished and defined to provide us with meaningful concepts for the specific setting with which we are concerned. Five major classes of these assets figure prominently in metropolitan development (and decision-making).

1. The qualities with which the members of the metropolitan population are endowed—the *human resources* of the region:

The development of a region is greatly influenced by the stock of productive "power" represented by its population—by its occupational skill and industrial distribution, by its energy, initiative, and imagination. The occupational-skill distribution represents simultaneously a level of investment in human resources and the existing productive capability of the local population; the industrial distribution of the population represents the kinds of productive experience—and hence the kind of specialization—which characterize the region's labor force. In general, the capacity of the region to produce a flow of valued economic goods and services stems largely from the producer characteristics of the region's population.

But urban populations consume as well as produce. They provide the final markets for the goods and services of the private sector. The functioning of such markets, the changing tastes and preferences of urban populations, the relationships of rising incomes to consumption patterns significantly influence metropolitan development. Urban populations are also the beneficiaries of public services —an important form of consumption. The allocation and financing of such services present some of the most difficult policy questions of the metropolitan region, since here no "invisible hand" of the market gears public wants and needs to output of the public sector or its distribution.

Production and consumption—broad as they are—cannot encompass adequately the full scope of the "human assets" concept (limited as even that term is). For human beings also give character and "tone" to a metropolitan community, and these have at least as much to do with the development of a region as the most concrete of the assets.

2. The physical endowment of the region—*the natural resources:* Where access to natural resources contributes to the competitive advantage of a region in local and national markets it can be a powerful force for metropolitan development. Needless to say, a region's natural resource endowment is intimately tied up with interregional transportation, for a resource advantage is simply an advantage in *relative* accessibility to resource stocks. Iron and coal deposits were important in Pittsburgh's economic development because they were immediately available. They are important in Baltimore's development not because of propinquity but because of Baltimore's accessibility to the sea lanes which connect it with foreign deposits.

The meaning of resource endowment changes over time. In a period when service industries, rather than agricultural or manufacturing industries, dominate the economic picture, it is necessary to expand the concept of natural resources to include all the features of the physical environment which influence in a major way the development of a region. A specific constellation of these environmental conditions has been labeled the "amenity resources"—that coincidence of climate, land, and shoreline which affords conditions of life highly sought after in an affluent and mobile society. It is no accident that the states rich in these resources are also the ones which have experienced the most rapid rates of economic growth: California, Florida, Texas, Arizona, and New Mexico. Increasingly, industry, liberated from its earlier direct geographic ties to natural resources and specific kinds of labor resources, is drifting toward such areas, pulling with it the labor and capital resources traditionally associated with the older areas of the nation.

A final aspect of resource endowment exerts a truly powerful leverage on regional development—the particular environmental qualities which help to sustain the conditions of metropolitan expansion: the quality and accessibility of developable land, the kinds of water resources available, the characteristics of the atmosphere which determine the impacts and costs of air pollution, and finally, the landscape—the wooded areas, fishing streams, scenic vistas, and intriguing open spaces which attract people for recreation and leisure-time activities. The conservation and use of these resources set the quality and special tone of metropolitan development.

3. The stock of facilities for the direct production of economic goods and services for the market—the reservoir of *private capital* in the region:

The stock of this productive wealth derives from the netting out of historical flows of investment into the region—new plants, new machines and tools, and inventory stocks—against the rates of obsolescence and depreciation.

The productivity of the regional economy depends heavily on the volume and quality of this capital stock, and a considerable proportion of local economic development activity in this country aims at increasing the rate of inflow of private investment in the form of new plant locations. Nevertheless, the older capital is vitally important to regional development also; for example, the New York Regional Study has pointed out the critical role of the old loft buildings in Manhattan in "hothousing" new small enterprises.

The existence of capital assets in a region is not the whole story, even if account is taken of its relative productive capacity; location is also significant. The way in which capital facilities locate with respect to each other in a region greatly influences the "externalities" among productive enterprises in the use of their capital—the good and bad effects for neighboring activities which spill over the boundaries of an enterprise.

Quantity, quality, location—all these have a potent impact on the pace and character of regional development.

4. The stock of community overhead, or servicing facilities—the *public capital:*

Public capital is distinguished from private capital in a number of ways. In the first place it is usually owned and operated by the public at large. Second, it services the community as a whole and thus produces services valuable to consumers and producers alike. Third, the volume and composition of public capital are not determined by conventional market conditions but by centralized decisions based on nonmarket as well as market factors. If private capital is the keystone relating human and natural resources in metropolitan development, public capital is the mortar that binds them all together. Public capital in the form of transportation facilities provides the framework for interaction among the region's producing and consuming activities. Public capital in the form of water and sewerage facilities provides a high quality consumer good and a vitally important industrial material at very low cost. Public capital in the form of schools and medical facilities enhances the conserves the region's human capital. The array of the region's public capital establishes the overhead conditions for its productive efficiency through kinds of services which the private sector generally cannot economically provide for itself.

These facilities are furnished and managed by all levels of government, from the massive river-basin facilities developed by the federal government down to the neighborhood tot lot. For this reason, and for others, the problem of rationalizing public investment to make its maximum contribution to metropolitan development is as complex as it is important.

5. The *organizational tools* available for the pursuit of community ends:

These are peculiarly amorphous, if critically important, metropolitan assets. We can conceive that a region richly endowed in other assets might fail to achieve a desirable rate and quality of development largely because of a poverty in the social inventiveness employed in the use of its endowment. Social inventiveness is essentially a matter of institutional arrangements: how creativity gets built into organizations; how freely and reliably informational flows necessary to carry out the business of the region take place; how wisely human and natural resources and investment can be brought into productive combinations—all these are dependent on the state of the organizational assets in a region.

For many planning purposes the existence of a metropolitan regional government would be counted an asset; for others a broad array of local citizens' organizations would have considerable asset value. For local enterprises, effective survey and research activities serving the region with a continuous monitoring of economic conditions would be reckoned as an invaluable organizational resource. New migrants into a region undoubtedly find employment and counseling services to be organizational assets in their adjustment to the new conditions of the region. The kinds of institutional endowment which qualify as organizational assets are those which expedite adjustments among the region's parts, identify alternative directions for regional development, facilitate the significant information flows, and generative effective and timely action.

These broad assets, then, are the essential elements in the progressive development of metropolitan regions. Regions which are well endowed with such assets have an imposing potential for the kinds of development which are most important to the people in the region, while a really severe deficiency in any one necessarily constrains the quality and kinds of metropolitan development which are possible. *Thus, it is a matter of highest importance for a region to assure the continuous strengthening of its assets; upon this the total quality of life and work in the region must depend.*

Even a brief description of the metropolitan assets is highly suggestive of the nature of the bonds of city planning to the significant modern social movements. This is so for a very good reason: all of the movements described earlier, just as much as city planning, are concerned ultimately with guiding metropolitan development so that there evolves a high quality of life and work in the region. This is true whether the focus is a single function or need (such as recreation and housing), or a broad aspect of life (such as jobs and income).

As each of the movements has matured and its views have become more sophisticated, its approach is increasingly characterized by an appreciation of its tie to other aspects of metropolitan development (even the most ardent houser or highwayman or human-dynamics type begins to sense this) and an appreciation of the importance of working on the "fundamentals" (or working on what we have called the metropolitan assets).

Thus, a sensible strategy for coming to understand the "natural" bonds of city planning to all of these diverse movements is to define as sharply as possible the relationship of city planning to the metropolitan assets. This, in turn, requires some sense of how they singly and jointly make their contributions to metropolitan development. In short, we need a useful scheme to put these concepts to work.

A Planning Development Framework: The Question of Scale

The key to an effective model of metropolitan development lies in the matter of the "scale" of analysis—as well as action. An issue of concern to a neighborhood is not necessarily an issue of concern to the metropolitan region as a whole; it becomes so only if the same issue troubles a number of neighborhoods and if its solution depends on the concerted action of a larger group. Reciprocally, the loss of a market for an important product of the region is not an appropriate concern at the neighborhood level—although it may well have an impact there—simply because the total impact is more diffuse so that a remedy lies again in the action of some larger community. Thus, scale makes a great difference. It is, as a matter of fact, *the* key "organizing" feature in metropolitan development. We will now demonstrate how the developmental issues of the region segregate themselves according to the relative regional scale of impact and the influential variables involved. Around the focal points that emerge in this way, the "natural" ties of city planning to the other social movements can be brought to the forefront. While it would take much more space than we have to draw out the implications for such natural bonds, it is our hope that the treatment of the framework will be suggestive enough to make more explicit description unnecessary. The main challenge in the first instance is to evolve a fruitful analytical framework.

We can discern three important regional levels (or scales) within which the critical metropolitan developmental problems come to rest: the suprametropolitan level, the metropolitan level, and the intrametropolitan level. In other words, some kinds of metropolitan problems exist because of the relationship of the region to a broader economic, political, and social environment; others because of important aggregative characteristics of the region; and still others because of special properties associated with its geographical parts. How the scale dimension should be treated will be indicated by pinning down some of the salient characteristics of the problem at each level.

What is suggested by analyzing the necessary and sufficient conditions of metropolitan development, and by focusing on the various levels of significance for the metropolitan region, is a joint consideration of the regional development assets and the scales at which they emerge as significant urban issues. This broad framework we refer to as the *metropolitan planning and development* model.

Conceptually, it can be thought of as a table which has for its rows the five metropolitan development assets: human resources, natural resources, private capital, public capital, and organizational resources. (See Table 1.) It has three columns, one for each of the major scales or levels of significance: suprametropolitan, metropolitan, and intrametropolitan. Each box in the table, then, identifies a specific asset group with a particular metropolitan scale, so that the exercise of considering each of the boxes successively should carry us through the crucial developmental questions confronting the metropolitan region. At the same time, attention to the relationships between and among the boxes should highlight many of the

TABLE 1 Elements in a planning and development framework.

ASSETS	LEVELS		
	SUPRAMETROPOLITAN	METROPOLITAN	INTRAMETROPOLITAN
Human resources	Quality of the labor force and "consumer power" of the region as factors in growth and development of the metropolis. Role of labor migration	Regional manpower budget and spatial patterns of household activities	Importance of working & living environments and interaction of economic, social, and physical factors
Private capital	Interregional capital flows, industrial location, and technology in regional economic expansion and incomes	Flow of investment into productive facilities as basic region *building* process; external economies as region *shapers*	Roles of markets and land use policies in meeting locational and service needs of economic activities
Natural resources	Material resources and amenity resources in growth of metropolitan economy	Environmental resources—land, air, water, landscape—and viability of the metropolis	Conservation and development of landscape resources at the neighborhood and community scale in livability of the region
Public capital	Interregional transportation and resource development as links to the the world at large	Centralized, interdependent service systems as crucial skeletal elements	"Incremental" services and distribution of the impacts of costs and benefits
Organization	Institutionalized information flows and response of region to national changes	Institutional arrangements as integrators for metropolitan development	Neighborhood and community organization to evaluate service levels and assert local needs

intricate interconnections among developmental factors and suggest a broader array of the consequences of public action than single-minded concentration on any one.

To identify the subjects that are pertinent to the understanding and control of the strategic factors in the economic, social, and political life of the community, there are certain questions that need to be answered, to produce an orderly (even if complex) picture of the main developmental issues confronting the metropolitan region. An appropriate slate of questions would include the following:

1. What is the nature of each asset at each scale—what role in the total fabric of urban life does it comprehend? How can it best be formulated in terms of the interaction of public decisions and policies with the private decisions of the region's firms and individuals?

2. What are the major interconnections between the "boxes"?

3. What kinds of flows (information, goods, persons, vehicles, money and credit, etc.) are important in these interconnections?

4. What kinds of analytical techniques are appropriate to describe and predict the ways in which the contents of each "box" change?

5. What are the current trends that can be identified in the state of each asset at each metropolitan level?

6. Given national and community values, what kinds of objectives are relevant to the development of each asset at each level?

7. What local and regional policies are likely to be involved in any community-wide program to develop this asset? More specifically, what is the relevance for city planning?

Other questions are of course possible—or even other ways of asking these—but these address the main issues in relating the role of metropolitan planning to the processes of metropolitan development. The nature of our specific problem points up the advantages of taking each of the metropolitan scales and examining the salient features of the metropolitan assets at that level; for other purposes we could as readily focus on any or all of the asset groups, studying the implications of each at the various scales.

THE SUPRAMETROPOLITAN SCALE

A frequently ignored dimension of the metropolitan region is its role as part of a larger whole. It is not a Greek city-state, nor can it sensibly act as one. It clearly participates in the national economy and society, whose developments reciprocally touch the metropolitan region. A recent study by the Committee for Economic Development has highlighted the impact of national foreign trade policy on the levels and composition of economic activities in metropolitan regions other than the great ports that thrive on the flows of goods, persons, and money between this country and the rest of the world. All of the broad *national* policies of the federal government are strongly selective in their impacts among cities. Changes in production technique which are virtually national in their effects, new tastes and preferences coupled with secularly rising *national* income, changes in the national stock of social overhead such as highways, river valley developments, drainage facilities—all these eventually come home to roost at the local level as changes in the broad economic and social milieu within which metropolitan development takes place.

The metropolitan region is also a part of a larger, multistate region which has its own dynamics within the national picture. A large part of the story of our national economic growth can be told in terms of the great historical shifts of economic activity among these regions, which have identities and characteristics of their own. Des Moines cannot escape the implications of its position in the Corn Belt; and the growth of Atlanta finds its roots in the changes which are transforming the entire Southeast. Cities take much of their functions, their special *élan*, their vigor from their larger regions, so that as New England differs from the rest of the nation, so will New England cities reflect the differences, and their future progress and prosperity will be closely linked to those of the larger region. On the other side, of course, the development of the individual metropolis has a great impact on the surrounding broad region.

Finally, a metropolitan region, as part of a complex *system of cities* distributed across the national landscape, has a number of special dimensions. First, it has a rank in the hierarchic structure of the system. A small number of great cities in which are concentrated great national functions and activities crown the hierarchy. A large set of small cities occupies the other end of the spectrum—cities whose primary function is to organize, service, and distribute the product of small regional hinterlands. In between we find the "capitals" of the great multistate regions, Los Angeles, Houston, Minneapolis–St. Paul, Atlanta, Boston. Indeed, a city's place in this hierarchy carries with it a large set of implications about its connections with the world at large.

Second, a city may be a relatively specialized or an unspecialized member of this system. Urban scholars have for years pointed to the tendencies of cities to demonstrate considerable variety in economic structure; for example, manufacturing cities have been distinguished from commercial cities, from institutional cities, from service cities. Clearly, some cities are better endowed than others to carry out some important national and regional activities, which then make disproportionate contributions to the economic flows of their regions: Chicago with its commodity markets, Detroit with its auto industries, Pittsburgh with its steel complex. The degree and kind of the region's specialization can contribute another layer of knowledge about the interaction of the region and its economic environment.

At some point we must see the system as it is structured in space, for this will also identify important aspects of the region's role in the larger society. Some cities participate in the great conurbations whose significance in our society increases with each passing decade. The most dramatic of these—so-called *Megalopolis*—stretches from Portsmouth, Virginia, to Portsmouth, New Hampshire; other cities enjoy a much larger degree of spatial and functional independence with regard to neighboring cities, as exemplified by Houston, Portland, Denver, and Atlanta. The critical difference between these two kinds of relationships lies in the extent to which boundaries and distinctions in economic and social phenomena are blurred in the conurbation. Local markets—and commuting patterns—can no longer be clearly defined; markets for local goods become proliferated; the siting opportunities for industries are richer and more extensive. In short, where a city stands in the spatial structure of the system of cities carries with it important potentials for the development of its region.

The first requirement in metropolitan policy, then, is to learn to adapt to the great "outside" forces at work and, if at all possible, to turn them to the community's advantage. If the service industries increasingly dominate the nation's economic scene and manufacturing employment has ceased to grow over-all, it will be like pushing a string for a community that has long been an agricultural center to become a great manufacturing center in the latter part of the twentieth century.

First and foremost concern for the future of a metropolitan area must mean coming to grips with the suprametropolitan elements. These can best be seen within the context of the five asset groups.

1. The Human Resources

The very first question in metropolitan development involves the quantity and quality of the regional population. The size and characteristics of the population today and the projections of its size and characteristics in years to come are primary elements in all planning and in all development and in all social movements (that is, whether the concern is jobs, transportation, housing, recreation, neighborhoods, or mental health).

At the suprametropolitan scale, the relationship between particular features of the region's population *and the nation at large* is the main interest. It is seen in the sharpest possible focus when related to the problems associated particularly with area (or economic) development. Two characteristics of urban populations attract our attention when viewed in terms of an evolving metropolitan economy: (1) the population as the source of the labor inputs for the production of goods and services, and (2) the population as consumers of goods and services. In both roles, population serves as a magnet of greater or lesser attraction for economic activities. This, of course, is only one aspect of human beings in the metropolis, but it is a highly significant one.

Workers and managers are key ingredients in all production, and increasingly businesses tend to locate where labor of the appropriate quantity and quality is to be found. The local region is a competitor of the other regions composing the national economy for economic activities. How well it does in this competition depends on the comparative advantages it can marshall to sell its product at home and in the external markets at costs less than those of its competitors. *A regional labor force can contribute to the competitive advantages and disadvantages of a region through the characteristics which contribute in a significant way to its productivity—through the quality of the labor force.*

The labor force at any level is always a complex mixture of skills, experience, and capabilities, some combinations of which are of higher quality in their ability to yield higher productivities. The short-run migration of labor into and out of the region can dramatically alter the labor force mix by the *net* results of the inflow and outflow of workers and their productive attributes. An outflow of high quality labor and an inflow of workers with a very low productivity can, if very large, substantially degrade a local labor force. A more common situation is revealed by the chronically depressed areas where the outmigration consists largely of the young, skilled, healthy, and ambitious workers, who leave behind a less productive fraction of the original. How the composition of the flows of migrants *among* regions relates to the composition of labor forces *in* the regions sets the short-run limits which labor productivity imposes on regional development.

Certain things can be done within a given region to influence the direction and character of migration. Very much more can be done directly about the quality of the resident labor force through investment in education, in training and retraining, and in vocational guidance. A wide understanding of the critical role of the quality of the labor force in the attraction of industry—and particularly of high-wage industry—can bring about an appreciation of the role of investment in human resources in the improvement of manpower quality.

Urban populations also consume, and consumer "power" is a mighty attraction for industry. The larger and richer the local market, the greater is the possibility that industries of all types will want to produce within the metropolis itself. But here, as in production, while sheer volume is important, the richness and diversity of demand set the pace for the development of a strong metropolitan economy. Any measures which contribute to the upgrading of incomes contribute to the attraction that the region holds out to industry.

2. The Stock of Private Capital

Parallel to the interregional flows of labor seeking more profitable employment are the interregional flows of investment funds pursuing profits in economic activities. These funds eventually end up in the form of new or replacement capital—new plants and equipment, or inventories of materials and goods held to assure a smooth flow of production. The rate of investment flow into any particular region responds to profit expectations, and this in turn will tend to determine the rate at which the region will grow.

Expanding regions find their strength in an intricate set of market relationships which have been described elsewhere as "input-output-access" advantages: industries tend to locate or expand where advantages in the cost of quality of their input requirements permit them to produce at advantageous unit costs, or where they can exploit advantages of excellent access to large markets for their output.

The future development of a metropolitan area is closely linked to its position in the area in which the forces making for growth and redistribution of economic activity are working themselves out. Every community has an existing stock of productive capital—all types of plants and machines. As capital facilities age, they become less efficient, and the likelihood increases that they will obsolesce as competing regions employ new machines and new methods of production. Merely to stand still in the competition among regions requires a constant flow of "modernizing" investment, the failure of which, for example, has been a significant factor in the limited economic growth of New England in recent decades.

The economic expansion of a region has a number of local dimensions. The most subtle consist of the decisions of local firms to expand their output as their markets expand. The location of *new* plants of existing firms in the region is the most dramatic form of economic expansion, for these new plants signify the massive injections of investment in the regional economy and are the lure of literally thousands of local "industrial development" programs seeking to precipitate plant location decisions in their favor. Finally, regional economies expand through high-risk investments to incubate new enterprises producing new goods and services which some day may compete for the consumer's dollar across the face of the nation (the Ford Motor Company was incorporated in Michigan on June 16, 1903, with a capital of $100,000). Each of these kinds of capital growth lean heavily on the region's relations with the rest of the world to serve their functions in metropolitan development effectively.

Private capital in a region meshes with the region's human resources in the labor markets. As a matter of fact, when an economist refers to the "technology of production" he is talking in large degree about the proportions in which capital and labor are put together with other inputs to produce the specified outputs, while the layman thinks in terms of machines. Technology in both senses affects the labor market. New capital means expanded output, of course, and if existing technology is merely expanded, the new capital will result in more jobs. However, new capital may bring with it new machines and methods which alter the productive relationships of labor and capital—which, indeed, substitute capital for labor. Fewer jobs requiring more highly skilled labor may be the result. In short, it is not at all certain that new capital in the region means expansion of employment generally; its impacts on the labor supply may be quite selective in terms of employment opportunities.

Ultimately the relationship of capital, labor, and technology is reflected in regional incomes. Capital inflows associated with a constant technology that requires an array of labor skills comparable to those available will work toward the full employment of local labor and rising wages. Capital inflows with changing technology requiring higher skills may well result in higher incomes for that part of the supply so equipped and lower incomes (or more *under*employment) for less skilled groups. Not only is the average family income affected by new investment flows, but the distribution of incomes among members of the community can be substantially altered by the character of new capital investment.

Two conclusions may be drawn from the dynamics of local private capital's relationship to "the rest of the world": (1) not only does the region have need for a positive rate of private capital accumulation, but also for balanced investment in modernizing, in expansion, and in the birth and location of new enterprises; and (2) some of the most crucial metropolitan problems stem from the joint effects of interregional flow factors affecting the labor supply—migration—and interregional factors in the flow of investments which influence the level and technology of local production.

We should not turn from the flows of private capital without recognizing the significance of "consumer capital," particularly housing. As regions grow in population, they must keep pace in the net increase of new dwelling units; otherwise, housing costs will rise, households will tend to lower housing levels as a result, and the "filtering mechanism" by which new housing additions are translated into increases in the stock of low income housing—a balky process at best—may break down. The federal government has taken a powerful position in channeling investment capital into housing generally, but increasingly attention should be focused not only on the degree to which housing investment flows are related to urban growth, but also on their ultimate effects on the composition of the housing stock in the region.

3. Natural Resources

For our purposes, "Natural Resources" embrace all the consequences of the natural endowment affecting the conduct of economic activity. Natural resources influence the character of metropolitan development in two ways: first, as basic material inputs into the processes of production; second, as influential environmental conditions affecting the welfare of the community as a whole.

The natural resource *advantages* of a region depend only in part on its natural resource endowment. The value of any resource to the region's economy is a function in the first instance, of its accessibility: coal a thousand feet underneath us is a "poorer" resource than coal a hundred miles away on a rail line. Regional development responds to the costs of the resource at the plant door, which varies in accordance with the quality of the resource and the costs of transporting it to that point; regions frequently reach out for basic industrial materials far beyond their own hinterlands when quality and transport costs make such importation economical. A region need not default on economic growth merely because of a poverty of nearby natural resources. Substitutions may be feasible among materials, capital, and labor which are not precluded by the competitive conditions in the consumer markets. Thus, the effect of natural resources as industrial materials on the region's economic base is, at best, ambiguous: a good endowment of valuable natural materials may add up to a powerful competitive advantage for a region in outside markets, but good access to external sources may achieve the same thing; similarly, poor access may inhibit growth or result in a form of growth paced by activities not dependent on resource materials.

The impact of other features of the natural metropolitan environment upon the conditions of life and work may completely overshadow the problems of resource materials. Certainly water, air, and land are fundamental resources simply because the viability of the urban system is extremely sensitive to them. Beyond this, these resources are now dramatically influencing the distribution of national economic activity among the various regions. The "amenity resources" of a congenial climate with attractive shoreline, open water, and landscape resources continue to be powerful levels in the growth of Florida, California, and other "favored" areas.

The development of these fundamental resources on broad regional and national bases will enrich even distant regions in the same way that local wastage of these resources imposes "spillover" effects far beyond local borders in ways which even now are major considerations of metropolitan development. State and federal programs to develop landscape resources for recreation and to provide for the multiple purpose development of our river valleys contribute important new assets for urban populations. The need for supraregional efforts to conserve the resource qualities of the environment confronts us daily in the fields of watershed protection, water pollution, air pollution, and erosion. Because these resource effects extend beyond the bounds of any metropolitan region, the conservation development programs needed to control them will require joint local, state, and national participation.

4. Public Capital as Social Overhead

Social overhead investments amplify the productivity of the region by developing and exploiting the benign features of the economic environment within which producing activities pursue their ends. They may reduce the costs of interaction among firms and individuals, as in the case of transportation and communication facilities; they may reduce the costs of important inputs, such as power, water, and even land; they may reduce external hazards, such as floods, fire, and felony. All of them taken together generate the special environmental conditions conducive to a high level of productive efficiency by the components of the region's economy. These are, indeed, collective services supported broadly throughout the region; the ultimate benefits are enjoyed in some degree—if differentially— by almost all of the region's citizens. Fundamentally, the role of social overhead investment is to exploit the potential external economies among activities in a way that cannot be pursued or enjoyed by any one or small group of firms and individuals.

The social overhead investment programs of public agencies can influence the relationship of the metropolitan region to the rest of the world in a number of ways: they can enhance the productivity of the region as a whole in such a way as to appeal explicitly to new investment in the region's productive plant; they can improve the region's access to external markets; and they can enhance the resource environment of the region as a whole.

Transportation and communication facilities—central elements in the national reservoir of social overhead—most dramatically link the region to the rest of the world. Efficient and inexpensive channels to handle tremendous flows of goods, persons, and information are essential for a region to play a useful role in the national economy. The maturing of the national railroad network early in this century left virtually every part of the nation interconnected by rail transportation, but the differential costs of transporting goods as exemplified by freight rates, became as powerful distributers of economic development as simple, physical accessibility had been in an earlier day. Now a national highway program promises again to raise the accessibility among the parts of the nation to a new level which will further facilitate the flows of goods and persons throughout the metropolitan regions of the nation.

The improvement of access, quality, and cost of socially produced or regulated resources imposes a second major responsibility on national and state social overhead investment. The emerging difficulties of supplying water to an urbanizing, industrial society demonstrates the critical nature of this problem. Maintenance of the physical volumes and flows has led to a focus on broad river-valley development of storage and distribution facilities, while the increasing deterioration of quality through pollution centers on issues of water purification and waste removal—again, on a scale much greater than that of the metropolitan region.

The exploitation of water power is part of this picture, but the securing to the region of an adequate capacity of electricity generation at an economic cost is a broader need involving public or quasi-public investment. Finally, the provision of a high quality supply of air is engaging regional attention. Although public investment has not played a large role here, public policy is increasingly likely to require firms and individuals to assume costs of maintaining this resource at some minimum level of quality. Social overhead investment in resources forges an important connection between the region and the rest of the world.

Finally, we should mention in passing the role of public investment in developing controlled industrial areas and in providing the kinds of services needed to support new industrial plants and activities.

Thus, public capital investment operates on metropolitan development both by improving its competitive position in external markets and by improving the character of regional endowments in the natural resources—land, water, and air.

5. Organizational Assets

Much of the contact of the region with the rest of the world takes place by virtue of its organizational links and services. Perhaps the most important aspect of this asset is in the organization of the markets for goods and services and for the factors of production which are of strategic importance in the region's development. Wall Street is an incomparable asset of the New York metropolitan region, as are the grain markets in the agricultural Midwest, and the livestock markets in Chicago and Kansas City; but these are also important to communicating cities whose economies are closely linked to these markets.

The region's organizational ties with the rest of the world should be judged by the extent to which they enhance the region's capability for swift and smooth adjustment to the broad changes taking place in the nation at large. The array and freshness of critical information available to the significant decision-makers in the region determine the limits of rational choices and policies in the region. Local manufacturers need to know not only anticipated developments in national markets for their products but what kinds of local advantages and disadvantages are likely to affect their competitive positions. Local governments need to understand how national changes are likely to influence the volumes and kinds of public services needed in the region, what kinds of welfare outlays they may confront, and what kinds of current policies will improve the region's position in the nation. Local households need information about the long-run employment prospects in their occupations, their industries, and their communities so that they can make the best decisions about themselves and their future. Organizational arrangements which can produce a full and continuing report on the relation of the region to the rest of the world will provide a region with an invaluable advantage in its ability to exploit the favorable and hedge against the unfavorable developments in the national environment.

More concretely, however, the kinds of organizational arrangements which encourage an integrated view of the region's external relations and its internal—that is, adaptive—responses can be of immense value. Such arrangements would tend to dissolve the unnatural barriers which compartmentalize the three critical aspects of metropolitan development—economic development, physical development, and development of the region's human resources by exploiting the common, long-range perspectives to relate these phases of metropolitan development more effectively. Area development, physical planning, and social planning would thus find more intimate ties which would permit all three to contribute much more powerfully to the broad development of the region as a whole within the framework of an evolving national economy and society.

Although the impact of individual organizational arrangements (or assets) in metropolitan development is difficult to assess, it is not difficult to conclude that the quality of a region's organizational contacts with the larger region and the world can aid or inhibit its ability to exploit these contacts fully. The sources and impetus for metropolitan growth and development lie essentially in the world beyond it. Its relationships with this world take the form of a complex set of flows—of persons, of money, of goods, of information. The impacts of these flows on the local region and their accumulation as assets or liabilities are the central problems of the suprametropolitan scale of regional development.

THE METROPOLITAN SCALE

An understanding of the complex relations of a metropolitan region to the outside world needs to go hand-in-hand with a clear view of the metropolis as an *entity* of a special sort. Certain problems and potentialities center on the metropolis as a total unit. This uniqueness rests on the degree to which the intensity of interaction among the parts of a metropolis normally exceeds that between any one of its parts and the rest of the world.

The metropolis, for example, forms a distinctive scale of labor market. In the short run, it represents a stock of occupational skills and industrial experiences to support the labor needs of the region's economic activities. The commuting patterns of workers in the metropolis normally leave few of a region's employment centers inaccessible to a worker in any part of the region. At the same time, the worker views the metropolis as a circumscribed set of job opportunities as he casts about for more advantageous employment. The concentration of most of the region's employment within the reach of most of the region's wage earners, coupled with the difficulties of commuting between metropolitan regions, gives the metropolis a critical dimension as a labor market.

The metropolitan region is similarly a unique market for space. In the short run its firms and households generate the demands for space for the efficient conduct of the region's activities; at the same time the supply of vacant and improved land in the region identifies almost exhaustively the physical supply of site available for present and future activities. Because of the immobility of land as site, the land markets in one region are influenced by market conditions in another only in very special cases. At the other extreme, we can clearly distinguish land submarkets which operate at less than metropolitan scales; however, extensive substitution possibilities among them exist not only for the ultimate occupants, but for the intermediate market activities of subdividers, builders, and developers. This intergrated metropolitan land market works to knit the whole region into a grossly rational spatial pattern of activities.

The metropolitan region also has unique characteristics as a market for goods and services. The concentration of purchasing power and the highly efficient organization of the distribution processes in the metropolitan area make it a natural target for the production plans of local firms—and the prize sought after by external producers whose outputs are imported into the region. Warehousing facilities and wholesaling activities are oriented to the metropolis as an economic entity, while the strategies of firms producing for consumption in the region are governed by the special characteristics of the regional market. Each important factor in the consumer market—population, income, and tastes—is conditioned by the characteristics of the metropolitan scale.

Finally, the metropolis is a unique and integral concentration of educational-cultural-recreational institutions and facilities which take their meaning from the metropolitan character of the region. Clearly, operas, symphonies, the legitimate theater, and art galleries are made possible by and addressed to the broad cultural elites which can support them only in metropolitan aggregations. Parallel to this we can find the specialized and advanced educational facilities which flourish in the rich stimulation of the metropolis. The concentrations of leisure also make the metropolitan area the focal market for a vast array of recreational activities many of which can be brought into being only by these metropolitan concentrations.

The unique importance of the metropolitan scale can be demonstrated in many more ways, but these dramatic features identify the special significance of the metropolitan scale resulting from intense concentration of persons and activities and the relative isolation of each concentration from others. For this reason the metropolitan scale presents some very special developmental issues.[1]

1. The Human Resources

The basic human resource "unit" at the metropolitan level is the household as a producer of labor and a consumer of goods and services. We will focus on the household against the perspective of the regional labor market and the ways in which consumption activities help to organize the region.

As we have suggested earlier, the metropolitan labor market is largely circumscribed and self-contained in the short run. Over the longer run the cumulative effects of migration flows will transform the stock of occupational skills and industrial experience represented in the region's population, just as investment flows will alter the demands for labor by the region's activities. These cumulative processes become significant only over time, and it is important at any point to understand the character of the existing stock of skills and experience against the backdrop of manpower needs. On the demand side of the labor market, the economic structure of the region exhibits the manpower needs which specify the kinds of industrial experience which are most valuable and the occupational skills called for by the kinds of tasks to be performed. The supply side is a labor force—a specific array of skills and experience. Metropolitan development is shaped in considerable degree by how well the supply and demand characteristics of the labor market can be meshed.

A good accommodation of labor force qualities and employment needs would find a close balance for each occupational-industrial class; no bottlenecks would impede production on the one hand, and no extraordinary surpluses would be evidenced by extensive underemployment and higher community relief loads.

The *regional manpower budget* offers a useful framework for examining the problem. Conceive of a set of accounts, one for each significant combination of occupation and industry endowment. The community labor force is inventoried across the debit sides of these accounts, identifying in each case a labor supply. Employment plus job openings are tallied on the credit side. Each account then nets out to a deficit in labor supply or a surplus representing

1. In those few cases where isolation has disappeared, it becomes very hard indeed to define the metropolitan scale with any precision. Note, for example, the difficulty of the Census Bureau in defining the New York metropolitan area. No matter how fuzzy the boundaries may be, however, metropolitan-wide issues come forcefully to the forefront even in areas like new York.

unemployment. For the accounts to be truly effective, they would have to be refined to identify *over* and *under*employment as well as a precise picture of supply and demand relationships. In some cases, for example, underemployment and overemployment may be found to exist side by side as a result of employment discrimination. The regional manpower budget can thus be a valuable tool in the analysis of the regional labor market.

It can help anticipate future difficulties in the market, also. Projections of the region's economy can be the basis for estimating future labor force needs by class. The gap between these figures and current supply can provide valuable information required for programs working for the appropriate supplies of skills and experience to meet future needs. New training institutions or programs may be required, or improved flows of market information, perhaps even more dramatic steps. It has become evident that regional agencies can play more active roles in the achievement of effective supply and demand relationships in the labor market. Our failure hitherto is manifest in the backwaters of the market where underemployed, unskilled, and "nonprime" workers stagnate in hopelessness and apathy—an extravagant waste even in this rich and powerful economy.

The metropolitan labor force exhibits a definite structure in space. Systematic distributions of various classes of households are brought about by the technical linkage of the worker with his work and by a broad class of social forces operating on the urban scene. The general impact of these factors is to sort the so-called metropolitan labor market into a complex set of smaller, short-run labor markets with significant spatial features.

Take the linkage between the worker and his work. For important economic reasons productive activities tend to agglomerate in centers of various sizes, the most significant of which is the central business district. The labor force is articulated with these centers by the daily journey-to-work, which, in conjunction with the transportation system over which it takes place, sets powerful limits on where he can live to carry out his functions at any particular employment center. In a static sense, then, we can visualize how worker households, constrained by the time and money costs of the journey-to-work, compete with each other for the accessible space (or housing stock). A structure of land values is created, and worker households find locations in the urban space in accordance with the impact of transportation costs and rents on the household budgets.

Social factors are also at work sorting out various fractions of the household sector in space. Minority group discrimination is perhaps the most dramatic of these processes. In recent years the racial barriers in jobs and housing have dammed up the migrant flows of Negroes, Puerto Ricans, and Mexicans in the older core of the metropolitan regions, while middle-class white households have fled outward. These processes of discrimination are centrifuging our metropolitan regions into a dense, depressed core of disadvantaged minority groups surrounded by broad rings of middle-income, pure-white suburbs. The various stages of the family cycle and income variations also sort out households according to their spatial needs and their ability to compete for valuable locations. All these processes operate continuously to create a very intricate labor-force structure in which a number of labor markets intermesh functionally and overlap spatially.

The consumer market also helps to organize the metropolis. First, the local consumer demand generates the production of a large array of local goods and services for local consumption—provides the demand for the "secondary" economic activities whose cost advantages largely exclude external competition. Local populations also consume a large flow of public goods and services, as recent urban budgets will attest.

The consumption activities (or shopping patterns) of urban households have a discernible influence on the spatial structure of the city also, differentiated by the kinds of products involved. Highly specialized consumer goods tend to be aggregated in the urban core; the distribution of the more general classes of goods and services takes place in a much more dispersed fashion throughout the region, a dispersion which is conditioned by the competition among firms for control of "market areas" which become defined in terms of spending power—population, income, and access.

2. The Stock of Private Capital

The physical artifact of the city is brought into being by the flows of private investment into the construction of new production facilities about a skeleton of public capital in the region: office buildings, factories, and stores are erected, improved, or demolished in accordance with the rewards anticipated from their services. The private capital assets in the metropolis at any one moment are composed of the stock of physical facilities which have accumulated from these flows of investment. The spatial dimensions of these investment flows has traditionally been the grist of urban land use planning.

The uses to which private capital is put derives from the industrial structure of the region and the technology of production in each industrial sector. "Industrial structure" is simply another term for the region's mix of economic activities, some of which produce essentially for local markets, while others compete in external markets. One of the facts of urban life is the constant transformation of this mix in response to the changing conditions of local and external demand, innovations in the methods of production, and the prices of inputs. This dynamically modulating structure is accompanied by changes in the investment flows and consequently, in the composition of new private capital, which constantly amend the course of metropolitan development.

The changing flows of investment show up in a number of ways in the physical plant of the community, in the use of urban space, and in the distribution of the demand for public services. New plants and vacant industrial buildings, great regional shopping centers and blighted ribbon commercial developments, vigorous new neighborhoods and acres of blighted housing are all symptomatic of great shifts in these investment flows as they respond to changes in profit expectations and entrepreneurship. As these changes accumulate among the various parts of the city, the spatial structure of the city becomes transformed.

In addition to the effects of changing demand and technology the organization of the region is influenced by certain kinds of cost and revenue advantages which can be enjoyed only jointly by several establishments located together—"external economies." These effects gave rise to the CBD; they are the rationale for the modern integrated shopping center; they have generated the "clumping" of industrial activity within the urban space. The opposite side of this coin consists of external *dis*economies—the proclivities of some activities to increase the costs to other nearby activities—which act centrifugally to disperse some mixes of activity. Rising site rents under the impetus of demand of industry for sites is the most widespread of these; the nuisance effects of smoke, noise, glare, and fumes are the most dramatic. All these externalities are powerful factors in the profitability of economic activity in the region; through the intricate network of relationships among activities they largely determine the way in which the spatial pattern of the metropolis comes into being.

One aspect of these interrelationships deserves special mention: many of them are realized through flows of goods, persons, and information among establishments. Thus, retail stores seek locations with advantageous access to a clientele for much the same reason that refineries locate near water transportation—to reduce the costs and inconveniences of moving goods. Thus, the spatial distribution of these economies—and even the levels which can be realized at any moment in time—depends heavily on the quality of the channels over which these relations are conducted and the institutions which facilitate them. These comprise important elements in the stock of "social overhead"—the array of public facilities which reduce the cost of conducting economic activities throughout the whole region.

These externalities by themselves cannot organize the city in space simply because the supply of space is limited. The profitable industrial advantage of a waterfront location, for example, cannot be enjoyed by all potential beneficiaries; they must bid for it and so create a structure of site values which allocates the scarce frontage to those to whom it is most valuable. Hence, each industry's locational needs must be moderated by the claims of all other potential users through the market mechanism. Locating—that is, land using—decisions are largely long-run investment decisions which take place one at a time and represent estimates about the future advantages of sites and reflect a complex array of prices set within the price system. One of the more urgent problems confronting city planning has emerged with a planning strategy that would severely constrain, if not replace, the price system largely in favor of arbitrary land use patterns as the technique for achieving key community objectives. A more reliable strategy may lie in the direction of regulatory tools *supplementing* and *improving* the allocative advantages of the price system in the achievement of these key objectives.

Anything that substantially influences the flows of private investment within the region is a "region-shaping" factor. The main external region shapers are the demand for the region's output abroad and the changing techniques of production, while within the region the relationships among activities and the facilities by which they are realized really find their expression in the changing form and spatial structure of the region.

3. Natural Resources

All sections of the metropolitan region are intertwined in their common dependency on its environmental resources: land, water, air, and the landscape. What happens to any one of these in any part of the region can impoverish all or produce effects whose benefits accrue to the total community. This kind of resource interdependence argues strongly for consistent region-wide policies for the development and conservation of the region's resources.

The resource attributes of land for urban purposes are essentially its spatial capabilities to satisfy the spatial needs of private activities. The demand for land ultimately depends on how land and capital are combined to create a productive facility, a relationship summarized by some measure of capital density, such as the "floor-area ratio." This relationship tends to vary with the price of land, which, in turn, is structured by the transportation system and other public facilities. The needs for land by urban activities then, are deeply influenced by the extent to which public investment and services have extended the supply of accessible sites. The enhancement of the social productivity of land by investments in social overhead, such as in transportation and utilities, is the sum and substance of the resource development of urban land.

The conservation of land is a different problem, however. The unregulated market in land can have a number of consequences which are wasteful of land resources. The outward progression of urban development may leave behind parcels of land impaired by adjoining uses or by uneconomic size either for urban use or for continued agriculture. The loss of product resulting from the withdrawal of such land from economic use is a consequence of the wastage of land. Land can be polluted or damaged for certain kinds of site purposes and so require a substantial investment in its restoration before it can be economically used: in part, this is the problem of urban renewal. Metropolitan land conservation, then, involves both the protection of the quality of site and the orderly transfer not only from nonurban to urban uses, but also among urban uses themselves as the city grows and changes.

The region-wide nature of water resources needs little exposition. The parts of a metropolitan area generally depend on common water sources for municipal supplies. The burgeoning demands of growing cities upon these sources throw into bold relief the intimate interconnections between urban waste disposal and water supplies in a rising water consumption accompanied *pari passu* by the deterioration of quality through pollution. These effects present a joint conservation and development problem which can be handled only on a metropolitan-wide basis; control of waste effluents entering the supply can be effective only when all parts of the region are party to regulations while the amounts of investment called for to develop water resources —to build dams, aqueducts, purification plants, and distribution systems—and the social benefits that flow therefrom make a region-wide approach indispensable.

Air is a commodity new to the resource field. Only recently have we awakened to the fact that air is not the "free good" that economics texts had casually described. How costly a resource high-quality air has turned out to be in metropolitan areas is suggested by the amount of social effort it is inducing. The air conditioning ("climate control," or what you like) of homes and offices, the growth of stringent antipollution measures, the increasing tempo of research on the relationship of air pollution to lung cancer and pulmonary disorders are symptomatic of this change in status. The rapid rise in the social costs of polluted air is likely to precipitate major problems in the conservation—if not the development—of aeroform resources.

Landscape resources are in a very real way the property of the whole region. In public or private hands, their aesthetic and recreational qualities attract people from all parts of the region. The growing awareness of regional populations to their landscape resources has created such pressure of usage that serious damage if not destruction is in the offing. These pressures will require redoubled efforts at conservation coupled with broad development programs to sustain even their current contributions to the well-being of the community at large.

The viability of the metropolis is a direct function of the quality of its environmental resources, and present trends suggest that the future of urban America will become increasingly involved in maintaining and extending the quality of its resource endowment.

4. Social Overhead at the Metropolitan Level

Fundamentally, public agencies produce two kinds of services for the metropolitan region. One kind is characterized by the comparatively small, technologically independent units of production which function in a decentralized fashion. Schools, fire stations, libraries, and recreational facilities exemplify these *decentralized service systems*. They are characterized also by their response to the growth and change of the metropolis; increases in the demand for services occasioned by urban growth are accommodated by the addition of new units serving new areas. Outside of the budget, the creation of such new units does not ordinarily affect the operation of other units. Maladjustments of supply and demand engender essentially local effects, although they may be widespread: one overcrowded or underutilized school will not ordinarily alter the performance of others. The significant implication of these decentralized service systems for metropolitan development resides in the extent to which they lend themselves technically to local operation, economies of scale notwithstanding. We will have more to say about them at a later point.

Contrasted to them are the large, technically centralized service systems which compose the truly skeletal elements of the region. Immediately regional transportation and water-sewerage systems come to mind, but the quasi-public utility systems—telephone, electric power, and natural gas distribution—tend to fit the description also. These systems exhibit a very high degree of technological interdependence among their parts, but an interdependence which is based on a special relationship between a set of core facilities and a distribution net. Consider the analogy of a generalized "tree." Its core is a trunk and a root subsystem which serves the whole tree; its distribution net is the structure of successively diminishing and proliferating branches terminating in a vast number of small twigs—the "end" of the system. Although the state of any one twig will be a matter of indifference to its neighbors in any direct sense, indirectly it exerts demands on the core of the system which in turn affects the state of the entire system. This is the basic aspect of a *centralized, interdependent system*, such as those which bind the metropolitan region together technologically.

Physical relationships rather than purely economic characteristics tend to dominate the manner in which these services are provided. The supply perspective focuses on physical capacities to serve flows of material, of persons, of information at some specified level of service, and the capacities at the core are very intimately related to the capacities as they are arranged in the distribution net. The demands confronting such a system tend to have very strong "peaking" tendencies, which may press the capacities in the system heavily and which, when they exceed capacities at points in the system, may produce rapid, if temporary, deterioration of service levels.

Secular growth of the region generally produces a complex systemic response in such services which generally begins with the growth of demand at the periphery of the distribution net and which may ultimately end with costly expansions in the core facilities. The process is triggered when service demands in a part of the distribution system at the "twig" level exceed capacities there as manifested by a sharp decline in service levels (e.g., traffic congestion or low water pressure at peak loads). This "bottleneck effect" will elicit local expansion of capacities and throw new demands on the succeeding parts of the net and engage a larger part of the system. By this process the bottleneck can travel through the distribution net to the core, where the service level of the entire system becomes involved. It follows quite clearly that under conditions of growth there are no purely local effects: all secular changes accumulate and soon involve the core of the system and the quality of its output for all parts of the region.

If the cost of such systems were trivial, one could conceive of several operating competitively in the region. But the capital costs are massive, especially in the core facilities. Thus, not only is the level of service a region-wide determination, but a rational service development program requires central planning and policy-making which can continuously weigh emerging demands and program investment rationally to avoid deterioration of service levels as well as premature and costly investments in surplus capacity.

We must view this problem not from the viewpoint of any one of these services, but from the perspective of all of them. The plans and policies in each can have dramatic effects over time in the form and direction of metropolitan growth. Where the collective impacts are capriciously distributed and uncoördinated, the region at large must bear not only the financial costs of inefficiency but the frustration of meaningful community objectives. The integration of these great, skeletal, centralized, service systems into a consistent regional development framework deserves a high place on the agenda of metropolitan affairs.

5. The Organizational Assets

It is almost superfluous to point out that the primary obstacles to a well-coördinated, region-wide effort toward metropolitan development lurk in the political ideals of extreme local self-government, "home rule," and the other entrenched and divisive concepts that have fragmented the metropolitan region. It is equally clear that the kind of organizational assets required at the metropolitan level consist of the institutions which can

1. Expedite the efficient provision of the skeletal systemic services which tie the region together;
2. Equip the region with the mechanisms for relating these services to the over-all development of the region; and
3. Improve the operation of the private choice mechanisms in the region—markets, ballots, interest organizations, and channels of communication—which alone can tie the future of the region to the aspirations of its citizens.

The proponents of metropolitan government may argue that their program meets these tests, and indeed it may. But our choices are not metropolitan government or nothing. Actually, we deal in incremental choices most of the time, so that the array of explicit alternative institutional arrangements at any point in time can be critical. Here the sole constraint is organizational creativity—the ability of the major institutions in the region to structure new flows of information and responsibility on both small and large scales to cope with quite specific problems and obstacles in the path of metropolitan development.

At the metropolitan scale, then, the problems of metropolitan development are largely subsumed in the need to integrate effectively the parts of the region into a developmental process which permits all parts of the region to share equitably in the benefits of its growth and change. In the over-all, one may well conclude that the most pressing need is for the evolution of the new organizational assets by which this can be achieved.

THE INTRAMETROPOLITAN SCALE

A concern for the specific functions carried out by the *parts* of the metropolitan region marks the intrametropolitan scale. Here our units are neighborhoods, retailing centers, industrial districts, the central business district and its satellite centers; our concern here is with the basic question of how well they fulfill their functions.

The thing that is particularly "metropolitan" about the metropolis is its almost unbelievable diversity of environments, activities, and opportunities; clearly a diversity of functions requires a diversity among the parts of the region fitted to serve these functions. Producing activities need to aggregate in subareas in which their economic efficiency is amplified: distribution activities cluster around points of high accessibility to consumer submarkets, while manufacturing firms assemble where services and transportation costs give them optimal advantages. The enhancement of these efficiency conditions in industrial and commercial areas places a major responsibility upon local governments.

Residential neighborhoods, on the other hand, not only need to be served efficiently in the narrow sense, but to offer the kind of environment in which families can evolve and individuals mature and realize their highest capacities. Efficiency in the development and servicing of residential neighborhoods depends not only on the service levels of the region-wide skeletal services but on the array of the local, decentralized services. Their relatively loose interdependencies permit them to expand simply by adding new units at regular intervals, as with schools, libraries, fire stations, and the like.

The design of neighborhoods stands out as a powerful factor in the degree to which the living environment of the region's population makes day-to-day—or even moment-to-moment—living a rewarding experience. The availability of useful open spaces, the minimizing of nuisances from abutting areas, a built-in sense of variety and individuation can be the fruits of effective neighborhood design. Hence, the servicing and the design process must go hand-in-hand in the development—and redevelopment—of viable urban residential areas.

1. The Human Resources

In the larger scales the nature of the problems and processes compelled us to look upon urban populations as aggregative elements —as flows of people and skills, as productive "stocks," as markets for goods and services. At the intrametropolitan scale, we must disaggregate these concepts and focus on the individual as he functions within the peculiar urban environment. Where in the first round we tied the metropolis to the world, here we can link it up with the individual, his needs and demands, his accommodation to the bewildering complex that is our cities.

Take the individual in his role as producer. For him, the problem is not how he may optimize the region's output, but how he may maximize his own growth and productivity over his life cycle. He has a right to expect that the economy will provide him with the opportunities for advancement. A careful matching of his talents, training, and attributes with the productive activity in which they can be usefully employed must go hand-in-hand with equipping him with the means of responding to the powerful exogenous changes that are the essence of a dynamic society. At the very least his physical vitality must be conserved.

The welfare of the citizen as consumer is closely bound up with how "good" the markets are in which he makes his wants known. Increasingly the economies of scale impose the threat of monopolistically biased markets for consumer goods and services, to which urban planners have done more than lend a little aid and comfort. Increasingly, city "plans" work to diminish the vigor of competition in the distribution of consumer goods with the unavoidable result that the favored entrepreneur can levy a rent on his output compared to a less favorably situated competitor. Information processes are vitally important in consumer welfare, and especially in the housing and land markets, where the ability of the consumer to behave rationally depends on his knowledge of the alternatives that are open to him. Hence, at the intrametropolitan level the enhancement of the consumer's welfare will depend heavily on the extent to which the region's market institutions can be made responsive and efficient.

The processes of the metropolitan economy, the large social issues and needs of an urban society, and the physical environment within which they work themselves out have complex and powerful interconnections. The urban slum exhibits one set of these relationships, for slums are the specialized areas of poverty in the intricate spatial structure of the metropolis. Slums exist not because buildings deteriorate but because too large a fraction of the urban population is too poor to live anywhere else; so here gather all those who are ill-equipped by training, experience, disposition, or by accident of birth to perform—or compete—effectively in the urban labor force. With them assembles the great majority of the social problems of the city. In this context urban redevelopment is not necessarily either cure or prevention for slums; too frequently it is only cosmetic surgery.

The interconnections between the economic, social, and physical factors in the city dramatized by the slum are part of a much larger set of relationships which have a natural focus on the neighborhood as the basic living environment of the region. The living and working environments of the urbanite are certainly among the things that matter to him. He chooses where he wants to work and where he wants to live, the one choice constraining the other. Not only need he be able to make these choices intelligently, but the quality of the alternatives must make choice worthwhile. If all of his choices of work involve an hour and a half journey-to-work at unrewarding work in dreary surroundings, freedom of choice may not be worth much. If he must live in even the best of the old buildings in rundown, high-density, low-service neighborhoods in order to do this, his freedom of choice about the meaningful things in his daily life dissolves into choices among trivia. This is really the crucial responsibility of the city planner to the urban citizen—to so order the internal development processes of the region that meaningful choices among rewarding living and working environments will exist for all segments of the population.

Human resources at the human scale bring us face to face with the individual and his needs in the urban region. Chief among these are provisions to maximize his worth to himself as a producer; perfection of the market mechanisms by which he makes his choices among the goods of the economy; and viable, congenial neighborhoods and working centers to enhance the quality of his daily experience.

2. Private Capital

The investment decisions of the firm loom as a principal element in the development of private capital assets at the intrametropolitan level. The entrepreneur sees these decisions as individual problems in maximizing his profits within the constraints set by local public policies, such as zoning and tax policies. The urban planner views these decisions as potential changes affecting the orderly disposition of land uses detailed by zoning maps and land use policies. Since the caprice of politics and nonmarket incentives frequently arbitrates the conflicts between these viewpoints, metropolitan development offers some prospects for a more orderly meshing of these public and private gears.

The issues surrounding private capital investment at the intra-metropolitan level find expression in two closely related aspects of the spatial organization of the metropolis: first, what kinds of inter-connections with the region—and the world at large—are possible in various parts of the region; second, what factors are important in the locational decisions of various kinds of economic units. These considerations come together forcefully in the land use policies pursued by local public authorities.

The location decision of firms and households do not take place in a vacuum; they respect the real alternatives available to them at any one moment. Basically the behavior of these units can be described as "efficiency-seeking." For producing units, efficiency is expressed in profits, and the locational behavior of firms is basically a search for an economic environment in the city that affords it the best possible array of the interconnections it needs. The real estate market moderates between the needs of any one firm and those of all the rest. Transportation facilities expedite such interconnections, certainly, but utilities and the broad regional resources of land, air, and water also influence the effectiveness of these linkages and indicate the important reasons why activities with similar kinds of linkage needs tend to agglomerate in various parts of the region. Households, it must be noted, evidence this process in their tendency to domicile with more than casual attention to the time and money costs of the journey-to-work.

The metropolitan region is broadly differentiated in space by the intensity and quality of the opportunities for households and businesses to exploit significant interconnections; the CBD, in contrast to outlying areas, provides an intensive environment for face-to-face communication and a high degree of accessibility to the region as a whole for specialized activities. The stock of older industrial and commercial structures ringing the CBD provides a favorable milieu not duplicated elsewhere in the region for the nurture of a variety of embryonic enterprises. The densely settled core of the region offers cultural and economic contacts which make it a highly amenable living environment for many kinds of nonchild-rearing households, while young families seeking different kinds of contact gravitate to the suburbs.

In short, there are powerful forces tending to sort out activities and groups within the metropolitan region. These are in large degree motivated by private efficiency considerations, which need to be moderated (and certainly not supplanted) by overriding considerations of broad social efficiencies. This is an important facet of the role of local government, but with it goes a second and equally important responsibility—to provide for all kinds of activities, environments within which individual units can operate at high levels of private efficiency. The real estate market operating within land use regulation provides the mechanism by which important classes of firms are satisfied. Where the land use policies do not explicitly account for these needs, either extraordinary rents may be imposed upon the costs of production, or formal and informal political processes may be invoked to remedy the misallocation. Firms seek to realize important external economies; to frustrate these in wholesale fashion can result in a loss to the region's welfare as a whole.

Public policy can help firms and households exploit the economies which the urban environment offers for the production—and consumption—of goods and services. At the same time, it can legitimately constrain some of the negative externalities which can seriously impair the orderly development of the region. Fundamentally, land use regulation and the locational activities of households and business enterprises are keyed to metropolitan development, a common interest to moderate their conflicts and disharmonies over the long run.

3. Natural Resources

A large part of the livability of the urban milieu is a function of the conservation and development of the natural environment and its integration in the location and design of residential areas. Neighborhoods intimately designed with green space and natural landscape offer relief in the living environment from the imposing demands the technological city makes upon its citizens. But even more, they provide the ranging ground which growing children require. This articulation of neighborhood design and natural resources of the land is frequently frustrated by the demands of mass production of housing and by the irresistible tendency to remake the topography. The purpose is to use the land more extensively, but the result is to pay a cost in the waste of the important benefits which development of the landscape resources of new neighborhoods could bring about. Here, the major issues of natural resources revolve around the spatial dimension in the use of land and capital; here, the design orientation and sensitivity of the planner can perform most effectively in the development of the region.

Conservation of natural resources has some very special features within the processes of urban growth and change. On the outer periphery of growth, rapid urbanization of land may cause a precipitous abandonment of intensive agricultural activity, such as fruit-growing and dairying, long before the land can be brought into urban use in an orderly fashion. At the core the gigantic build-up of land values threatens the survival of the landscape resources which still grace the intensely developed part of the region. Those in private hands succumb to the market forces; those in public hands are eroded away by competing public uses such as highways, public buildings, and utility installations—all with the argument that the values of landscape cannot compete with those of more instrumental urban needs. Conservation will require a rationale within the framework of metropolitan development, if such areas are to be held.

4. Public Investment in Social Overhead

As distinguished from the skeletal metropolitanwide services, at the intrametropolitan scale we are concerned with the *incremental* types of public goods—those whose parts are not so rigorously interconnected that expansion of any part requires modification of the system in a larger sense. Many of these services are associated with property development directly or indirectly, such as fire protection, streets, and waste disposal. Others are more closely related to the number of persons who are users, such as schools, public health, and cultural facilities. A major issue for the various parts of the region is the array and quality of services which are expected of the public agencies and the financial resources available to provide them.

Suburbs on the periphery of urban growth generally demand a high level of public services, and the costs come high simply because new capital such as streets and sidewalks, schools, and utilities, must be built and put into operation. In the older areas, more intensive public services are required of old and inefficient capital, so that operating costs skyrocket. Public health, welfare, and educational programs are the main sources of these costs, although public safety also ranks high. In the best of circumstances in a growing city, most of these effects would be unavoidable, but the constant processes reorganizing, restructuring, and redistributing the city's activities exacerbate this process considerably. Thus, we sometimes find suburban schools used to an excessive degree while schools in the center of the region may be substantially underutilized. Residential areas in the central city may feel the impact of the growing streams of suburban auto traffic on what used to be quiet neighborhood streets. In large degree the scale of public inputs needed to maintain some consistent service position derives largely from the scale of these broad shifts.

At the intrametropolitan level we are compelled to consider the distribution of the impacts of public decisions and investment programs. Here "who gains?" and "who loses?" are legitimate and important questions, for where considerable divergences exist between those who reap the benefits of a public investment and those who pay for them, it is important to ascertain that this subsidy is consistent with public policy. Otherwise, the net benefits will no longer count for much against inequities which the program engenders. Do we really believe that low income families should subsidize urban renewal when they are dislocated, or when rents are increased to cover the costs of upgrading properties? Is it equitable for the worker in the new and distant suburb to impose some of his costs of commuting to an in-town job on the older city neighborhoods whose streets he appropriates? Perhaps we do, but it is essential for rational public policy to make this determination explicitly.

Public investment at the intrametropolitan level takes place at a lower scale and so confronts different kinds of problems. It concerns itself with increments to existing stocks of facilities rather than with the expansion of tightly integrated systems. Its dimensions are related to the vast changes taking place among the parts of the region. Its issues are more likely to be those of equity rather than of net benefits. For these reasons organizational assets need to meet some special responsibilities. Here, also, the planner-designer comes into his own.

Industrial districts designed with a careful eye to maximizing the external economies of industrial establishments working in close proximity, neighborhoods whose use of space and resources can stimulate and soothe, retailing centers which can bring the household into easy contact with a rich array of consumer goods and services, and regional centers which are visually exciting and functionally vital with all of the activities of which the region's urbanity is a result—all these elements plead for the imagination and creativity of the architect-planner working within the current urban artifact to engender the meaningful urban environments which can maximize the really unique benefits of metropolitan development for the region's citizenry.

5. Organizational Assets

The failure of formal institutional channels to provide in every case for the information flows necessary to relate local area needs and assets to the metropolis as a whole provides a unique role for *informal* channels and institutions. Neighborhoods threatened by juggernaut public investment programs are defenseless in the absence of an institution that can make their case for them at the higher levels of decision-making. Recreation groups and nature lovers could have their activities banished to the outer limbo of the region except for their capacity to organize. Local industry and commerce can become indiscriminately the happy hunting ground for the needed increments to local revenues unless they can place the issues in a developmental light with a responsible voice. Formal governmental institutions and procedures do not lend themselves to making the critical determinations of equity which are central to the relative welfare of the smaller parts of the region. Interest groups, voluntary citizens organizations, trade and business associations are essential parts of the organizational paraphernalia of metropolitan decision-making. The real problem emerges from the fact that many groups and localities may be poorly endowed with organizational assets of this sort so that their claims go unheard. Since these are usually the groups that are most exposed to the impact of inequities, positive and creative organizational arrangements urgently need to be developed to assure a fair hearing for such groups.

Again, local organization is needed to allow local areas to participate in the decisions which literally choose the kind of environments in which its residents will live. Every public agency will have its own tests for the adequacy of its own programs in the various parts of the region. At the neighborhood level—where all these individual policies come to rest—someone must be able to determine whether the whole bundle of public services adds up to something sensible for the neighborhood as a whole, whether all important needs and wants are met, whether extravagances are accidental attributes of the convergence of these policies on the neighborhood. This critical kind of local policy evaluation depends on the effectiveness of informal neighborhood and civic organizations whose passionate interests in the quality of urban life are needed to complement the dispassionate appraisal by public agencies of the performance of their programs.

SOME IMPLICATIONS OF THE MODEL

This, then, is our metropolitan development model. It focuses on the great development assets of the region and on the ways in which they relate the metropolis to the world and to the citizen. The vital issues of an urban industrial civilization fall into place here, and the issues which really matter to the citizen, the nation, and the future are embraced with all of their interconnections of purpose, policy, and predictability. It remains only for us to set city planning within this perspective explicitly.

First, it is clear that if city planning is to matter greatly, it must come to play a vital central role within certain of the forces and factors through which metropolitan development works itself out.

Of equal importance is recognition that the developmental process is a vast, confused, chaotic, innovative hurly-burly of public and private decisions against which highly formalized city plans sometimes appear more than a little incongruous. Not so much control as civic vigor is the essential quality needed to exploit these forces for the welfare of the region; not so much static order as the essential disorder of creativity; not so much regularized governmental processes as a vital responsiveness to the turbulent succession of opportunities and perils which unfold within and without the region. In short, it is the *process* of effective planning that can integrate the city planner powerfully into the processes of development, not the preparation of a plan.

Finally, this process of development absorbs the energies of a vast and heterogeneous set of public agencies and private groups, each of which is straining to plug into these forces in a useful way, albeit sometimes for narrow and ephemeral purposes. All contribute to this process; all have rights and responsibilities in it. Should any attempt by city planning be made to usurp these roles, the very ties which are essential to a strategic role in this whole arena will be destroyed. Rather, it must constantly forge and reforge these ties by helping these agencies and groups to fulfill their responsibilities in an expeditious, long-range, and socially optimal way.

With these "facts of life" in mind, we can search out some of the signal dimensions that emerge from this model as points of connection for city planning.

It is, for example, too easy to dismiss the suprametropolitan scale as being beyond the range of the city planner. It is not sufficient for him to make well-hedged predictions about it and then proceed as if he had solved the problem. His first responsibility here surely is to predict well—and to plan under the certainty that his predictions will not be realized. To do this effectively demands an emphasis on creativity in regional analysis which has several dimensions: first there must be a careful identification of the main factors conditioning the rates and directions of the region's development; second, techniques for integrated procedures of projection *cum* metering need to be built into the planning process; then, long-range planning needs a capacity to "change heading" when the information flows from the research "boxes" so indicate. In some such process of relating relevant information flows to planning decision-making lies one important key to the city planner's contribution to metropolitan development.

Other more active roles await the planner in creating beneficial links between the region and the rest of the world. The kind of contribution he can make to the economic development of the region is not the least of these. This can involve a number of aspects. The quality of economic growth will depend on the nature of the net flows of investment and migrants between the region and the rest of the world, which are frequently influenced by something as insubstantial as the kind of image which a metropolitan region puts forth: is it actively developing its assets and creatively making a place for itself in the development of the greater region and the nation? In the last analysis, this image will reflect the quality and vitality of planning in the region and especially its awareness of its role in the development process. Then planners can work specifically to create the kinds of public capital and environmental conditions to attract new capital—such as the creation of industrial estates with home not too far distant—and to retain existing industries through industrial redevelopment to make expansion and high-quality public services possible. It can ally itself directly and functionally with the total complex of area development activity in such a way as to supplement its research and informational needs as well as to build into the flow of planning recommendations those elements needed in the area development effort.

The city planner has an increasingly important tie to federal programs addressed to urban needs generally. Urban renewal and highway transportation are the most dramatic of these, but they are constantly expanding with new kinds of national concern in open space, transit, and public facilities programs. The effective use of these programs by the region is a powerful way of exploiting these external links of the region to the world at large.

Finally, the city planner has the potential to relate regional development to the large state and national resource development programs. The liveliest of these connections currently involves the multiple purpose development of the great river basins whose benefits —and costs—will increasingly accrue to the metropolitan regions. Their voices must be heard in these programs, and the city planner's commitment to the longrange makes him a most valuable spokesman.

The really critical need at the suprametropolitan level centers on the development of new organizational assets by which the contribution of the city planner can be exploited. The key to this need undoubtedly involves new institutions and relations between the metropolis, the state, and the federal governments which can make it possible for all of the many state and federal programs to add up to something meaningful to the regional level; certainly this is the appropriate juncture by which "area redevelopment" can be linked to urban redevelopment, where public roads can be articulated with mass transportation, where open spaces for the city can be related to a national recreation program. Something more than piecemeal coördination is needed; the city planner with a strong, developmental view of the region may be the missing ingredient.

At the metropolitan level the role of the city planner is somewhat more clearly defined: he is inevitably caught up in the great long-range issues of the future, the form and pattern of the region as a whole; he is confronted with the key decisions about the conservation and development of the environmental resources of the region and about the costly, skeletal, systemic services about which the growth of the region will take place.

The city planning contact with natural resources has grown out of a traditional involvement with land and landscaping. These are things which are familiar and which the city planner understands. However, the broad regional perspective introduces elements and dimensions which are new and strange, at least in American city planning. The green wedges of the *Year 2000 Plan for the Nation's Capital* are unique not only in a design sense, but in the need they create for new criteria to relate land *development* and land *conservation*, for new authorities and powers to create them, for new institutions to carry them out. The increasing pressure of urban populations on water supplies and on the capital needed to develop them magnifies tremendously the importance of decisions about the expansion of the region. After all, water runs downhill, and the complex balancing out of natural flows with the spatial distribution of the region's needs and the pollution potential of its wastes involves the system-wide kinds of decision that can be rationally made only on the basis of developmental considerations.

As far as public capital is concerned, the core problem is not only how planners can coördinate regional investment in such capital (so that mistiming and incomplete services do not plague the region), but more basically to set out for the region as a whole the broad spatial criteria for the sequential development of its parts. This developmental posture of decision-making approaches its objectives through the regional distribution of relative service levels and arrays, which are not so much coördinated as integrated stage by stage.

A number of serious obstacles are to be overcome: political Balkanization is perhaps not the most important of these, for it is rivaled by a growing propensity to allocate responsibilities for the development of these services to autonomous agencies whose single-mindedness can jeopardize any effective developmental program for the region. This functional Balkanization can do more to usurp and thwart the regional planning processes simply because it cannot be corrupted by compromise or coerced into coördination. The city planner will have to move fast to create the urgently needed institutions to prevent these barriers from hardening, for he is a primary focus of long-range, region-wide developmental reponsibility. To fail here will seriously restrict the role of the planner in formulating the strategy of development.

In short, although the important functions to be served by the city planner at the metropolitan or regional level flow quite clearly from the nature of the problems, the organizational arrangements are still to be perfected by which metropolitan planning can mediate among the claims and demands of the region's parts through a vigorous resources and "core" services program intimately bound up with lively images of an appropriate course for regional development.

At the intrametropolitan (or local) level, the primary focus is on the interactions of people with private and public capital and natural resources as the principal elements in the urban environment. Here the design orientation of traditional city planning looms large and important, and the human response to this environment is the ultimate criterion of success. Arrangement in space, the quality of the space, the level of services to people and to the land, the imaginative juncture of structure and nature, all appropriately organized—with sufficient diversity—can provide the kind of urban environments which appeal to the urban citizen; failure here can debase the living and working environment almost beyond belief.

There are challenges for organizational innovation here, also. Although the planner and designer can have a powerful influence on the new environments brought forth from urban redevelopment, the new development of the region involves a much freer flow of private capital and private decisions by developers and builders. In the past the planner had made his impact on design in a negative sense: he has regulated out the really appalling breaches of taste by imposing certain kinds of standards. He may very well have eviscerated much of the creativity which suburban development stands so much in need of. Although this negative approach may improve the *average* level of design, it may do so at the expense of good design and innovation. A relationship between the planner and the supplier of the housing market is needed in which the planner can take a more positive role in harnessing the aesthetic creativity of the community to the building of more vital living environments.

The other side of this coin is the relationship of the planner *qua* designer with his ultimate clients—the residents of his neighborhoods. How do their needs and wants fit into the design framework? How can a constant flow of communication be maintained between them and the planner so that urban design is not only more aesthetically pleasing, but is more humanly satisfying, as attested to by the human subject? Hence a new role is suggested for the planner—mediating between the technical proclivities of the producer, the aesthetics of design, and the responses of the region's citizenry to the quality of their environment.

Thus, today there is a whole series of choices confronting city planning which will influence its place in the strategy of regional development. For a half century and more it has been absorbing new objectives—beautifying the city, efficiency in the provision of public services, changing and revitalizing the urban core. It has been evolving in specific directions and reaching out for new ties with significant movements on the American scene. Now we have reached a state where social forces are giving us some new and vivid indications of what really matters to people in our metropolitan regions. These create at the same time a most serious need for city planning to relate itself conceptually to these meaningful issues, and to devise the new techniques and organizational arrangements which will permit it to move powerfully among the public and private groups involved. The metropolitan development framework is the appropriate and powerful device by which the planner can relate himself to these issues and identify the new institutional arrangements and information flows that will allow city planning to exploit its immense assets in the service of the vitality and creativity of regional development.

The clear lesson which emerges is that to bring the terms "planning" and "development" together in the same title is not enough. The city planner must relate himself in an effective way to the activities and groups who are instrumentally involved. But above all, he must take his objectives, his inspiration, his motivation from the powerful forces which are shaping our metropolitan regions and which will not be denied.

16

BRITTON HARRIS

The City of the Future: The Problem of Optimal Design

This paper draws attention to a major distinction between planning design on the one hand and analysis, theory building, and simulation of human social and economic systems on the other hand. The distinction revolves around questions of policy-making and optimality, and in the course of examining it, I think I shall be able to demonstrate that there is at least one major aspect of purposeful social activity which is somewhat intractable and not fully responsive to systematic and scientific approaches. If this be true, there is an important residuum of art in the practice of planning that may resist the efforts of regional science to systematize the world.

For purposes of illustration, I shall later develop this distinction with the example of the city of the future as a specific instance. Meanwhile, I maintain that the process of planning has common features that apply equally well to the engineering design of a bridge, the architectural design of a building, the design of the city of the future, or the design of a viable and effective program of national economic development.

We may distinguish three main but overlapping phases in this planning or design process. The first is design proper or the delineation of a selected set of feasible alternatives. The second phase might be called plan testing or forecasting the outcome of policy and the impacts of its parts, severally and jointly. These effects are often very complex and difficult to trace, and the understanding of the relationships that govern them is perhaps the central focus of a great deal of academic research. The third phase is one of evaluation of and selection between alternative designs or plans based on more or less general social criteria applied to the delineated outcomes.

We must, of course, regard this process as cyclic. The outcomes and evaluations of one set of designs will lead us back to the drafting board for improvements and amendments. The evaluative criteria themselves will reflect social goals that will influence the very first step of selecting interesting alternatives and, indeed, may suggest some of the elements which go into these alternatives.

Let us now attempt to refine the distinction between the scientist

Reprinted from Papers and Proceedings of the Regional Science Association, *19 (1967), 185–95, by permission of the publishers and the author.*

and the planner. One of the trickiest parts of this distinction has to do with the problem-solving orientation of the planner or engineer as contrasted with the academic posture of the scientist, who may be assumed to be interested in knowledge for its own sake. This contrast is blurred from both sides. The problem which many planners address may be very broadly generalized to include a long-run preoccupation with producing a better environment or making possible the good life. These general goals coincide with the general objective of society as a whole and do not reflect any trivial obsession with immediate problems and squeaking wheels such as might be regarded as *infra dig* by academicians. On the other hand, the potentially sterile preoccupation of the academic world with knowledge for its own sake is in fact modified by the strong social commitment of many scientists and by an historic, though perhaps latent, recognition that a true goal of science is the betterment of the human condition. It is very likely true that the planner and the scientist take different starting points for their examination of the world, and I believe that an emphasis on the need for knowledge and understanding is apt to be more productive than an emphasis on the existence of large problems. Nevertheless, there is a coincidence between some aspects of these two functions, and the activities of the planner and scientist frequently are more convergent than divergent. Therefore, I feel that, outside of the field of academic administration, one may set this question aside as containing its own solution.

The strongest coincidence between the process of planning and the process of scientific investigation arises in the area the planner might call testing alternatives and the scientist, predicting the outcomes of alternative policies. These two activities are, in fact, identical and involve relevant theories of the real world embodied in models competent to make accurate projections that discriminate between the effects of differing policies and groups of policies. When we consider the nature of these theories, we discover one of the main sources of confusion and difference between the two fields.

Many social scientists have come to the conclusion that one of the moving forces in social and economic life, and in location, is a tendency toward equilibrium arising out of the actions and decisions of individuals in a free or partially free market. This line of argument is not seriously damaged by the assumption that in a dynamic society equilibrium is always sought but never achieved. It is also true that the conditions of equilibrium frequently correspond with the conditions for the existence of an extreme value of a welfare function. Most often this extreme value is an optimum, but, occasionally, as in the case of the prisoner's dilemma, it may be a "pessimum."

There are two essential distinctions to be made between the

economic or social optimum related to the equilibrating process which the scientist can identify and the optimum or best plan which the planner or engineer seeks to generate. The first point is that the scientist's optimum is not normative but refers to the state of a system and an optimum measured by a social or economic objective function which is defined by the nature of the system. The optimum can be given a normative interpretation only if society accepts the scientifically defined objective function as a desirable goal. In the second place, the scientist's optimum exists with the structure of the problem defined at least in part outside of the system of interest. Thus, laws, customs, and the existing cultural artifacts must be in general taken as given. The planner, in turn, is concerned with the conscious change of these given elements and consequently is seeking to optimize a different problem. We will now turn our attention to that problem in some detail.

The problem of optimizing the operation of a complex system by changing or redefining its structural characteristics is essentially a problem of design. Quite generally, design might therefore be defined as a process of inventing new elements and recombining known or existing elements so as to produce a desired whole. The terms "elements" and "whole" are purposely left undefined except for their hierarchical relationship; viewed from one aspect, an element may be a lower-level whole consisting of still smaller elements, and the whole for one design purpose may be an element in a larger whole for other purposes. At the moment, I also leave undefined the term "desired," not specifying whether this is to be judged by standards of optimizing or satisficing. The idea of combining elements can readily be extended to the idea of combining policy measures, activities, and like entities in variable amounts. Thus, the design process is defined in terms of the process of invention and the process of combination. A determination to include an element in the whole at any specified level will be called a design decision. It is unlike a real-world decision in that it can be revised or reversed without cost.

A little reflection will, I think, show that this definition of design can be applied to a wide range of different types of human activity. The architect or engineer, for example, invents forms and occasionally structural methods and recombines rooms, spaces, materials, etc. These may all be regarded as elements. The final product or products of his efforts are judged as more or less satisfactory according to the budget and program of his client and according to certain ill-defined canons of aesthetics and of functional efficiency. In an entirely different realm, a national economic planner may be regarded as a policy designer. His elements are people, financial resources, capital investments, modes of organization, laws, regulations, taxes, tariffs, and even public political campaigns. His problem in designing a coordinated set of policies may be to maximize gross national product, to guarantee military preparedness, or to optimize a growth pattern for the entire economy. In the sense which we have defined, he is a policy designer and pursues inventive and combinatorial activities purposively in exactly the same manner as the architect or engineer. The city planner, regional planner, and resource planner occupy an intermediate position, being somewhat more concerned with physical elements and engineering solutions than the national economic planner and somewhat more concerned with laws, customs, and influences on behavior as instruments in attaining objectives than is the architect or engineer. In the discussion that follows, I intend to focus on the problems of the policy designer in seeking somehow to achieve the best possible results from the design process.

The more prosaic and self-assured planners and policy makers have a very smug name for design of this type—they call it end-reduction. This naive title implies that design is indeed a mechanical task, that a simple correspondence between ends and means is easily established, and indeed that the whole process of design, forecast, and evaluation is thus comprehended in one swift leap. Unless end-reduction is more complex than its name implies, there is little room for policy design, no need for cost-benefit analysis of the results, and no problem of choice. Because of these implications, perhaps not justly drawn, I shall not use this term in my discussion.

The essential difficulties in the analytic treatment of the design process are twofold. First, owing to the possibility of inventing new elements, the design decision space is not bounded and, in fact, has an unknown dimensionality. This fact in itself guarantees that we can never state unequivocally that a given design or proposed policy is the best. Quite aside from the uncertainties introduced into life by technology, changes in taste, war, famine, and pestilence, the best policy may be immediately available and feasible yet never have been discovered. This might be called a technological uncertainty of the policy design process itself. A second, and in some ways more intriguing, difficulty arises from the fact that the predictable effects of design decisions, if they become settled policy, are not mutually independent. Policy A in combination with policy B may and most probable will have effects which differ from the sum of the effects of policies A and B taken individually. Perhaps this problem is more intriguing because it seems that it should be susceptible to straightforward analysis and thus teases us more unmercifully than uncertainties about which we know we can do little. In order to explore the nature of this problem somewhat more fully, I propose to develop a few specific and easily comprehended examples.

I am indebted for the first example to Professor Zofia Dembowska of the Instytut Urbanistyki i Architektury, Warszawa, who encountered it in the course of planning for the expansion of an existing Polish metropolis. Let us assume that the expansion will occur in a planned fashion along a number of radial fingers from the existing body of the metropolis. The areas in which this expansion may be planned are not developed in any urban uses and do not contain any urban engineering improvements. In order to accomplish the expansion, each new district will have to be served by transportation routes and utility lines that will follow a corridor outward from the existing body of development. The costs of these installations depend in part linearly on the distance of the farthest developed precinct from existing development and in part on the number of precincts actually developed along each corridor. The incidence of these costs on the development is roughly inverse to the number of precincts developed. Normally, this is a problem in marginal analysis but we introduce the fact that the terrain is not uniform and that costs of development vary between areas, with some lower site development costs occurring farther out in certain corridors. Thus, a decision not to develop a close-in precinct may save on land development costs but throw a heavier burden for the provision of urban services on the remaining precincts. It appears that for any given corridor, the optimum combination for the development and non-development of precincts can only be determined by a complete enumeration of combinations. If, for example, there are ten possible precincts, there will be 1,024 combinations, of which perhaps half will be worthy of examination. Considering, say, half a dozen different corridors and the constraint that all the anticipated population must be located, there is obviously an additional level of analysis, in that a selection of the best combinations for each corridor must somehow be made under an over-all optimizing criterion.

I have purposely omitted from this example many additional complications that could be included without any distortion of the problem. For example, the outlying precincts will in general incur higher travel costs to their residents, but, on the other hand, under certain circumstances, groups of these precincts may develop subsidiary business centers that will reduce these costs. The addition of these and others would greatly complicate the process of costing out the very large number of combinations that the simplest problem of this type can generate.

My second example is even more striking; it was first clearly defined by Roger L. Creighton, Director of the Transportation Planning and Programming Subdivision, New York State Department of Public Works, and represents a special case of a general and very important problem which might be called the optimum network problem. Imagine a state containing 20 major cities of various sizes currently connected by a highway network providing 30 m.p h. service. The state proposes to upgrade this network by the provision of a number of links providing 60 m.p.h. service. To simplify the problem, we may assume that we have defined a subset of 40 out of all possible direct city-to-city links, such that these 40 links define a generally satisfactory network configuration. The state is operating under budget constraints that make it impossible to build, say, more than half of the mileage of the high-grade links defined by this network. The problem may be simply stated: what subset of the 40 links will satisfy the budget constraint and provide the greatest benefits to the state?

In order to examine this problem more explicitly, we may assume that an objective function for maximizing benefits can be formulated and even, for purposes of simplicity, that it is linear in the policy variable, travel time between cities. Such an objective function, for instance, might be

$$\text{Max} \sum_i \sum_j -P_i P_j T_{ij}.$$

Any straightforward analytical solution to this deceptively simple problem founders, because the addition of any link of improved facilities to the system effects the variable T_{ij} which depends on the precise links previously added to the improved system. Once again, the only possible thorough approach is to denumerate all possible combinations, in this case 2^{40}, or a million million. Even if we assume that only one in a million combinations is at or near the budget constraint and that these combinations can be rapidly and cheaply identified, there still remain a million combinations to be evaluated. At a most optimistic estimate of one second per evaluation on a high-speed computer, these would require nearly 300 hours!

This case is of some interest because of the great importance of transportation costs in regional science theory and analysis. I am not aware that this discipline has usually done other than take the existence of a network as given. Yet many development problems in which it is or might be interested probably turn out to involve resource allocation for transportation improvements. It is difficult to see how these allocational problems can be solved, for discrete variables, by ordinary optimizing or partial equilibrium methods.

The multiplicity of design solutions for problems can be still more stupefying than in our previous example if we look at cases where we are dealing not with combinations but with permutations. These arise naturally in instances where we consider the design of a process or sequential steps. The permutations of ten program steps in all possible sequences is over a million and of fifteen, over a million million. This problem in its simplest form has the ludicrous name of the Traveling Salesman Problem, which turns out to be remarkably difficult and, at the same time, isomorphic to many serious realworld, program-planning and design problems. Some spice is lent to its discussion at the moment, since the Bell Telephone Laboratories have just spent several thousand dollars advertising their achievement of a partial and approximate solution method. If this (mathematical) solution can bring such credit to the Bell Laboratories, our hats must be off to either the gall or the genius of countless engineers and planners who have defended the optimality of their own endless practical solutions of the same problem.

It is, as the last case indicates, undoubtedly true that by careful planning and with further analysis, short-cut methods can be developed for attacking these or any similar problems with some hope of guaranteeing an approximately optimal solution. The general point, which bears repetition, is that extensive combinatorial problems of this type are thoroughly resistant to bounded search procedures and even more resistant to those optimizing methods which depend essentially on marginal analysis and thus on some form of hill climbing. The designer who devises a selection procedure in this context is, in the first place, engaged in much more than analysis; in fact, his conclusions may not be analytically defensible (or analytically impeachable either). He will make use of his intimate knowledge of the structure of the problem and of the real world to guide him intuitively toward regions richer in useful answers. Such intuition is, in part, based on knowledge and experience and, in part, is the unconscious product of the remarkable combinatorial powers of the human mind. Its danger lies in the fact that, as an internalized and personal process, it may suffer from unconscious biases and limitations. In dealing with problems of this type, this last difficulty is sometimes attacked by way of so-called team efforts and brainstorming.

So far, we have dealt with examples of optimal design decisions in which all of the choices are binary, either yes or no. This restriction has enabled us to lay bare the essential nature of the problem. The usual case is indeed much more complex because the policies available to the designer usually represent a mixture of binary and continuous variables. Thus, for example, budget allocations for many activities are frequently regarded in analysis as continuously variable, and this may be a useful artifice in spite of the fact that the budgets apply to programs which are indeed lumpy and discontinuous. In the general case where all policy variables are continuous, we rarely find that the connections of policies with outcomes are independent and linear. Some policies reinforce each other and others conflict. Consequently, even if all relations are clearly defined and analytically tractable, the conventional processes of optimizing lead only to local optima. Since it is to be expected that the criterion function is not unimodal in the policy space, this result is unsatisfactory.

The usual approach to this problem is to select a number of widely separated points in the policy space, that is, a number of plans of sketches differing as widely as possible from each other, and to explore their implications. This is becoming accepted practice in metropolitan planning and transportation planning. I shall revert to the implications of this for the city of the future after a brief examination of three other approaches to the problem.

In spite of the recent introduction of the explicit and deliberate consideration of widely separated alternatives, we most commonly observe in regional and city planning a process of sequential design decisions which results ordinarily in only *one* final plan. Aside from the technical difficulties in preparing detailed alternatives, I believe that there exist very real but unsound reasons for this practice. Sequential planning depends for its justification on one or both of two assumptions. The first such assumption is that the latitude available to the designer is very narrow and that it is, in fact, impossible to choose two or more widely separated policies. In a policy space narrowly circumscribed by law, custom, and economic conditions, system performance could indeed be regarded as unimodal and optimizing procedures using marginal adjustments might be readily applicable. This is the viewpoint historically embraced by the Bureau of Public Roads and by many transportation studies under its general aegis. The second general assumption, of a somewhat different character, is that the goals to be pursued in the planning process are strongly hierarchical in nature and that interactions and tradeoffs between them can largely be neglected. Thus, the sequential design steps will be related to these goals in declining order of importance, and the decisions necessary to achieve the first goal will be frozen regardless of their effects on subordinate goals. This approach is common among architectural and engineering designers and land planners. The two types of assumptions may interact in a variety of interesting ways, the most usual being the case in which engineering and policy restraints are regarded as circumscribing most closely the avenues for achieving the most important goal.

Quite clearly, even a minor exercise in sequential decision making can greatly reduce the dimensionality of the design problem. In the combinatorial case, each design decision that can be made independently reduces the total number of combinations by a factor of two. The essential problem, however, remains. Each such decision must be judged on its own merits. This then assumes that the interactions with other decisions can indeed be neglected, but, in many instances, this seems unlikely. Sequential decision making thus effectively bars the testing of unusual and fruitful combinations of policy, where the benefits derive from the active combination rather than from the individual policies.

An interesting variation on the circumscribed policy space can result in the use of the apparatus of optimizing in a misleading way. When social criteria for design are specified in substantial detail, and, even more, when they are translated into detailed minimum standards, the first stage of design of alternatives may turn into a simple search for a *feasible* solution. If such a solution can be found and if nearly all restraints are binding, then there is no merit in seeking other alternatives or improvements in this one. Otherwise, a real but somewhat specious optimizing search may ensue. In either case, there is no need for evaluation, since all performance standards have been prespecified and are by definition met by a feasible solution. This approach, all too common in the planning profession, obviously begs the question of tradeoffs between different goals which are an important aspect of the whole planning process. These tradeoffs are uniquely implied by the levels at which different standards are set, and it is difficult to tell whether, in fact, they reflect the values of the community. Using this approach, tradeoffs can be explored but only by a parametric variation of the restraints. The whole problem of optimal design has then been shifted into the setting of standards, where it is latent rather than manifest. Still worse, the uncritical observer may be deceived into feeling that any later steps are indeed truly optimizing in nature.

Another approach to recalcitrant problems of design explicitly recognizes the major problem of the nonindependence of design decisions. Christopher Alexander and others have suggested methods whereby the goals to be satisfied by design effort may be explicitly listed, and, through a knowledge of the technical nature of the problem, the interactions between pairs of goals may be set out in matrix form. Various methods are then proposed, partly using graph theoretic procedures, to decompose the matrix in a hierarchical fashion, so that, at any level, the interaction between goals or decisions in a subset is greater than the interaction between subsets. This then provides a basis on which the designer seeks to find a satisfactory or even optimal solution to a subproblem where interdependencies are important and then proceeds to resolve the joint problems which arise between subproblems. This procedure is extraordinarily interesting and useful because of its explicit and sophisticated exploration of the design process. It is especially useful for heuristic or exploratory use. Its weaknesses are almost self-evident. It is unable to deal with the case where a large number of design decisions are inextricably interrelated. It is unclear, in fact, whether the attack on the problem is by way of goals or by way of means, except where there may be a one-to-one correspondence between the design decisions and the satisfaction of goals, and this is seldom the case. Depending on the structure of the problem, allowance should be made for the occasional importance of inverting the decomposition so as to place particularly difficult design conflicts of superordinate character at the top of a decision tree. Most important, the emphasis in this procedure is on finding a design fit rather than an optimum or quasi-optimum. This implicitly assumes either that the latitude for optimization is very small or that the failure to optimize is not significant. In the first case, as we argued above, the restraints are probably over-specified, and insufficient allowance is made for tradeoffs between goals. The assumption that optimization is not important might be valid for engineering and architectural works of limited size, if it were not for their great number, but for national, regional, and metropolitan development policy, where the resources to be committed are very large, it is not admissible.

After this extended overview of the problem of design in principle, of selected examples, and of a number of partial solutions, we may turn briefly to the relation between these issues and the design of the city of the future.

The general context in which most of these problems have come forcibly to my attention is that of rapid and pejorative change in the American urban environment. Our cities are growing mightily in population, in wealth, and in geographic extent but with social and environmental consequences which most of us find distasteful. Our general view of society suggests that by conscious intervention in this developmental process we can change its course and invent a more desirable future than presently seems likely. It is also clear that the changes we can bring about may take many decades to effect. Likewise, we may assume that big problems may require drastic remedies. Thus, it is possible that the present framework of social, economic, legal, and technological arrangements of our cities and metropolitan areas may be the object of major change and modification.

Considering the commitment of resources that any society must make to urban living arrangements, we must, I think, concede that the design process must seek some sort of social optimum. We may now usefully review the extent to which regional science, urban economics and sociology, and related analytical disciplines can and cannot solve these problems of optimization.

Quite clearly, the process of theory building and analytical understanding of the metropolitan area is of key importance in the whole planning process. Without this understanding, it is impossible to predict the consequences of policy decisions and hence impossible to evaluate alternative bundles of policy. At least equally important, a direct engagement in analytic research provides a wealth of insights into urban processes which may be of critical importance in suggesting new policy designs and in guiding the process of evaluation. Therefore, although I have tried to make a conceptual distinction between analysis and design and between analysis and planning, I think that we could usefully consider means by which these processes can maintain an intimate connection in the real world. Nothing is more self-defeating than a design effort which is not based on an intimate knowledge of goals, of means, and of interrelationships.

There are at least two directions within the strict limitation of theory and analysis in which the preceding discussion suggests directions for improvement. When we examine in detail the problem of designing the future city, we find that in many aspects this becomes the problem of designing a setting for all society. Insofar as this difficulty must be faced, it suggests that economic models of equilibrium and optimization are not enough and, indeed, that the objective function and the means by which it is maximized must cover a wider range of social forces and social values. A second aspect which deserves consideration is the importance of nonlinear and possibly of time-dependent systems. Even elementary economic considerations regarding economies and diseconomies of scale, as well as considerations of individual behavior, suggest that interactions in the urban system are strongly nonlinear. Yet we still cast much of our analysis in linear terms because these systems are more tractable. As an addendum, perhaps a third point could be made regarding the importance of exploiting equilibrium considerations more explicitly as a basis for theory building and analysis. Steps have been made in all of these directions, but perhaps they could be longer and more firm.

In contrast to the possibility of direct contributions to planning by theory, we must identify certain areas in which the contributions will be indirect and where, in fact, an independent approach to the theory of design may be required. In the discussion of these cases, we will again assume away those circumstances that are the consequence of general uncertainty and focus only on those inherent in the design process itself.

Policy planning, in the first instance, may be devoted to changing the rules of the game and thus the structure of the world to which analysis and theory apply. Mortgage insurance, urban renewal, and the interstate highway program may be taken as examples of the type of structural change greatly influencing the development of urban areas. Prior to their invention, they were not in general a part of the world which the analyst examined. In the future, we may expect that to deal with urgent urban problems, many new devices of similar magnitude will have to be invented. Frequently, perceptive analysts may actually originate these suggestions. In general, even though basic qualities of human behavior and economic reality will persist, we may expect that some such changes will so drastically alter the structure of urban affairs that they may even call for new theories and certainly for new models.

A second problem, somewhat peripheral to design but of great interest to economists, is the fact that the objective functions used in equilibrating a market or submarket may not coincide with the objective functions proposed for measuring social welfare. This is quite clearly the case, for example, when we consider the environmental effects of transportation improvements, which have become an important issue in the urban highway construction program. The fact that present engineering criteria for optimality do not take into account the externalities of highway construction might suggest to the economist that there is an imperfection in the market. He might then recommend either a new objective function which places arbitrary prices on externalities, or an actual revision of the effective pricing system, with a similar but more explicit effect. It might thus be suggested that a careful examination of mismatches between broad social and narrow economic optimizing procedures could reveal important means for improving efficiency by redefining market relations. In this context, economists could participate directly in some of the innovative aspects of policy planning design.

A narrow line divides the invention of new policy measures, our third area of difficulty, from the process discussed above of changing the rules. It might be suggested, for example, that entirely new methods of taxation of real estate could be devised with anticipated effects radically different from those of existing tax policies. Yet it is quite conceivable that the analysis of these proposals could proceed in the existing framework of economic theory and partial equilibrium treatment of the system. Despite the fact that such measures are analyzable, it would indeed be a rash economist who would suggest that he has reviewed all such possible innovations. It would be even more rash to suggest that all such measures are arranged in a continuum (of however many dimensions) and that their exploration can be made a matter of systematic search and of pushing presently known concepts to the limit. However useful this technique may be, it is clearly not exhaustive.

We come, finally, to the most troublesome aspect of exploring the consequences of alternative bundles of policies, the combinatorial aspect which has been stressed in the preceding discussions. The design of a future metropolis probably involves several hundred interdependent decisions, many of which can already be delineated. These include the sites, future land uses, and methods to be used for urban renewal; zoning over scores of districts and including the location and densities of many classes of activities and residence; and the provision of transportation facilities. They also include operating policies regarding taxes, prices, and the provision of public welfare services such as health, education, and social service. Quite apparently, the interactions of these decisions are nontrivial; for example, in a multitude of ways both large and small, the designation of land uses and the design of transportation systems interact with each other. In spite of our best efforts to restructure and simplify the problem, it seems likely to me that there exist for any given city many thousand defensible alternatives with a wide range of as yet unpredicted costs and benefits. Even assuming that we had adequate analytical methods for examining alternatives, it is quite clear that practicality and economy would dictate that we must select a restricted subset for detailed examination. When, for example, four plans are selected for detailed study out of perhaps a possible thousand, the planner puts a substantial emphasis on his professional ability to select useful alternatives. It is indeed a fearsome responsibility for the regional scientist or the planner to take the initiative in circumscribing the problem or recommending short-cut methods, since these steps are tantamount to excluding a wide class of combinations from further consideration.

The solution to this problem requires much more careful and explicit consideration of the processes involved in design and the selection of designs for testing. At the same time, it requires a detailed knowledge of the policy space in which design is proceeding and some intuition as to the probable effects of jointly determined design decisions. Thus, the design process stands with one foot in an increasingly self-conscious creative effort and the other foot in an increasingly detailed scientific knowledge of society's relation to its environment. It would indeed, I think, be foolish for people on either side of this fence to maintain that they can operate without the other side.

The acuteness of this problem is being daily increased by a variety of trends in relation to our policy toward our cities. The increasing determination for action, the increasing recognition of the importance of a long-range view, the growing willingness to use new policy measures, the increasing flexibility and virtuosity of our technology, and the increasing affluence of our society all tend to create additional degrees of freedom within which the problems will hopefully be solved. These added degrees of freedom greatly increase the complexity of the design process and its intractability under ordinary economic or behavioral analysis. I hope, therefore, that this effort to delineate the inherent nature of the problem will arouse a constant awareness of its existence and stimulate efforts to reduce its intransigencies.

INDEX

Index